PSYCHOANALYSIS AND ART

PSYCHOANALYSIS AND ART
Kleinian Perspectives

edited by

Sandra Gosso

KARNAC

LONDON   NEW YORK

First published in 2004 by
H. Karnac (Books) Ltd.
6 Pembroke Buildings, London NW10 6RE

First published in Italian in 2001 by Bruno Mondadori, Milan, under the title, *Psicoanalisi e arte, Il conflitto estetico,* © 2001 Paravia Bruno Mondadori Editori.

Preface, Introduction, Chapter 15 (Donald Meltzer, "New Considerations on the Concept of the Aesthetic Conflict"), Chapter 18 (Donald Meltzer, "Disorders of Thought"), translated by Geoffrey Elkan.

Chapter 9 (Donald Meltzer, "The Aesthetic Object"), translated by Mathias Koenig-Archibugi.

British Library Cataloguing in Publication Data

A C.I.P. for this book is available from the British Library

ISBN: 1-85575-968-3

10 9 8 7 6 5 4 3 2 1

Edited, designed, and produced by Communication Crafts

Printed in Great Britain

www.karnacbooks.com

Dedicated to Geoffrey Elkan

CONTENTS

ANTHOLOGY **II**
Post-Kleinian thought

COPYRIGHT ACKNOWLEDGEMENTS

Chapter 1: Melanie Klein, "Infantile anxiety-situations reflected in a work of art and in the creative impulse" (1929): reprinted from M. Klein, *Love, Guilt and Reparation and Other Works* (London: Hogarth Press, 1975), pp. 210–218.

Chapter 2: Hannah Segal, "A psycho-analytical approach to aesthetics" (1952): reprinted from M. Klein, P. Heimann, & R. Money-Kyrle, *New Directions in Psycho-Analysis* (London: Tavistock, 1955), pp. 384–405.

Chapter 3: Joan Riviere, "The unconscious phantasy of an inner world reflected in examples from literature" (1955): reprinted from M. Klein, P. Heimann, & R. Money-Kyrle, *New Directions in Psycho-Analysis* (London: Tavistock, 1955), pp. 346–369.

Chapter 4: Marion Milner, "The role of illusion in symbol formation" (1955): reprinted from M. Klein, P. Heimann, & R. Money-Kyrle, *New Directions in Psycho-Analysis* (London: Tavistock, 1955), pp. 82–108.

Chapter 5: Adrian Stokes, "The invitation in art" (1965): reprinted from A. Stokes, *The Invitation to Art* (London: Taylor & Francis [Tavistock], 1965), pp. 260–266.

Chapter 6: Donald Meltzer, "The apprehension of beauty" (1973): reprinted from D. Meltzer & M. Harris Williams, *The Apprehension of Beauty: The Role of Aesthetic Conflict in Development, Art and Violence* (Strath Tay, Perthshire: Clunie Press, 1988), pp. 1–6.

Chapter 7: Donald Meltzer, "The delusion of clarity of insight" (1975): reprinted from the *International Journal of Psycho-Analysis, 57* (1976): 141–146.

Chapter 8: Donald Meltzer, "The relation of dreaming to learning from experience in patient and analyst" (1984): reprinted from D. Meltzer, *Dream-Life: A Re-Examination of the Psycho-Analytical Theory and Technique* (Strath Tay, Perthshire: Clunie Press, 1984), pp. 163–169.

Chapter 9: Donald Meltzer, "The aesthetic object" (1984), originally published in French in *Revue Française de Psychanalyse, 5* (1985), then in Italian in *Quaderni di psicoterapia infantile, 14* (Rome: Borla, 1985), pp. 203–205.

Chapter 10: Donald Meltzer, with Eve Cohen, "Concerning the perception of one's own attributes and its relation to language development" (1986): reprinted from D. Meltzer, *Studies in Extended Metapsychology: Clinical Applications of Bion's Ideas* (Strath Tay, Perthshire: Clunie Press, 1986), pp. 175–186.

Chapter 11: Donald Meltzer, "On turbulence" (1986): reprinted from D. Meltzer, *Studies in Extended Metapsychology: Clinical Applications of Bion's Ideas* (Strath Tay, Perthshire: Clunie Press, 1986), pp. 187–190.

Chapter 12: Donald Meltzer, "Dénouement" (1986): reprinted from D. Meltzer, *Studies in Extended Metapsychology: Clinical Applications of Bion's Ideas* (Strath Tay, Perthshire: Clunie Press, 1986), pp. 203–211.

Chapter 13: Donald Meltzer and Meg Harris Williams, "The aesthetic conflict: its place in the developmental process" (1988): reprinted from D. Meltzer & M. Harris Williams, *The Apprehension of Beauty: The Role of Aesthetic Conflict in Development, Art and Violence* (Strath Tay, Perthshire: Clunie Press, 1988), pp. 7–33.

Chapter 14: Donald Meltzer: "The place of aesthetic conflict in the analytic process" (1988): reprinted from D. Meltzer & M. Harris Williams, *The Apprehension of Beauty: The Role of Aesthetic Conflict in Development, Art and Violence* (Strath Tay, Perthshire: Clunie Press, 1988), pp. 134–144.

Chapter 15: Donald Meltzer, "New considerations on the concept of the aesthetic conflict" (1990): originally published in S. Gosso, *Paessaggi della mente* (Milan: Franco Angeli, 1997), pp. 107–116.

Chapter 16: Donald Meltzer, "The geographic dimension of the mental apparatus" (1992): reprinted from D. Meltzer, *The Claustrum: An Investigation of Claustrophobic Phenomena* (Strath Tay, Perthshire: Clunie Press, 1982), pp. 57–60.

Chapter 17: Donald Meltzer: "The compartments of the internal mother" (1992): reprinted from D. Meltzer, *The Claustrum: An Investigation of Claustrophobic Phenomena* (Strath Tay, Perthshire: Clunie Press, 1982), pp. 61–67.

Chapter 18: Donald Meltzer: "Disorders of thought" (1994): passages taken from lectures held at the Institute of Calambrone, 23rd Conference on Child Psychotherapy, 21 July 1994; published in *Attidel xxiii Stage di Psicoterapia infantile del 21 Iuglio 1994, del Istituto di Calambrone*.

Chapter 19: Donald Meltzer and Meg Harris Williams, "The lobby of dreams" (1988), from "The undiscovered country: The shape of the aes-

COPYRIGHT ACKNOWLEDGEMENTS xiii

thetic conflict in *Hamlet*": reprinted from D. Meltzer & M. Harris
Williams, *The Apprehension of Beauty: The Role of Aesthetic Conflict in Development, Art and Violence* (Strath Tay, Perthshire: Clunie Press, 1988), pp. 97–106.

Chapter 20: Donald Meltzer and Meg Harris Williams, "Aesthetic appreciation through symbolic congruence" (1988), from "Holding the dream: the nature of aesthetic appreciation": reprinted from D. Meltzer & M. Harris Williams, *The Apprehension of Beauty: The Role of Aesthetic Conflict in Development, Art and Violence* (Strath Tay, Perthshire: Clunie Press, 1988), pp. 178–187.

Chapter 21: Meg Harris Williams, "Keats: Soul-making" (1991): reprinted from M. Harris Williams & M. Waddell, *Chamber of Maiden Thought: Literary Origins of the Psychoanalytic Model of the Mind* (London: Routledge, 1991), pp. 109–125.

Chapter 22: Meg Harris Williams, "Entry to the Claustrum" (1992), from "Macbeth's equivocation, Shakespeare's ambiguity": reprinted from D. Meltzer, *The Claustrum: An Investigation of Claustrophobic Phenomena* (Strath Tay, Perthshire: Clunie Press, 1982), pp. 165–171.

Chapter 23: Margot Waddell, "Parallel directions in psychoanalysis" (1991): reprinted from M. Harris Williams & M. Waddell, *Chamber of Maiden Thought: Literary Origins of the Psychoanalytic Model of the Mind* (London: Routledge, 1991), pp. 170–183.

ACKNOWLEDGEMENTS

During the Christmas period of 2002, Geoffrey Elkan finished translating my anthology on *Psychoanalysis and Art*. Of course, we were happy: Geoffrey, his wife Judith, who has helped in the final stages of the translation, and I were all very happy at the completion of the work.

Geoffrey did an excellent job. He noticed a large number of mistakes about which we used to joke via email, such as my writing that Othello was the lover of Ophelia. Before leaving for a Christmas vacation Geoffrey sent me a large envelope in which he indicated all mistakes that needed to be corrected in the next Italian edition of the book. He then left for Israel in order to play in a concert for peace and reconciliation in Israeli–Palestinian relations.

I never imagined that Geoffrey would be taken ill with a stroke and that his life would end so suddenly six days after his concert in Jerusalem.

Geoffrey loved music, art, and psychoanalysis. We met just twice, in London and in Lucca, at a conference where I heard him playing the clarinet. We did not know each other very well, but I believe that we greatly enjoyed the work we did together, and therefore I feel that I have lost a friend; I often feel the need to see him, or to read one of his emails written in a funny Italian–English language, which only he could have invented, and which I can still read on my computer.

Sandra Gosso, Christmas 2003

Which psychoanalytic theory for art?

When he introduced his first writings on clinical psychoanalysis, the *Studies on Hysteria*, Freud affirmed that these were "short stories", similar to those that might issue from the pen of a writer. The reference to narrative, mentioned from the very beginning, marks all Freud's work: the histories of the patients are "short stories", Gradiva a "psychoanalytic romance", while "Moses and Monotheism" is presented to the reader in the manner of a historical novel. In a letter of 14 May 1922, Freud admits to Schnitzler that the difficulties in the way of reciprocal knowledge were due to "a kind of awe of meeting my double" (letter of Freud to A. Schnitzler, 14 May 1922, in Jones, 1957)—an admission of envy, but also an awareness of an identification with the artist who knows intuitively what the father of psychoanalysis discovered only by "laborious work".

The analogy between psychoanalysis and literature dates back to the beginning of the psychoanalytic era, if one thinks that the most enthusiastic review of the *Studies on Hysteria* were made by a literary historian.[1] In effect, in the course of Freud's forty years of productive life in the sphere of the new science, while the fundamental metapsychological presuppositions were changing, the narrative style remained firm and became sharper in the course of time. This occurred not only in the so-called psychoanalytic romances from which psychoanalytic theory began, but also in the clinical accounts, which freed themselves from the heavy medical and neurophysiological terminology that Freud used in seeking acceptance and appreciation from the scientific community. Disappointment at his ostracism by the medical and academic "establishment" led Freud to new discoveries and to the consolation of contributions from far afield, allowing him to use freely his narrative gift: one need only think of the Schnitzlerian climate of the case of Dora and of the slightly Tolstoyan flavour of the Wolf Man, with the lively Russian character of the figures in the patient's childhood.

But besides the Freud the clinician and writer of monumental historical frescoes, there is Freud the literary theorist—here much less convincing. The essay on "Creative Writers and Day-dreaming", which attempts a scientific approach to the creative personality, ends by asserting an estrangement of the poet from the real world, seeing the artist as never disengaged from the pleasure principle, imprisoned in his perpetual immaturity. Freud's writings on artists, in particular the paper on Leonardo, consider the work of art as a symptom, and this, together with the biography of the artist, ends up leading us to where it is of little use, to the pathology of the artist. This was the beginning of "psychobiography", which consisted of a psychoanalytic enquiry into the artist starting from a study of his work. This form of enquiry, initiated by Freud, has had a long life, made difficult by hostility from the literary world, which objected to the juxtaposition of psychoanalysis and art and criticized the way in which a work of art was "interpreted" in accordance with psychoanalytic theory, often no differently from the analysis of material presented by a patient.

* * *

An interesting corrective to so-called psycho-criticism was perhaps shown from the outset in the numerous essays in which psychoanalysis searched in literary works to show the existence of psychical processes that were gradually being observed in the clinical situation. The many authors who came together around the review *Imago*[2] were aware that everything that psychoanalysis was discovering had already been better described in the field of art. To this direction of research, which has its point of departure in the Freudian account of the *Oedipus* of Sophocles, belong essays such as those of Ernest Jones on *Hamlet* (Jones, 1954) and of Melanie Klein on the *Oresteia* (Klein, 1963). In this case psychoanalysis does not interpret but, on the contrary, has recourse to literature, that incomparable illustration of the human mind, to find a language suited to the complexity of the material. Could Freud have proposed for consideration by his contemporaries the Oedipal triangle, without Sophocles and without Oedipus? It seems plausible to me that Freud would never have given up making these public, but this would have had a different outcome from that which actually occurred. We would have had some sort of dictionary of the perversions, a *psychopathia sexualis à la* Krafft Ebing, or a psychopathology *à la* Kraepelin, while the germ of psychoanalysis remains in the initial impetus of Freud, whose turning from the outset to literature to give form to the internal work lead to the discovery of the Oedipus complex. It is this that makes unavoidable, even if often criticized as useless and superfluous, the binominal "psychoanalysis-literature", on the grounds of the incontestable evidence that in the beginning there was art, and it was to art that psychoanalysis had to turn to bring to a conclusion the travail of its birth.

So what are we to make of this inseparable couple, which yet seems to have borne fruit that has not always been good? Confronted by the criticisms levelled against psychobiography, in recent times psychoanalytical criticism—above all by the French school—has wanted to equip itself with more sophisticated heuristic instruments, such as structuralism, structural linguistics, and the *nouvelle rhetorique*. This has, however, involved a violation of the text through the use of an extrinsic conceptual apparatus whereby the text itself is dissected in order to demonstrate the existence of a remote signified and of a "deep" formal structure. In the work of Julia Kristeva this operation is accompanied by an explicitly anal view of the "art material", which, taking as its origin the importance that Freud attributed to marginal aspects of culture (the joke, the dream), put forward a real apologia to all art as a urethral and anal *rejet*.[3]

In contrast to this, British psychoanalysis developed, in the same years, a positive vision of the artistic event, far from the influx of a variety of negative forms of thought developed in middle Europe, including the thoughts of Freud. It is this interpretative view that we wish to place for the attention of students of aesthetics and literature through the present anthology. This is a view of art that takes off from the ideas of Bion to focus attention on the identical nature of the processes set in motion in the experience of psychoanalysis and those in aesthetic perception and in artistic creativity. Meltzer, developing Bion's ideas, has put the link between beauty and mental life at the centre of his thinking. Bion, in his pre-psychoanalytic period, was able in his study of groups to note a basic mental functioning in which the individual is moved by primitive mechanisms that exclude thinking. At the level of "basic assumptions", the mind functions bi-dimensionally, so that the absence of emotional perception impedes the development of the capacity for thought. In this mental world, behaviour, unthinking and imitative, prejudices at one and the same time thinking, feeling, and the perception of beauty.

* * *

Louis Malle's film *Lacombe Lucien*, set in the time of the Nazi occupation of Paris, tells the story of the life of a young man impelled only by an unreflective impulse to action. After a first crime he happens to seek refuge from justice by joining the Vichy government, enjoying privileges ensured for him by collaboration with the Gestapo. What moves him in his violent and barbaric deeds is something other than wickedness. It is a more banal matter of a modality of action based on thoughtless behaviour, linked to the evacuation of impulses and to immediate gratification of desire: Lucien Lacomb does not have the capacity (or the wish) to insert, in a Freudian way, thought between impulse and action. Having infiltrated the home of an old Jewish tailor through blackmail and violence, and protected by the Nazis who exploit his skill as a craftsman, he becomes attracted by the highly emotional, artistic, and affective level that infuses, even in fear and suffering, the family's life. He is split between his possessive impulses and his desire for the tailor's young daughter, struck as he is by her qualities, which are so alien to him: shyness, politeness, artistic ability. The girl's beauty is the effect of nature but also of thought and of education, and this stirs his curiosity and indeed attracts him to this unknown type. The girl, while not succeeding in avoiding his attentions, hopes at least to use her power to exert enough influence over the young man to allow her to save her life and that of her old father. But to Lacombe carnal possession is not enough. What disturbs him is just the beauty which, he feels, eludes his grasp so enigmatically. To beauty he cannot respond other than with destructiveness, shown in the film in shots of the progressive vulgarizing of the girl's personality. Under the influence of terror and barbarity, sexuality offers itself as the last refuge with some semblance of humanity, leading to a perverse attachment between the young lady and the ignorant executioner. The world of Lacombe Lucien (first the surname, then the first name, as with all men of the establishment) is the world of "basic assumptions", where obedience to the slogan is accompanied by acts that provide immediate gratification of impulse.

Thought, beauty, art, aesthetic perception are highly evolved categories, prerogatives of the capacity to think, whereas envy, violence, and barbarity, generated by intolerance of frustration, represent the psychotic part of the mind. The more mature work of Bion offers a vast panorama of the struggle between the psychotic and non-psychotic parts of the personality, describing mental life as an epic battlefield for the forces of thought and the forces of anti-thought.

Starting from these theoretical presuppositions, Donald Meltzer has integrated and completed the ideas of Bion, elaborating a theory in which aesthetic sensibility is understood as a primary event in life, and the aesthetic conflict fashions the beginnings of our imagination and phantasy, just as it does the disturbances in our mental life. On the literary side, Meg Harris Williams puts forward a psychoanalytic critique of the work of art modelled on concepts that harmonize with the psychoanalytic process. This implies valuing, within psychoanalytic criticism, the modality of the relationship that the subject entertains with his primary loved objects; the critic respects the mystery of art, avoiding interpretations that appropriate, in the same way as the baby comes to respect the mystery that the riches of the maternal body represent for him.

The point of view put forward here distances itself implicitly from the interpretative models that, since structuralism, had been advanced to give a scientific foundation to the interpretation of literary texts. The hermeneutic plan has primarily undermined this view, breaking down the one-sidedness of interpretations in favour of the subjectivity of the reading of the text. Currently, aesthetic criticism derived from the post-Kleinian model finds itself in agreement with those versions of contemporary thought that make an appeal to the imagination, to wonder, to the gratuitous gift of the moment, like the "illumination" of Maria Zambrano (1988 [1977]) and the "poetic writing" of Martha Nussbaum who, trusting her style, chooses to write in a way that will show "the complete spectrum of my reactions to the texts, attempting to evoke identical reactions in the reader" (Nussbaum, 1987).

The riches of the values of subjectivity and the evocative quality of poetic communication appropriate to these directions of thought, which foster a close rapport between the work of art and its interpreter and between interpreter and reader, can fairly be compared to the model of the intimacy of mother–baby, to their reciprocal giving to and questioning of one another, so that we can imagine a mother who tells of the beauty of her baby and a baby who wonders at the beauty of the mother as the prototype of the never-ending interpretation.

Notes

1. See in this connection Meltzer (1978, Vol. 1), p. 8.
2. The journal, founded in 1927 by Otto Rank and Hanns Sachs, was dedicated to the application of psychoanalysis to the human sciences.
3. See, in this connection, Kristeva (1984).

GLOSSARY

With the impossibility of expounding, even in summary, Bion's dense and difficult theorizing, we have restricted ourselves to providing an essential glossary of the concepts presented in the Introduction and in the anthology that follows, but only insofar as they are relevant to our text.

Alpha elements: Attributes of a thinker who is in the process of making sense of his emotions, including pre-existing thoughts.

Alpha function: Describes the primary activity by which the mother, in the course of the care that she instinctively provides for the baby, attributes meaning to its sensory and emotional perceptions, transforming them into symbolic elements. This transformation is accomplished through projective identification, the process by which the suckling projects his fears and anxieties together with part of his own mind, into a "container", the maternal breast, capable of modifying them.

Beta elements: Raw perceptual data that carry indescribable emotions, which are, therefore, without sense. They lend themselves to being evacuated as indigestible elements, but in the presence of a container (the maternal breast) are modified into alpha elements.

Contact barrier: Membrane that divides the non-symbolic from the symbolic part of the mind, i.e. beta elements from alpha elements.

The contact barrier is sufficiently permeable to allow the passage of beta elements in symbolic form, maintaining the process of symbolization.

Grid: Table that, by analogy with the periodic table of Mendeleev, puts psychoanalytic elements in vertical order (developmental axis) and horizontal order (axis of usage) (Bion, 1977).

Intrusive projective identification: Pathological inverting of projective identification in which there is a reduction of relational and communicative experience, since, in the absence of separation, the projective mechanism becomes a massive removal of the self into the maternal body, while the identificatory mechanisms assert, in a delusional way, an identity with the object.

Learning from experience: A way of learning linked to the development of a capacity for thinking. It is related to the capacity for maternal *reverie*, which modulates the emotional experience of the neonate: "One cannot learn from experience, nor can there be mental growth without having from birth a maternal container" (Bléandonu, 1994).

Links L, H, K: Indicate the links of Love, Hate, Knowledge between two persons or parts of a person. The ability to install links of love and of hate makes possible emotional experience and the development of the personality. The K-link in particular represents the feeling of sadness connected with the search into the truth of oneself.

Male and female ♀♂:   Relationship of container–contained, i.e. of what is projected into an object (the fear and anxiety of the baby) and the object that can function as container of the projection. ♀♂ is a crucial outcome of projective identification.

Mystical: In our context, the concept of "mystical" compares in terms of the part of the personality capable of putting itself in contact with O and to pursue a development in O.

O: On the epistemological plane, represents absolute truth unknowable and ineffable (Kant); in psychoanalytic terms it is the "quintessence" or "central characteristic" of an emotional situation. Its reality is present from the moment of *transformations*, which imply a catastrophic change. At such moments the analysand achieves an *evolution in O*, moving to a unison with that which transcends him insofar as it is the ultimate reality.

Projective identification: This concept is considered by Bion to be a universal mode of thought. It is the most primitive method of the infant for communicating with its mother (as also for the patient with the analyst), achieved by removing a part of the self into the inside of the object.

Ps ↔ D: Oscillation between processes of splitting and integration, which operates together with ♀♂.

Selected fact: Element that introduces order into the fragmented, leading to the establishment of a synthesis. Represents the simplest clement for approaching *D* (the depressive position).

Symbol: In Bion's theory, the concept of symbol tends to be treated in terms of a theory of mind. We restrict ourselves to mentioning the formulation: "No breast—therefore a thought", where the symbolic function consists in the capacity to recognize and live with absence. In a different but convergent vertex, the attribution of "symbolic" connotes the area of alpha elements transformed by the function of *maternal reverie.*

Thoughts in search of a thinker: In Bion's epistemological theory, thoughts pre-date the thinker. When the hitherto unthought thought comes into the mind of the thinker, a persecutory feeling is generated, which leads to splitting (*Ps*). This impact gives rise to *catastrophic change.*

PSYCHOANALYSIS AND ART

Introduction

From reparation to the aesthetic conflict

Melanie Klein: art as reparation

History of the concept of "reparation" (1927–1940)

Melanie Klein's essay, "Infantile Anxiety Situations Reflected in a Work of Art and in the Creative Impulse" (chapter 1, this volume), which first appeared in the *International Journal of Psycho-Analysis* in 1929, constitutes a prologue to the reflections on the creative process within British psychoanalysis. The essay is of theoretical and historical relevance, since for the first time artistic creativity was related to the concept of "reparation". Because for a long time the theory of "art as reparation" was considered as a relic of Kleinian thought about art, a brief digression is made here on Melanie Klein's thinking to help us understand its development.

In 1929 Klein had recently discovered the phantasy life of the infant, describing the deep psychic processes observed by her in the course of play sessions. She started out from the postulate of the existence in the baby of a quotient of aggression, the expression of the death instinct, intrinsic to the organism, which is expressed in sadistic and destructive attacks on the maternal body and on such phantasied contents—aggressive attacks that, however, turn against the baby himself by reason of the projection of his aggression into the objects: he imagines that the objects attacked are really bad and persecutory, he fears being devoured by them, torn to pieces, poisoned, fears that they are destroying

1

him with a sadism equal to that with which he, in phantasy, has destroyed the maternal object. Describing infantile play, Klein showed the way in which sadistic phantasies generate intense persecutory anxieties even if experienced in solitude. In a later period of her thinking, Klein designated this period of infantile life as "paranoid–schizoid", since to deal with the persecutory (paranoid) anxieties, the baby has recourse to mechanisms of defence: splitting the breast—and, successively, the mother and the world—into "good" and "bad", the projection of undesired aspects (e.g. aggression) into the other, and idealization. If the breast—and as a consequence the mother and the world—are totally bad and destructive, the baby creates in his phantasy a breast, a mother, a world that are exclusively good in which to take refuge. Splitting, projection, and idealization are the mechanisms of defence of the paranoid–schizoid "position", a distortion of reality that is at the root of a series of psychic disturbances that can lead to various clinical syndromes. Only with the advent of the "depressive position"[1] does the baby reconstruct the reality of the object in its wholeness, which signifies accepting the co-existence of good and bad. This is a reality that the baby can only accept by becoming aware of his own aggression and of the feelings of depression consequent on this. The feeling of guilt connected to depression is, for Klein, the beginning of mental health.

This theorizing about mental life, put together here, had begun with Melanie Klein's 1935 essay, "A Contribution to the Psychogenesis of Manic-Depressive States", to be completed in 1946 with "Notes on Some Schizoid Mechanisms", with its description of the paranoid–schizoid position (Ps). Among the concepts elaborated in this period, the concept of "reparation" found a special place: the infant passes from the paranoid–schizoid position to the depressive position—that is, from dissociative anxiety to depressive anxiety—a process that was subsequently indicated by the symbols $Ps \leftrightarrow D$. This means that after having sadistically destroyed, broken into pieces, devoured his primary love-object, the maternal breast, he is afraid on account of the damage inflicted, feels pity for the destroyed object, and grieves in the attempt to repair it. The approach to the depressive position begins when the baby puts into action all his talent, his love, and his creativity, succeeding in repairing the object. Reparation is "a powerhouse for mature energy and creativity in the actual external world" (Etchegoyen, 1991). From the outset, Melanie Klein showed how remorse, compassion, and genuine concern for destroyed objects can mobilize extraordinary creative and reconstructive forces. Even if she does not abandon the Freudian term "sublimation" and often accompanies it with that of "reparation", there is no doubt that the two concepts refer to differing views of psychic life. Sublimation developed within the Freudian theory of the libido, according to which a drive from the id is transformed, under pressure from the external world, into a socially acceptable creative potential. Reparation is, instead, the outcome of a primary relational view, in which the baby experiments with aggression towards the mother and the contents of her body, which, finally lead to concern and remorse—feelings from which arise the concern and love that are at the origin of the urge to create. At the same time as she was developing her theory, Melanie Klein abandoned the idea of sublimation while developing that of reparation, "which comes out of real concern for the object, a pining for it. It may involve great self-sacrifice in the external world into which damaged objects have been projected" (Etchegoyen, 1991).

It must be emphasized that this theorization belongs to a period of Kleinian thought that followed the essay of 1929. It should perhaps be said that Klein observed, from the outset, the tendency to reparation in the play of her little patients. In a 1927 essay on "Criminal Tendencies in Normal Children", Klein asserts that "The manifestation of these 'destructive' tendencies is invariably followed by anxiety, and by performances in which the child now tries to make good and to atone for what he has done. Sometime he tries to mend the very same dolls, trains, and so on that he has just broken. Sometimes drawing, building, and so on express the same 'reactive tendencies'" (p. 190). It is to be noted how Klein here defines the reparative impulse as merely "reactive"—that is to say, as a move intended to oppose an undesired event. In this move from reparation as merely reactive (1927) to reparation as a nuclear process in psychic life (1935–40) belongs the 1929 essay (chapter 1, this volume) with which we began, the first of Klein's works devoted to the creative process.

In this essay the author examines two works of art. The first is a composition by Ravel, who set to music a story written by Colette.[2] The protagonist is a child who, tired of studying and frustrated by his mother's hardness, becomes prey to a sadistic and destructive will, which leads him to strike the wooden animals and to destroy household objects. The animals and the objects then revolt against him until he has a feeling of pity for a toy and helps it, bandaging its wounded paw. There then occurs a reconciliation with the animals, and the boy whispers "Mamma", which the animals repeat with him. A reparative act (binding the paw of the toy, sowing a feeling of pity) ends the persecution of the boy and reconciles him with his mother. Here Klein does not mention the term "reparation", implicit in the event. The term appears, instead, in a story by the Danish writer, Karin Michaelis, which tells of the painter Ruth Kjär, a young woman who begins to suffer from depressive episodes when a painting is removed from the walls of her room. The space, remaining empty, "grinned hideously down at her". To overcome the sense of empty space, she begins to paint, starting on a profession that brings her to recompose, through painting, the destroyed maternal figure, thus overcoming the feeling of emptiness. The story ends with the description of two paintings, which the artist paints successively. They represent two old women: the first bearing the signs of years and of disillusionments of an old woman declining towards death, the second like a mother, full of energy, of pride and vitality. Klein shows how the painting of the woman full of life activates a reconciliation with the maternal figure:

> It is obvious that the desire to make reparation, to make good the injury psychologically done to the mother and also to restore herself was at the bottom of the compelling urge to paint these portraits of her relatives. That of the old woman on the threshold of death seems to be the expression of the primary, sadistic desire to destroy. The daughter's wish to destroy her mother, to see her old, worn out, marred, is the cause of the need to represent her in full possession of her strength and beauty. By so doing the daughter can allay her own anxiety and can endeavour to restore her mother and make her new through the portrait. In the analysis of children, when the representation of destructive wishes is succeeded by an expression of reactive tendencies, we constantly find that drawing and painting are used as means to restore people. [Chapter 1, this volume]

Here is recognized a fundamental value of reparation, both in overcoming anxiety and in setting in motion the creative process—even though it is still defined as a "reaction formation"—that is, the substitution for a repressed desire of an opposite attitude. In *The Psycho-Analysis of Children* (1932), the concept of reparation had been presented in terms of reaction formation.

In "A Contribution to the Psychogenesis of Manic-Depressive States" (Klein, 1935), Melanie Klein attributes a more important role to reparation: "We know that at this stage the Ego makes a greater use of introjection of the good object as a mechanism of defence. This is associated with another important mechanism: that of reparation to the object . . . it is far more than a mere reaction-formation." This mechanism of defence, in contradistinction to reaction-formation, has a structural valence, in so far as it is employed for defence and plays a part in the formation of the ego.

Another step forward occurs in the 1940 essay in which Melanie Klein, dealing with the problem of mourning, describes the outcome of the process in terms of reparation:

The pining for the lost loved object also implies dependence on it, but dependence of a kind which becomes an incentive to reparation and preservation of the object. . . . We know that painful experiences of all kinds sometimes stimulate sublimations, or even bring out quite new gifts in some people, who may take to painting, writing or other productive activities under the stress of frustrations and hardships. Others become more productive in a different way—more capable of appreciating people and things, more tolerant in their relation to others—they become wiser. . . . any pain caused by unhappy experiences . . . reactivates the depressive position; the encountering and overcoming of adversity of any kind entails mental work similar to mourning. [Klein, 1940]

As we see, here she is no longer speaking of creativity in terms of reaction formation, nor of mechanism of defence. Hanna Segal, too, dealing with the problem of reparation, asserts that it cannot be understood in terms of defence. It is, on the contrary, the driving force in the integration of the ego, in its growth and its adaptation to reality, "the strongest element of the constructive and creative urges" (Hinshelwood, 1989, p. 396) and "the cornerstone of the maturational processes that forge a way out of the depressive position" (p. 399).

Klein had also observed in the 1934 essay that:

the attempts to save the loved object, to repair and restore it, attempts which in the state of depression are coupled with despair, since the ego doubts is capacity to achieve this restoration, are determining factors for all sublimations and the whole of the ego-development. . . . It is a "perfect" object which is in pieces; thus the effort to undo the state of disintegration to which it has been reduced presupposes the necessity to make it beautiful and "perfect". The idea of perfection is, moreover, so compelling because it disproves the idea of disintegration. [Klein, 1935, p. 270]

As we see, the Kleinian route here begins to touch clearly on two aesthetic themes: the origin of the creative process and the concept of beauty. This is a topic that was to be developed particularly by Hanna Segal, one of the most eminent students of Klein.

Art as the expression of early processes

In the last years of her life, Melanie Klein devoted herself to a wider application of her psychoanalytic method. We have already said how, in the course of time, with the consolidation of her thinking, she drew away from classical theory, abandoning specifically Freudian concepts, including "sublimation", to develop the concept of "reparation" (Hinshelwood, 1989, p. 398). In the Kleinian view, reparation, just like the creative process, is part of the depressive position, including the putting together of the split object and the integration of the ego, which proceed *pari passu*: the theory of art as reparation links with the creative process in *D* (the depressive position). But what is to be said about all the shattered and split aspects, of the kernel of the more-or-less manifest perversions that we see in the art of every period, from Michelangelo to Bosch, not to speak of modern art? The fact that objects are cut, attacked, destroyed—or, conversely, idealized—that form is born from semantically opposed elements, is found in the art of every period. Among the many examples, Leonardo da Vinci's "Lady with the Ermine" shows a perfect feminine beauty, made disturbing by the "grafting" on of the male hand with which the lady controls the animal.

Confronted by the "disturbing" element of the work of art, the concept of "art as reparation" emphasizes maturity and the act of composition, risking underestimating the creative possibilities from within the paranoid–schizoid position. In this regard, we are helped by some illuminating intuitions presented in Melanie Klein's last papers.

In her 1958 essay "On the Development of Mental Functioning", Melanie Klein offers a vision of art that underlines and re-evaluates the role of *Ps* in artistic creativity:

> The more the ego can integrate its destructive impulses and synthe-size the different aspects of its objects, the richer it becomes; for the split-off parts of the self and of impulses which are rejected because they arouse anxiety and give pain also contain valuable aspects of the personality and of the phantasy life which is impoverished by split-ting them off. Though the rejected aspects of the self and of internal-ized objects contribute to instability, they are also at the source of inspiration in artistic productions and in various intellectual activi-ties. [Klein, 1958, p. 245]

This is an affirmation that goes side by side with a declaration in "Reflections on the Oresteia"[3], which anticipates a new line of investi-gation. Klein, in fact, affirms there that her "main concern is to establish the connection between the earliest processes and the productions of the adult artist". Implicit here are the lines of a very different route to a psychoanalytic aesthetics, in which an interest in the restorative ele-ment of which the form is composed allows for an interest in the disintegrated, split, fragmented, attacked, and devoured object, to the experiences of persecution, revenge, and the sequence of defences of idealization, omnipotence, and magic into which descend the perverse universe of Bosch and the deformed fragmentation of Picasso. This is primary in art, the wild tangle of the relation of the suckling with his part object (the breast) and his whole object (the mother), with his phantasied inside, which includes the paternal-penis/source-of-milk, and the internal siblings, felt as treasure to attack or steal from the mother.

This new way opens up possibilities from which we may follow various routes. What is worth underlining is the necessary integration of *Ps* and *D* in the creative process, whence we see the breaking up of a passionate and conflictual (*Ps*) tangle, which can only find representation in a form operated by *D*. In the words of an old Chinese poetic saying, "Heaven and Earth are trapped in the cage of form" (taken from Archibald MacLeish, in Harris Williams, 1987, p viii). It is our opinion that to insist on reparation, and therefore on harmony, does not allow for the fact that the artistic process, as also the creative process, is born from the chaos of primary impulses and affects.

With this second view Melanie Klein's discussion opens up a complex but clear view of art.

The interest in art in the 1950s

In the course of the 1950s there developed, within British psycho-analytic thought, a series of initiatives that had at their centre the problem of art, and these were not without influence from outside the Bloomsbury Group. Alix and James Strachey—sister-in-law and brother, respectively, of Lytton Strachey—were the first to foster enthusiasm for the ideas of Melanie Klein, making them known to the British Psycho-Analytical Society. In the course of 1925 Alix often visited Melanie Klein in Berlin, where both were in analysis with Abraham. During his stay in Berlin, Alix persuaded Melanie to come to London to give a series of lectures, which were held in the home of Adrian Stephen, brother of Virginia Woolf. We know that the writer made a habit of attending his lectures, continuing to admire her "subtlety; something working underground" (Grosskurth, 1986, p. 137). Joan Riviere, who became a student of Klein, also became part of the Bloomsbury Group, though she was less committed. On the whole, the British Psycho-Analytical Society was in varying degrees linked to Bloomsbury, as is shown by the fact that it was the Hogarth Press, the publishing house founded by Leonard Woolf, that was to publish the series "The International Psycho-Analytical Library".

In 1926, thanks to the intervention of the Stracheys, Melanie Klein moved to London at the invitation of Ernest Jones. She soon felt at her ease in the environment of London, so full of art and literature and extremely receptive to her ideas. While her genius showed itself in clinical work, her theories, just because they revealed hitherto unknown psychic processes, led to new approaches in the social sciences and in particular in the field of art. This highly productive melting-pot of interests led to the founding, in the 1950s, of the Imago Group by the well-known art historian Adrian Stokes, who was also analysed by Melanie Klein. Some dozen persons, linked to Melanie Klein by having been analysed by her and having become her pupils, participated in the group, which met in the home of Ernest Jones's widow. Among them, we would like to mention Donald Meltzer, Wilfred R. Bion, Roger Money-Kyrle, and Marion Milner.

While there are no accounts extant of the meetings in the Jones's home, some published documents show the range of this sector of applied psychoanalysis. Two contributions read by Meltzer at the Imago Group in 1964–65 and later published in the volume *The Apprehension of Beauty* (see Meltzer, 1994, chapters 6 & 7), deal with sociological and historical themes, testifying to the interest of the students of Melanie Klein in extending Kleinian thinking to the whole range of the human sciences, just as in his time Freud had foreseen for his psychoanalytic theories.

Of greater importance, which also relates to our argument, is Adrian Stokes's book, *Painting and the Inner World* (1963a), in which he puts forward a theoretical and interpretative model for application to works of art. The second part of the volume, containing a discussion on art between Stokes and Meltzer (Stokes, 1963b), was published in *The Apprehension of Beauty*. The debate presupposes an understanding of the Kleinian psychic apparatus as a sequence of movements between states of fragmentation and states of integration, summarized in the formula $Ps \leftrightarrow D$. Unlike Freud, who had described mental health as a point reached through a series of phases, in their turn coincident with the psycho-sexual developmental phases, Melanie Klein did not view mental health as a state reached definitively with the approach to the depressive position. The subject is, on the contrary, constantly obliged to renegotiate his mental state, passing between the paranoid–schizoid position, in which primitive anxieties and defences are shown, and the depressive position, in which the corresponding anxieties are overcome in the re-creative processes of reparation. A reading of the discussion allows one to see the variety of problems that then worried the small group, among which was the ambitious intention of "formulating a theory of art" (Stokes, 1963b, p. 212) based on Kleinian concepts and on the Kleinian model of the mind. The principles on which the members of the group agreed can be summarized: art accepted as being within the movement $Ps \leftrightarrow D$, artistic creativity as derived from projective identification and the overcoming of anxiety, the responsibility of the artist to nurture and promote the values of the depressive position. The controversial element is the value of idealization, which, while it has a role in relation to art, is in psychoanalysis seen as a mechanism of defence. In the following years Meltzer himself, with other students, proposed a re-evaluation of the "values of the paranoid–schizoid position", but the positive view of the depressive position and of reparation was dominant at the time when Stokes's book appeared, so that Meltzer could conclude the discussion praising the "world of art" in so far as it was "the expression of beauty and of the goodness of psychic reality" (Stokes, 1963b, p. 225) and "the institutionalization of the social forces in the direction of integration"—a view of the social role of art about which Meltzer himself would, much later, show himself to be strongly disillusioned.[4]

The debate between Stokes and Meltzer can at times be difficult to understand insofar as it puts forward a series of arguments that are not adequately supported, being based on a theoretical system still under-developed in relation to its subject matter.

As of now, the construction of a psychoanalytic theory of literature appears to be a matter of hope. In this sense the affirmations made during the discussions can be considered as points of departure: the idea of art as a therapeutic process that may facilitate a passage from the paranoid–schizoid to the depressive position[5]; the existence of values of the paranoid–schizoid position (well-being, gratification, omnipotence) and of values of the depressive position (solicitude, responsibility, gratitude): in short, the concept of art as a representation of the passage of internal objects from a state of fragmentation to integration and vice-versa, which implies a large reduction of anxiety with a lesser use of defence mechanisms.

"New directions in psychoanalysis"

If the Imago Group, active in the 1950s and 1960s, is the first sign of the breadth of interest of Kleinian psychoanalysis in the widest fields of knowledge, another enterprise, this time published, is evidence of the intention of the British School to propose the broadening of clinical theory to include interpretations far removed from the immediately therapeutic. The authors of the book, in addition to being medical and psychoanalytic, were familiar with the world of art; some of them came from other disciplines: Money-Kyrle came from the world of philosophy but with a considerable interest in social phenomena, and Bion, before becoming a doctor and psychoanalyst, had been a history teacher. Many had strong philosophical leanings, including Bion, as is testified by his work. Obviously, each of them could not do other than to read and interpret with a psychoanalytic lens their own areas of interest. From this cultural richness was born the project of a volume of collected papers: *New Directions in Psycho-Analysis*, published in 1955.

The particular feature of *New Directions in Psycho-Analysis* was to gather together writings of purely Kleinian origin with members from the Middle Group, who, in the split within the British Psycho-Analytical Society between the followers of Melanie Klein and those of Anna Freud, maintained an equidistant position, developing an independent line of thought that was less aligned with the opposed orthodoxies of the two schools.[6] The book, divided into two parts, the first devoted to the clinical and the second to what is again termed, on the Freudian model, "applied psychoanalysis", intends to offer a panoramic view of the point reached through the Kleinian perspective not only in the clinical field but also in a variety of areas of the social sciences. We will restrict ourselves to the essays relating to aesthetics and to art, tracing, so to say, a map of the theoretical views presented in those years insofar as they deal with the problem of aesthetic perception and the creative processes.

From the book we can pick out three different routes to an aesthetic and critical approach. We have chosen also to add a fourth route: that represented by Donald Winnicott in an essay on "Transitional Objects and Transitional Phenomena", originally written for the 1955 volume of but rejected by Melanie Klein, who did not accept, for theoretical reasons, the existence of "transitional objects". This episode well illustrates the belligerent climate in British psychoanalysis in those years.

Melanie Klein's essay on "projective identification", like the two essays of Joan Riviere, shows clearly her involvement in the field of art. In her paper, which opens the section devoted to "applied psychoanalysis", Klein describes the operation of projective identification and envy through the analysis of a story by Julien Green, *Si j'étais vous* (Klein, 1955, pp. 309 ff). At the same time, the author demonstrates the function of a process of integration that works against disintegration (*Ps*), directing positively the internal life of the protagonist.

Klein's point of view is shared by Joan Riviere, who in two essays demonstrates the important part played in poetry by primitive defence mechanisms, in particular that of projective identification (chapter 3, this volume). In the second essay, on Ibsen (Riviere, 1959, pp. 370ff), she gives us perhaps the first example of an interpretative method that develops from the analytic tradition of dream interpretation, by which the various characters in a poetic or theatrical tale can be understood as figures of the internal world, so that "the whole drama can be said to be a representation of that".[7]

Hanna Segal develops, instead, in a masterly way the Kleinian concept of art as reparation, connecting artistic creation to the depressive position, understood in terms of the elaboration of mourning. Her essay (chapter 2, this volume) is based, in addition to her clinical examples, on a reading of Proust's *A la Recherche du Temps Perdu*, through which the author shows how artistic creativity presupposes loss, renunciation, abandonment. Segal confronts the nature of the aesthetic experience and art as the bringing together of the "ugly"—destructiveness, aggression, death instinct—and of the "beautiful"—union, life instinct—expressed through form.

Adrian Stokes (1955, pp. 406ff) takes up Hanna Segal's theme, developing it particularly in relation to figurative art. He elaborates the concept of form, whether in its benign aspects of the depressive position or in its various elements belonging to the paranoid–schizoid position—idealization, ferocity, obsessive and paranoid characteristics—for which art offers a harmless expression. Stokes's essay develops a view of the creative process as a union of Eros and Thanatos, where the experience of fusion with the breast is accompanied by recognition of the otherness of the object. The artistic object, understood as form, succeeds paradoxically in yoking together two contrary elements: fusion and otherness.

A third perspective is offered by the writings of Marion Milner, who was equally close to Melanie Klein and Donald Winnicott. Milner illustrates the concept of "symbolization" as the foundation of every type of creativity, so that the emphasis is moved from "reparation" to "symbolization" (chapter 4, this volume). The symbol of which Milner speaks is that described by Melanie Klein, which is created through a transfer of interest from the primary object—the breast—to an object in the outside world which, from an emotional point of view, is felt as analogous. In this way the baby transfers his curiosity and his love of the maternal body to the outside world, enlarging his intellectual and emotional life. This is the point at which Milner almost imperceptibly modifies the Kleinian discourse, affirming here that the process of moving from the maternal body to the external world is possible in so far as it is possible through "finding the familiar in the unfamiliar".[8] For Milner, the baby perceives the external world as all united and harmonious because he invests it "with something of himself" which makes it "familiar and comprehensible" (chapter 4, this volume).[9] It is in this sense that the author can coin a felicitous phrase when she asserts that "Art creates Nature", which is to say that without a unified mental universe (art) nature (the external world) would not be for us a harmonious, unified world, the source of beauty. At the same time it should be noted that Wordsworth's phrase "identity in diversity" alludes implicitly to the transitional area described by Winnicott.

Milner's essay uses many concepts such as "illusion", "phantasy", "oceanic feeling", "blurring of boundaries"—categories all related to pre-logical thinking.

It should be emphasized that Marion Milner is the first psychoanalyst to attribute particular importance both to the beauty of analysis and to the sensation of beauty in particular moments of analysis, thus raising the question of its importance clinically.

Donald Winnicott, in his essay on "Transitional Objects and Transitional Phenomena" (1951), introduces concepts that were to have great importance within psychoanalysis: the transitional object is the first external object onto which the baby transfers the feelings for his mother. It constitutes an intermediate place between internal and external, easing the process of separation between the baby and the mother, which occurs for Winnicott in an intermediate zone, which he calls "potential space" or "area of illusion" in which the area of the mother and that of the baby overlap, allowing play, where the baby expresses its creativity. Winnicott's now well-known theory of "transitional phenomena" appears of extreme importance not only in the clinical field but also for a theory of the creative processes, since that theory brings together the origins of "creativity and artistic taste, of religious feeling and of the dream".

Donald Meltzer: the aesthetic conflict

The premises

Psychoanalytic thought aimed, from its beginnings, at putting forward the bases of a *Weltanschauung* that could explain almost all of the social sciences. Freud in particular, in his theoretical journeyings, moved from anthropology to poetry, from literature to myth, from folklore to the plastic and figurative arts. Even if so-called "applied" psychoanalysis in various fields combined in itself the aim of understanding those fields and at the same time of putting forward new psychoanalytic concepts, this ended by developing in two directions, exactly as was organized in the book *New Directions in Psycho-Analysis*. This was the dual route to which Freud had in his time set his seal with the creation of the review *Imago*, devoted to "applied" psychoanalysis and generating, in the course of time, a division between this and so-called "clinical" psychoanalysis.

What is special about Donald Meltzer is how he has put together the two aspects, clinical and aesthetic, born not only from a theoretical aim, but also tied to a natural capacity to "read" a clinical case in terms of beauty: beauty as the driving force of the "aesthetic conflict", beauty as a primary function of the mind, and, furthermore, beauty as an intrinsic component of the psychoanalytic method. This way of working is present in his first writings, supported by a theorization that developed during the following years, which brings together a complete congruence between the concepts of "aesthetic object" and "aesthetic conflict", preceding the Oedipus complex, and active probably from birth or even in the last period of intra-uterine life. The author locates his theoretical presuppositions in the Freud of the clinical cases and of the second, topographical, model (id, ego, superego), whereas the first theory, that of drives and libido, appears to him to have been still infused with neuropsychological thinking, which lacks the interpersonal dimension that is at the base of Kleinian theory. Melanie Klein brought to light a fantastic world of objects endowed with particular concreteness: the "internal objects" (mother, father, babies, paternal penis, maternal breast, combined object, etc.) weave among themselves and with the baby a rich series of shifting relationships and combinations in addition to the "positions", paranoid–schizoid or depressive, within which they come together. Each of the two positions is distinguished by specific mechanisms of defence, which Meltzer understands in terms of "values".[10]

Meltzer's main source of reference is the thinking of Wilfred R. Bion, who developed psychoanalysis in an epistemological direction, having as its subject the birth of thinking. For Bion, unlike Freud and Klein, the mind is no longer essentially intrapsychic, but relational. This implies a dependence on the other, an interaction. In Bion's model, alongside an innate predisposition or unconscious phantasy (Susan Isaacs) in the baby, there is a very important maternal function—the function of reverie—which allows the baby in its turn to develop alpha function.

Bion's thinking, while not explicitly dealing with aesthetic problems, was stated by Meltzer to have been like an inspiration for the "new idea" that revolutionized his way of understanding psychoanalysis. The "new idea", affirms Meltzer, "is clearly something like 'in the beginning was the aesthetic object, and the aesthetic object was the breast and the breast was the world' . . ." (chapter 12, this volume). (For an explanation of Bion's terminology, see Glossary.)

*The first phase of Donald Meltzer's theories:
clinical studies and the post-Kleinian model*

Donald Meltzer's interest in the problem of aesthetics is documented from the time of his arrival in London to have analysis with Melanie Klein, linked, as we have shown, with the Imago Group.

With the dissolution of the group, Meltzer devoted himself to an impressive clinical research, which occupied him for more than a decade, in which the aesthetic dimension appeared in many ways, particularly in terms of an analogy between psychoanalytic work and artistic creativity.

Here we make only brief references to that period, so full of clinical interest. Of particular importance, also for its guiding role, which was gradually to unfold, is the 1965 essay on "Anal Masturbation and Projective Identification" (Meltzer, 1966), in which the author describes the important role of masturbation in supporting the unconscious phantasm of intrusion into the mother's rectum: "this derives from a confusion of identity, in which the baby who explores the inside of his own body, with the unconscious phantasm of exploring the mother's inside, identifies in a delusional way with the internal mother" (Fano Cassese, 2002). In his first book, *The Psycho-Analytical Process* (1967), Meltzer reconfigures this confusion of identity in terms of geographical confusion, used to deny the separation of the self from the object for fear of experiencing a separate identity. These problems of intrusion linked to anal masturbation and to the denial of separation will be redefined, in the last phase of Meltzer's theories, in terms of the *claustrum*.

Meltzer's interest in aesthetics, re-appearing in his first London period, is shown in the short 1973 essay "On the Apprehension of Beauty" (chapter 6, this volume) and runs through the three volumes of *The Kleinian Development* (Meltzer, 1978), where the author traces a single route, starting from Freud, passing through the work of Melanie Klein, and reaching Bion, giving birth to the line of thought that will be defined as "post-Kleinian". In the same field belongs the critique of the Freudian concept of sublimation found in *Sexual States of Mind* (1973). This work, devoted to the subject of psycho-sexual development, particularly in adolescence, also contains illuminating pointers to problems of creativity. In particular, the author substitutes for the Freudian concept of sublimation his own view: that sexuality and passion are the driving forces of creativity. Inventiveness in every field (scientific or artistic) is connected to the realm of idealization and the ideal, implicates affects and passions, and has a sexual origin and significance.

The clinical and historical writings, run through with frequent references to the aesthetic dimension, led to a turning point in Meltzer's thinking, in which we can discern three periods. The first we have already mentioned: having begun in the middle of the 1960s with *The Psycho-Analytical Process*, it was developed in the monumental clinical work of the 1970s, which includes, in addition to the works already mentioned, *Explorations in Autism* (Meltzer et al., 1975). In 1984, in the second phase, he offers the first elaboration of what will be the "aesthetic psychoanalysis". The third phase sees his full elaboration, in the 1980s and 1990s, with *The Apprehension of Beauty* (1988) and *The Claustrum* (1992).

The second phase: towards a psychoanalysis of aesthetics

Two papers in 1984 open the second phase of Meltzer's thought. The first, "The Aesthetic Object" (chapter 9, this volume), is a short but illuminating contribution. In the space of one weekend of work on infantile autism, the author sets out the innovative directions of a psychoanalysis of the future: the concept of the "aesthetic object"; the uterus as a claustrum; birth as "the primary aesthetic experience"; the hypothesizing of an "aesthetic conflict", which arises in connection with the relationship between external beauty and the internal contents of the mother; the reversal of the precedence of the paranoid–schizoid position to assert the precedence of the depressive position. The extempore contribution constituted a true and fitting manifesto, which contains in a nutshell all that Donald Meltzer was to develop in the years that followed.

In the same year appeared *Dream Life* (1983), an elaborate volume that puts forward a revision of the Freudian theory of the dream in an aesthetic mode. To the neuro-physiological and quantitative model of the *Interpretation of Dreams* (Freud, 1900a), Meltzer counterposes "the world of Romantic literature and art . . . characters were repeatedly being depicted as haunted by their dreams, fearful of sleep lest they be repeated" (Meltzer, 1983, p. 12). Interest is shifted from the mechanism of dream-formation, which for Freud did not imply thought, to a view of the dream as "essentially the function of the mind which deals with our aesthetic experience of the world where 'beauty is truth, truth beauty'" (Meltzer, 1983, p. 29). Meltzer's theory put to fruition, here more than anywhere else, Bion's ideas: "Dreaming *is* thinking; dream life. . . (p. 46). The problem of dreams also relates to the problem of language, the profoundly emotional roots of which Meltzer demonstrates in a view of mental life that puts emotions and their meaning at its centre.

The key to the passage from these first illuminating anticipations about aesthetics is his pointing out the particular and important role of beauty in mental life that is consolidated in the *Studies in Extended Metapsychology* (Meltzer, 1986). This book was written in two very productive years, starting from 1984. As stated in the *Introduction*, the book occasioned a qualitative leap from a causal view of mental life to an artistic one. Following Bionic theory, Meltzer places at the origins of symbolic life the "mystery" of alpha function, the source of a process in which the imagination, a function of the "mystical" part of the personality, works to restore the impenetrable void at its centre.

Thus psychoanalysis discovers the need for a new vocabulary that includes terms such as imagination, excitement, emotion, passion, affect, intimacy, mystery, tyranny, trust, hope: a vocabulary of "sentimental education", which will become enriched in the following years in the writings in the supervision workshops.

It must be emphasized that the term "extended psychoanalysis" implies an extension of the field of psychoanalysis to include the aesthetic dimension, which is here for the first time linked explicitly and organically to the clinical. It is no longer a matter of intuitions and analogies between psychoanalytic and artistic work—rather, it is one of pointing out the aesthetic roots of mental processes, of pathology as much as of creativity. This movement occurred gradually and can be seen in the successive interpretations of autism, beginning with *Explorations in Autism* (Meltzer et al., 1975), in which the author describes in the autistic personality a typical mechanism that he terms "dismantling"— that is, giving up the act of concentrating his "attention", which is how the autistic child reacts to difficult situations. The second interpretation is expressed by Meltzer in his use of the term "improvisation" in his "Study Days on Autism" (see Meltzer, "The Aesthetic Object", chapter 9, this volume), where autism is described as a flight from the paranoid–schizoid position to defend against the impact of the aesthetic object and of the disturbing question about the aesthetic congruence between the inside and the outside of the object; in Meltzer's terms, the baby, confronted by the mother's beauty, asks itself: "but is her inside beautiful?" This question constitutes "the very essence of the depressive position", from which one defends oneself by taking refuge in the paranoid–schizoid position which is always a defence against the depressive position.

Two years later, in *Studies in Extended Metapsychology*, Donald Meltzer reworks *Explorations in Autism* in terms of the "aesthetic conflict" and in his latest explication of a concept already referred to in 1984, that of the claustrum understood as a refuge inside an internal mother operated through what he calls "intrusive identification", a pathological use of projective identification, which aims to invade another's personality and body through subterfuge and fraud. This occurs in the predatory and devastating ways described by Melanie Klein. Insofar as the violence of the intrusion leads to the fragmentation of the container, intrusive identification is at the root of a series of severe mental disturbances, from claustrophobic phenomena to perversions to schizophrenia.

In *Studies in Extended Metapsychology* is developed the line of thought that will lead to "Love and Fear of Beauty", a re-evaluation of the aesthetic conflict through the bringing together of two disciplines, clinical psychoanalysis and literary criticism. Meltzer brings to this a significant move: clinical psychoanalysis and literature no longer represent parallel or concurrent sectors but, rather, come together in the aesthetic "apprehension" of the mental. "Love and Fear of Beauty", says Meltzer, is born from a "joint family venture" in which the reciprocal influences of sensitivity and thought have woven together psychoanalysis and literary criticism.

Third phase: aesthetic psychoanalysis

The aesthetic conflict

"My own first glimpse of the problem was recorded in a paper called 'The Apprehension of Beauty', where I also failed to grasp what I had glimpsed, as I think had Hannah Segal in her famous paper on aesthetics", wrote Meltzer at the end of the *Studies in Extended Metapsychology*. What had then not been grasped was "the enigma of the inside and the outside of the aesthetic object" with its "ability to evoke emotionality . . . only equalled by its ability to generate anxiety, doubt, mistrust" (see "Dénouement", chapter 12, this volume). This conflict contained for Meltzer the key to symbol formation.

This concept is made fully explicit in the 1988 volume *The Apprehension of Beauty*, in which the authors, Donald Meltzer and Meg Harris Williams, describe, in a series of clinical–literary essays, the phenomenology of the aesthetic conflict: two authors because, as Meltzer explains, it was "a joint venture, interdigitating clinical psychoanalysis and literary criticism"—"the two sciences of psycho-analysis and of art or . . . literary criticism are so intertwined with one another when approached from a descriptive vertex" (Meltzer & Harris Williams, 1988, p. 203).

The concepts which form the basis of the work are those of "the aesthetic object", the maternal breast, and the "aesthetic conflict", which originate from the questioning by the baby of the match between the mother's interior and her exterior.

The function of the breast has been, furthermore, understood, in psychoanalytic literature, in terms of protecting against fragmentation: the warmth of the milk which reaches inside the body gives well-being and reassurance, allowing the newborn baby to gain a unified perception of the self, which contrasts with the persecutory anxiety generated by hunger, while the nipple in the mouth ensures an external bulwark which leads to a primary security in space. But the maternal object very soon generates a series of insecurities about its real intentions: what is in the mother's mind? Is she beautiful in her invisible inside, or is she hiding dangerous intentions? Another range of insecurities assails the neonate in regard to the inadequacies of the maternal figure, so that the aesthetic impact of her beauty generates an experience of being over-whelmed if the mother does not set in motion a reciprocity that leads her, in her turn, to see her newborn as "beautiful". Many mothers tell that when they see their child for the first time, they are struck by an "enchantment", experiencing "love at first sight", which is "the sine qua non of the baby's tolerance to the aesthetic blow it receives from the mother" (Meltzer & Harris Williams, 1988, p. 57).

The mother presents her baby with "a complex object of over-whelming interest . . . her outward beauty, concentrated as it must be in her breast and her face, complicated in every case by her nipples and her eyes" (chapter 13, this volume) generates in the baby the first, intense perception of beauty. But at the same time the baby does not understand the meaning of the mother's behaviour, her appearance and disappearance, the emotional changes that he perceives in the changes in her face. He then perceives the existence of an invisible inside of the mother, which is for him an unknown and disturbing country. The mother becomes enigmatic, her voice changes in tone, and her words are indecipherable. Even in the course of lactation at the breast she gives ambiguous messages, since if, on the one hand, it takes away the pangs of hunger, leading to well-being and calm, the milk then changes into an internal content which generates unpleasant tensions, of which the newborn must rid himself. Who, then, is the mother: is she Beatrice or the Gioconda or his Belle Dame Sans Merci? Is she beatific or will she lead him to perdition?

The question in the mind of the mother, of her real intentions, leads the baby to ask itself about her sincerity. The words that Hamlet asks Ophelia—"are you honest?"—are for Meltzer allegoric of the aesthetic conflict.

The primary conflict between "the beautiful mother" perceptible to the senses and that which is enigmatic internally leads to a construction of the inside through creative imagination, as is testified by so much figurative art and literature. Because the infant can use its imagination, it can be asserted that there is activated the curiosity that Melanie Klein had understood as the "epistemological instinct", a thirst for knowl-edge that Bion has designated with the sign K (*Knowledge*), linked to L (*Love*) and H (*Hate*). In this fluctuation between love and hate (love which is generated through the continuity of the relationship to the breast and in the togetherness of care, hate from maternal ambivalence, her disappearing, her being uncontrollable externally and internally) what saves the object is K, the desire for knowledge, which becomes a potent stimulus to creativity.

But it can be that in place of knowledge there supervenes the "need to possess", which opens the way to every sort of vandalizing intrusion, while the lack of imaginative ability blocks creativity and generates envy of beauty. This negative outcome of the aesthetic conflict is accompanied by cynical attacks meant to vilify the object, and to the violation of its inside through intrusive identification. In *The Apprehension of Beauty* Meltzer describes convincingly the process of relapse in terms of the vulgarization of taste, violence, and tyranny. The book, assembled by two pairs of hands, reviews various aspects of the aesthetic conflict, alternating clinical essays and those of literary criticism, the latter importantly not bearing the author's signature, serving to demonstrate how the process set in motion both in analysis and in the coming to fruition of a work of art are essentially one.

This courageous turn within psychoanalytic thought should come to be fully accepted by many workers, additionally because it brings together diverse disciplines. If it is true that psychoanalysis and art are, at their roots, stories based on analogous/similar mental processes, at a more superficial level we know that the two disciplines came together within historically different contexts, with different jargons and different levels of competence.

In reality the invitation to put together the two disciplines encounters obstacles both from psychoanalysis, which is in many respects anchored in a pseudo-scientific medical, biological, and positivist matrix, and from literary criticism, which from the 1970s onwards privileged formalizations based on a logico–mathematical model. This model, in its various forms of structuralism, semiology, and linguistics, has rendered more distant an approach to art in the Bionic sense of *learning from experience*.

Starting from this understanding, Meg Harris Williams proposes a critical method based on the model of the mind described by psychoanalysis, emphasizing at the same time the existential value of bringing to fruition the work of art.

Aesthetic criticism

A preview of Harris Williams's thinking is contained in an essay on Wordsworth, in which are demonstrated the theoretical presuppositions of an "aesthetic critique" which bears a strong imprint of the psychoanalytic model. The author models her approach on that of Adrian Stokes, with its sensitivity, Stokes having himself been influenced by the ideas of Bion and Meltzer. From Stokes comes the proposal for an aesthetic listening analogous to "holding on to the feeling of the dream": "The contents that reach us in terms of aesthetic form have the 'feel' of a forgotten dream" (see chapter 20, this volume), which cedes its mystery to the viewer only on condition that he "tolerate the cloud of unknowing" that emanates from the aesthetic object.

Harris Williams shows how this implies "thinking with" the work of art in place of "speaking about the work of art", developing a symbolic congruence between the structure of the self and the structure of the aesthetic object, thus moving in the direction of a process rather than an interpretation. The effect of enchantment or of "enveloping oneself" in the work of art at first leads the viewer to be overcome by the "cloud of unknowing". Only gradually does there emerge from the object a pattern, which leads the viewer to respond to the work of art with words modelled on the struggle of the poet to produce a symbolic form. This is the "symbolic equivalence" of which Harris Williams speaks, meaning "the intense concentration on the process of finding a containing, descriptive language congruent to the artist's own symbolic exploration" (Meltzer & Harris Williams, 1988, p. 190), "the first that ever burst / Into that silent sea" (Coleridge) (chapter 20, this volume).

A felicitous formulation of Harris Williams is "the deep-laid metaphor" with which the author points to "the symbol of form . . . which offers a container for the 'feel' of a dream otherwise forgotten" (Meltzer & Harris Williams, 1988, p. 187). This is a concept that supported the structure of a book by Meg Harris Williams and Margot Waddell, *The Chamber of Maiden Thought* (Keats), the various chapters of which take their names from the metaphors through which the processes of symbol formation are expressed: "Soul Making" (Keats), "Unmapped Country" (George Eliot), "The Mind's Own Place" (Milton), "The Visionary Gleam" (Wordsworth), and so on. The "deep-laid metaphor" is the end product of the process of symbol formulation that enables the reader/ viewer to entertain the dream in his mind, bearing the weight of the mystery represented by the aesthetic object. The critic employs, in Bion's terms, an "identification with the evolution of O", which modifies his mental make-up analogously with the formal qualities of the aesthetic object. This choice is the opposite of interpretation, which requires definition and makes use of presumed scientific concepts, and which, in various ways, claimed to reach "the heart of the mystery".

Harris Williams's opposition to "intrusive" criticism, which aims to "reveal" or, conversely, "trap" the aesthetic object in an extrinsic formal structure or cage is restated by Meltzer in terms of a deficiency of symbolic capacity, which leads to his placing the mystery of beauty in what, at a recent conference, he called "the skeleton of the symbol" (chapter 18, this volume).

The claustrum

While *The Apprehension of Beauty* shows the function of maternal reverie in transforming things perceived into symbols through alpha function, *The Claustrum* (1992) takes us into a dark claustrophobic and claustrophilic world. Unlike the maternal container, which wraps round and protects the baby, adjusting itself to its spatial and mental needs and favouring creativity, the claustrum is a rigid container, without elasticity, which imprisons like the "mother–Prague" of Kafka: "Prague does not get soft. It does not soften us two. This mother has claws. One must adapt or. . . . At two points we must apply fire to her . . . and in this way it will be possible to free ourselves".[11]

The focal point of the book is "life in the claustrum", the closed maternal space into which the infantile part penetrates and in which it remains trapped. It brings to our attention again the clinical studies in autism and on the psychoses of the 1970s, alongside more recent writings, which move within the literary and artistic dimensions of Meltzer's aesthetic period. This procedure, in its riches, makes for difficult reading, increased by the analysis of phenomena drawn from early and pre-verbal material, the reality of which is difficult to communicate in conventional language. Meltzer himself warns us that his description of patients fixated in the infantile world of the claustrum could seem to be the products of the therapist's imagination, or, rather, a fiction, and, in accordance with his new way of proceeding, he chooses to deal with the clinical material in an evocative way with the help of a vast literary and artistic store that can provide forms for perceptions derived from *insight* and *countertransference*, from dreams and infantile phantasies. To choose in this situation to set out the basic processes of the claustrum can thus seem a contrary approach, even though it appears necessary to help understand the phenomenology of the claustrum for those who do not know its internal dynamics.

The origins of the claustrum are intrinsically bound up with projective identification, a concept described by Melanie Klein as a defence mechanism of the paranoid–schizoid position, whereby the subject frees himself from an unwanted part of himself, uniting himself with the object (originally the maternal object), with serious consequences for mental health. Projective identification is strictly linked to splitting processes: it has to be hypothesized that the personality would be in a state of falling to pieces, to be then able to think that a piece can be inserted, in phantasy, into an external object (Klein, 1946).

The role attributed to projective identification changed during the years that followed, when its universal function as pre-requisite for communication came to be understood. Bion in particular put into relief its important role in mother–infant communication, essential for the establishment of alpha function. A large part of our adult life is based on projective identification, present in all intimate relations, for example love, the psychoanalytic process, and also in emotional but non-verbal relationships, as in the case of mutism or of our relations with animals.

Projective identification, the cornerstone of alpha function, is transformed in a negative way when it becomes "intrusive", a concept which, in *The Psycho-Analytical Process*, Meltzer had described with the term "massive projective identification"—that is, originating from an excessive projective identification by which the subject invades the object, doing harm to the container on account of this excess. This quantitative criterion Meltzer later abandoned in favour of a qualitative view of the process, which he termed "intrusive identification"—that is, penetration into the inside of the object (the maternal body or, in analysis, the analyst) through all available orifices in ways which are based on "violence, stealth and trickery" (Meltzer, 1992, p. 71). Intrusive identification loses every aspect of communication insofar as it is based on the phantasy of fusion with the object. The violent nature of intrusive identification destroys the container, the place for maternal alpha function. The container is now transformed into a claustrum, a rigid prison brought about by the intrusive process either of active penetration or of being sucked in passively.

The claustrum, like the maternal container, also has its internal space, which, by contrast, is terrifying on account of the violence of the intrusion. While the working of the maternal alpha function, linked to aesthetic reciprocity, creates the conditions for respect for the integrity of the object, intrusive identification invades and devastates the container. In this case "consciousness (may) be found only by penetrating and scavenging within the object, with the risk of remaining trapped in the black hole of the maternal body and devoured by monsters" (Fano Cassese, 1998, p. 50).

The unconscious operations peculiar to the claustrum carry material that is naturally "confused", expressed in psychoanalytic categories that were understood, in earlier psychoanalytic literature, in terms of geographical confusion, misunderstandings, self-deceptions, lies. A reading of *The Claustrum* conveys in many places this sensation of confusion, which is plausible because all the categories of the claustrum are about confused objects. It appears incorrect, however, to attribute two contradictory functions to projective identification: one that generates the symbol-forming alpha function, in contrast to another that forms the basis for the confused objects of the claustrum. The difference is, rather, between projective identification, the great weaver of the

world of the mind, and intrusive identification, generator of disturbances leading to the vast field of the psychoses. In the same way, the
term "confusion" is understood in a positive sense, as one can see in the
genesis of that eminently psychoanalytic object, the inside of the internal object, coloured by the emotions, phantasies, desires, and fears of
the infant.

To indicate the movements that bear on the creation of the inside of
the internal object, one has to begin from the two aspects of projective
identification: that which is identificatory and that which is projective;
as we have seen, the subject splits off an unwanted part of the self and
projects it into the object (or into the mother), installing himself in a
receptive space. There occurs at this point a first process of con-fusion
between the projected and the receptive parts, which come to be understood as a single object: successively the subject introjects (or internal-
izes or *identifies* with) the external object into which the projection
occurred—or, rather, he identifies with the con-fused object. It is precisely this internalization of an external object with which there has
been a projective identification that introduces the idea that external
objects can be internalized: the confusion in this case is [to be] understood in terms of fusion between two objects (con-fusion), differentiated but not necessarily psychotic or autistic, but at the service of the
process of internalization.

Maps and compartments

When he comes to describe the six areas or zones of the mental
apparatus, it seems that after having struggled with all the demons of
Milton's *Pandemonium*, Meltzer submits to the necessity to create a map
(Meltzer, 1992, p. 118)—or, rather, as is asserted in the preface to the
book, he creates "an architectural model as seen from inside", outlining
a geography of the mental apparatus and of the compartments of the
internal mother, in an attempt to put some order to the confusion,
which is not only that of the claustrum, but also that described in *The
Psycho-Analytical Process* (of which *The Claustrum* recapitulates many
parts) in terms of geographical and zonal confusion. Here it is sufficient
to say that the first is related to the confusion between the self and the
object, aimed at avoiding the process of individuation, the second splits
the mother horizontally, confusing the zones of her body and the erogenous zones and their object.

We shall attempt now to illustrate the six areas of the mental apparatus: (1) the external world; (2) the mother's womb; (3) the interior of
external objects; (4) the interior of internal objects; (5) the internal
world; (6) the delusional world, or "nowhere".

(1) Deals with the concrete reality which rules mainly over the processes of adaptation, but the impact of events can assume for us an emotional significance, setting in motion processes of imagination, symbol formation and thought.

(6) The delusional system is without meaning and does not belong to the area of alpha function, that is to say, of "symbols". Such a system has no emotional links but only formal qualities derived from the detritus of the world previously destroyed. It is the world of the psychotic part of the personality.

(2–5) These areas have real psychic meaning.

(2) The mother's womb nourishes, for example, phantasies of re-entering the womb or in addition, according to Bion, there exists a part of our psyche which we have lost at birth and which we may imagine as having remained in her womb.

(3) The interior of the external objects sets in motion the question of the aesthetic conflict: "The outside (of the breast, of the mother, of the world) is beautiful. But what is her interior like?" The question "what is her interior like?" refers not only to the external mother, available to the senses, but also to the interior of the internal objects, created by the phantasy life of the baby. The interior of the external objects is also the receptacle for the projective identifications of the baby or for the infantile transference in analysis.

(4) The interior of the internal objects is created, as has been described, by the introjection of the external object. The psychoanalytic approach is concerned principally with the interior of the internal objects, coloured by the infant's emotions and phantasies. Projective identification, in its dual character of projective and identificatory processes, is directed principally at the interior of the internal objects. When the identification is intrusive, the interior of the internal objects is transformed into the theatre of the claustrum, whose compartments are described in chapter 5 of *The Claustrum* (1992; see especially chapter 16, this volume).

(5) By internal world is understood the game which the internal objects play amongst themselves. As contrasted with the outside world, which sacrifices intimacy for the purposes of adaptation and defence, the internal world is the place of privacy and mystery, described by Meltzer as "nuptial chamber" where meaning is generated and "where the alpha function takes place, where the creative act of symbol formation quietly proceeds through the night" (Meltzer & Harris Williams, 1988, p. 83).

The second compartment deals with the internal world of the internal mother. Although the places for re-entering the mother's body are many (sense organs, bodily orifices, skin, and so on), the zones in which the intrusive part of the personality takes refuge are, in Meltzer's description, the head–breast, the genital area, the rectum. I recall Silvia Fano Cassese's description of the processes that lead to the formation of the internal maternal compartments, which

> are imaginative constructs formed by analogy between the mother's functions and what the baby experiences through its own orifices in the mother–baby relationship. Thus the infant's eyes are attracted to the mother's eyes, its mouth to the nipple, its ear to the words coming from her mouth, and all these together form a compartment of experiences and phantasies pertaining to the baby's head-the maternal head-breast (mind). The other two compartments are formed in the same fashion around the excretory processes and the erotic genital trends. These three compartments inside the mother must be kept separate: the internal babies in the genital compartment must not receive nourishment from the head-breast either in the form of food from the breast or by occupying the mother's mind. The excrements in the rectum must in no way contaminate the breast or poison the babies in the genital compartment. During the maturational process, the conflicts pertaining to each compartment must be resolved in order to achieve integration; it is only once the pre-genital conflicts in the head-breast and in the rectal compartments have been resolved that the integration of these with the genital compartment becomes possible. [Fano Cassese, 2002, p. 86]

The world of the claustrum is sustained primarily by masturbatory processes and then by "phantasies claustrophobic and claustrophilic, of the space inside the internal maternal object as a life space, a world with its own qualities and values" (Meltzer, 1992, p. 46). The claustrum is the enclosed space into which the infantile part has penetrated or within which it remained trapped. It derives from changes that are generated by intrusive projective identification into the three compartments of the inside of the internal mother, to which various claustrophobic pathologies correspond. Meltzer chooses a famous painting by Bosch, *The Garden of Earthly Pleasures*, to illustrate the world of the claustrum, which, like works of art, is also a world of beauty. It must be emphasized that all the descriptions of the compartments of the claustrum are described with reference to artistic sources: Proust and *Oblomov* for the head–breast, Titian, Bosch, and Goethe for the genital area, and Orwell for the anal area, which appears to us above all as a representation of the persecutory and hallucinatory world of Kafka, where cockroaches and mice dominate.[12]

How can one explain, in metapsychological terms, the world that art describes and which is really born from within pathology? The claustrum is the generator of pathology and of mental disorder, ranging from claustrophobia to delusion. This is a question to which Freud refers in 1897 in a very brief note, "Poetry and 'fine frenzy'" (Freud, 1950 [1892–1899], Draft N, p. 208): poetry and madness, an intuition that seems confirmed with the choice, for the end of the book, of Meg Harris Williams's beautiful essay on Shakespeare's *Macbeth*. The author illustrates the claustrum–witch who imprisons Macbeth and Lady Macbeth first in ambition, then in crime, and finally in madness, confirming that the artist is dealing with the claustrum.

The beauty of the claustrum

In his previous writings on beauty, Meltzer described artistic creativity as the outcome of alpha function and of the internal parental objects in their reproductive functions, employing a frankly romantic formulation linked to Keats's affirmation that "Beauty is Truth, Truth Beauty". How can one reconcile this positive view with an artist's account of the densely packed group inhabiting the claustrum? One's thoughts run first to Franz Kafka, imprisoned in the intestinal corridors of the courthouse (*The Trial*), in the surreal prison of *The Castle*, in the bachelor room (*Metamorphosis*), in the chosen torture chamber (*In the Penal Colony*). Yet it is here that we rediscover a disturbing beauty, sick, partly torn apart in a corrosive and death-dealing environment:

> At last the steam thinned a little, and K. was gradually able to make things out. It seemed to be a general washing day. Near the door clothes were being washed. But the steam was coming from a different corner, where in a wooden tub . . . two men were bathing in steaming water. . . . From a large opening, the only one in the back wall, a pale snowy light came in, apparently from the courtyard, and gave a gleam as of silk to the dress of a woman who was almost reclining in a high armchair. She was suckling an infant at her breast. Several children were playing around her, peasant children as was obvious, but she seemed to be of another class, although of course illness and weariness give even peasants a look of refinement . . . the woman in the armchair lay as if lifeless staring at the roof without even a glance towards the child at her bosom. She made a beautiful, sad, fixed picture, and K. looked at her for what must have been a long time; then he must have fallen asleep. [Kafka, 1924/1987, pp. 18–19]

This is a description of the impossibility of a mother–baby relationship, preventing any containment. The claustrum is, nevertheless, a place of pale and ghostly beauty, where no medium that could make possible a reciprocal mirroring between "Madonna and child" exists. But this is the environment in which a large part of the modern world finds itself.

Hanna Segal addressed the problem in her essay on aesthetics, written in 1952 and extended in 1991, emphasizing the importance of "the ugly" in a work of art: "The terms I need are 'ugly' and 'beautiful'. [Ugliness] includes tension, hatred and its results—the destruction of good and whole objects and their change into persecutory fragments" (chapter 2, this volume). Segal comes to grips with the problems using concepts from aesthetics, in terms of the essential co-presence of the polarities ugly/beautiful, contents (ugly)/form (beautiful), destruction/rhythm, life instinct/death instinct. She also has recourse to the theory of literary types and their use of ugly or beautiful contents.

With Bion, the problem of the ugly–deformed–disturbing conflicting but co-existing with the beautiful is addressed in terms of alpha function. This allows us to understand the co-presence of the ugly and the beautiful in psychoanalytic terms: "beautiful" (harmonious, whole, endowed with meaning) is the alpha element, "ugly" (tension, destructiveness, disharmony) is the beta element. The relationship between the alpha element (the realm of thinking) and the beta element (realm of anti-thinking) may be conflictual, as occurs in the case of disturbances in mental life of various kinds and various degrees of severity, or it can appear as a continuous exchange across the permeable membrane of the contact barrier. In the latter case there occurs a continuous passage from beta to alpha—that is, beta elements, held in the *storage evacuation*[13] to be expelled as indigestible elements, are pushed from the *input* of the dream towards the contact barrier, where they are submitted to the work of alpha function, which makes them thinkable.

Bion's work allows us to understand in these terms the artist's work, which is intended to give form to his confused anxiety—the "thing in itself"—the beta element. Here is the work of "gestation" in art, in the course of the waiting that drives it towards "thinkability"; it may find its form at the moment when it appears as the "selected fact",[14] transforming into form, thinkability, and beauty the anxiety of the singular, which now becomes universal and shareable. Kafka, prisoner of the claustrum, bore his inexpressible anxiety (gestation) until there was within him an image or a word (selected fact) for the creation of a beautiful work. This process has many analogies with psychoanalytic work, and it can be turned into a therapeutic tool: at the end of his life Kafka frees himself from the claws of Mummy–Prague, gives up the bachelor room–claustrum, and meets Dora Dyamant, to choose, in the splendour of a love finally shared, his creative journey, which illus-trated the anguish of modern man.

Notes

1. Melanie Klein substituted for the Freudian term "phase" that of "position", to give a different emphasis to her model of development. In contradistinction to a "phase", which is passed, a "position" is a constellation of anxieties, defences, and impulses that recurs in infancy and in the course of adult life.

2. The original title of Ravel's lyric fantasy on a text of Sidonie-Gabrielle Colette is *L'enfant et les sortilèges.*

3. The essay on the Oresteia was published posthumously (Klein, 1963).

4. "My view at that time was expressed in the 'Dialogue' which Adrian Stokes published in *Painting and the Inner World* and was, I now think, a pessimistic one as regards the social role of psycho-analysis and analysts. It tended to shift the entire burden on to artists, or rather the 'art world', of carrying on the social equivalent of the psycho-analytical method of interpretation with a view to lessening of paranoid anxieties and strengthening the bonds of relationship to good objects by which greater capacities for depressive pain might develop. Its hope was that the findings of psycho-analysis might percolate through the 'art world', especially through the analytic treatment of artists. It might be said to have left the field to humanism as the heir to the church" (Meltzer, 1973, p. 148).

5. An example of this function of art is illustrated in Ronald Britton's essay on Rilke, "Existential anxiety: Rilke's *Duino Elegies*" (1999).

6. The success of Melanie Klein's theories in England, which already worried the Freuds, became the cause of a bitter dispute when the latter moved to London following the promulgation of the racial laws in Germany. Very soon the proximity of Anna Freud and Melanie Klein, both child analysts, became unsustainable. This led to the formation of two sections within the British Psycho-Analytical Society. The theoretical positions of the two opposed positions are recorded in the "Contro-versial Discussions" (Steiner & King, 1994).

7. This interpretative model is not, moreover, outside literary criticism, if one thinks of Gianfranco Contini's Introduction to Dante Alighieri, *Rime* [Verses] (1946), who has recourse to the concept of "theatre of the mind" for his interpretation of Dante's *Vita Nuova* [New style of life], understanding the characters as aspects of the author's inner life.

8. The formulation is Wordsworth's.

9. Milner writes: "The process is described as depending upon the identifica-tion of the primary object with another that is in reality different from it but emotionally is felt to be the same" (chapter 4, this volume).

10. "The values of the paranoid–schizoid position are gradually replaced by those of the depressive position, with the relinquishment of egocentricity in favour of concern for the welfare of the loved objects of psychic and external reality. This gradual shift in values has a seeping effect upon judgement and the estimation in which are held the various attributes of human nature. Thus goodness, beauty, strength, and generosity replace in esteem the initial enthralment to size, power, success and sensuality" (chapter 6, this volume).

11. Letter to Oskar Pollack of 20 December 1902, in Kafka *Letters*. Mummy, metaphorically Prague, a city that is enchanting but at the same time dismal and disturbing, from which one cannot escape, is an extraordinary exemplification of the claustrum.

12. See, e.g., F. Kafka, "Metamorphosis" and "Josephine, the Singer and the Mice People".

13. This concept is from Alessandro Bruni [in English in the original].

14. The application of Bion's concept of the "selected fact" is shown in *La sindrome di Stendhal* (1995), pp. 15–16.

ART AS REPARATION

Infantile anxiety-situations reflected in a work of art and in the creative impulse

(1929)

Melanie Klein

My first subject is the highly interesting psychological material underlying an opera of Ravel's, now being revived in Vienna. My account of its content is taken almost word for word from a review by Eduard Jakob in the *Berliner Tageblatt*.

A child of six years old is sitting with his homework before him, but he is not doing any work. He bites his pen-holder and displays that final stage of laziness, in which *ennui* has passed into *cafard*. "Don't want to do the stupid lessons", he cries in a sweet soprano. "Want to go for a walk in the park! I'd like best of all to eat up all the cake in the world, or pull the cat's tail or pull out all the parrot's feathers! I'd like to scold everyone! Most of all I'd like to put mama in the corner!" The door now opens. Everything on the stage is shown very large—in order to emphasize the smallness of the child—so all that we see of his mother is a skirt, an apron and a hand. A finger points and a voice asks affectionately whether the child has done his work. He shuffles rebelliously on his chair and puts out his tongue at his mother. She goes away. All that we hear is the rustle of her skirts and the words: "You shall have dry bread and no sugar in your tea!" The child flies into a rage. He jumps up, drums on the door, sweeps the tea-pot and cup from the table, so that they are broken into a thousand pieces. He climbs on to the window-seat, opens the cage and tries to stab the squirrel with his pen. The squirrel escapes through the open window. The child jumps down from the window and seizes the cat. He yells and swings the tongs, pokes the fire furiously in the open grate, and with his hands and feet hurls the kettle into the room. A cloud of ashes and steam escapes. He swings the tongs like a sword and begins to tear the wallpaper. Then he opens the case of the grandfather-clock and snatches out the copper pendulum. He pours the ink over the table. Exercise-books and other books fly through the air. Hurrah! . . .

The things he has maltreated come to life. An armchair refuses to let him sit in it or have the cushions to sleep on. Table, chair, bench and sofa suddenly lift up their arms and cry: "Away with the dirty little creature!" The clock has a dreadful stomach-ache and begins to strike the hours like mad. The tea-pot leans over the cup, and they begin to talk Chinese. Everything undergoes a terrifying change. The child falls back against the wall and shudders with fear and desolation. The stove spits out a shower of sparks at him. He hides behind the furniture. The shreds of the torn wallpaper begin to sway and stand up, showing shepherdesses and sheep. The shepherd's pipe sounds a heartbreaking lament; the rent in the paper, which separates Corydon from his Amaryllis, has become a rent in the fabric of the world! But the doleful tale dies away. From under the cover of a book, as though out of a dog's kennel, there emerges a little old man. His clothes are made of numbers, and his hat is like a pi. He holds a ruler and clatters about with little dancing steps. He is the spirit of mathematics, and he begins to put the child through an examination: millimetre, centimetre, barometer, trillion—eight and eight are forty. Three times nine is twice six. The child falls down in a faint!

Half suffocated, he takes refuge in the park around the house. But there again the air is full of terror, insects, frogs (lamenting in muted thirds), a wounded tree-trunk, which oozes resin in long-drawn-out bass notes, dragon-flies and oleander-flies all attack the newcomer. Owls, cats and squirrels come along in hosts. The dispute as to who is to bite the child becomes a hand-to-hand fight. A squirrel which has been bitten falls to the ground, screaming, beside him. He instinctively takes off his scarf and binds up the little creature's paw. There is great amazement among the animals, who gather together hesitatingly in the background. The child has whispered: "Mama!" He is restored to the human world of helping, "being good". "That's a good child, a very well-behaved child", sing the animals very seriously in a soft march— the finale of the piece—as they leave the stage. Some of them cannot refrain from themselves calling out "Mama".

I will now examine more closely the details in which the child's pleasure in destruction expresses itself. They seem to me to recall the early infantile situation, which in my most recent writings I have described as being of fundamental importance both for neurosis in boys and for their normal development. I refer to the attack on the mother's body and on the father's penis in it. The squirrel in the cage and the pendulum wrenched out of the clock are plain symbols of the penis in the mother's body. The fact that it is the *father's* penis and that it is in the act of coitus with the mother is indicated by the rent in the wallpaper, "which separates Corydon from his Amaryllis", of which it has been said that to the boy it has become "a rent in the fabric of the world". Now what weapons does the child employ in this attack on his united parents? The ink poured over the table, the emptied kettle, from which a cloud of ashes and steam escapes, represent the weapon which very little children have at their disposal: namely the device of soiling with excrement.

Smashing things, tearing them up, using the tongs as a sword— these represent the other weapons of the child's primary sadism, which employs his teeth, nails, muscles and so on.

In my paper at the last Congress (Klein, 1928) and on other occasions in our Society, I have described this early phase of development, the content of which is the attack made on the mother's body with all the weapons that the child's sadism has at its disposal. Now, however, I can add to this earlier statement and say more exactly where this phase is to be inserted in the scheme of sexual development proposed by Abraham. My result leads me to conclude that the phase in which sadism is at its zenith in all the fields whence it derives precedes the earlier anal stage and acquires a special significance from the fact that it is also the stage of development at which the Oedipus tendencies first appear. That is to say, that the Oedipus conflict begins under the complete dominance of sadism. My supposition that the formation of the superego follows closely on the beginning of the Oedipus tendencies, and that, therefore, the ego falls under the sway of the superego even at this early period, explains, I think, why this sway is so tremendously powerful. For, when the objects are introjected, the attack launched upon them with all the weapons of sadism rouses the subject's dread of an analogous attack upon himself from the external and the internalized objects. I wanted to recall these concepts of mine to your minds because I can make a bridge from them to a concept of Freud's: one of the most important of the new conclusions which he has put before us in *Inhibitions, Symptoms, and Anxiety* [1926d (1925)], namely the hypothesis of an early infantile situation of anxiety or danger. I think that this places analytic work on a yet more exactly defined and firmer basis than heretofore and thus gives our methods an even plainer direction. But in my view it also makes a fresh demand upon analysis. Freud's hypothesis is that there is an infantile danger-situation which undergoes modification in the course of development, and which is the source of the influence exercised by a series of *anxiety-situations*. Now the new demand upon the analyst is this—that analysis should fully uncover these anxiety-situations right back to that which lies deepest of all. This demand for a *complete* analysis is allied to that which Freud suggests as a new demand at the conclusion of his "History of an Infantile Neurosis" [1918b (1914)], where he says that a complete analysis must reveal the primal scene. This latter requirement can have its full effect only in conjunction with that which I have just put forward. If the analyst succeeds in the task of discovering the infantile danger-situations, working at their resolution and elucidating in each individual case the relations between the anxiety-situations and the neurosis on the one hand and the ego-development on the other—then, I think, he will achieve more completely the main aim of psychoanalytic therapy: removal of the neuroses. It seems to me, therefore, that everything that can contribute to the elucidation and exact description of the infantile danger-situations is of great value, not only from the theoretical, but also from the therapeutic point of view.

Freud assumes that the infantile danger-situation can be reduced ultimately to the loss of the beloved (longed-for) person. In girls, he thinks, the loss of the object is the danger-situation which operates most powerfully; in boys it is castration. My work has proved to me that both these danger-situations are a modification of yet earlier ones. I have found that in boys the dread of castration by the father is connected with a very special situation which, I think, proves to be the earliest anxiety-situation of all. As I pointed out, the attack on the mother's body, which is timed psychologically at the zenith of the sadistic phase, implies also the struggle with the father's penis in the mother. A special intensity is imparted to this danger-situation by the fact that a union of the two parents is in question. According to the early sadistic superego, which has already been set up, these united parents are extremely cruel and much dreaded assailants. Thus the anxiety-situation relating to castration by the father is a modification, in the course of development, of the earliest anxiety-situation as I have described it.

Now I think that the anxiety engendered in this situation is plainly represented in the libretto of the opera which was the starting-point of my paper. In discussing the libretto, I have already dealt in some detail with the one phase—that of the sadistic attack. Let us now consider what happens after the child has given rein to his lust for destruction.

At the beginning of his review the writer mentions that all the things on the stage are made very large, in order to emphasize the smallness of the child. But the child's anxiety makes things and people seem gigantic to him—far beyond the actual difference in size. Moreover, we see what we discover in the analysis of every child: that things represent human beings, and therefore are objects of anxiety. The writer of the review writes as follows: "The maltreated things begin to live." The armchair, the cushion, table, chair, etc., attack the child, refuse to serve him, banish him outside. We find that things to sit and lie upon, as well as beds, occur regularly in children's analyses as symbols for the protecting and loving mother. The strips of the torn wallpaper represent the injured interior of the mother's body, while the little old number-man who comes out of the book-cover is the father (represented by his penis), now in the character of judge, and about to call the child, who faints with anxiety, to his reckoning for the damage he has done and the theft he had committed in the mother's body. When the boy flees into the world of nature, we see how it takes on the role of the mother whom he has assaulted. The hostile animals represent a multiplication of the father, whom he has also attacked, together with the children assumed to be in the mother. We see the incidents which took place inside the room now reproduced on a bigger scale in a wider space and in larger numbers. The world, transformed into the mother's body, is in hostile array against the child and persecutes him.

In ontogenetic development sadism is overcome when the subject advances to the genital level. The more powerfully this phase sets in, the more capable does the child become of object-love, and the more able is he to conquer his sadism by means of pity and sympathy. This step in development is also shown in the libretto of Ravel's opera; when the boy feels pity for the wounded squirrel and comes to its aid, the hostile world changes into a friendly one. The child has learnt to love and believes in love. The animals conclude: "That is a good child—a very well-behaved child." The profound psychological insight of Colette—the author of the libretto of the opera—is shown in the way in which the conversion in the child's attitude takes place. As he cares for the wounded squirrel, he whispers: "Mama". The animals round him repeat this word. It is this redeeming word which has given the opera its title: "The Magic Word" [Das Zauberwort]. But we also learn from the text what is the factor which has ministered to the child's sadism. He says: "I want to go for a walk in the park! I want most of all to eat up all the cakes in the world!" But his mother threatens to give him tea without sugar and dry bread. The oral frustration which turns the indulgent "good mother" into the "bad mother" stimulates his sadism.

I think we can now understand why the child, instead of peaceably doing his homework, has become involved in such an unpleasant situation. It *had* to be so, for he was driven to it by the pressure of the old anxiety-situation which he had never mastered. His anxiety enhances the repetition-compulsion, and his need for punishment ministers to the compulsion (now grown very strong) to secure for himself actual punishment in order that the anxiety may be allayed by a chastisement less severe than that which the anxiety-situation causes him to anticipate. We are quite familiar with the fact that children are naughty because they wish to be punished, but it seems of the greatest importance to find out what part anxiety plays in this craving for punishment and what is the ideational content at the bottom of this urgent anxiety.

I will now illustrate from another literary example the anxiety which I have found connected with the earliest danger-situation in a girl's development.

In an article entitled "The Empty Space", Karin Michaelis gives an account of the development of her friend, the painter Ruth Kjär. Ruth Kjär possessed remarkable artistic feeling, which she employed especially in the arrangement of her house, but she had no pronounced creative talent. Beautiful, rich and independent, she spent a great part of her life travelling, and was constantly leaving her house upon which she had expended so much care and taste. She was subject at times to fits of deep depression, which Karin Michaelis describes as follows: "There was only one dark spot in her life. In the midst of the happiness which was natural to her, and seemed so untroubled, she would suddenly be plunged into the deepest melancholy. A melancholy that was suicidal. If she tried to account for this, she would say something to this effect: 'There is an empty space in me, which I can never fill!'"

The time came when Ruth Kjär married, and she seemed perfectly happy. But after a short time the fits of melancholy recurred. In Karin Michaelis's words: "The accursed empty space was once more empty." I will let the writer speak for herself: "Have I already told you that her home was a gallery of modern art? Her husband's brother was one of the greatest painters in the country, and his best pictures decorated the walls of the room. But before Christmas this brother-in-law took away one picture, which he had only lent to her. The picture was sold. This left an empty space on the wall, which in some inexplicable way seemed to coincide with the empty space within her. She sank into a state of the most profound sadness. The blank space on the wall caused her to forget her beautiful home, her happiness, her friends, everything. Of course, a new picture could be got, and would be got, but it took time; one had to look about to find just the right one.

"The empty space grinned hideously down at her.

"The husband and wife were sitting opposite one another at the breakfast table. Ruth's eyes were clouded with hopeless despair. Suddenly, however, her face was transfigured with a smile: 'I'll tell you what! I think I will try to daub a little on the wall myself, until we get a new picture!' 'Do, my darling,' said her husband. It was quite certain that whatever daub she made would not be too monstrously ugly.

"He had hardly left the room when, in a perfect fever, she had rung up the colour-shop to order the paints which her brother-in-law generally used, brushes, palette, and all the rest of the "gear", to be sent up at once. She herself had not the remotest idea of how to begin. She had never squeezed paint out of a tube, laid the ground-colour on a canvas or mixed colours on a palette. While the things were coming, she stood before the empty wall with a piece of black chalk in her hand and made strokes at random as they came into her head. Should she have the car and rush wildly to her brother-in-law to ask how one paints? No, she would rather die!

"Towards evening her husband returned, and she ran to meet him with a hectic brilliance in her eyes. She was not going to be ill, was she? She drew him with her, saying: "Come, you will see!" And he saw. He could not take his eyes from the sight; could not take it in, did not believe it, *could* not believe it. Ruth threw herself on a sofa in a state of deadly exhaustion: "Do you think it at all possible?"

"The same evening they sent for the brother-in-law. Ruth palpitated with anxiety as to the verdict of the connoisseur. But the artist exclaimed immediately: "You don't imagine you can persuade me that you painted that! What a damned lie! This picture was painted by an old and experienced artist. Who the devil is he? I don't know him!"

"Ruth could not convince him. He thought they were making game of him. And when he went, his parting words were: 'If you painted that, I will go and conduct a Beethoven Symphony in the Chapel Royal tomorrow, though I don't know a note of music!'

"That night Ruth could not sleep much. The picture on the wall had been painted, that was certain—it was not a dream. But how had it happened? And what next?

"She was on fire, devoured by ardour within. She must prove to herself that the divine sensation, the unspeakable sense of happiness that she had felt could be repeated."

Karin Michaelis then adds that after this first attempt, Ruth Kjär painted several masterly pictures, and had them exhibited to the critics and the public.

Karin Michaelis anticipates one part of my interpretation of the anxiety relating to the empty space on the wall when she says, "On the wall there was an empty space, which in some inexplicable way seemed to coincide with the empty space within her." Now, what is the meaning of this empty space within Ruth, or rather, to put it more exactly, of the feeling that there was something lacking in her body?

Here there has come into consciousness one of the ideas connected with that anxiety which, in my last paper, already mentioned (1928), I described as the most profound anxiety experienced by girls. It is the equivalent of castration-anxiety in boys. The little girl has a sadistic desire, originating in the early stages of the Oedipus conflict, to rob the mother's body of its contents, namely, the father's penis, faeces, children, and to destroy the mother herself. This desire gives rise to anxiety lest the mother should in her turn rob the little girl herself of the contents of her body (especially of children) and lest her body should be destroyed or mutilated. In my view, this anxiety, which I have found in the analyses of girls and women to be the deepest anxiety of all, represents the little girl's earliest danger-situation. I have come to see that the dread of being alone, of the loss of love and loss of the love-object, which Freud holds to be the basic infantile danger-situation in girls, is a modification of the anxiety-situation I have just described. When the little girl who fears the mother's assault upon her body cannot *see* her mother, this intensifies the anxiety. The presence of the real, loving mother diminishes the dread of the terrifying mother, whose introjected image is in the child's mind. At a later stage of development the content of the dread changes from that of an attacking mother to the dread that the real, loving mother may be lost and that the girl will be left solitary and forsaken.

In seeking the explanation of these ideas, it is instructive to consider what sort of pictures Ruth Kjär has painted since her first attempt, when she filled the empty space on the wall with the life-sized figure of a naked negress. Apart from one picture of flowers, she had confined herself to portraits. She has twice painted her younger sister, who came to stay with her and sat for her, and, further, the portrait of an old woman and one of her mother. The two last are described by Karin Michaelis as follows: "And now Ruth cannot stop. The next picture represents an old woman, bearing the mark of years and disillusionments. Her skin is wrinkled, her hair faded, her gentle, tired eyes are troubled. She gazes before her with the disconsolate resignation of old age, with a look that seems to say: 'Do not trouble about me any more. My time is so nearly at an end!'

"This is not the impression we receive from Ruth's latest work—the portrait of her Irish–Canadian mother. This lady has a long time before her before she must put her lips to the cup of renunciation. Slim, imperious, challenging, she stands there with a moonlight-coloured shawl draped over her shoulders: she has the effect of a magnificent woman of primitive times, who could any day engage in combat with the children of the desert with her naked hands. What a chin! What force there is in the haughty gaze!

"The blank space has been filled."

It is obvious that the desire to make reparation, to make good the injury psychologically done to the mother and also to restore herself was at the bottom of the compelling urge to paint these portraits of her relatives. That of the old woman, on the threshold of death, seems to be the expression of the primary, sadistic desire to destroy. The daughter's wish to destroy her mother, to see her old, worn out, marred, is the cause of the need to represent her in full possession of her strength and beauty. By so doing the daughter can allay her own anxiety and can endeavour to restore her mother and make her new through the portrait. In the analyses of children, when the representation of destructive wishes is succeeded by an expression of reactive tendencies, we constantly find that drawing and painting are used as means to restore people. The case of Ruth Kjär shows plainly that this anxiety of the little girl is of greatest importance in the ego-development of women, and is one of the incentives to achievement. But, on the other hand, this anxiety may be the cause of serious illness and many inhibitions. As with the boy's castration-dread, the effect of his anxiety on his ego-development depends on the maintenance of a certain optimum and a satisfactory interplay between the separate factors.

CHAPTER TWO

A psycho-analytical approach to aesthetics

(1952)

Hanna Segal

> "*Denn das Schöne ist nichts*
> *als des Schrecklichen Anfang, den wir noch gerade ertragen,*
> *und wir bewundern es so, weil es gelassen verschmäht,*
> *uns zu zerstören.*"[1]

In 1908 Freud wrote: "We laymen have always wondered greatly like the cardinal who put the question to Ariosto—how that strange being, the poet, comes by his material. What makes him able to carry us with him in such a way and to arouse emotions in us of which we thought ourselves perhaps not even capable?"[2] And as the science of psychoanalysis developed, repeated attempts were made to answer that question. Freud's discovery of unconscious phantasy life and of symbolism made it possible to attempt a psychological interpretation of works of art. Many papers have been written since, dealing with the problem of the individual artist and reconstructing his early history from an analysis of his work. The foremost of these is Freud's book on Leonardo da Vinci. Other papers have dealt with general psychological problems expressed in works of art, showing, for instance, how the latent content of universal infantile anxieties is symbolically expressed in them. Such was Freud's paper "The Theme of the Three Caskets",[3] Ernest Jones's "The Conception of the Madonna through the Ear",[4] or Melanie Klein's "Infantile Anxiety Situations Reflected in a Work of Art and the Creative Impulse".[5]

Until recently such papers were not mainly concerned with aesthetics. They dealt with points of psychological interest but not with the central problem of aesthetics, which is: what constitutes good art, in what essential respect is it different from other human works, more particularly from bad art? Psychological writers attempted to answer questions like: "How does the poet work?" "What is he like?" "What does he express?" In the paper "Creative Writers and Day-Dreaming",[6] Freud has shown how the work of the artist is a product of phantasy and has its roots, like the children's play and dreams, in unconscious phantasy life. But he did not attempt to explain "why we should derive such pleasure from listening to the day-dreams of a poet". How he achieves his effects is, to Freud, the poet's "innermost secret". Indeed, Freud was not especially interested in aesthetic problems. In "The Moses of Michelangelo",[7] he says: "I have often observed that the subject-matter of works of art has a stronger attraction for me than their formal and technical qualities, though to the artist their value lies first and foremost in this latter. I am unable rightly to appreciate many of the methods used and the effects obtained in art." He was also aware of the limitations of analytical theory in approaching aesthetics. In the preface to the book on Leonardo da Vinci,[8] he says that he has no intention of discussing why Leonardo was a great painter, since to do that, he would have to know more about the ultimate sources of the creative impulse and of sublimation. This was written in 1910. Since that time the work of Melanie Klein has thrown more light on the problem of the creative impulse and sublimation, and has provided a new stimulus to analytical writers on art. In the last fifteen years a number of papers have appeared dealing with problems of creation, beauty, and ugliness. I would mention, in particular, those by Ella Sharpe, Paula Heimann, John Rickman, and Fairbairn in Britain, and H. B. Lee in the United States.

Maybe it is possible now, in the light of new analytical discoveries, to ask new questions. Can we isolate in the psychology of the artist the specific factors which enable him to produce a satisfactory work of art? And if we can, will that further our understanding of the aesthetic value of the work of art, and of the aesthetic experience of the audience?

It seems to me that Melanie Klein's concept of the depressive position makes it possible at least to attempt an answer to these questions.

The "depressive position", as described by Melanie Klein, is reached by the infant when he recognizes his mother and other people, and among them his father, as real persons. His object relations then undergo a fundamental change.[9] Where earlier he was aware of "part objects" he now perceives complete persons; instead of "split" objects— ideally good or overwhelmingly persecuting—he sees a whole object both good and bad. The whole object is loved and introjected and forms the core of an integrated ego. But this new constellation ushers in a new anxiety situation: where earlier the infant feared an attack on the ego by persecutory objects, now the predominant fear is that of the loss of the loved object in the external world and in his own inside. The infant at that stage is still under the sway of uncontrollable greedy and sadistic impulses. In phantasy his loved object is continually attacked in greed and hatred, is destroyed, torn into pieces and fragments; and not only is the external object so attacked but also the internal one, and then the whole internal world feels destroyed and shattered as well. Bits of the destroyed object may turn into persecutors, and there is a fear of internal persecution as well as a pining for the lost loved object and guilt for the attack. The memory of the good situation, where the infant's ego contained the whole loved object, and the realization that it has been lost through his own attacks, gives rise to an intense feeling of loss and guilt, and to the wish to restore and re-create the lost loved object outside and within the ego. This wish to restore and re-create is the basis of later sublimation and creativity.

It is also at this point that a sense of inner reality is developed. If the object is remembered as a whole object, then the ego is faced with the recognition of its own ambivalence towards the object; it holds itself responsible for its impulses and for the damage done to the external and to the internal object. Where, earlier, impulses and parts of the infant's self were projected into the object, with the result that a false picture of it was formed, that his own impulses were denied, and that there was often a lack of differentiation between the self and the external object, in the depressive phase a sense of inner reality is developed and in its wake a sense of outer reality as well.

Depressive phantasies give rise to the wish to repair and restore, and become a stimulus to further development, only in so far as the depressive anxiety can be tolerated by the ego and the sense of psychic reality retained. If there is little belief in the capacity to restore, the good object outside and inside is felt to be irretrievably lost and destroyed, the destroyed fragments turn into persecutors, and the internal situation is felt to be hopeless. The infant's ego is at the mercy of intolerable feelings of guilt, loss, and internal persecution. To protect itself from total despair the ego must have recourse to violent defence mechanisms. Those defence mechanisms which protect it from the feelings arising out of the loss of the good object form a system of manic defences. The essential features of manic defences are denial of psychic reality, omnipotent control, and a partial regression to the paranoid position and its defences: splitting, idealization, denial, projective identification, etc. This regression strengthens the fear of persecution and that in turn leads to the strengthening of omnipotent control.

But in successful development the experience of love from the environment slowly reassures the infant about his objects. His growing love, strength, and skill give him increasing confidence in his own capacities to restore. And as his confidence increases he can gradually relinquish the manic defences and experience more and more fully the underlying feelings of loss, guilt, and love, and he can make renewed and increasingly successful attempts at reparation.

By repeated experiences of loss and restoration of the internal objects they become more firmly established and more fully assimilated in the ego.

A successful working through of the depressive anxieties has far-reaching consequences; the ego becomes integrated and enriched through the assimilation of loved objects; the dependence on the external objects is lessened and deprivation can be better dealt with. Aggression and love can be tolerated and guilt gives rise to the need to restore and re-create.

Feelings of guilt probably play a role before the depressive position is fully established; they already exist in relation to the part object, and they contribute to later sublimation; but they are then simpler impulses acting in a predominantly paranoid setting, isolated and unintegrated. With the establishment of the depressive position the object becomes more personal and unique and the ego more integrated, and an awareness of an integrated internal world is gradually achieved. Only when this happens does the attack on the object lead to real despair at the destruction of an existing complex and organized internal world and, with it, to the wish to recover such a complete world again.

* * *

The task of the artist lies in the creation of a world of his own. In his introduction to the second Post-Impressionist Exhibition, Roger Fry writes: "Now these artists do not seek to give what can, after all, be but a pale reflex of actual appearance, but to arouse a conviction of a new and different reality. They do not seek to imitate life but to find an equivalent for life." What Roger Fry says of post-impressionists undoubtedly applies to all genuine art. One of the great differences between art and imitation or a superficial "pretty" achievement is that neither the imitation nor the "pretty" production ever achieves this creation of an entirely new reality.

Every creative artist produces a world of his own. Even when he believes himself to be a complete realist and sets himself the task of faithfully reproducing the external world, he, in fact, only uses elements of the existing external world to create with them a reality of his own. When, for instance, two realistic writers like Zola and Flaubert try to portray life in the same country, and very nearly at the same time, the two worlds they show us differ from each other as widely as if they were the most phantastic creations of surrealist poets. If two great painters paint the same landscape, we have two different worlds.

> . . . and dream
> Of waves, flowers, clouds, woods,
> Rocks, and all that we
> Read in their smiles
> And call reality.
>
> [Shelley]

How does this creation come about? Of all artists the one who gives us the fullest description of the creative process is Marcel Proust: a description based on years of self-observation and the fruit of an amazing insight. According to Proust, an artist is compelled to create by his need to recover his lost past. But a purely intellectual memory of the past, even when it is available, is emotionally valueless and dead. A real remembrance sometimes comes about unexpectedly by chance association. The flavour of a cake brings back to his mind a fragment of his childhood with full emotional vividness. Stumbling over a stone revives a recollection of a holiday in Venice which before he had vainly tried to recapture. For years he tries in vain to remember and re-create in his mind a living picture of his beloved grandmother. But only a chance association revives her picture and at last enables him to remember her, and to experience his loss and mourn her. He calls these fleeting associations: *"intermittences du coeur"*, but he says that such memories come and then disappear again, so that the past remains elusive. To capture them, to give them permanent life, to integrate them with the rest of his life, he must create a work of art. *"Il fallait . . . faire sortir de la pénombre ce que j'avais senti, de le reconvertir en un equivalent spirituel. Or ce moyen qui me paraissait le seul, qu'était-ce autre chose que de créer une oeuvre d'art?"* ["I had to recapture from the shade that which I had felt, to reconvert it into its psychic equivalent. But the way to do it, the only one I could see, what was it, but to create a work of art?"]

Through the many volumes of his work the past is being recaptured; all his lost, destroyed, and loved objects are being brought back to life: his parents, his grandmother, his beloved Albertine. *"Et certes il n'y aurait pas qu'Albertine, que ma grandmère, mais bien d'autres encore dont j'aurais pu assimiler une parole, un regard, mais en tant que creatures individuelles je ne m'en rappellais plus; un livre est un grand cimetière où sur la plupart des tombes on ne peut plus lire les noms effacés."* ["And indeed it was not only Albertine, not only my grandmother, but many others still from whom I might well have assimilated a gesture or a word, but whom I could not even remember as distinct persons. A book is a vast graveyard where on most of the tombstones one can read no more the faded names."]

And, according to Proust, it is only the lost past and the lost or dead object that can be made into a work of art. He makes the painter, Elstir, say: *"On ne peut recréer ce qu'on aime qu'en le renonçant."* ["It is only by renouncing that one can re-create what one loves."] It is only when the loss has been acknowledged and the mourning experienced that re-creation can take place.

In the last volume of his work Proust describes how at last he decided to sacrifice the rest of his life to writing. He came back after a long absence to seek his old friends at a party, and all of them appeared to him as ruins of the real people he knew—useless, ridiculous, ill, on the threshold of death. Others, he found, had died long ago.

And on realizing the destruction of a whole world that had been his, he decides to write, to sacrifice himself to the re-creation of the dying and the dead. By virtue of his art he can give his objects an eternal life in his work. And since they represent his internal world too, if he can do that, he himself will no longer be afraid of death.

What Proust describes corresponds to a situation of mourning: he sees that his loved objects are dying or dead. Writing a book is for him like the work of mourning in that gradually the external objects are given up, they are reinstated in the ego, and re-created in the book. In her paper "Mourning and its Relation to Manic-Depressive States",[10] Melanie Klein has shown how mourning in grown-up life is a re-living of the early depressive anxieties; not only is the present object in the external world felt to be lost, but also the early objects, the parents; and they are lost as internal objects as well as in the external world. In the process of mourning it is these earliest objects which are lost again, and then re-created. Proust describes how this mourning leads to a wish to re-create the lost world.

I have quoted Proust at length because he reveals such an acute awareness of what I believe is present in the unconscious of all artists: namely, that all creation is really a re-creation of a once loved and once whole, but now lost and ruined object, a ruined internal world and self. It is when the world within us is destroyed, when it is dead and loveless, when our loved ones are in fragments, and we ourselves in helpless despair—it is then that we must re-create our world anew, reassemble the pieces, infuse life into dead fragments, re-create life.

If the wish to create is rooted in the depressive position and the capacity to create depends on a successful working through it, it would follow that the inability to acknowledge and overcome depressive anxiety must lead to inhibitions in artistic expression.

I should now like to give a few clinical examples from artists who have been inhibited in their creative activities by neurosis, and I shall try to show that in them it was the inability to work through their depressive anxieties which led to inhibitions of artistic activity, or to the production of an unsuccessful artistic product.

Case A is a young girl with a definite gift for painting. An acute rivalry with her mother made her give up painting in her early teens. After some analysis she started to paint again and was working as a decorative artist. She did decorative handicraft work in preference to what she sometimes called "real painting", and this was because she knew that, though correct, neat, and pretty, her work failed to be moving and aesthetically significant. In her manic way she usually denied that this caused her any concern. At the time when I was trying to interpret her unconscious sadistic attacks on her father, the internalization of her mutilated and destroyed father and the resulting depression, she told me the following dream: "*She saw a picture in a shop which represented a wounded man lying alone and desolate in a dark forest. She felt quite overwhelmed with emotion and admiration for this picture; she thought it represented the actual essence of life; if she could only paint like that she would be a really great painter.*"

It soon appeared that the meaning of the dream was that if she could only acknowledge her depression about the wounding and destruction of her father, she would then be able to express it in her painting and would achieve real art. In fact, however, it was impossible for her to do this, since the unusual strength of her sadism and her resulting despair, and her small capacity to tolerate depression, led to its manic denial and to a constant make-believe that all was well with the world. In her dream she confirmed my interpretation about the attack on her father, but she did more than this. Her dream showed something that had not been in any way interpreted or indicated by me: namely, the effect on her painting of her persistent denial of depression. In relation to her painting the denial of the depth and seriousness of her depressive feelings produced the effect of superficiality and prettiness in whatever she chose to do—the dead father is completely denied and no ugliness or conflict is ever allowed to disturb the neat and correct form of her work.

Case B is that of a journalist aged a little over thirty, whose ambition was to be a writer, and who suffered, among other symptoms, from an ever-increasing inhibition in creative writing. An important feature of his character was a tendency to regress from the depressive to the paranoid position. The following dream illustrates his problem: "*He found himself in a room with Goebbels, Goering, and some other Nazis, He was aware that these men were completely amoral. He knew that they were going to poison him and therefore he tried to make a bargain with them; he suggested that it would be a good thing for them to let him live, since he was a journalist and could write about them and make them live for a time after their death. But this stratagem failed and he knew that he would finally be poisoned.*"

An important factor in this patient's psychology was his introjection of an extremely bad father-figure who was then blamed for all that the patient did. And one of the results was an unbearable feeling of being internally persecuted by this bad internal father-figure, which was sometimes expressed in hypochondriacal symptoms. He tried to defend himself against it by placating and serving this bad internal figure. He was often driven to do things that he disapproved of and disliked. In the dream he showed how it interfered with his writing: to avoid death at the hands of internal persecutors he has to write for them to keep them immortal; but there is, of course, no real wish to keep such bad figures alive, and consequently he was inhibited in his capacity for writing. He often complained, too, that he had no style of his own; in his associations to the dream it became clear that he had to write not only for the benefit. of the poisoners, and to serve their purposes, but also at their command. Thus the style of his writing belonged to the internal parental figure. The case, I think, resembles one described by Paula Heimann.[11] A patient of hers drew a sketch with which she was very displeased; the style was not her own, it was Victorian. It appeared clearly during the session that it was the result of a quarrel with another woman who stood for her mother. After the quarrel the painter had introjected her as a bad and revengeful mother, and, through guilt and fear, she had to submit to this bad internal figure; it was really the Victorian mother who had dictated the painting.

Paula Heimann described this example of an acute impairment of an already established sublimation. In my patient his submission to a very bad internal figure was a chronic situation preventing him from achieving any internal freedom to create. Moreover, although he was trying to appease his persecutors, as a secondary defence against them, he was basically fixed in the paranoid position and returned to it whenever depressive feelings were aroused, so that his love and reparative impulses could not become fully active.

* * *

All the patients mentioned suffered from sexual maladjustments as well as creative inhibitions. There is clearly a genital aspect of artistic creation which is of paramount importance. Creating a work of art is a psychic equivalent of procreation. It is a genital bisexual activity necessitating a good identification with the father who gives, and the mother who receives and bears, the child. The ability to deal with the depressive position, however, is the precondition of both genital and artistic maturity. If the parents are felt to be so completely destroyed that there is no hope of ever re-creating them, a successful identification is not possible, and neither can the genital position be maintained nor the sublimation in art develop.

This relation between feelings of depression and genital and artistic problems is clearly shown by another patient of mine. C, a man of thirty-five, was a really gifted artist, but at the same time a very ill person. Since the age of eighteen he had suffered from depression, from a variety of conversion symptoms of great intensity, and from what he described as "a complete lack of freedom and spontaneity". This lack of spontaneity interfered considerably with his work, and, though he was physically potent, it also deprived him of all the enjoyment of sexual intercourse. A feeling of impending failure, worthlessness and hopelessness marred all his efforts. He came to analysis at the age of thirty-five because of a conversion symptom: he suffered from a constant pain in the small of his back and the lower abdomen, which was aggravated by frequent spasms. He described it as "a constant state of childbirth". It appeared in his analysis that the pain started soon after he learned that the wife of his twin brother was pregnant, and he actually came to me for treatment a week before her confinement. He felt that if I could only liberate him from the spasm he would do marvellous things. In his case identification with the pregnant woman, representing the mother, was very obvious, but it was not a happy identification. He felt his mother and the babies inside her had been so completely destroyed by his sadism, and his hope of re-creating them was so slight, that the identification with the pregnant mother meant to him a state of anguish, ruin, and abortive pregnancy. Instead of producing the baby, he, like the mother, was destroyed. Feeling destroyed inside and unable to restore the mother, he felt persecuted by her; the internal attacked mother attacked him in turn and robbed him of his babies. Unlike the other three patients described, this one recognized his depression and his reparative drive was therefore very much stronger. The inhibition both in his sexual and artistic achievements was due mainly to a feeling of the inadequacy of his reparative capacity in comparison with the devastation that he felt he had brought about. This feeling of inadequacy made him regress to a paranoid position whenever his anxiety was aroused.

* * *

Patient E, a woman writer, was the most disturbed of the patients described here. She was a severe chronic hypochondriac, she suffered from frequent depersonalization and endless phobias, among them food phobias leading at times to almost complete anorexia.

She had been a writer, but had not been able to write for a number of years. I want to describe here how her inability to experience depression led to an inhibition of symbolic expression.

One day she told me the following dream: *"She was in a Nursing Home, and the Matron of this Home, dressed in black, was going to kill a man and a woman. She herself was going to a fancy dress ball. She kept running out of the Nursing Home in various fancy disguises, but somehow something always went wrong, and she had to come back to the Nursing Home, and to meet the Matron.* At some point of the dream *she was with her friend Joan."*

Her friend, Joan, was for my patient the embodiment of mental health and stability. After telling me the dream she said: "Joan was not in a fancy dress, she was undisguised, and I felt her to be so much more vulnerable than me." Then she immediately corrected herself: "Oh, of course I meant she was so much less vulnerable than me." This slip of the patient gave us the key to the dream. The mentally healthy person is more vulnerable than my patient, she wears no disguises and she is vulnerable to illness and death. My patient herself escapes death, represented by the Matron, by using various disguises. Her associations to this dream led us to a review of some of her leading symptoms in terms of her fear of, and attempted escape from, death. The disguises in the dream represented personifications, projective and introjective identifications, all three used by her as means of not living her own life and—in the light of the dream—not dying her own death. She also connected other symptoms of hers with the fear of death. For instance her spending almost half her lifetime lying in bed, "half-dead", was a shamming of death, a way of cheating death. Her phobia of bread, her fear of sex, appeared to her now as ways of escaping full living, which would mean that one day she would have "spent her life" and would have to face death. So far, she had almost lived on "borrowed" life. For instance, she felt extremely well and alive when she was pregnant, she then felt she lived on the baby's life; but immediately after the baby's birth she felt depersonalized and half-dead.

I mention here only some of her more striking symptoms, which all pointed in the same direction: to a constant preoccupation with the fear of death. The analyst, represented by the Matron, tears off her disguises one after another and forces her to lead her own life and so eventually to die.

After some three sessions completely taken up with the elaboration of this theme, she started the next one with what appeared to be a completely new trend of thought. She started complaining of her inability to write. Her associations led her to remember her early dislike of using words. She felt that her dislike was still present and she did not really want to use words at all. Using words, she said, made her break "an endless unity into bits". It was like "chopping up", like "cutting things". It was obviously felt by her as an aggressive act. Besides, using words was "making things finite and separate". To use words meant acknowledging the separateness of the world from herself, and gave her a feeling of loss. She felt that using words made her lose the illusion of possessing and being at one with an endless, undivided world: "When you name a thing you really lose it."[12] It became clear to her that using a symbol (language) meant an acceptance of the separateness of her object from herself, the acknowledgment of her own aggressiveness, "chopping up", "cutting", and finally losing the object.

In this patient the loss of the object was always felt as an imminent threat to her own survival. So we could eventually connect her difficulties in using language with the material of the earlier sessions. Refusing to face this threat of death to her object and to herself, she had to form the various symptoms devised magically to control and avoid death. She also had to give up her creative writing. In order to write again, she would have to be stripped of her disguises, admit reality, and become vulnerable to loss and death.

I shall now describe briefly a session with the same patient two years later.

She had known for some time that she would have to give up her analysis at the end of the term, through external circumstances. She came to thus session very sad, for the first time since it became clear that she would end her analysis. In preceding sessions she felt nausea, felt internally persecuted and "all in bits and pieces". She said at the beginning of the session that she could hardly wait to see me for fear that her sadness would turn into a "sickness and badness". She thought of the end of her analysis, wondered if she would be able to go on liking me and how much would she be able to remember me. She also wondered if she in any way resembled me. There were two things she would wish to resemble me in: the truthfulness and the capacity to care for people which she attributed to me. She hoped she may have learned these from me. She also felt I was an ordinary kind of person, and she liked that thought. I interpreted her material as a wish to take me in and identify herself with me as a real "ordinary" feeding breast, in contrast to an earlier situation when an idealized breast was internalized, which subsequently turned into a persecuting one.

She then told me the following dream: "*A baby has died—or grown up—she didn't know which; and as a result her breasts were full of milk. She was feeding a baby of another woman whose breasts were dry.*"

The transference meaning of that dream was that I weaned her—my breast was dry—but she had acquired a breast and could be a mother herself. The baby who "died or grew up" is herself. The baby dies and the grown woman takes its place. The losing of the analyst is here an experience involving sadness, guilt (about the rivalry with me in relation to the baby), and anxiety (will she be able to go on remembering me?). But it is also an experience leading to the enrichment of her ego—she now has the breasts full of milk and therefore needs no longer depend on me.

Towards the end of the hour, she said: "Words seem to have a meaning again, they are rich", and she added that she was quite sure she could now write "provided I can go on being sad for a while, without being sick and hating food"—i.e. provided she could mourn me instead of feeling me as an internal persecutor.

Words acquired a meaning and the wish to write returned again when she could give up my breast as an external object and internalize it. This giving up was experienced by her as the death of the breast, which is dried up in the dream and the death of a part of herself—the baby part—which in growing up also dies. In so far as she could mourn me words became rich in meaning.[13]

This patient's material confirmed an impression derived from many other patients, that successful symbol formation is rooted in the depressive position.

One of Freud's greatest contributions to psychology was the discovery that sublimation is the outcome of a successful renunciation of an instinctual aim; I would like to suggest here that such a successful renunciation can only happen through a process of mourning. The giving up of an instinctual aim, or object, is a repetition and at the same time a re-living of the giving up of the breast. It can be successful, like this first situation, if the object to be given up can be assimilated in the ego, by the process of loss and internal restoration. I suggest that such an assimilated object becomes a symbol within the ego. Every aspect of the object, every situation that has to be given up in the process of growing, gives rise to symbol formation.

In this view symbol formation is the outcome of a loss, it is a creative act involving the pain and the whole work of mourning. If psychic reality is experienced and differentiated from external reality, the symbol is differentiated from the object; it is felt to be created by the self and can be freely used by the self.

I cannot deal here extensively with the problem of symbols; I have brought it up only in so far as it is relevant to my main theme. And it is relevant in that the creation of symbols, the symbolic elaboration of a theme, are the very essence of art.

* * *

I should now like to attempt to formulate an answer to the question whether there is a specific factor in the psychology of the successful artist which would differentiate him from the unsuccessful one. In Freud's words: "What distinguishes the poet, the artist, from the neurotic day-dreamer?" In his paper "Formulations on the Two Principles in Mental Functioning" [1911b], Freud says: "The artist finds a way of returning from the world of phantasy back to reality, with his special gifts he moulds his phantasies into a new kind of reality." Indeed, one could say that the artist has an acute reality sense. He is often neurotic and in many situations may show a complete lack of objectivity, but in two respects, at least, he shows an extremely high reality sense. One is in relation to his own internal reality, and the other in relation to the material of his art. However neurotic Proust was in his attachment to his mother, his homosexuality, his asthma, etc., he had a real insight into the phantasied world of the people inside him, and he knew it was internal, and he knew it was phantasy. He showed an awareness that does not exist in a neurotic who splits off, represses, denies, or acts out his phantasy. The second, the reality sense of the artist in relation to his material, is a highly specialized reality assessment of the nature, needs, possibilities, and limitations of his material, be it words, sounds, paints, or clay. The neurotic uses his material in a magic way, and so does the bad artist. The real artist, being aware of his internal world which he must express, and of the external materials with which he works, can in all consciousness use the material to express the phantasy. He shares with the neurotic all the difficulties of unresolved depression, the constant threat of the collapse of his internal world; but he differs from the neurotic in that he has a greater capacity for tolerating anxiety and depression. The patients I described could not tolerate depressive phantasies and anxieties; they all made use of manic defences leading to a denial of psychic reality. Patient A denied both the loss of her father and his importance to her: Patient B projected his impulses on to an internal bad object, with the result that his ego was split and that he was internally persecuted: Patient C did the same, though to a lesser extent: Patient E regressed to the schizoid mechanisms of splitting and projective identification which led to depersonalization and inhibition in the use of symbols.

In contrast to that, Proust could fully experience depressive mourning. This gave him the possibility of insight into himself, and with it a sense of internal and external reality. Further, this reality sense enabled him to have and to maintain a relationship with other people through the medium of his art. The neurotic's phantasy interferes with his relationships in which he acts it out. The artist withdraws into a world of phantasy, but he can communicate his phantasies and share them. In that way he makes reparation, not only to his own internal objects, but to the external world as well.

* * *

I have tried, so far, to show how Melanie Klein's work, especially her concept of the depressive position and the reparative drives that are set in motion by it, and her description of the world of inner objects, throws new light on the psychology of the artist, on the conditions necessary for him to be successful, and on those which can inhibit or vitiate his artistic activities. Can this new light on the psychology of the artist help us to understand the aesthetic pleasure experienced by the artist's public? If, for the artist, the work of art is his most complete and satisfactory way of allaying the guilt and despair arising out of the depressive position and of restoring his destroyed objects, it is but one of the many human ways of achieving this end. What is it that makes a work of art such a satisfactory experience for the artist's public? Freud says that he "bribes us with the formal and aesthetic pleasures".

To begin with, we should distinguish between the aesthetic pleasure and other incidental pleasures to be found in works of art. For instance, the satisfaction derived from identification with particular scenes or characters can also arise in other ways, and it can be derived from bad as well as from good art. The same would apply to the sentimental interests originating in memories and associations. The aesthetic pleasure proper, that is, the pleasure derived from a work of art and unique in that it can only be obtained through a work of art, is due to an identification of ourselves with the work of art as a whole and with the whole internal world of the artist as represented by his work. In my view all aesthetic pleasure includes an unconscious re-living of the artist's experience of creation. In his paper on "The Moses of Michelangelo", Freud [1914b] says: "What the artist aims at is to awaken in us the same mental constellation as that which in him produced the impetus to create."

We find in Dilthey's philosophy a concept called by him "nach-erleben"[14] This means to him that we can understand other people from their behaviour and expression, we intuitively reconstruct their mental and emotional state, we live after them, we re-live them. This process he calls *"nach-erleben"*. It is, he says, often deeper than introspection can discover. His concept, I think, is equivalent to unconscious identification. I assume that this kind of unconscious re-living of the creator's state of mind is the foundation of all aesthetic pleasure.

To illustrate what I mean, I will take as an example the case of "classical" tragedy. In a tragedy the hero commits a crime: the crime is fated, it is an "innocent" crime, he is driven to it. Whatever the nature of the crime, the result is always complete destruction—the parental figures and child figures alike are engulfed by it. That is, at whatever level the conflict starts—*Oedipus Rex*, for instance, states a genital conflict—in the end we arrive at a picture of the phantasies belonging to the earliest depressive position where all the objects are destroyed. What is the psychological mechanism of the listener's *"nach-erleben"*? As I see it, he makes two identifications. He identifies himself with the author, and he identifies the whole tragedy with the author's internal world. He identifies himself with the author while the latter is facing and expressing his depression. In a simplified way one can summarize the listener's reaction as follows: "The author has, in his hatred, destroyed all his loved objects just as I have done, and like me he felt death and desolation inside him. Yet he can face it and he can make me face it, and despite the ruin and devastation we and the world around us survive. What is more, his objects, which have become evil and were destroyed, have been made alive again and have become immortal by his art. Out of all the chaos and destruction he has created a world which is whole, complete and unified."

It would appear then that two factors are essential to the excellence of a tragedy: the unshrinking expression of the full horror of the depressive phantasy and the achieving of an impression of wholeness and harmony. The external form of "classical" tragedy is in complete contrast with its content. The formal modes of speech, the unities of time, place and action, the strictness and rigidity of the rules are all, I believe, an unconscious demonstration of the fact that order can emerge out of chaos. Without this formal harmony the depression of the audience would be aroused but not resolved. There can be no aesthetic pleasure without perfect form.[15]

In creating a tragedy I suggest the success of the artist depends on his being able fully to acknowledge and express his depressive phantasies and anxieties. In expressing them he does work similar to the work of mourning in that he internally re-creates a harmonious world which is projected into his work of art.

The reader identifies with the author through the medium of his work of art. In that way he re-experiences his own early depressive anxieties, and through identifying with the artist he experiences a successful mourning, re-establishes his own internal objects and his own internal world, and feels, therefore, re-integrated and enriched.

* * *

But is this experience specific to a work of art that is tragic, or is it an essential part of any aesthetic experience? I think I could generalize my argument. To do so I shall have to introduce the more usual terminology of aesthetics and re-state my problems in new terms. The terms I need are "ugly" and "beautiful". For Rickman, in his paper "The Nature of Ugliness and the Creative Impulse",[16] the "ugly" is the destroyed, the incomplete object. For Ella Sharpe[17] "ugly" is destroyed, arrhythmic, and connected with painful tension. I think both these views would be included if we say that "ugliness" is what expresses the state of the internal world in depression. It includes tension, hatred and its results—the destruction of good and whole objects and their change into persecutory fragments. Rickman, however, when he contrasts ugly and beautiful, seems to equate "beautiful" with what is aesthetically satisfying. With that I cannot agree. Ugly and beautiful are two categories of aesthetic experience and, in certain ways, they can be contrasted; but if beautiful is used as synonymous with aesthetically satisfying, then its contradictory is not "ugly", but unaesthetic, or indifferent, or dull. Rickman says that we recoil from the ugly; my contention is that "ugly" is a most important and necessary component of a satisfying aesthetic experience. The concept of ugliness as one element in aesthetic satisfaction is not uncommon in the tradition of philosophical aesthetics; it has been most strikingly expressed, however, by the artists themselves. Rodin writes: "We call ugly that which is formless, unhealthy, which suggests illness, suffering, destruction, which is contrary to regularity—the sign of health. We also call ugly the immoral, the vicious, the criminal and all abnormality which brings evil—the soul of the parricide, the traitor, the self-seeker. But let a great artist get hold of this ugliness; immediately he transfigures it—with a touch of his magic wand he makes it into beauty."

What is "beautiful"? Taking again the beautiful as but one of the categories of the aesthetically satisfying, most writers agree that the main elements of the beautiful—the whole, the complete, and the rhythmical—are in contrast with the ugly. Among analytical writers— Rickman equates the beautiful with the whole object; Ella Sharpe considers beauty essentially as rhythm and equates it with the experience of goodness in rhythmical sucking, satisfactory defaecation and sexual intercourse. I should add to this rhythmical breathing and the rhythm of our heart-beats. An undisturbed rhythm in a composed whole seems to correspond to the state in which our inner world is at peace.

Of non-analytical writers, Herbert Read comes to a similar conclusion when he says that we find rhythmical, simple arithmetical proportions which correspond to the way we are built and our bodies work. But these elements of "beauty" are in themselves insufficient. If they were enough then we would find it most satisfactory to contemplate a circle or listen to a regular tattoo on a drum. I suggest that both beauty, in the narrow sense of the word, and ugliness must be present for a full aesthetic experience.

I would re-word my attempt at analysing the tragic in terms of ugliness and beauty. Broadly speaking, in tragedy "ugly" is the content the complete ruin and destruction—and "beautiful" is the form. "Ugly" is also an essential part of the comic. The comic here is ugly in that, as in caricature, the overstressing of one or two characteristics ruins the wholeness—the balance—of the character. Ugly and tragic is also the defeat of the comic hero by the same world. How near the comic hero is to the tragic can be seen from the fact that outstanding comic heroes of past ages are felt, at a later date, to be mainly tragic figures; few people today take Shylock or Falstaff as figures of fun only; we are aware of the tragedy implied. The difference between tragedy and comedy lies then in the comic writer's attempt to dissociate himself from the tragedy of his hero, to feel superior to it in a kind of successful manic defence. But the manic defence is never complete; the original depression is still expressed and it must therefore have been to a large extent acknowledged and lived by the author. The audience re-lives depression, the fear of it, and the aggression against it which are expressed in a comedy and its final successful outcome.

It is easier to discover this pattern of overcoming depression in literature, with its explicit verbal content, than in other forms of art. The further away from literature, the more difficult is the task. In music, for instance, we would have to study the introduction of discords, disharmonies, new disorders which are so invariably considered to be ugly before they are universally accepted. New art is considered "difficult", it is resisted, misunderstood, treated with bitter hatred, contempt; or, on the other hand, it may be idealized to such an extent that the apparent admiration defeats its aim and makes its object a butt of ridicule. These prevalent reactions of the public are, I think, manifestations of a manic defence against the depressive anxieties stirred by art. The artists find ever new ways of revealing a repressed and denied depression. The public use against it all their powers of defence until they find the courage to follow the new artist into the depths of his depression, and eventually to share his triumphs.

The idea that ugliness is an essential component of a complete experience seems to be true of the tragic, the comic, the realistic, in fact of all the commonly accepted categories of the aesthetic except one— and this single exception is of great importance.

There is, undoubtedly, a category of art which shows to the greatest extent all the elements of beauty in the narrow sense of the word, and no apparent sign of ugliness; it is often called "classical" beauty. The beauty of the Parthenon, of the Discobolos, is whole, rhythmical, undisturbed. But soulless imitations of beauty, "pretty" creations, are also whole and rhythmical, yet they fail to stir and rouse nothing but boredom. Thus classical beauty must have some other not immediately obvious element.

Returning to the concept of *nach-erleben*, of experiencing along with another, we may say that in order to move us deeply the artist must have embodied in his work some deep experience of his own. And all our analytical experience as well as the knowledge derived from other forms of art suggest that the deep experience must have been what we call, clinically, a depression, and that the stimulus to create such a perfect whole must have lain in the drive to overcome an unusually strong depression. If we consider what is commonly said about beauty by laymen, we find a confirmation of this conclusion. They say that complete beauty makes one both sad and happy at the same time, and that it is a purge for the soul—that it is awe-inspiring. Great artists themselves have been very much aware of the depression and terror embodied in works of classical beauty which are apparently so peaceful. When Faust goes in search of Helen, the perfect classical beauty, he has to face unnamed terrors; to go where there is no road:

> *Kein Weg! Ins Unbetretene*
> *Nicht zu Betretende; ein Weg ins Unerbetene,*
> *Nicht zu Erbittende.*

He must face endless emptiness:

> *Nichts wirst du sehn in ewig leerer Ferne,*
> *Den Schritt nicht hören den du tust,*
> *Nichts Festes finden, wo du ruhst.*

Rilke writes: "Beauty is nothing but the beginning of terror that we are still just able to bear."

Thus to the sensitive onlooker, every work of beauty still embodies the terrifying experience of depression and death. Hanns Sachs, in his "Beauty, Life and Death" [1940], pays particular attention to the awesome aspect of beauty; he says the difficulty is not to understand beauty but to bear it, and he connects this terror with the very peacefulness of the perfect work of art. He calls it the static element; it is peaceful because it seems unchangeable, eternal. And it is terrifying because this eternal unchangeability is the expression of the death instinct—the static element opposed to life and change.

Following quite a different trend of thought, I come to similar conclusions about the role of the death instinct in a work of art. Thus far my contention has been that a satisfactory work of art is achieved by a realization and sublimation of the depressive position, and that the effect on the audience is that they unconsciously re-live the artist's experience and share his triumph of achievement and his final detachment. But to realize and symbolically to express depression the artist must acknowledge the death instinct, both in its aggressive and self-destructive aspects, and accept the reality of death for the object and the self. One of the patients I described could not use symbols because of her failure to work through the depressive position; her failure clearly lay in her inability to accept and use her death instinct and to acknowledge death.

Re-stated in terms of instincts, ugliness—destruction—is the expression of the death instinct; beauty—the desire to unite into rhythms and wholes—is that of the life instinct. The achievement of the artist is in giving the fullest expression to the conflict and the union between those two.

This is a conclusion which Freud has brought out in two of his essays, though he did not generalize it as applicable to all art. One of these essays is that on Michelangelo's Moses [1914b], where he clearly shows that the latent meaning of this work is the overcoming of wrath. The other essay is his analysis of the "Theme of the Three Caskets" [1913f]. He shows there that in the choice between the three caskets, or three women, the final choice is always symbolical of death. He interprets Cordelia in *King Lear* as a symbol of death, and for him the solution of the play is Lear's final overcoming of the fear of death and his reconciliation to it. He says: "Thus man overcomes death, which in thought he has acknowledged. No greater triumph of wish-fulfilment is conceivable."

All artists aim at immortality; their objects must not only be brought back to life, but also the life has to be eternal. And of all human activities art comes nearest to achieving immortality; a great work of art is likely to escape destruction and oblivion.

It is tempting to suggest that this is so because in a great work of art the degree of denial of the death instinct is less than in any other human activity, that the death instinct is acknowledged, as fully as can be borne. It is expressed and curbed to the needs of the life instinct and creation.

Notes

1. "... For Beauty is nothing but beginning of Terror we're still just able to bear and why we admire it so is because it serenely disdains to destroy us...." Rilke, *Duino Elegies* (1923).

2. "The Relation of the Poet to Day-dreaming", *Collected Papers, Vol. IV* (London, 195) [Freud, "Creative writers and day-dreaming", 1908e (1907)].

3. (1913). Ibid. [1913f].

4. (1914). *Essays in Applied Psycho-Analysis, Vol. II* (London, 1951).

5. (1925). *Contributions to Psycho-Analysis, 1921–45* (London, 1948). [see chapter 1, this volume].

6. (1908). *Collected Papers*, Vol. IV (London, 1935). [1908e (1907)]

7. (1914). Ibid. [Freud, 1914b].

8. (1920). *Leonardo da Vinci* (London, 1922).

9. For the description of the preceding phase of development see Melanie Klein's Contributions to Psycho-Analysis, 1921–45, and Herbert Rosenfeld's [1962] paper.

10. (1940). op. cit.

11. A contribution to the problem of sublimation and its relation to processes of internalization. *International Journal of Psycho-Analysis, 23*, Part 1, 1942.

12. This theme became later linked with the "Rumpelstiltskin" theme of stealing the baby and the penis, but I cannot follow it up here.

13. I have given here only the transference meaning of the dream in order not to detract from my main theme. This transference situation was linked with past experiences of weaning, birth of the new baby, and the patient's failure in the past to be a "good" mother to the new baby.

14. Hodges, H. A., *Wilhelm Dilthey: Selected Readings from his Works and an Introduction to his Sociological and Philosophical Work* (London).

15. Roger Fry says, "All the essential axthetic quality has to do with pure form", and I agree, but he adds later: "The odd thing is that it is, apparently, dangerous for the artist to know about this." Fry feels that it is odd, I think, because of an inherent weakness of the formalist school he represents. The formalists discount the importance of emotional factors in art. According to Fry, art must be completely detached from emotions, all emotion is impurity, and the more the form gets freed from the emotional content the nearer it is to the ideal. What the formalists ignore is that form as much as content is in itself an expression of unconscious emotion. What Fry, following Clive Bell, calls "significant form", a term he confesses himself incapable of defining, is form expressing and embodying an unconscious emotional experience. The artist is not trying to produce pretty or even beautiful form, he is engaged on the most important task of re-creating his ruined internal world and the resulting form will depend on how well he succeeds in his task.

16. *International Journal of Psycho-Analysis, 21*, Part III (1940).

17. Certain aspects of sublimation and delusion (1930). Similar and divergent unconscious determinants underlying the sublimations of pure art and pure science (1935).

CHAPTER THREE

The unconscious phantasy of an inner world reflected in examples from literature

(1955)

Joan Riviere

The inner world which in our unconscious phantasy each of us contains inside ourselves is one of those psychoanalytical concepts that most people find especially difficult to accept or understand. It is a world of figures formed on the pattern of the persons we first loved and hated in life, who also represent aspects of ourselves. The existence even in unconscious phantasy of these inner figures and of their apparently independent activities within us (which can be as real, or more real and actual, to us in unconscious feeling than external events) may seem incredible and incomprehensible; it might therefore perhaps be useful to approach the problem from the opposite end, as it were, that is from the conscious level. My aim in this contribution is essentially to forge a link between certain conscious experiences, which will be familiar to most people, and the proposition that phantasies of our containing other persons inside ourselves, though deeply unconscious, do exist. For this purpose I have selected some relevant passages from literature. Before discussing these, however, I will consider shortly the question why this proposition of internal objects seems so difficult to accept.

It was of course Freud who first recognized the existence of the "introjected object" as a regular phenomenon, a normal part of the personality, namely, in his formulation of the mental institution he called the superego, mainly based on the person of the father and represented consciously in our minds by what we call the conscience in each of us. Melanie Klein, however, in her explorations of unconscious phantasy through her work with very young children, has pursued this theme and brought to light much more concerning the persons in the inner world whom each of us individually has felt or feels to be part of himself. There is a difference between Freud's superego, a single differentiated function of our mental make-up, modelled though it may be on the personalities of parents, and the "personal relations", however primitive and fantastic, we have had with the figures who people our inner worlds. When Freud published his *The Ego and The Id* his concept of the internalized parent as the superego did not rouse much resistance; it is true that it had already been introduced in a more acceptable form under the title of ego-ideal. Nevertheless, before very long an emotional reaction to the concept of the superego was manifested in a new view of analytic therapy; a move for the "dissolution of the superego" was even initiated by Alexander at the Salzburg Congress, 1924, and found considerable support at the time. (This view is to be distinguished from the general recognition that the curative effects of analysis are in part attributable to a reduction of the severity of the superego.) The point I wish to recall here is the emotional enthusiasm greeting Alexander's idea which virtually stigmatized the independent internal object in the self as something morbid. In the enthusiasm for this view, which Freud himself did what he could to discourage, we had, I think, the first flicker of the suspicion and intolerance often enough manifested against the concept of internal objects.

The "inner world", like other psychoanalytical concepts, meets with a twofold resistance: on the one hand, the incapacity to understand it, and on the other a direct emotional rejection of it as an unwelcome suggestion which is hardly rationalized by serious discussion. Emotional rejection is an acute reaction which arises, as experience teaches, from an acute anxiety; arguments and explanation have little influence on it. When anxiety is not too over-mastering, however, one means of allaying it consists in obtaining control of the alarming phenomenon by knowledge and understanding. The urge to master the terrors of superstition and so to find and to make life and the world safer for ourselves was undoubtedly one main source from which scientific curiosity sprang.

The debatable point in question here is that we all had originally and still have in some form an emotional relation with persons felt to exist inside ourselves. When this proposition meets with an intense emotional rejection, there is clearly a direct association in the hearer's mind of this idea with danger, as though anything inside one which is not "oneself" pure and simple is and must be dangerous—or pathological; in fact the association of such an idea with madness is often conscious. Less acute reactions can yet be seen to have a similar quality even when the objects inside are not directly imagined as dangerous, but are felt to be unknown and therefore alarming. This condition is similar to the common experience of looking into a medical book with drawings of internal organs and feeling extremely repelled—and in effect alarmed—at the sight of things which we "did not know" were inside us. This tendency to fear the unknown[1] plays its part in our difficulties in forming a conscious idea of the internal objects which unconsciously have so much reality to us; on this line of feeling any such unknown relation to objects inside one must be morbid and dangerous. There is, nevertheless, another quality of feeling in us towards such figures, one entirely distinct from this apprehensiveness or suspicion about them. From this other angle these internal figures represent what we most love, admire and crave to possess—they constitute the good properties and aspects in our lives and personalities.[2] The value and beneficence of these figures in us is usually even less in evidence consciously than their bad aspects, since in their good aspects they do not give rise to fear reactions which then become noticeable.

Freud formulated the pleasure–pain principle, but the degree to which it rules our lives often seems overlooked. Melanie Klein's work has emphasized a fact that sounds like a platitude in its obviousness, yet seems not fully recognized in all its simplicity. The life of the emotions which is continuously active in us from birth to death is based on a simple pattern: fundamentally everything in it is either "bad" or "good", nothing is neutral. Events, circumstances, things, people, everything we have to deal with in life and, above all, our own feelings and experiences are felt in the depths as essentially bad, i.e. disappointing, alarming, sad or painful; or good, i.e. satisfying, reassuring, hopeful, happy. Less fundamentally we may be aware of experiences and of our own feelings as mixed good and bad; but offhand and spontaneously, as it were, things in us and about us seem to split naturally into "good" or "bad". One day "all's right with the world", another day "all's wrong"; instinctively there are often no half-measures. I am not to be misunderstood to mean that apparently normal adults are consciously in a mental state approximating to a manic–depressive condition— though that may be less uncommon than is generally supposed. I am saying that there is always a general undertone of feeling even consciously in normal adults, which can be defined as predominantly good or bad, although the condition will be by no means entirely related to external causes, or even appropriate to the external situation of the person at the moment. There is, however, less conscious awareness of feelings of contentment and satisfaction (unless they arise suddenly

from changes for the better) than of unpleasant feelings, because satisfying feelings are taken for granted as our right, whereas ail unpleasant
state tends to rouse a reaction of protest immediately.

This brings me back to the inner world: good inner objects are to
some extent taken for granted. Unless their presence has to be emphasized unconsciously and demonstrably insisted on (e.g. as in people
who are continually needing praise and recognition—unconsciously—
about their internal goodness), the good things within us do not excite
attention and they remain unconscious. This state of things again has its
corollary in our relation to our physical bodies; so long as our digestive
or other organs are functioning well and are in a "good" condition, we
take them for granted and either remain unconscious of them, or it may
be that in so far as we are aware of pleasurable bodily sensations they
are frequently felt consciously to be self-ordained and self-induced and
thus suggest no connection with any other agency internally. It is especially when such sensations are "bad" in some way or may become so
that we pay them much attention and recognize their existence; thus it
happens that when we are required to recognize the existence of anything inside us, we may almost automatically expect it to be bad and
think of it as bad. Along with this expectation there goes as a corollary
a constant claim by us that all should be perpetually well and giving no
trouble within us, namely, that everything in us should be "good".[3]

At first sight there appears to be no connection between the proposition that we imagine ourselves to contain within us other persons and
the sharp differentiation in feeling just described between good or bad
states of mind or body which colour all our emotional experiences. But
in fact the connection is simple: the people we unconsciously feel to be
within us, parts of ourselves or alien to ourselves are not neutral, they
also are felt as either good or bad. They are essential parts of ourselves
and as such we require them to be "good"—perfect, in fact; all our
vanity and self-esteem is disturbed if they are not. Melanie Klein's work
has clearly shown that the phenomenon of narcissism—one's relation to
oneself—is unconsciously bound up with the inner world, the relation
one has to the figures inside one and their relation to oneself. But if we
feel wrong, guilty, and bad, then one of the purposes for which we need
or use our internal objects is that of attributing our own badness to them
inside us. Thus our narcissism is relieved and enabled to escape blem-
ish in some degree. This demand that we should have everything in
perfection and without pain or effort of course extends beyond our own
persons and internal economy to what is outside us, to our external
needs, circumstances and belongings; obviously, our narcissism requires that we should have the best of everything outside us as well as

inside, e.g. our possessions, reputations, or, say, our children particularly, should have no flaws. The demands of external reality, however, the pressure of Necessity, to quote Freud's phrase, train us to inhibit or modify these egoistic claims in the external world to some degree and at least superficially; whereas in our inner worlds we tend to maintain our infantile assumption of autocratic intolerance of all interference with our self-satisfaction and well-being.

It is not my aim here to give a description of the inner world of unconscious phantasy, still less to give a theoretical exposition of how or why this phenomenon occurs. The work of Melanie Klein and Paula Heimann contains such accounts. But it seems that the following illustrations, which may help to bridge the gap between a difficult concept and conscious understanding, should be prefaced with a few provisos to obviate misunderstandings.

Although in psychoanalysis we speak of the inner world, it must be remarked that this phrase does not denote anything like a replica of the external world contained within us. The inner world is exclusively one of *personal* relations, in which nothing is external, in the sense that everything happening in it refers to the self, to the individual in whom it is a part. It is formed solely on the basis of the individual's own urges and desires towards other persons and of his reactions to them as the objects of his desires. This inner life originates at least at birth and our relation to our inner world has its own development from birth onwards, just as that to the external world has. Our relation to both worlds is at first of an extremely primitive character, based on bodily needs such as sucking at the breast; this relation comprises also the emotional elements, the love and hate, spring in from our two main instincts—desire and aggression—at first felt only in relation to such limited objects as the nipple or breast. (But to the baby this one and only object is to begin with the be-all and end-all of existence.) The bodily sensations of taking in and containing are accompanied by the emotional corollary of pleasure, or of pain when frustration occurs, in varying degrees.

These early experiences of taking in, with their accompaniment of emotional pleasure, constitute the foundation and prototype of the phantasy-process of internalization, which persists throughout life in more developed forms as a main feature of our mental functioning. The inner world of our instinctual objects in its primitive form is thus first peopled with our mother and father or the parts of them internalized at this time, e.g. by the sucking act or by looking, perceiving and registering within; and those two persons remain as the prototypes of all our later developed reactions with other persons. In later life, moreover, these objects, external or internal, no longer need be exclusively persons, but may be represented by non-human, inanimate, or abstract interests. To the infant in particular, in whom life is governed by pleasure and pain, both his own feelings and the objects to whom they refer are never neutral; both his feelings and his objects are either pleasurable or painful, good or bad. For the infant, moreover, it is especially characteristic that his own bad painful sensations and impulses may be projected internally and attributed to his inner people or parts of them, which to some extent he feels are not himself, thus helping to relieve his fears about inherent or uncontrollable evil or danger in himself. The sway of pleasure or pain diminishes with growth and the course of later development progresses beyond the stage at which the internalized figures are so much needed in their original primitive forms; we can become less dependent on our objects, both external and internal, less subject to the crudely violent forces felt both in our own spontaneous impulses and in the good and bad objects whom we love and hate. As we gradually assimilate and work over into components of ourselves the good and bad properties we recognized in our loved and hated parents, or with which we endowed them, their nature as distinct and separate entities in ourselves alters, recedes and diminishes. The residue of these primitive figures in us, formed so largely on our own primitive characteristics, will ultimately consist mainly of qualities or characters in our personality which still retain and crystallize the strong charges of emotional feeling once attaching to the original persons from whom they are derived.

Nevertheless, in the depths our loving or hating relationships to the good or bad mother and father remain—an experience in our past life which is unconsciously indestructible and which on occasions becomes reactivated and relived, its reality re-established. At moments such as these in adult life, poets and writers have become aware of this reality in the depths and have sometimes been able to transmute it into convincing expression.

In my first example a poet describes his inward possession of his beloved who in the outside world is far away, while he nevertheless has her clasped within himself.

Absence, hear thou my protestation
Against thy strength,
Distance and length;
. . . . . .
To hearts that cannot vary
Absence is presence;
rime doth tarry.

My senses want their outward motion,
Which now within
Reason doth win,
Redoubled by her secret notion;
Like rich men that take pleasure
in hiding more than handling treasure.

By absence this good means I gain,
That I can catch her
Where none can watch her,
In some close corner of my brain:
There I embrace and kiss her,
And so enjoy her, and none miss her.[4]

These lovely lines express with matchless simplicity a happening that no one who has ever loved can have failed to experience—undisclosed and unconsidered though it may ordinarily be. It constitutes a feature of human experience, part of the human heritage. We should find allusions to it in most of the famous love-letters of history; but a poet alone can bring such an experience out into full daylight.

Yet the description given in this poem of a relation to another person inside oneself confirms the proposition of the existence of an emotional inner world only to a special and limited extent. It relates to only one person contained within the speaker—his beloved—and she and his relation to her are in the highest degree "good"—in fact, they are idealized, as is typical in a highly developed love-relation. This idealization of the loved one is achieved, as we know, by the process of divesting him or her of all unwelcome or evil associations and locating them elsewhere; a splitting into two, good and bad aspects, of the original single object of both love and hate has taken place. A strong denial is then set up that the pair, the good and bad figures, can have anything in common; they are kept at opposite poles. The denial or banishment of all "badness"—pain, deprivation or danger—in the relation to the loved one is very explicitly represented in the poem quoted. Its message consists in a denial, a "protestation" against the plain emotional fact that the absence of the loved one is painful, and this denial it is which produces the idealization of the situation and also results in its fantastic quality.

The driving force behind the poetic creation reveals itself, though in the setting of an adult love-relation, as one of the simplest, if not the most primordial of all human reactions—namely, fear of the loss and the craving for possession of something outside oneself, here another person, on which one's life seems to depend. The inevitable reaction to this need must be the drive to obtain possession of such an object, to acquire it, absorb it and make it one's own. Food would be the evident prototype of such a desire and need; and the earliest experience in life of such a longing, and of the joy expressed in the poem, must be the infant's craving for his or her mother along with the life-giving breast she represents, and the phantasy of taking her into the self in order nevermore to be without her. This primordial human phantasy belongs of course to the order of instinctual impulses classed as cannibalistic, although the overmastering intensity of the love-longing and the terror of loss which are inherent elements in it were not originally appreciated by those psychoanalysts who first recognized the existence of such impulses in all human beings.[5] It is through Melanie Klein's work that we are now able to understand the common meaning and origin of what appear to be two such totally unrelated human experiences of incorporation as that of the poem and those cannibalistic acts which take place in dreams or in savage rites. Yet there is again an undeniable link between the two in the physical impulse that often becomes conscious in the intensity of sexual passion to incorporate the loved one by biting and absorbing, as well as by clasping and embracing. Devouring with the eyes, too, is perhaps the commonest, because the least prohibited, of all activities between lovers.

In all these forms the wish to incorporate a desired object is manifest and conscious; as such it cannot be denied. What is denied, however, to conscious recognition is that all these and many similar manifestations are but varied expressions of a major human tendency. Each of such examples can be treated as an isolated phenomenon, belittled as unimportant or without significance; the associations between them which build them into a whole are kept unconscious, so that the inevitable inferences are ignored. In referring above to the infant's earliest experience of this desire to incorporate whatever is intensely craved and needed, I quoted the fear of its loss as one great incentive. This fear is in fact an indissoluble element of the wish; desire on the one hand, and fear of frustration, still more of total deprivation of desire's fulfilment on the other, are but two aspects of one emotion. Now the superficial disregard of the intensity and significance of human impulses to possess and incorporate operate largely by admitting the wish to some extent, it is true; though denying it any "meaning". But it operates still more by total denial and exclusion of the great factor of *fear of loss* from which so largely springs the dynamic process of this wish to possess. The fundamental connection between the two is plainly manifest in one universal human response, namely, in the reflex action of hugging and embracing, clasping and clinging to a person (or a thing) which one has regained after a parting or loss. Because it is regarded as so natural, the significance of this quite unequivocal expression of a desire to incorporate what has been (and therefore may be again) lost remains unrecognized.[6] In my view it is our rejection of and blindness to our dread of total loss and deprivation of good objects which results in the lack of understanding of these manifestations and the failure to recognize that in the vast field of human life this dynamic causation is a constant force.

In the poem I have quoted this fear is actually expressed, though the main content of ecstatic joy in it almost entirely outweighs the allusions in it to fear. "To *hearts that cannot vary*, absence is presence; time doth tarry": it is clear that the pain which is being extinguished by the thought of the beloved's secret presence inside himself, her "secret notion", is not that merely of her absence, but of the fear that her heart may vary; if she is not with him she is loving and giving herself to another, *she has left him*, not merely in the flesh but with her love, and he has *lost her finally*. It is hinted at too in the last verse, where he insists on the secrecy of his possession, as if he would have lost her if she were known to be his. Those who are familiar with Donne's love-poems will know how constant and repetitive in them, despite their wealth of unique imagery and the varied forms of love-relation described, these two themes are: the rapturous union of the lovers is yet invariably shot through with the dread of loss of her and her love. A few of the poems consist simply of the certain expectation of this loss, or of his absolute conviction of it and his own intense despair.

I will digress here from my main point for a moment to refer to the middle verse of the poem in question:

> My senses want their outward motion
> Which now within
> Reason doth win,
> Redoubled by her secret notion
> . . . . . .

In the poem's plainspoken description of the incorporation of an object it is interesting to find direct illustrations of the following themes: a withdrawal of cathexis from external objects leading to the reinforcement of narcissistic pleasure (Freud); compensation for disappointment by an external object by turning to the internal counterpart object (Klein); the suggestion contained in it that narcissistic well-being depends on or is greatly augmented by the existence of good internal objects (Klein); and the "manic" quality (Klein) of the idea that the phantasy of inward possession of the loved one "redoubles reason". Even if "Reason" in the seventeenth century did not mean exactly what it connotes to us today, the prevalent split between reason and feeling was already well established; no doubt it was born or reborn in the Renaissance. Was Donne's peculiar melancholy and tendency to despair, which epitomizes one aspect of the Renaissance spirit, perhaps an

expression of grief and mourning for the coming degradation in Western life of the status of feeling and for the foreseen victory of intellect
and objectivity over feeling and subjective experiences? And is his use
of the word "reason" here a flat repudiation of the truth that he does
not possess the objective person of the beloved, and a direct assertion
that the omnipotence of his subjective thought can override and arro-
gate to itself the omnipotence of external reality? "Time doth tarry!"

To revert to my theme: that the fear of loss is a dynamic factor in the
need to possess and incorporate. There is much to be understood about
this fear of loss, and the more so by reason of our blindness to it and
refusal to take it into account. Why should we unconsciously have such
an "unreasoning" expectation and terror of loss? To begin with, all
terrors are to be regarded as fears of some kind of loss. Freud regarded
castration as the greatest fear in man (and woman) and that consists of
the loss of the penis. This view did not satisfy everyone. Ernest Jones
found a deeper and broader explanation of anxiety in his suggestion
that it is rooted in the fear of "aphanisis", the loss of the capacity for
experiencing pleasure in life, ultimately sexual pleasure. Finally, the
work of Melanie Klein has shown that whereas both these roots of
anxiety are true and valid, there is a yet deeper source of fear—fear of
the loss of life itself.[7] All fears are intrinsically related to the deepest fear
of all: that in the last resort any "loss" may mean "total loss": in other
words, if it persists or increases, loss may mean loss of life itself and
unconsciously any loss brings that fear nearer. All fears come back to
the fear of death: to the destructive tendency that might be called the
capacity for death in oneself, which must be turned outward in aggression if it is not to work out in and on oneself. Yet in turning this
destructive force outward the loved and needed objects become its
target and so the danger of their loss arises. Faced with the loss of them
and their death, as a result of one's own destructiveness and hate, one's
own death appears imminent; thus the fear of "total loss" takes shape.
It is ultimately the fear of death which is behind our cravings to acquire,
possess, and incorporate, behind our greed and sadism and the predatory aspects of our modes of life.

And why should this fear be so acute in human beings and lead to so
many differences between us and the rest of animal life? Here I think
Freud gave us an answer, though he did not explicitly link it with the
craving to possess and acquire: Freud was always impressed with the
lengthy period of immaturity which human beings alone are subject to,
with the long condition of dependence and helplessness of our early
years. He clearly felt that it had fateful consequences on our psychical
development, even if he did not altogether succeed in formulating
them.[8] Thus, as I see it, the helplessness and dependence of human

children must, in conjunction with their phantasy-life, presuppose that the fear of death is even part of their experience. They cannot maintain themselves; absence of the parents, the means of life, entails loss of life. Even today in this country children die of neglect by the parents; older children see it happening. Many people have conscious memories of their terror as small children of being turned out by their parents to starve, as it might be. The small child's ego is quite sufficiently rational to appreciate its dependence on adults, and in addition in its phantasies the angry and revengeful parents threaten it with starvation, exposure, and all the terrors of death at their hands, which the child has willed that the parents shall undergo. It may well be that the id, which represents the mental expression of life and death instincts in fusion, cannot experience their total defusion and the extinction of life until bodily death ensues. But the ego, of which there is some nascent core from the very beginning of life, must have some capacity in that direction, since self-preservation is its primary function. To the unconscious of the child the worst terror, as Freud recognized, is that of the loss of the parents' love, and that loss means loss of all their needed goodness and in its place incurring their hate and revenge, so being alone and destitute with death as the consequence. This frightful thought is plainly dealt with by many and various methods of defence, among which denial of any such possibility or any such fear will be one of the first. Such an idea thus becomes inaccessible and taboo.[9]

We cannot escape the conclusion that an intense fear of dying by active aggression or passive neglect is a fundamental element in our emotional life, is as deeply-rooted in our unconscious minds as life itself and is barricaded off from conscious experience by every known mechanism of defence.[10] My thesis is that this fear is one fundamental source of the danger and terror giving rise to the drive to *incorporate* whatever is longed for and needed and the loss of which is dreaded. But in what sense does life depend on security in the love and possession of loved and needed persons, so that they must be internalized and kept alive within? It is true that people as well as animals are known to pine away and die when their loved ones vanish. We are not concerned here with material realities only; death is not only a matter of whether the breath leaves the body and the heart ceases to beat. That is one item of the experience of death, it is true; but is that all that death means to us? It is probably the most important factor in death because it is irrevocable, and thus all else that death means becomes irrevocable: namely, the cessation, the disappearance, so comparatively sudden, of a living existence, an entity, a person, a personality, a most complex and composite structure of attributes, tendencies, experiences, memories, idiosyncrasies good and bad, as well as the body they belong to. It is all this which disappears; from one moment to the next it was here and it is gone. So when one fears one's own death, it is all that which one will lose, one's "life"—in both senses—one's present breath of life, and one's "past life" out of which one's identity is constituted. And evidently it is to the loss of the latter, bound up with the death of the body, that the fear of death largely relates; the belief in the immortality of the soul even points to the wish that the death of the body might be negligible if only the personality could survive.

This complex personality of ours, unique in every individual, then, is what we cling to in life.[11] And now I must consider what this personality consists of, how it is composed. We tend to think of any one individual in isolation; it is a convenient fiction. We may isolate him physically, as in the analytic room; in two minutes we find he has brought his world in with him, and that, even before he set eyes on the analyst, he had developed inside himself an elaborate relation with him. There is no such thing as a single human being, pure and simple, unmixed with other human beings. Each personality is a world in himself, a company of many. That self, that life of one's own, which is in fact so precious though so casually taken for granted, is a composite structure which has been and is being formed and built up since the day of our birth out of countless never-ending influences and exchanges between ourselves and others. They begin with heredity and are succeeded by every emotional experience undergone as the days of life pass; and every one of these emotional experiences is bound up in feeling with one or more other persons in our lives, with "loved and hated objects". From the earliest and simplest infantile situations of receiving or giving pleasure, of receiving or giving frustration and pain, of love of power, of hatred of authority or necessity, of fear of losses— from life itself to loss of the imperatively claimed, needed and desired persons on whom and on whose life our life depends—from these ultimates have expanded all our experiences, memories, qualities and idiosyncrasies which form our own identity—our loves and hates, our likes and dislikes, our habit of mind, our tendencies and reactions— every one of which is ultimately founded on experiences with other persons in our lives and every one of which is an integral part of our personality. These other persons are in fact therefore parts of ourselves, not indeed the whole of them but such parts or aspects of them as we had our relation with, and as have thus become parts of us. And we ourselves similarly have and have had effects and influences, intended or not, on all others who have an emotional relation to us, have loved or hated us.[12] We are members one of another.

All this, which must be theoretically well known and obvious to any analyst, still seems to be insufficiently appreciated by us emotionally.

We cling to the fiction of our absolute individuality, our independence, as if we owed nothing to anyone and nothing in us had been begged, borrowed or stolen. I will not go into the motives which create and maintain this fiction—the deep-rooted egoisms omnipotent self-importance, the denial of debts which demand to be repaid; I will only point in passing to this attitude as another facet of the lack of comprehension of resistance against the notion of other individuals being within us and yet parts of ourselves. Nevertheless, there are moods and there are moments when we can be and are deeply conscious of the extent to which our lives and our being are interwoven with those of others. Everyone realizes at times, and normally with strong feeling, how much his life and his experience, if not his character and personality, is or has been enriched by a relation with other men and women (whether or not consciously he includes his parents among them). One thinks of the phrase "To have loved her is a liberal education".

Now it is not without significance that such moments most commonly occur in two particular situations: on the one hand, it is characteristic that the awareness of boons and benefits derived through the relation with another is part of the state of being in love, and especially when the love is returned; the other situation in which such emotions are typical is that of mourning the death or loss of someone whose value to one has been very great.[13] When, however, the awareness of all that one has gained in experience and personality from other people is connected with their loss this recognition of what such a person has meant to one is manifestly bound up with conscious *memories*. It can be said perhaps that the nearest a normal person, at any rate in the Western culture, comes to conscious realization of his own inner world is through the processes of memory. When we think such a thought as "I shall always have him or her with me wherever I go", what we consciously mean is that our memory of the person is so vivid and established so firmly in us that it is part of ourselves and cannot be lost. We can see them with "that *inward eye* which is the bliss of solitude", as Wordsworth says.

The experience and functions of "memories" in the life of the emotions is a large subject, not yet adequately explored. Memories have perhaps been awarded a somewhat back-handed evaluation in psychoanalysis. To begin with, Freud credited them with being the origin of neurotic symptoms, after which we all expected to unearth traumatic incidents in the childhood of our patients. Since those days other factors in aetiology have come into the foreground, and we hear far less of "memories". But this is too superficial a description of what has happened. Analysis is not now seen so much as the process of recovering the memory of certain specific early events, but as a process in which every significant *relation* to others throughout life, whether permanent, constant, temporary, or incidental, has to be recalled and realized; all the important emotional experiences of one's life comprise the "memories" which the analysis of today finds it necessary to recover, and these important experiences consist, as we know well, as much or more of feeling and phantasy in reference to other persons as of real occurrences in which they figured. What matters is what we "did with them inside ourselves" (a phrase used by a patient) "in our own minds", usually much more than what happened with them outside in "real life". The memories to be recovered in analysis consist so much of these inner happenings, to which external events such as we consciously call memories are often not much more than labels or signposts—in a sense but "screen-memories". As such nevertheless they have their great emotional importance to us; just as a person's name, which is but a label, can represent his whole being to us.

I will now illustrate this significance of past memories in our lives with another verse—a more familiar and, because it expresses such a universal experience, even a hackneyed one.

> At moments which he calls his own,
> Then, never less alone than when alone,
> Those whom he loved so long and sees no more,
> Loved and still loves—not dead, but gone before—
> He gathers round him.[14]

The meaning which is conveyed to us consciously by these lines is that the poet, when alone, becomes so deeply immersed in his thoughts and memories of those whom he has loved and lost by death that they seem to him to be still alive as they were in the past and their death and absence is thus for the time annulled. We recognize this to be a natural and familiar experience and so we attribute this meaning to the poem. In fact, however, the poet does not say that at all; he says nothing whatever about memory or the past. He simply says that when he is alone loved ones whom he no longer sees can be called to him, and he is then not alone, for he has them round him. His words are based on the assumption that they are *still present* and available to him; his words contradict the supposition that his relation with them lies in the past and can be enjoyed no longer. Yet it is incontestable that what this poetic phantasy relates to in external reality is his acts of absorption when alone in thoughts and memories of his *past*. The contradiction which is so remarkable here between past and present is to be resolved only in one way, namely, by the realization that the two opposites, past and present experience, are one and the same thing—two aspects of *one phenomenon.* It represents very much more than the banal fact that memories are always present with us to be called up when required. The appeal of these lines to so many thousands rests on their forthright statement that all those who have been emotionally important to us are still with us and inseparable from us—the unconscious truth behind the words being that they are *in us* and part of us and therefore inseparable and available to us. Memory, relating to external events and to the corporeal reality of loved figures as beings distinct from ourselves, is one facet of our relation to them; the other facet is the life they lead within us indivisible from ourselves, their existence in our inner worlds.[15]

I will digress here to give a significant instance of these two facets of a relation to another, past and present, coming to expression in one and the same breath, as it were. R. L. Stevenson was a writer whose mind was unusually open to the idea that other persons can be contained in oneself, whether for good or ill; such stories as *Dr. Jekyll and Mr. Hyde* and *The Bottle Imp,* for instance, are evidence enough. In his essay, "The Manse", he gives a picture of his grandfather's house and the grandfather himself, as he saw him and remembered him from his own childhood—silver hair, pale face, aloofness, the solemn light in which he was beheld in the pulpit, a somewhat awful figure. He wonders what of himself derives from this old minister, and would like to have inherited his noble presence.

"I cannot join myself on with the reverend doctor; yet all the while, no doubt, and even as I write the phrase, *he moves in my blood and whispers words to me,* and sits efficient in the very knot and centre of my being."[16] The whimsical R. L. S. then goes on most sensibly and plausibly to describe the converse: not only is the grandfather alive in him now, but he, R. L. S., was alive (part of him) in the grandfather when *he* was young, and went to school in him and was thrashed perhaps by Dr. Adam, and fell in love and married a daughter of Burns's Dr. Smith, and heard stories of Burns at first hand. "I have forgotten it but I was there all the same." So his past memories of the actual grandfather he knew in his childhood slide imperceptibly into his present phantasies of containing his grandfather alive in him now and of being alive in him before he himself was born. Time doth tarry in this inner world, indeed.

The two poems I quoted represent first and foremost the psychological truth that other persons can exist within us; besides expressing this thought more or less unequivocally, however, both these poems at the same time refer manifestly to situations of the loss of loved objects in external reality by death or absence. I tried to show in these two cases the special compensatory connection between external loss and internal acquisition or possession. This particular causative connection does not, however, exhaust the functions or significance of internal objects in our minds; and though I am not inclined to suppose that this dynamic element can ever be entirely inoperative during life, there are other and equally important factors at work which create and maintain our inner worlds.

It is an essential element in these poems that the persons inside, or spoken of as "round", the speaker are exclusively those he feels great love for. Not only is there no question in these instances of any alarm or revulsion at the idea of alien entities existing within the self; on the contrary, it is precisely the assurance that "good", loved and loving, ones are present that serves to ward off alarm in the speaker's mind and recoil from thoughts of loneliness, sadness and despair. In the case of Donne's poem about *Absence* I pointed to the extreme idealization in it as an inherent feature of the phantasy-situation: the implied idealization and perfection of the beloved herself has radiated and extended into the ecstasy of possessing her which the poet actually describes. In the lines from *Human Life*, too, there is a strong idealization of the man's relation with the dead men and women from his past: there is in it the asseveration that nothing but love is felt for them or by them. What is assumed in the first poem is explicit in the second, that it is the presence of the *love*-feelings between the speaker and those he can recall and possess that gives rise to the happiness, the fulfilment, reassurance, and peace they express and constitutes the effective barrier against the depression, loneliness, and alarm more natural in such a situation.

It appears therefore that these two poems would have had no meaning and served no purpose without their content of strong predominating love-feelings: anything indifferent or antagonistic in the speaker's relation with those within him must be totally excluded. And it is equally clear that just as it is the strong accentuation on possessing love which successfully excludes the thoughts of loss, so the emphasis on the loving relation between those concerned just as effectively averts the thought of any hostility, hurtfulness, or pain between them. What is explicitly denied in the poems is the experience and the fear of loss, as I commented to begin with; what is implicit in the poems is that the loss feared and denied is specifically of the *love* in the relation with another human being. Thus we see, what as analysts we already know, that the loss and absence of loved ones can be equivalent in our unconscious to *lack of love*, hostility, hate, even malevolence, in them to us and in us to them. Donne's poems betray the failure of love, the tendency to cynicism and despair, behind which lies the dread of hate, in his jealous expectations of losing the beloved. The second poem, about those who have died, cannot fail to remind us that the dread, guilt, and hate felt towards the dead in the unconscious, and the projected hate they feel for us, which psychoanalysis recognized so early, inevitably play their part here, and that the essential impulse prompting the verse is to dispel this fear. If love is not present there will be hate, there must be hate. Deep in the dynamic reservoir of instinctual forces, in the id, Eros the life and Thanatos the death force are in never-ending strife, one always aiming at ascendancy over the other. Whether in absence, or in death, or in other situations of estrangement, the intolerable fear rises that it is our own deadly hate which brings about the loss; and the greater is the love, the more hate is feared.

This brings me back to the split between love and hate, and between loved and hated, good and bad, objects, which I discussed to begin with; the simple "good or bad" pattern of our emotional life. I referred to the prevailing expectation we have that anything unknown, "not oneself" and alien inside us must be bad and dangerous, and to the corresponding claim and assumption that everything belonging to and part of us *must* be good—in itself a denial of the fear that it is not. I have further tried to show that our loving and hating of others relate as much (and more crudely) to their aspects inside us as to those outside us. In our earliest days, but later in life too, when the self within feels full of ruthless egoism or hate, destructive and painful, intense anxiety arises, both for ourselves and for the endangered objects; the violence of the fierce greed and hate raging within, and felt to be uncontrollable, is unutterably terrifying. It is then omnipotently denied and dissociated from the self, but is attributed instead to the persons inside who are the objects of the hate or greed, and are then felt to have provoked hate by their hate. It is they who are felt as bad: envious, robbing, ruthless, murderous. Thus it happens that a good helping person or part of a person, who was needed and craved, changes shape and turns into a terrifying and dangerous enemy inside one; one is felt to be "possessed of a devil" inside.

The bad objects within thus take their origin from our own dangerous and evil tendencies, disowned by us; characteristically therefore they are felt as "foreign objects", as an incubus, a nightmare, an appalling, gratuitous and inescapable persecution.[17] This phantasy-situation takes particular symptomatic form in hypochondriasis, in which the feelings about the evil persons who are parts of oneself are replaced consciously by feelings about various organs or parts of the body supposed to be diseased and dangerous.[18] Thus the persons outside us whom we once needed and depended on as life-giving come to be taken into us in phantasy; as they then become attacked and hated for further satisfactions they come to represent our own evil, until they are at the opposite pole and personify death-dealing influences. Then a defence against this danger will be sought by externalizing them again, projecting and finding them outside in the external world, in the effort to rid the self of them again.

The projection of persecutory phantasies concerning the inner world has manifestly found its most widespread expression in the myths of frightful and horrible forms of existence, e.g. as in nether worlds, notably in the Hell of medieval times. Such regions are explicitly of an "inner" description, circumscribed and contained, and the inmates are immured *within* them; their underground siting links, among other things, with the inner depths of the unconscious and the "bad" inner worlds.[19] Hell is a mythological projection of a personal region within the individual in which all one's own "bad", cruel, torturing and destructive impulses are raging against the "badness" of others and vice versa; the fires of Hell too symbolize the guilt and shame, not felt by the persecuted as part of them and arising spontaneously, but as attacking them aggressively. Dante's *Inferno is* the classic portrayal of this inner life.

Apart from descriptions of such terrible regions, there are in literature of course innumerable instances of less generalized representations of the bad inner world, transposed into the external world. Modern poetry abounds in them; such, for instance, as in T. S. Eliot's *Waste Land* and also in his *Murder in the Cathedral,* where the action takes place in the innermost sanctuary *inside* a sacred building. The cathedral represents both the person of the thinker in his most precious and valued aspects, his highest aspirations and capacities—love, truth, nobility and so on—as well as the inside of the idealized mother's body. In the depths, nevertheless, the bloody outrage happens with its accompaniments of desecration, ruin, and corruption. The idealization of creative love and goodwill breaks down and the persecution by evil, in the murder of the father by the son, resurges within it.

The fears of malevolent and dangerous beings inside us unconsciously representing those we love, desire, hate, misuse, and treat despitefully, and thus by our own persecution of them transform into persecutors of us, are, moreover, bound up in a particularly complex and specific way with the detailed phantasies relating to the act of their incorporation. I have already attempted to give some general idea of the way our lives and personalities are interwoven with those of others and how we become integral parts of them and they of us. I shall now quote a passage from a love-story which puts into words something of the emotion belonging to the act of incorporating another and even expresses some details in the process which are part of the underlying unconscious phantasy itself.

In this story, a man who believes his beloved to be far away comes back unexpectedly at night to a house where he and she had once spent much time, but actually he discovers her there. They talk; and then after a silence:

> "What are you thinking of?" she said.
>
> "Can I think of anything but you?" I murmured, taking a seat near the foot of the couch. "Or rather, it isn't thinking; it is more like a consciousness of you always being present in me, complete to the last hair, the faintest shade of expression, and that not only when we are apart but when we are together, alone, as close as this. I see you now lying on this couch, but it is only the insensible phantom of the real you: the real you is in me. How am I to know that the image is anything else but an enchanting mist?
>
> "I will tell you how it is. When I have you before my eyes there is such a projection of my whole being towards you that I fail to see you distinctly. I never saw you distinctly till after we had parted and I thought you had gone from my sight for ever. Then you took body in my imagination and my mind seized on a definite form of you for all its adorations—for its profanations too."[20]

Not only does the writer give us here an absolutely explicit description of one human being's act of incorporation of another, but he tells us of several accompaniments of the process. There is again the association of it with parting and loss which I have dwelt on already. There is the statement that the other whom he has within him is *more real* than the woman outside him, thus bringing into the foreground the connection between the directness and immediacy of the experience and the unconscious instinctual sources of our being, the *reality* of sensation, emotion, and the surges of instinct in us being so much more actual and vivid than any perceptions of the external world. It is here that lies the origin of the mystical tendencies in human nature, bound up as they are with immediate experience of body and mind; their explanation is found in phantasies of bodily incorporation, union, fusion, and inner possession.[21] In the quotation above there is, further, a direct statement of the phantasy of *self-projection* into the object which appears to be bound up and simultaneous with the process of *introjection* of the object; this is a most remarkable direct intuitive emergence into the author's conscious thought of the deepest unconscious processes which only through the work of Melanie Klein have now been uncovered and recognized in a scientific sense. Finally and most important is the last sentence in the passage: "you took body" in me and my mind "seized" you, "for its adorations *and its profanations too*".

This final utterance it is which completes the picture; with this nothing is left out. In spite of the intensity of the love which infuses the speaker and his words, the phantasy of incorporating another person is not here bound up, as it is in the other cases quoted, with an idealization of the lover's feelings. Ruthless and egoistic impulses towards the woman are scarcely veiled in his speech and purely antagonistic hate and revenge are almost manifest in it. The egoism of the lover and his hate of the frustrating object are here felt by him *as part of his love of her* and are recognized by him as such. There is a differentiation of his motives indeed into "adorations and profanations", but here it does not develop fully into the split between love and hate, good and bad, the split of idealization versus persecution, with the persecutory aspects denied and obliterated; in this passage the fundamental truth of their coexistence is laid bare. The open admission of intense love, longing, craving for possession, hand in hand with the impulse to profane—to maltreat, abuse, and degrade—is almost unique and it yields the solution to all our problems about the inner world. Those whom we love and crave for—first the mother, and later the long procession of all who come after her—who "take body" in us, whom we seize, devour, and immure, we have not only loved, not only yearned to be fed by and to feed, not only longed to satisfy and delight, but have craved to engulf and possess for ourselves and to use for our own ruthless purposes, in total disregard of their needs, and have wreaked on them the greed and savage impulses that are inherent in us along with our capacity for love. These savage impulses gain ground when love and desire are frustrated; they spring from the forces of death in us which are reinforced when love fails, and the fear of such danger to the self within impels us to direct them outward on to the other. In its primitive form perhaps the impulse to possess and incorporate the desired object can be regarded as a sort of half-way process, a manifest fusion of Eros and Thanatos, a compromise between loving and killing, in which both have a share but neither prevail and by means of which the life of both subject and object is felt to be secured. Nevertheless, in one of its aspects it entails the imprisonment, subjection, and torture of the loved, desired, and hated objects, and from that circumstance spring the torments and agonies suffered by them and by us in our inner worlds. Thus it is that one and the same figure in our inner worlds can bear two different aspects, can be felt as ideally perfect, without a flaw, or as vile and monstrous, as bounteously loving and protecting, or as terrifying and persecuting.

Now to conclude I will come back from the theme that good and bad cannot be isolated from each other, that all life and therefore ourselves contain them both in varying degrees, to the corollary of this that none of us can be isolated, that each of us is a company of many, and that our being is contained in all those others we have been and are occupied with as we live, just as they are contained in us. The following translation of verses by a French poet expresses this aspect of life with the peculiar concrete realism of such phantasies.

> The stream of life went past me and I looked for my body there
> All those who followed on and on and who were not myself
> Were bringing one by one the pieces of myself
> There I was built up piece by piece as one erects a tower
> The men and women piled up high and I appeared—myself
> Who had been made of all the bodies all the stuff of man
>
> Times past—passed out—ye gods who made me
> As you lived so I in passing only live
> My eyes averted from the empty future
> Within myself I see the past all gaining growth
>
> Nothing is dead but what is yet to come
> Beside the luminous past to-morrow is colourless
> And shapeless too beside what perfectly
> Presents at once both effort and effect[22]

My attempt has been to convey some introductory idea, as it were, of the phantasies we all unconsciously create of harbouring others inside ourselves. I have scarcely touched on what they are, what we feel they do with us or we do with them.[23] I have wished to show that even the *conscious* phantasy of other beings existing within us is not in the least uncommon in the imagination of man, and is far from being an outrage on human nature or a sign of derangement. The understanding of the part played in our lives by the *unconscious* phantasy can only come through the widening knowledge of psychoanalysis.

Notes

1. The tendency discussed by Freud in "The Uncanny", *Collected Papers, Vol. IV* (London, 1925) [1919h].

2. Cf. Freud on the good, protective, tender aspects of the superego in "Humour", *Collected Papers, Vol. V* (London, 1950) [1927d].

3. The words "good" and "bad" are obviously used here in the simplest possible sense—in fact, much as a small child would use them—as expressing the quality of feeling concerned and unrelated to any other standard. Moral judgments, for instance, as to what is good or bad do not necessarily coincide with what is spontaneously felt by the person in himself to be so often quite the contrary. The same applies to matters of health, of pleasure, of taste; the sole criterion is the pleasure-principle. In the cradle we were all originally in the condition of the

despised person who "knows nothing about" any external criteria but "simply knows what he likes", namely, what gives hint pleasure or unpleasure; and however much the forms taken by our pleasures may alter as life proceeds, it is fundamentally always on that same principle that our good and bad experiences arise.

4. John Donne [1573–1631].

5. Cf. Freud, "Mourning and Melancholia" [1917e (1915)], for the relation between loss and incorporation of the object.

6. The relation between the symptom of kleptomania and experiences of deprivation in early life has been to some extent recognized.

7. See her papers, especially "Anxiety and Guilt", Ch. VIII; also "Notes on the Life and Death Instincts", Ch. X, by Paula Heimann, in *Developments in Psycho-Analysis*, London, 1952.

8. Freud's decisive rejection of the possibility of an unconscious fear of death evidently played its part in this. Even if this view represents an aspect of truth, it appears to be only a partial one.

9. I mention these objective factors in their bearing on a child's feelings and phantasies, not because I believe them to be a first cause of the fears in question, the root of which lies in a child's own instinctual endowment, but because such factors and their influence are denied and ignored by adults.

10. I cannot here discuss the point further, but would refer the reader to recent papers on the topic by Melanie Klein and Paula Heimann, notably Chapters VIII and X in *Developments in Psycho-Analysis* (London, 1952).

11. The fear of the *loss of one's own identity*, by the disintegration and splitting of the ego, can be seen to be one of the most acute and painful anxieties accompanying or underlying schizophrenic disorders.

12. As will be seen, what I have here attempted to describe in non-technical terms is something of the operation of introjection and projection in the formation of the personality, though excluding arbitrarily for the moment the dynamic instinctual forces behind their functioning.

13. It would seem to be worth remarking that they are both situations in which a measure of defusion of instincts has taken place; for the time being either Eros or Thanatos has gained some victory and the equilibrium which balances on so many compensatory denials has given way.

14. Samuel Rogers, *Human Life* [1819].

15. It will be seen that in the lines from *Human Life* the poet does not actually state in words that these men and women are alive *in him*. The phrase he uses is that they can be gathered "round him". The content of the poem, however, states that they are not dead but are *still present to him*, and it is of interest to find that he chooses the idea that they are "round him" to express this thought since it is one of the most frequent symbols for internal objects. As Melanie Klein has mentioned in *Contributions to Psycho-Analysis*, p. 303, also p. 333 note, a house, a car, a train or whatever contains people commonly represents the inner world; and conversely, whatever is closely round a person or on top of him (close but invisible) may represent his internal objects. Another aspect of the inner world, its mysterious, inaccessible quality, is also commonly represented symbolically by *far away*, by *looking into space*, both not tangible, incapable of exploration; again, by *farthest away*, equivalent to nearest, one's own inside; by *looking into a mirror*, into one's own inside; or by *the sky, heaven high above*, inaccessible, unknowable and again *above*.

In the lines quoted the explicitly omnipotent character of the poetic phantasy, together with the speaker's solitude, are further indications of inner world phantasy-manipulation.

16. (My italics) *Memories and Portraits*.

17. The classical and emotionally most significant example of these unconscious phantasies of inner activities with and by inner objects is that of the primal scene, the parents in intercourse, typically of a monstrous and unutterably terrifying character, inside one. By the child originally they are felt as enacting what one set of urges in him is aiming at with each of them, but these aims are denied as his own and transferred on to them.

18. For a study of hypochondriasis, see Paula Heimann, *Developments in Psycho-Analysis* (London, 1952), Ch. IV.

19. The symbolic association of the lower parts of the body and the "lower" aspects of human nature with the deep internal regions of Hell and the sadistic—anal and genital allusions in this context have long been recognized by psychoanalysis.

20. Joseph Conrad, *The Arrow of Gold*, p. 283.

21. These phantasies of "projective identification" are the kernel of the "cannibalistic" stage of development, already mentioned; they accompany the earliest oral phase of breast-feeding, the former being in any case an offshoot of impulses and phantasies belonging to the latter.

22. *Le cortège passait et j'y cherchais mon corps*
    Tous ceux qui survenaient et n'étaient pas moi-même
    Amenaient un à un les morceaux de moi-même
    On me bâtit peu à peu comme on élève une tour
    Les peuples s'entassaient et je parus moi-même
    Qu'ont formé tous les corps et les chores humaines
    Temps passés Trépassés Les dieux qui me formâtes
    Je ne vis que passant ainsi qui vous passâtes
    Et détournant mes yeux de ce vide avenir
    En moi-même je vois tout le passé grandir

    Rien n'est mort que ce qui n'existe pas encore
    Près du passé luisant demain est incolore
    Il est informe aussi près de ce qui parfait
    Présente tout ensemble et l'effort et l'effet
            Guillaume Apollinaire (1914), *Alcools*, p. 57.

23. In my paper on "The Inner World in Ibsen's *Master-Builder*" [1959] some pathological aspects of the activities of internal objects are illustrated.

CHAPTER FOUR

The role of illusion in symbol formation

(1955)

Marion Milner

Psychoanalytic concepts of the two functions of the symbol

Much has been written by psychoanalysts on the process by which the infant's interest is transferred from an original primary object to a secondary one. The process is described as depending upon the identification of the primary object with another that is in reality different from it but emotionally is felt to be the same. Ernest Jones and Melanie Klein in particular, following up Freud's formulations, write about this transference of interest as being due to conflict with forces forbidding the interest in the original object, as well as to the actual loss of the original object. Jones, in his paper "The Theory of Symbolism" (1916), emphasizes the aspects of this prohibition which are to do with the forces that keep society together as a whole. Melanie Klein, in various papers, describes also the aspect of it which keeps the individual together as a whole; she maintains that it is the fear of our own aggression towards our original objects which makes us so dread their retaliation that we transfer our interest to less attacked and so less frightening substitutes. Jones also describes how the transfer of interest is due, not only to social prohibition and frustration and the wish to escape from the immanent frustrated mouth, penis,

---

This paper originally appeared in a slightly longer form, under the title "Aspects of Symbolism in Comprehension of the Not-Self". A postscript has been added to this version.

vagina, and their retaliating counterparts, but also to the need to endow the external world with something of the self and so make it familiar and understandable.

The identification of one object with another is described as the forerunner of symbolism, and Melanie Klein, both in her paper "Infant Analysis" (1923) and in the "The Importance of Symbol Formation in the Development of the Ego" (1930), says that symbolism is the basis of all talents. Jones describes this identification as a process of symbolic equivalence through which progress to sublimation is achieved, but adds that symbolism itself, in the sense in which he uses the word, is a bar to progress. Leaving aside for a moment this difference over the use of the word symbol, there is one point about wording which, I feel, requires comment. Jones describes the process of identification that underlies symbol formation as being not only the result of the forbidding forces, but also a result of the need to establish a relation to reality. He says that this process arises from the desire to deal with reality in the easiest possible way, from "the desire for ease and pleasure struggling with the demand of necessity". It seems to me that this way of putting it is liable to lead to misunderstanding. The phrase "desire for ease and pleasure" set against the "demand of necessity" gives the impression that this desire is something that we could, if we were sufficiently strong-minded, do without. The phrase reflects perhaps a certain Puritanism which is liable to appear in psychoanalytic writing. Do we really mean that it is only the desire for ease and pleasure, and not necessity, that drives us to identify one thing with another which is in fact not the same? Are we not rather driven by the internal necessity for inner organization, pattern, coherence, the basic need to discover identity in difference without which experience becomes chaos? Actually I think Jones himself implies such an idea when he says that this confounding of one thing with another, this not discriminating, is also the basis of generalization; and he indicates the positive aspect of this failure to discriminate, in relation to discovery of the real world, when he says:

> . . . there opens up the possibility . . . of a theory of scientific discovery, inventions, etc., for psychologically this consists in an overcoming of the resistances that normally prevent regression towards the infantile unconscious tendency to note identity in differences.

This was written in 1916. In 1951 Herbert Read writes:

> The first perceptions of what is novel in any science tend to assume the form of metaphors—the first stages of science are poetic.

Jones quotes Rank and Sachs when they make a distinction between the primary process of identification which underlies symbolism and symbolism itself. He quotes their description of how the original function (demonstrable in the history of civilization) of the identification underlying symbolism was a means of adaptation to reality, but that it " . . . becomes superfluous and sinks to the mere significance of a symbol as soon as this task of adaptation has been accomplished". He quotes their description of a symbol as the "unconscious precipitate of primitive means of adaptation to reality that have become superfluous and useless, a sort of lumber room of civilization to which the adult readily flees in states of reduced or deficient capacity for adaptation to reality, in order to regain his old long-forgotten playthings of childhood". But they add the significant remark that what later generations know and regard only as a symbol had in earlier stages of mental life full and real meaning and value.

Jones goes on to quote Rank's and Sachs' statement that symbol formation is a regressive phenomenon, and that it is most plainly seen in civilized man, in conditions where conscious adaptation to reality is either restricted, as in religious or artistic ecstasy, or completely abrogated, as in dreams and mental disorders. Here it seems to me that a valuable link has been made between symbolism and ecstasy, but the context in which these two ideas have been brought together leaves out, in respect of the arts, what Jones has described in respect of scientific invention: that is, that it may be a regression in order to take a step forward. Thus Rank's and Sachs' statement does not draw attention to the possibility that some form of artistic ecstasy may be an essential phase in adaptation to reality, since it may mark the creative moment in which new and vital identifications are established. In fact Rank and Sachs do not here allow for the possibility that truth underlies the much quoted aphorism that Art creates Nature; and so also they miss the chance of indicating an underlying relation between art and science.[1]

I think some of the difficulty arises here from lack of a sufficiently clear distinction between the two uses of the process which has been given the name of symbolization. Fenichel (1946) has made this distinction more clear. He says:

> In adults a conscious idea may be used as a symbol for the purpose of hiding an objectionable unconscious idea; the idea of a penis may be represented by a snake, an ape, a hat, an airplane, if the idea of penis is objectionable. The distinct idea of a penis had been grasped but rejected.

But he then goes on to say that symbolic thinking is also a part of the primal prelogical thinking and adds:

> . . . archaic symbolism as a part of prelogical thinking and distortion by means of representing a repressed idea through a conscious sym-

bol are not the same. Whereas in distortion the idea of penis is avoided through disguising it by the idea of snake, in prelogical thinking penis and snake are *one and the same;* that is, they are perceived by a common conception: the sight of die snake provokes penis emotions; and this fact is later utilized when the conscious idea of snake replaces die unconscious one of penis. [italics added]

A distinction between two uses of the word symbol has also been described by a non-analyst. Herbert Read (1950) says:

> But there is a very general distinction to be made between those uses of the word which on the one hand retain the sense of a throwing together of tangible, visible objects, with each other or with some immaterial or abstract notion, and those uses which on the other hand imply no such initial separation, but rather treat the symbol as an integral or original form of expression. A word itself may be a symbol in this sense, and language a system of symbols.

The similarity between this second use of the word symbol and Fenichel's second use of it, is clear; although Read says earlier that he feels that it is a pity that he and analysts have to use the same word to describe different things.

Illusion and fusion

It is the use of symbolism as part of what Fenichel calls prelogical thinking that I wish to discuss here. In particular I wish to consider what are the conditions under which the primary and the secondary object are fused and felt as one and the same. I want to study both the emotional state of the person experiencing this fusion and what conditions in the environment might facilitate or interfere with it; in fact, to study something of the internal and external conditions that make it possible to find the familiar in the unfamiliar—which, incidentally, Wordsworth (1798) said is the whole of the poet's business.

When considering what concepts are available as tools for thinking about thus process of fusion or identification, the concept of phantasy is obviously essential, since it is only in phantasy that two dissimilar objects are fused into one. But this concept is not quite specific enough to cover the phenomenon; the word illusion is also needed because this word does imply that there is a relation to an external object of feeling, even though a phantastic one, since the person producing the fusion believes that the secondary object *is* the primary one. In order to come to understand more about the meaning of the word illusion I found it was useful to consider its role in a work of art. I had already, when trying to study some of the psychological factors which facilitate or impede the painting of pictures,[2] become interested in the part played by the frame. The frame marks off the different kind of reality that is within it from that which is outside it; but a temporal spatial frame also marks off the special kind of reality of a psychoanalytic session. And in psychoanalysis it is the existence of this frame that makes possible the full development of that creative illusion that analysts call the transference. Also the central idea underlying psychoanalytic technique is that it is by means of this illusion that a better adaptation to the world outside is ultimately developed. It seemed to me that the full implications of this idea for analytic theory had still to be worked out, especially in connection with the role of symbolism in the analytic relationship.

In considering the dynamics of the process the concept of anxiety is clearly needed. Melanie Klein has laid great stress on the fact that it is dread of the original object itself, as well as the loss of it, that leads to the search for a substitute. But there is also a word needed for the emotional experience of finding the substitute, and it is here that the word ecstasy may be useful.

There is also another ordinary English word, not often used in psychoanalytic literature, except to talk about perversion, or lack of it, in neurotic states, and that is the word concentration. I wish to bring it in here because, in analysing children, I have found myself continually noticing the varying moods or quality of concentration shown by the children, and have tried to understand the relation of these variations to the kind of material produced. These observations have not been confined to the analytic situation; I have often noticed, when in contact with children playing, that there occurs now and then a particular type of absorption in what they are doing, which gives the impression that something of great importance is going on. Before becoming an analyst I used to wonder what a child, if he had sufficient power of expression, would say about these moods, how he would describe them from inside. When I became an analyst I began to guess that the children were in fact trying to tell me, in their own way, what it does feel like. And I thought I recognized the nature of these communications the more easily because I had already tried for myself, introspectively, to find ways of describing such states, most particularly in connection with the kinds of concentration that produce a good or a bad drawing.

Before going on to present and discuss some clinical material, there is one other concept which I think needs clarifying; and that is, the meaning of the term "primary object". Earlier psychoanalytic discussions of symbol formation most often emphasized the child's attempts to find substitutes for those original objects of interest that are the parents' organs. But some also emphasized the aspect of the child's attempts to find his own organs and their functioning in every object. In more recent work these two views tend to be combined and the idea develops that the primary "object" that the infant seeks to find again is a fusion of self and object, it is mouth and breast felt as fused into one. Thus the concept of fusion is present, both in the primary situation, between self and object, and in the secondary one, between the new situation and the old one.

Case material: a game of war between two villages

Moments when the original "poet" in each of us created the outside world for us, by finding the familiar in the unfamiliar, are perhaps forgotten by most people; or else they are guarded in some secret place of memory because they were too much like visitations of the gods to be mixed with everyday thinking. But in autobiographies some do dare to tell, and often in poetry. Perhaps, in ordinary life, it is good teachers who are most aware of these moments, from outside, since it is their job to provide the conditions under which they can occur, so to stage-manage the situation that imagination catches fire and a whole subject or skill lights up with significance. But it is in the analytic situation that this process can be studied from inside and outside at the same time. So now I will present some material from child analysis which seems to me to be offering data about the nature of the process.

The patient is a boy of eleven who was suffering from a loss of talent for school work. During his first school years, from four to six, he had been remarkably interested and successful and always top of his form; but he had gradually come to find himself very near the bottom, and at times had been totally unable to get himself to school at all.

The particular play that I wish to discuss had been preceded by a long period in which all the toys had been set out in the form of a village, full of people and animals; the boy would then bomb the village by dropping balls of burning paper upon it, my role being to play the part of the villagers, mid try to save all the toys from actual destruction. The rules of the game were such that this was often very difficult, so that gradually more and more of the toys were burnt, and from time to time I had replaced them by new ones. (This boy had, in fact, lived through part of the blitz on London, and had started this play some time after my own house had been damaged by blast; and he had shown delayed interest in the extent of the damage when he came to my house for his analysis.)

In the session which I have chosen to describe, he begins by saying that we are to have two villages and a war between them, but that the war is not to begin at once. My village is to be made up of all the people and animals and houses; his of toy trucks, cars, etc., and "lots of junk and oddments to exchange", though I am to have some oddments as well. He begins by sending along a truck from his village with half a gun in it, and takes various things in exchange. He then brings a test-tube and exchanges it for a number of objects, including a little bowl, bits of metal, a ladder, etc. When I comment on the amount taken in exchange he says: "Yes, the test-tube is equal to a lot", but on the return journey to his own village he adds: "I think those people were a bit odd, I don't think I like those people much, I think I will give them just a little time-bomb." So he takes back his test-tube, sticks some matches in it, and drops it over my village. He then drops a whole box of matches on my village, and says the villagers have to find it and put it out before it explodes. But then I have to come and bomb his village, and when I drop a flare, instead of putting it out he adds fuel to it. Then he says: "You have got to bring all your people over to my village, the war is over." I have to bring the animals and people over in trucks, but at once he says they must go back because they all have to watch the burning of the whole stack of match boxes (which he has bought with his own money). He makes me stand back from the blaze, and shows great pleasure.

He now decides that his "people" (empty trucks) are to call on mine; his are explorers and mine are to think his are gods. The trucks arrive, my people have to be frightened. He tells me to make them say something; so I make the policeman ask what they want; but he replies: "You've forgotten, they think it's gods." He now borrows the "Mrs. Noah" figure from my village and stands her in one of his trucks. Then, in a god-like voice, he commands that the villagers go into their houses and prepare food.[3] It is now the end of the session and while I am beginning to tidy up he plays with some melting wax, humming to himself the hymn-tune "Praise, my soul, the King of Heaven". He smears some wax on both my thumbs and says he is double-jointed, and asks if I am too.

At first I saw this material in terms of his bisexual conflict and I tried to interpret it in that way. I told him that I thought the war between the two villages was expressing his feeling that 1, as the mother, the woman, have all the human values, while he has only the mechanical ones. Thus interpretation linked with earlier material in which he had spent weeks making Meccano models with sets that he brought to the session, and had continually shown me the models illustrated in the handbook, assuring me that "You can make anything with Meccano"; but this play had stopped suddenly after lie had tried to make a mechanical man, as specified in the book, and it had failed to work, i.e. move. And I had told him then how disappointed he was that he could not make a live baby out of his Meccano. So, in this village play, I pointed out how he lead now attempted some rearrangement and exchange in which I was to be given some of the maleness (gun and test-tube), and he was to have something of the femaleness (ending up with getting the "Mrs. Noah" figure). I explained also how this compromise had not entirely worked, since jealousy had broken through, as was shown in his attempt to justify his impending envious attacks by saying "I don't like these people"; that is to say "I am not guilty because they are bad anyway, so it doesn't matter hurting them." Also I told him that by burning his own village he was not only punishing himself, but at the same time expressing (externalizing) the state of anxiety in which he felt full of explosive faeces which might at any moment blow up his own body; and added that he had returned to the attempt to avoid the cause of jealousy by trying to mitigate the absoluteness of his split between "mechanized" male and "human" female. I suggested that he was trying to tell me how he could not stand the empty, depersonalized gods (trucks), so effected a compromise by borrowing the good mother figure to fill the empty truck. I pointed out how, after this, he could tell me that he was double-jointed; that is, he combined both positions, and he hoped I could too.

In the next session immediately following this one, he spent the whole hour mending his satchel, a job that he said ordinarily his mother would do for him. Here I interpreted that the two villages were also mother and father, and that he felt he had succeeded in bringing them together inside him.

Certainly he did seem to be working out his conflicts about the relation between father and mother, both internally and externally, and trying to find ways of dealing with his jealousy and envy of his mother in what Melanie Klein (1928) has called the "femininity phase". Considered in this light, his mechanized village then also stood for his feeling about his school. For at this time he was constantly complaining how utterly uninteresting and boring his school work was, and lie frequently brought material to do with waste lands and desert places: this being in marked contrast with the early school years during which he had been interested and successful. Thus one way of trying to describe the situation was in terms of the idea that the school, the place in which he must seek knowledge, had become too much identified with the destroyed mother's body, so that it had indeed become a desert; for the game of attacking and burning the village had been played throughout the period of his most acute school difficulties. But at the same time it was also too much identified with the desired mother's body, for such material certainly also pointed to intense conflict in the direct Oedipus situation, as well as in the "femininity phase"; and for a long time it had seemed to me that the school difficulty was being presented largely in these terms. Thus the entry into the world of knowledge and school work seemed to be identified with the entry into the mother's body, an undertaking at once demanded by the schoolmaster–father figure but forbidden under threat of castration by the sexual rival father. In fact one could describe the situation here in terms of the use of symbolism as a defence, and say that because the school had become the symbol of the forbidden mother's body this was then a bar to progress.

The defence against the anxiety aroused by this symbolic identification took the form of a reversal of roles in his play with me; he himself became the sadistic punishing schoolmaster and I had to be the bad pupil. For days, and sometimes weeks, I had to play the role of the persecuted schoolboy: I was set long monotonous tasks, my efforts were treated with scorn, I was forbidden to talk and made to write out "lines" if I did; and if I did not comply with these demands, then he wanted to cane me. (When asked if he were really treated as badly as this at school he always said "no"; he certainly was never caned, and the school, though of the conventional pattern, did try most generously to adapt to his difficulties.) Clearly then there was a great amount of resentment and fear to be worked through in the Oedipus situation, but I did not feel this was the only reason for the persistence of this type of play. It was other aspects of the material which finally led me to see the problem as also something to do with difficulties in establishing the relation to external reality as such.

One of these was the fact that he frequently adopted a particularly bullying tone when talking to me, even when he was not playing the schoolmaster game, but he always dropped this tone as soon as he began imaginative play with the toys. This observation suggested that perhaps this boy could drop the hectoring tone, during this kind of play, because it was a situation in which he could have a different kind of relation to external reality, by means of the toys; he could do what he liked with them, and yet they were outside him. He nearly always began the session with the bullying tone and insistence that I was not ready for him at the right time, whatever the actual time of starting; but as soon as he had settled down to using the toys as a pliable medium, external to himself, but not insisting on their own separate objective existence, then apparently he could treat me with friendliness and consideration, and even accept real frustration from me.

The receptive role of the toys

This observation set me wondering about the exact function of this relation to the toys, and in what terms it could be discussed. I noticed how, on days when he did play with the toys, there seemed to develop a relationship between him and them which reminded me of the process I had myself tried to observe introspectively when doing "free" drawings (1950). I thought that there was perhaps something useful to be said about the actual process of playing with the toys as compared with, on the one hand, pure day-dreaming, and on the other, direct expedient muscular activity directed towards a living object. In the play with the toys there was something halfway between day-dreaming and purposeful instinctive or expedient action. As soon as he moved a toy in response to some wish or phantasy then the play-village was different, and the new sight set off a new set of possibilities; just as in free imaginative drawing, the sight of a mark made on the paper provokes new associations, the line as it were answers back and functions as a very primitive type of external object.

About two months after the war-of-the-villages play something occurred which seemed to offer a further clue as to what was happening when he played with the toys; for the bullying tone suddenly vanished for four days, beginning with a day when he told me about something that had happened at school which clearly gave him great pleasure. For many weeks before he had been intensely preoccupied with a photography club that he and his particular friends had organized in their out-of-school hours; now he reported that their form master had given him permission to hold their meetings in school, during a time set aside for special activities, and had even given them a little room in which to work.

This sudden disappearance of his dictatorship attitude gave me the idea that the fact of his spontaneously created activity being incorporated in the framework of the school routine was a fulfilling, in external life, of the solution foreshadowed in the war between the villages play. What he had felt to be the mechanized, soulless world of school had now seemed to him to have become humanized, by the taking into its empty trucks of a bit of himself, something that he had created. But what was particularly interesting was the fact that he had only been able to respond to the school's gesture at this particular moment; for there had been many efforts on their part to help him before this, such as special coaching after his continual absences. One could of course say that it was because of the strength of his own aggression and his anxiety about it, that he had not been able to make more use of the help offered; but it seemed to me that these earlier efforts on the part of the school had not had more apparent effect also because they had not taken the particular form of the incorporation of, acceptance of, a bit of his own spontaneous creation. Now the school, by being receptive, by being in-giving as well as out-giving, had shown itself capable of good mothering; it was a male world which had become more like his mother, who had in fact been a very good mother. Much earlier he had foreshadowed this same need by one of his rare dreams, in which his mother had been present at school in his Latin class, Latin being the bugbear of his school subjects.

This view of the meaning of the villages play as partly to do with problems of this boy's whole relation to what was, for him, the unmitigated not-me-ness of his school life, threw light on one of the elements in the original situation when his difficulties first became apparent. Not only had his father been called away to the war just at the time when his baby brother had been born and when London was being bombed, but he had also lost his most valued toy, a woolly rabbit. As the analysis advanced I had come to realize how significant this loss had been, for it became more clear that one of my main roles in the transference was to be the lost rabbit. He so often treated me as totally his own to do what he liked with, as though I were dirt, his dirt, or as a tool, an extension of his own hand. (He had never been a thumb sucker.) If I was not free the moment he arrived, even though he was often thirty minutes early, I was reprimanded or threatened with punishment for being late. In fact it certainly did seem that for a very long time he did need to have the illusion that I was part of himself.

Play and the boundary between inner and outer

Here I tried to review the various psychoanalytic concepts of mechanisms that can be forerunners of or defences against object relations, and see which might be useful to explain what was happening. Certainly he split himself and put the bad bit of himself into me when he punished me as the pupil. Certainly he used threatening words which were intended to enter into me and cow me into doing what he wanted and being his slave. Certainly he tried to make me play the role of the all-gratifying idealized phantasy object; he once told me that he did feel himself quite special and that the frustrating things that happened to other people would not happen to him. I thought that this did mean that he felt at times that he had this marvellous object inside him which would protect and gratify him. And this linked with the fact that he would sometimes hum hymn tunes, such as "Praise, my soul, the King of Heaven", although he explicitly expressed great scorn for religion. Certainly also he found it very difficult to maintain the idea of my separate identity; in his demands he continually denied the existence of my other patients or any family ties. The way he behaved could also be described by saying that he kept me inside him, since he continually used to insist that I knew what he had been doing or was going to do, when I had in fact no possible means of knowing. Yet I did not feel that these ways of talking about what happened were entirely adequate; for all of them take for granted the idea of a clear boundary, if I am felt to be inside him then he has a boundary, and the same if a bit of him is felt to be projected into me.

But there was much material in this analysis to do with burning, boiling down, and melting, which seemed to me to express the idea of the obliteration of boundaries. And I had a growing amount of evidence, both from clinical material and introspective study of problems in painting, that the variations in the feeling of the existence or non-existence of the body boundary are themselves very important. In this connection Scott (1949) restates Winnicott's view (1945, 1948) about how a good mother allows the child to fuse its predisposition to hallucinate a good situation with the earliest sensations of a good situation. Scott then describes this as an "oscillation between the illusion of union and the fact of contact, which is another way of describing the discovery of an interface, a boundary, or a place of contact, and perhaps at the same time is another way of describing the discovery of 'the me' and 'the you'". He goes on to say "But I think only a partial picture of union and contact is given by discussing the good situation. Equally important is the evil union and the evil contact and the discovery of the evil me and the evil you.[4] He also talks of the extremes of the states in which all discriminations and interfaces are destroyed as in what he calls "cosmic bliss" and "catastrophic chaos". And these extremes relate, I think, to behaviourist observations that can be made, both in and out of analysis, of the variations of facial expression between extreme beauty and extreme ugliness. I had, for instance, a child patient of six who would at times show an extremely seraphic face, and it occurred in connection with great concentration on the use or lack of use of outline in painting. I also observed a schizophrenic patient (adult) who would at times have moments of startling physical beauty counterbalanced by moments of something startlingly repellent.

One could certainly think of this phenomenon in terms of complete union with a marvellous or atrocious inner object, with the obliteration of inner boundaries between the ego and the incorporated object. But there was also the question of where the actual body boundary was felt to be. Did it mean that the skin was felt to include the whole world and therefore in a sense was denied altogether? Certainly the introspective quality of what have been called oceanic states seems to include this feeling, as does also the catastrophic chaos that Scott refers to. For the schizophrenic patient described above constantly complained that she could not get the world outside her and that this, rather than being a source of bliss, was agony to her. Certainly there is very much here that

I do not understand. Also the whole question of beauty appearing in analysis, perceived by the analyst either as a varying physical quality of the patient or as a quality of the material, has not been much discussed in the literature, though Sharpe (1937) does mention dreams that the patient describes as beautiful. When perceived by the analyst it can clearly be described in terms of the countertransference, and used, just as any other aspect of the countertransference can be used (Paula Heimann, 1950), as part of the analytic data. Thus in trying to understand all that this boy was trying to show me I had to take into account the fact that at times there was a quality in his play which I can only describe as beautiful—occasions when it was he who did the stage managing and it was my imagination which caught fire. It was in fact play with light and fire. He would close the shutters of the room and insist that it be lit only by candle light, sometimes a dozen candles arranged in patterns, or all grouped together in a solid block. And then he would make what he called furnaces, with a very careful choice of what ingredients should make the fire, including dried leaves from special plants in my garden; and sometimes all the ingredients had to be put in a metal cup on the electric fire and stirred continuously, all this carried out in the half darkness of candle light. And often there had to be a sacrifice, a lead soldier had to be added to the fire, and this figure was spoken of either as the victim or the sacrifice. In fact, all this type of play had a dramatic ritual quality comparable to the fertility rites described by Frazer in primitive societies. And this effect was the more striking because this boy's conscious interests were entirely conventional for his age; he was absorbed in Meccano and model railways.

Aesthetic experience and the merging of the boundary

The fact that in this type of material the boy's play nearly became "a play", in that there was a sense of pattern and dramatic form in what he produced, leads to many questions about the relation of a work of art to analytic work, which are not relevant here. But the particular point I wish to select for further consideration is that he seemed to me to be trying to express the idea of integration, in a variety of different ways. Thus the fire seemed to be here not only a destructive fire but also the fire of Eros; and not only the figurative expression of his own passionate body feelings, not only the phantasy representative of the wish for passionate union with the external object, but also a way of representing the inner fire of concentration. The process in which interest is withdrawn temporarily from the external world so that the inner work of integration can be carried out was, I think, shown by the boiling or melting down of the various ingredients in what he called "the fire cup", to make a new whole. And the sacrifice of the toy soldier by melting it down both expressed the wish to get rid of a bad internal object, particularly the cramping and cruel aspect of his superego, and also his sense of the need to absorb his inner objects into his ego and so modify them. But in addition to this I think it represented his feeling of the need to be able, at tunes, to transcend the common-sense ego; for common sense was very strong in him, his conscious attitude was one of feet firmly planted on the ground. For instance, when he did tell a dream, which was rarely, he usually apologized if it was at all nonsensical. And formerly also this boy had told me that he was "no good at art" and he was extremely tentative in any attempts at drawing. But later this changed. For he told me one day, with pride, that he was good at both science and art, which he felt was not very usual among his schoolfellows; though he was still inclined to be apologetic about his aesthetic experiences. When he told me of the delight he took in the colours of the various crystals he had studied in his chemistry he added, "It's childish to like them so much."

Although an important factor in this development of his capacity to feel himself "good at art" was his growing belief in his power to restore his injured objects, this is not the aspect of the material that I wish to discuss here; for I am concentrating on the earlier problem of establishing object relationships at all, rather than on the restoration of the injured object once it is established. Granted that these two are mutually interdependent and that anxiety in the one phase can cause regression to the earlier one, there is still much to be said about the earlier phase as such. Thus a central idea began to emerge about what this boy was trying to tell me; it was the idea that the basic identifications which make it possible to find new objects, to find the familiar in the unfamiliar, require an ability to tolerate a temporary loss of sense of self, a temporary giving up of the discriminating ego which stands apart and tries to see things objectively and rationally and without emotional colouring. It perhaps requires a state of mind which has been described by Berenson (1950) as "the aesthetic moment".

> In visual art the aesthetic moment is that fleeting instant, so brief as to be almost timeless, when the spectator is at one with the work of art he is looking at, or with actuality of any kind that the spectator himself sees in terms of art, as form and colour. He ceases to be his ordinary self, and the picture or building, statue, landscape, or aesthetic actuality is no longer outside himself. The two become one entity; time and space are abolished and the spectator is possessed by one awareness. When he recovers workaday consciousness it is as if he had been initiated into illuminating, formative mysteries.

Now I think it is possible to add something to my attempts to describe what happened in this boy during the play when his whole behaviour to me changed, and to link this with what an artist or a poet does. For observations in analysis suggest that experiences of the kind described by Berenson are not confined to the contemplation of works of art, but that art provides a method, in adult life, for reproducing states that are part of everyday experience in healthy infancy. Sometimes poets have explicitly related such states to their early experience: for instance, Traherne, and also Wordsworth, in his note on "Intimations of Immortality from Recollections of Early Childhood". Thus Wordsworth says that as a child he was unable to think of external things as having external existence, he communed with all he saw as something not apart from but inherent in his own immaterial nature; when going to school he would often grasp at a wall to recall himself from the abyss of idealism. I suggest that it is useful, in child analysis, to look out for the ways in which the child may be trying to express such experiences, when he has not yet sufficient command of words to tell what he feels, directly, but can only use words or whatever other media the play-room offers him, figuratively: for instance, as this child used candle light and fire and the activities of melting and burning, as well as the actual toys. And I think it may be useful also to bear in mind that if, when talking about this state, one uses only those concepts, such as introjection and projection, which presuppose the existence of the organism within its boundaries in a world of other organisms within boundaries, one may perhaps distort one's perception of the phenomenon. Thus it is important not to forget the obvious fact that we know the boundaries exist but the child does not; in the primal state, it is only gradually and intermittently that he discovers them; and on the way to this he uses play. Later, he keeps his perception of the world from becoming fixed, and no longer capable of growth, by using art, either as artist or as audience; and he may also use psychoanalysis. For, as Rank (1932) says, art and play both link the world of "subjective unreality" and "objective reality", harmoniously fusing the edges but not confusing them. So the developing human being becomes able deliberately to allow illusions about what he is seeing to occur; he allows himself to experience, within the enclosed space–time of the drama or the picture or the story or the analytic hour, a transcending of that common-sense perception which would see a picture as only an attempt at photography, or the analyst as only a present-day person.

The need for a medium between the self-created and external realities

What I want to suggest here is that these states are a necessary phase in the development of object relationships and that the understanding of their function gives a meaning to the phrase "Art creates Nature". In this connection a later phase in the transference phenomena shown by this boy is relevant. It was after lie had become deeply interested in chemistry that there occurred in analysis, for several weeks, a repeated catechism. He would say "What is your name?" and I would have to say "What is my name?" Then he would answer with the name of some chemical, and I would say "What is there about that?" And he would answer "It's lovely stuff, I've made it!"; and sometimes he would give me the name of the chemical which is used as a water-softener.

Here then is the link with the artist's use of his medium, what the *Concise Oxford Dictionary* defines as an "intervening substance through which impressions are conveyed to the senses"; and this pliable stuff that can be made to take the shape of one's phantasies, can include the "stuff" of sound and breath which becomes our speech. (This boy would sometimes tell me that I was a gas, or that he was going to dissolve me down or evaporate me till I became one.) So it seemed that he had become able to use both me and the play-room equipment as this intervening pliable substance; he had become able to do with these what Caudwell (1937) says the poet does with words, when he uses them to give the organism an appetitive interest in external reality, when he makes the earth become charged with affective colouring and glow with a strange emotional fire.

As regards the use of the medium of speech,[5] there was a stage, after the war of the villages play, when it was very difficult to get this boy to talk. He would play, but silently, and when he did talk, it was always to try and teach me something; sometimes it was the language of chemistry, which he knew and I did not. And this I think expressed the need of the artist in him (and also the scientist, for he soon became determined to make science his career) to have a bit of his own experience incorporated in the social world, just as he had been able to have his own club incorporated in the world of school. For, as Caudwell points out, the artist is acutely aware of the discrepancy between, on the one hand, all the ways of expressing feeling that are provided by the current development of speech and art, in our particular culture and epoch; and, on the other hand, our changing experiences that are continually outstripping the available means of expression. Thus the artist wishes to cast his private experiences in such form that they will be incorporated in the social world of art and so lessen the discrepancy. Caudwell points out that it is not only the artist who feels this discrepancy and not only the discrepancy between feeling and current forms of expression of it; it is also the scientist, in respect not of feeling, but of perception and currently accepted ways of formulating it, currently accepted views of "reality", who wishes to contribute something of his own to the changing symbols of science. Perhaps even he must do this if the already discovered symbols are to become fully significant for him.

Effects of premature loss of belief in the self-created reality

The phenomenon of treating the world as one's own creation is mentioned by Fenichel. He says:

> There always remain certain traces of the original objectless condition, or at least a longing for it "oceanic feeling"). Introjection is an attempt to make parts of the external world flow into the ego. Projection, by putting unpleasant sensations into the external world, also attempts to reverse the separation of ego from non-ego.

And he goes on to refer to the child who "when playing hide-and-seek closes his eyes and believes he now cannot be seen". Fenichel then says, "The archaic animistic conception of the world which is based on a confusion of ego and non-ego is thus illustrated."

Although there are differences of opinion about what he calls here "the original objectless condition", about whether or not there is some primitive object relation from the very beginning, which alternates with the "objectless" or fused condition, I think Fenichel's description is valuable. The example of the child playing hide-and-seek vividly shows the belief in a self-created reality, just as analytical material shows related phenomena such as the child's belief that when he opens his eyes and sees the world, he thereby creates it, he feels it is the lovely (or horrible) stuff that he has made.

The idea that these states of illusion of oneness are perhaps a recurrently necessary phase in the continued growth of the sense of twoness leads to a further question: What happens when they are prevented from occurring with sufficient frequency or at the right moments?

This boy had had in general a very good home and been much loved. But he had suffered very early environmental thwartings in the feeding situation. In the early weeks of his life his mother had had too little milk and the nurse had been in the habit of not getting the supplementary feed ready in time, so that he had had to wait to finish his meal and had shown great distress: an experience that was re-lived in the transference, when whatever time I was ready for him, he always said I was too late.

Although it is obvious that a child must suffer frustration, there is still something to be said about the way in which it should occur and the timing of it. I suggest that, if, through the pressure of unsatisfied need, the child has to become aware of his separate identity too soon or too continually, then either the illusion of union can be what Scott calls catastrophic chaos rather than cosmic bliss, or the illusion is given up and premature ego-development may occur; then separateness and the demands of necessity may be apparently accepted, but necessity becomes a cage rather than something to be co-operated with for the freeing of further powers. With this boy it was clear how the imposed necessities, regulations, non-self-chosen tasks, of a conventional school, had provided a setting for a repetition of his first difficulties in relation to the environment. In fact he often told me what his ideal school would be like, and it amounted to being taught by a method very like what modern educationists call the project method.

If one asks the question, what factors play an essential part in the process of coming to recognize a world that is outside oneself, not one's own creation, there is one that I think has not been much stressed in the literature. Thus, in addition to the physical facts of the repeated bodily experiences of being separated from the loved object, and being together with it, and the repeated physical experiences of interchange with the not-self world, breathing, feeding, eliminating: in addition to the gradually growing capacity to tolerate the difference between the feeling of oneness, of being united with everything, and the feeling of twoness, of self and object, there is the factor of a capacity in the environment. It is the capacity of the environment to foster this growth, by providing conditions in which a recurrent partial return to the feeling of being one is possible; and I suggest that the environment does this by the recurrent providing of a framed space and time and a pliable medium, so that, on occasions, it will not be necessary for self-preservation's sake to distinguish clearly between inner and outer, self and not-self. I wish to suggest that it was his need for this capacity in the environment that my patient was telling me about in his village play, when he said there was to be a war, "but not yet". It was as if he were saying that the true battle with the environment, the creative struggle of interacting opposites, could not begin, or be effectively continued, until there had also been established his right to a recurrent merging of the opposites. And until this was established necessity was indeed a mechanized god, whose service was not freedom but a colourless slavery.

Looked at in this way the boy's remark, "I don't like those people", was not only due to a denial of an uprush of feared uncontrollable jealousy and envy, it represented also the re-enactment of a memory or memories of a near breakdown of relationship to the outside world. It

was the memory, I suggest, of actual experience of a too sudden breaking in on the illusion of oneness, an intrusion which had had the effect
of preventing the emergence from primary narcissism occurring gradually in the child's own time. But it represented also a later situation; for
the premature ego-development, referred to by Melanie Klein as inhib-
iting the development of symbolization (or, in Jones's terms, of symbolic equivalents) was also brought about by the impingement of the
war. For the sake of self-preservation, it had been necessary for him
continually and clearly to distinguish between external and internal
reality, to attend to the real qualities of the symbol too soon. Thus it was
reported to me that this boy had shown remarkable fortitude when,
with his father away in the Navy, he and his baby brother and mother
had lived through the blitz on London. And also, later on, his reports
indicated that he was very self-controlled in school, in that situation
where self-preservation demands a fairly continual hold upon objectivity, since day-dreaming and treating the external world as part of one's
dream are not easily tolerated by schoolmasters. But the fact that this
amount of objectivity was only achieved at a fairly high cost in anxiety
was shown in his analysis, for at one time he was continually punishing
me for imagined lapses into forgetfulness, inattention, unpunctuality. It
was only later that he was able to tell me about what he now called his
absentmindedness, in a tolerant way and without anxiety.

Implications for technique

The considerations I have tried to formulate here are not only matters
for theory, they have direct bearings upon technique. With this boy
there was always the question of whether to emphasize, in interpreting,
the projection mechanisms and persecutory defences and to interpret
the aggression as such; but when I did this the aggression did not seem
to lessen and I was sometimes in despair at its quite implacable quality.
At times he treated me as if I were like the man in the Bible from whom
a devil was driven out, but into whom seven more came, so that he
went on attacking me with almost the fervour of a holy war. But when
I began to think along the lines described above, even though I knew
that I was not succeeding in putting these ideas clearly into words in
my interpretations, the aggression did begin to lessen and the continual
battle over the time of the beginning of each session disappeared. Of
course I may be mistaken in thinking that the change in the boy's
behaviour which accompanied the change in my idea of the problem
was a matter of cause and effect, since the issue is very complicated and
brings in many debatable questions of theory. But I think that it was
significant that, near the end of his analysis, this boy told me that when

he was grown up and earning his own living he would give me a papier-mâché chemical clock, which would keep perfect time and would be his own invention. He said it would be of papier-mâché because I had an ornament, a little Indian dog, made of this, and also I remembered how he himself had tried, during his play with me, to make papier-mâché bowls, but unsuccessfully. Granted that the idea of the giving of the clock stood for many things, including returning to me the restored breast and restored penis, and also represented his gratitude for the recovery of his own potency, I thought he was telling me something else as well. I thought that the malleability of the papier-mâché provided him with a way of expressing how he felt about part of the curative factor in his analysis. It was his way of saying how, in the setting of the analytic play-room, he had been able to find a bit of the external world that was malleable; he had found that it was safe to treat it as a bit of himself, and so had let it serve as a bridge between inner and outer. And it was through this, I suggest, as well as through the interpretations I had given about the content of his wishes towards outer and inner objects, that he had become able to accept the real qualities of externality, objective time standing as the chief representative of these. And in those phases when he could not make this bridge, because the fact that I had to work to a time-table forced on him an objective reality that he was not yet ready for, then I became merely the gap into which he projected all his "bad" wishes, or internal objects representing these. When he could not feel that he had "made" me, that I was his lovely stuff, then I was the opposite, not only bad but also alien, and bad because alien; so I became the receptacle for all that he felt was alien to his ego in himself, all the "devil" parts of himself that he was frightened of and so had to repudiate. It seemed as if it was only by being able, again and again, to experience the illusion that I was part of himself, fused with the goodness that he could conceive of internally, that he became able to tolerate a goodness that was not his own creation and to allow me goodness independently. Exactly how an infant does come to tolerate a goodness that is recognized to exist independently of himself seems to me to have not yet been entirely satisfactorily explained; though the factor of the relief obtained from giving up the illusion of omnipotence is mentioned in the literature and was clearly apparent in this boy. The repeated discovery that I went on being friendly, and remained unhurt by him, in spite of the continual attacks on me, certainly played a very important part. For instance, there was another ritual catechism which would begin with "Why are you a fool?" and I had to say, "Why am I a fool?" Then he would answer, "Because I say so". Clearly if he had to feel that all the foolishness of adults was his doing, as well as their goodness, then he was going to bear a heavy burden. But I think he could not proceed to the stage of experiencing the relief of disillusion until he had also had sufficient time both to experience and to become conscious of the previous stage; he had to become aware that he was experiencing the stage of fusion before he could reach the relief of de-fusion. And it was only when lie could become conscious of the relief of de-fusion that we were then able to reach his depression about injuries that he had felt he was responsible for, both internally and externally, in his family situation and in relation to me.

On looking back it seems to me that the greatest progress in his analysis came when I, on the basis of the above considerations, was able to deal with the negative countertransference. At first, without really being aware of it, I had taken for granted the view of infantile omnipotence which is described by Fenichel:

> Yet even after speech, logic, and the reality principle have been established we find that pre-logical thinking is still in operation and even beyond the role it plays in states of ego regression or as a form of purposeful distortion. It no longer fulfils, it is true, the function of preparing for future actions but becomes, rather, a *substitute* for unpleasant reality.

I had accepted this view but grown rather tired of being continually treated by this boy as his gas, his breath, his faeces, and had wondered how long the working through of this phase would take. But when I began to suspect that Fenichel was wrong here, and that this pre-logical fusion of subject and object does continue to have a function of preparing for future action, when I began to see and to interpret, as far as I could, that this use of me might be not only a defensive regression, but an essential recurrent phase in the development of a creative relation to the world, then the whole character of the analysis changed; the boy then gradually became able to allow the external object, represented by me, to exist in its own right.

Caudwell says that the artist and the scientist

> are men who acquire a special experience of life—affective with the artist, perceptual with the scientist which negates the common ego or the common social world, and therefore requires refashioning of these worlds to include the new experience.

This boy had, I think, indicated the nature of this process by his reaction to the school's refashioning of a tiny bit of itself and its routines. For this had happened in response to the vividness of his belief in the validity of his own experience; a vividness which also had contributed to a refashioning in me of some of my analytic ideas.

Conclusion

On the basis of the study of such material as I have described here, and also from my own experiments in painting, I came to see the pertinence of Melanie Klein's statement that symbolization is the basis of all talents; that is, that it is the basis of those skills by which we relate ourselves to the world around us. To try to restrict the meaning of the word symbolization, as some writers tend to do, to the use of the symbol for purposes of distortion, may have the advantage of simplification, but it has other disadvantages. One of these is that it causes unnecessary confusion when one tries to communicate with workers in related disciplines, such as epistemology, aesthetics, and the philosophy of science; it interferes with what might be a valuable collaboration in the work of clarifying some of the obscure issues about the nature of thought. This isolation of psychoanalysis, by its terminology, from related fields, may not have been a disadvantage in the early days of the struggle to establish analytic concepts in their own right, but now such isolation, can, I think, lead to an impoverishment of our own thinking.

Another advantage of not limiting the meaning of the word symbol to a defensive function would be a clarification of theory by bringing it more in line with our practice. The analytic rule that the patient shall try to put all that he is aware of into words does seem to me to imply a belief in the importance of symbolization for maturity as well as for infancy; it implies the recognition that words are in fact symbols by means of which the world is comprehended. Thus in the daily battle with our patients over the transference we are asking them to accept a symbolic relation to the analyst instead of a literal one, to accept the symbolism of speech and talking about their wants rather than taking action to satisfy them directly. And, as all analytic experience shows, it is when the patient becomes able to talk about all that he is aware of, when he *can* follow the analytic rule, then in fact he becomes able to relate himself more adequately to the world outside. As he becomes able to tolerate more fully the difference between the symbolic reality of the analytic relationship and the literal reality of libidinal satisfaction outside the frame of the session, then he becomes better.

Postscript

After completing this paper I began the analysis of another child, also aged eleven, who presented a somewhat similar problem of persistence in what looked like aggressive attacks. This child, a girl, fervently and defiantly scribbled over every surface she could find. Although it looked as if it were done in anger, interpretation in terms of aggression only led to increase in the defiance. In fact, the apparent defiance did not change until I began to guess that the trouble was less to do with faeces given in anger and meant to express anger, than with faeces given in love and meant to express love. In this sense it was a battle over how she was to communicate her love, a battle over what kind of medium she was going to use for the language of love.

So intense were her feelings about this that, after the first two days of analysis, she did not speak to me again, except when outside the play-room, for six months, although she would often write down what she wanted to say. Gradually I had come to look at the scribbling in the following way: by refusing to discriminate and claiming the right to scribble over everything, she was trying to deny the discrepancy between the feeling and the expression of it; by denying completely my right to protect any of my property from defacement she was even trying to win me over to her original belief that when she gave her messes lovingly they were literally as lovely as the feelings she had in the giving of them. In terms of the theory of symbolism, she was struggling with the problem of the identity of the symbol and the thing symbolized, in the particular case of bodily excretions as symbols for psychic and psychosomatic experiences. She was also struggling with the very early problem of coming to discriminate not only between the lovely feelings in giving the mess and the mess itself, but also between the product and the organ which made it.

When I began to consider what she was doing in these terms I also became able to see the boy's battle of the villages in a wider perspective. Both the children were struggling with the problem of how to communicate the ecstasies of loving, as well as the agonies; and the boy's "lovely stuff" was certainly both the lovely stuff of his lovely dreams *and* his lovely sensations which, at one level, lie could only think of in terms of "lovely" farces. The phrase "denial by idealization" is familiar, but the denial here is, I suggest, in the nature of the mess, not in the nature of the psychic experience of which it is the symbol. For this is the maximum experience of joy, ecstasy, which is a psychic fact, a capacity for heavenly or god-like experience possessed by everyone. The psychic agony came, and the anger, when this boy had to face the fact that there was discrepancy between the objective qualities of his messes, that is, how they looked to other people, and his subjective evaluation of them as actually being the same as the god-like experiences. Thus both children were struggling with the agony of disillusion in giving up their belief that everyone must see in their dirt what they see in it: "my people" are to see his empty trucks and "think it's gods". In fact, he is saying what the poet Yeats said: "Tread softly, because you tread on my dreams."

But was this struggle to make me see as they saw in essence any different from the artist's struggle to communicate his private vision? I have suggested that both the artist and the scientist are more acutely aware than the "average" man of the inadequacies of what Caudwell calls "the common ego", the commonly accepted body of knowledge and ways of thinking about and expressing experience, more sensitive to the gap between what can be talked about and the actuality of experience. If this is true, then it is also true to say that what is in the beginning only a subjective private vision can become to future generations, objectivity. Thus the battle between the villages seemed to me to be not only a symbolic dramatization of the battle of love and hate, the struggle with ambivalence towards the object, but also a genuine work of dramatic art, in which the actual process by which the world is created, for all of us, is poetically represented.

The battle over communicating the private vision, when the battleground is the evaluation of the body products, has a peculiar poignancy. In challenging the accepted objective view and claiming the right to make others share their vision, there is a danger which is perhaps the sticking point in the development of many who would otherwise be creative people. For to win this battle, when fought on this field, would mean to seduce the world to madness, to denial of the difference between cleanliness and dirt, organization and chaos. Thus in one sense the battle is a very practical one; it is over what is a suitable and convenient stuff for symbols to be made of; but at the same time it is also a battle over the painful recognition that, if the lovely stuff is to convey the lovely feelings, there must be work done on the material.

Notes

1. Rank, in his later work, does in fact take a much wider view of the function of art.

2. This study was published under the pseudonym "Joanna Field" (1950).

3. I have had to omit some of the play in the middle of the session for reasons of space. It was connected with the theme of the previous months, in which there had been only one village, which he had continually bombed and burnt. I had interpreted it as partly an attempt to gain reassurance about his attacks on his mother's body, by acting them out in this comparatively harmless way and with my approval; I had also linked it with the aggression he had actually shown when his mother was pregnant.

4. Winnicott, in a private communication, states that he does not entirely agree with Scott's restatement of his view, as quoted above. He adds the following modification:

"I agree with Scott's comment only if he is looking back at early infancy, starting from the adult (or child). Regression is a painful and precarious business partly because the individual regressing goes back with experiences of forward emotional development and with more or less knowledge in his pocket. For the person regressed there must be a denial of 'evil union' and of 'evil me' and 'evil you' when an 'ideal union' between 'good self' and 'good mother' is being lived (in the highly specialized therapeutic environment provided, or in the insane state).

"This begs the whole question, however, of the earliest stages of an individual's emotional development studied there and then. For an infant, at the start, there is no good or bad. only a not yet de-fused object. One could think of separation as the cause of the first *idea* of union; before this there's union but no *idea* of union, and here the terms good and bad have no function. For union of this kind, so important for the founding of the mental health of the individual, the mothers active adaptation is an absolute necessity, an active adaptation to the infant's needs which can only come about through the mother's devotion to the infant.

"Less than good enough adaptation on the part of a mother to her infant's needs at this very early stage leads (it seems to me) to the premature ego-development, the precocious abandonment of illusion of which M. Milner writes in this paper."

5. Unfortunately I was not able, before writing this paper, to read Susan Langer's (1942) detailed discussion of the nature and function of symbolism, as it was not yet published in England and I could not obtain a copy. Had I been able to obtain the book in time I would have made specific reference to some of Langer's statements about speech and symbolism. Particularly relevant to my problem is her emphasis on the advantages of small sounds made with part of one's own body as a medium for symbol formation. One of these advantages is the intrinsic unimportance, in their own right, of these sounds. This relates to my point about the effectiveness of the toys as a medium for thought and communication being due to their pliability; that is, that their real qualities are unimportant for practical expedient living, so they can be given arbitrary or conventional meanings and thus be used as a language. I would also like to have elaborated on the relation of Langer's conception of the function of symbols to Jung's (1933) and to have considered the bearing of both on the material presented here.

CHAPTER FIVE

The invitation in art

(1965)

Adrian Stokes

Since the time, nearly fifty years ago, that Marcel Duchamp sent to an exhibition in New York a porcelain urinal (described as a fountain) with the signature of the manufacturer that he, Duchamp, had attached in his own writing, we have had an excellent occasion with which to associate new reflections upon the values of art. We realize that adepts at scanning an object for the less immediate significance of its shape, a manner of looking at things that has been cultivated from looking at art, will contemplate a multitude of objects, and certainly, in an august setting, the regular curves and patterns of light on that porcelain object, with aesthetic prepossessions. With less thought for the object's function than for its patterns and shape, we project on to them a significance learned from many pictures and sculptures. But are we projecting separate experiences of art; are we not projecting an aspect of ourselves that has always been identified with them; and is not the identification an integral factor, therefore, of aesthetic experience and an aim for art? This has seemed even more likely since psychoanalysis uncovered a mechanism called projective identification by which parts of ourselves or of our inner objects may be attributed even to outside objects that, unlike artefacts, at first sight seem inappropriate for their reception. It is possibly in this manner as well that we might discover ourselves to be assimilated in an active aesthetic transformation of the urinal, an object that does not itself communicate to us with the eloquence of art. We, the spectators, do all the art-work in such a case, except for the isolating of the object by the artist for our attention.

Structure is ever a concern of art and must necessarily be seen as symbolic, symbolic of emotional patterns, of the psyche's organization with which we are totally involved. This reference of the outer to the inner has been much sharpened by psychoanalysis, which tells, for instance, of parts of the self that are with difficulty allied, that tend to be split off, and of internal figures or objects that the self has incorporated, with which it is in constant communication or forcible ex-communication. Pattern and the making of wholes are of immense psychical significance in a precise way, even apart from the drive towards repairing what we have damaged or destroyed outside ourselves.

In distinction from projections that ensue upon any perceiving, aesthetic projection, then, contains a heightened concern with structure. The contemplation of many works of art has taught us this habit. I think it is so strong only because in every instance of art we receive a persuasive invitation, of which I shall write in a moment, to participate more closely. In this situation we experience fully a correlation between the inner and the outer world which is manifestly structured (the artist insists). And so, the learned response to that invitation is the aesthetic way of looking at an object. Whereas for this context it is simpler to speak of structure, of formal relations, such a presentation is far too narrow. Communication by means of precise images obtains similarly in art a wider reference whenever the artist has created for the experience he describes an imagery to transcend it, to embrace parallel kinds of experience that can be sensed. Poetic analogy or image is apt; felicitous overtones coexist; the musical aptness of expression hazards wider conjunctions than those immediately in mind.

In visual art, too, we see without difficulty that form and representation enlarge each other's range of reference. Similarly, the same formal elements are used to construct more than one system of relationship within a painting itself, and with us who look at it. Whatever the total meaning, the perennial aspect reveals a heightened close connexion between sensation significance, that is to say, impact on the perceiving instrument as it organizes the data, and more purely mental content that we then apprehend in the outside terms of sensation significance.

Referring to the character of perception, I have in mind what might be called the prejudices of vision uncovered by psychologists. I take these "prejudices" to be an important link between the outer world and the empathic projection thereon, in ordinary and in aesthetic perception alike, of inner process. The "forces" uncovered by the psychology of vision provide the words, the language of visual art. Whereas wide disagreement exists among psychologists as to the way that the visual world is perceived or constructed, none would deny, I believe, that the perceiver participates in what might be called the quandary of units of the visual field, which do not, or do not easily, achieve restful status. Thus, there is tension in any perceived obliquity, in any departure from an open framework: there is pull, direction, the sense of weight and movement. Even a vertical ellipse strives upward in the top half, downward in the lower. A vertical line seems to be far longer than a horizontal line of equal length; and so on. Such forces, such bents, I repeat, are the words, the language, of visual art. Not only are their implications of direction, compression, weight, pull, interference, employed by the painter to communicate the sentiment of a pictorial subject-matter, but they mirror, in their inter-working, the power that one part of the self, or one inner object, can exert over the others. Indeed, I hope it is not an outrageous conjecture concerning perception to say that stereotypes for psychical tension may be projected thereby, and that these projections in some part may have reinforced the perceptual bents to which I am referring. In any case, whether or not immured biologically in perception, internal situations remark themselves therein. We are dynamically implicated with visual stress, particularly with the enveloping use that art makes of it. When the final balancing, the whole that is made up of interacting parts, is suspended for a time by the irregularities of stresses, these same stresses appear to gain an overwhelming, blurring, and unitary action inasmuch as the parts of a composition are thereby overrun, and inasmuch as the spectator's close participation, as if with part-objects, removes distance between him and this seeming process. Much of the attraction of the sketch lies in this situation, which arises also whenever we think we find the artist at work, in his calligraphy or flourish, his gesture or touch, and, even more generally, in the accentuations of style. I have particularly in mind the extreme example of Baroque paintings with a diagonal recession, invaded by a represented illumination, cast diagonally, that cuts across figures, that binds the composition as a movement of masses, without respect for integrity of parts of the scene, of distinct figures, voids and substances. A principle, a process at work, seems to override the parts. It is one aspect of the "painterly" concept formulated by Wölfflin, in which values of what some psychologists have called "the visual field" dominate certain values in "the visual world" of ordinary, everyday, perception. We very often associate creativeness first of all with an ability to disregard an order elsewhere obtained, to ignore an itch for finality in favour of a harder-won integration whose image may still suggest an overpowering process, no less than its integration with other elements.

Hence the invitation in art, the invitation to identify empathically, a vehemence beyond an identification with realized structure, that largely lies, we shall see more fully, in a work's suggestion of a process in train, of transcending stress, with which we may immerse ourselves, though it lies also in that capacious yet keen bent for aptness, for the embracing as a singleness of more than one content, of one mode for "reading" the elements of its construction, to which I have already referred in regard to form and image. Though they always have the strong quality of co-ordinated objects on their own, the world's arte-facts tend to bring right up to the eyes the suggestion of procedures that reduce the sense of their particularity and difference; even, in part, the difference between you and them, though the state with which a work is manifestly concerned be the coming of the rains, or redemption and damnation, or the long dominance of the dead. Most painting styles are what we call conceptual: objects are rendered under conformity to an idea of their genus, to hierarchic conceptions (with a comparative ne-glect of individual attributes and changing appearances) favouring the power to lure us into an easy identification with an expression of attitude or mood. The depicting of incident thus receives a somewhat timeless imprint, offers a relationship that at first glance saps the sym-bolism of an existence completely separate from ourselves. As we merge with such an object, some of the sharpness that is present when differentiation of the inner from the outer world is more accentuated, the sharpness and multiplicity of the introjectory–projectory processes, are at first minimized. Yet I shall note, on the other hand, that under the spell of this enveloping pull, the object's otherness, and its representa-tion of otherness, are the more poignantly grasped. But I want also to stress the opposite point by indicating in naturalistic styles, which boast far greater representation of the particular and of the incidental, that these works, if they are to be judged art, must retain, and indeed must employ more industriously, procedures to qualify the intimation of particularity, to counter the strong impression of events entirely foreign to oneself by an impression of an envelopment that embraces distinc-tiveness.

I now call the envelopment factor in art—this *compelling* invitation to identify—the incantatory process. I have often written of it, princi-pally in terms of part-object relationship, particularly of the prime enveloping relationship to the breast where the work of art stands for the breast. I adopt the word "incantatory" to suggest the empathic, identificatory, pull upon adepts, so that they are enrolled by the formal procedures, at any rate, and then absorbed to some extent into the subject-matter on show, a relationship through whose power each content in the work of art can be deeply communicated. I shall try to indicate further methods and characteristics of visual art whereby the incantatory process comes into being. I believe that much formal structure has this employment, beside entirely other employment, and that a part of the total content to be communicated is often centred upon unitary or transcending relationships, though they contrast with the work's co-ordination between its differing components, this, another content no less primary, whereby the integration of the ego's opposing facets and the restored, independent object can be symbolized. I believe that the incantatory quality results from the equation enlisted between the process of heightened perception by which the willing spectator "reads" a work of art—often with a difficulty of which the artist makes use to rivet attention to his patterns—and inner as well as physical processes; an equation constructed or reinforced by at least an aspect of the formal treatment that encourages the sense of a process in action. There is vitality in common that suggests an unitary relationship, as if the artefact were a part-object.

I shall continue to touch on a few manifest elements in the case of naturalistic art. For it goes without saying that dance, song, rhythm, alliteration, rhyme, lend themselves to, or create, an incantatory process, a unitary involvement, an elation if you will. Thus when I wrote of this matter in 1951, I did so in terms of the manic. During the next year, 1952, there appeared in the *International Journal of Psycho-Analysis* Marion Milner's paper, renamed in the Melanie Klein Symposium of 1955, "The Role of Illusion in Symbol Formation", where, not only in matters of art, she emphasized a *state* of oneness as a necessary step in the apprehension of twoness. Her key-word here is "ecstasy" rather than "part-object". Her paper derived partly from ideas she had already put forward in her book, *On Not Being Able to Paint* (Milner, 1950).

Of the principal aesthetic effects an incantatory element is easiest grasped. By "grasp" I refer also to being joined, enveloped, with the aesthetic object. But whereas we easily experience the pull of pleasant poetic, pictorial subject-matter—classical idylls, *fêtes champêtres*, and so on—there is not so much readiness to appreciate the perennial existence of a wider incantation that permeates pictorial formal language whatever the subject or type of picture. Similarly a poem, like a picture, properly appreciated, stands away from us as an object on its own, but the poetry that has gripped, the poetry of which it is composed, when read as an unfolding process, combines with corresponding processes in a reader who lends himself. Therefore my description is the incantatory process, since I feel that all art describes processes by which we find ourselves to some extent carried away, and that our identification with them will have been essential to the subsequent contemplation of the work of art as an image not only of an independent and completed object but of the ego's integration. Since, as a totality, it is an identification with the good breast, I have often submitted that the identification with processes that are thought of as in train allows a sense of nurture to be enjoyed from works of art, even while we view them predominantly in the light of their self-sufficiency as restored, whole objects, a value that thereby we are better prepared to absorb.

The first power that the work of art has over us, then, arises from the successful invitation to enjoy relationship with delineated processes that enliven our own, to enjoy subsequently as a nourishment our own corresponding processes, chiefly, it appears to me, the relationships between the ego and its objects, though concurrently the unitary power, inseparable from part-object relationship, that transcends or denies division and differences. To take the instance once more of this last relationship from painting, light and space-extension can be employed to override each particularity in favour of a homogeneity with which we ourselves are enveloped. And so, such effects in the picture—their variety is vast—construct an enveloping *mise-en-scène* for those processes in ourselves that are evoked by the picture's other connotations.

It is easily agreed that pictorial composition induces images of inner process as we follow delineated rhythms, movements, directions with their counter-directions, contrasts or affinities of shape with their attendant voids, as well as the often precarious balancing of masses. Predominant accents do not achieve settlement without the help of other, and perhaps contrary, references: hence the immanent vitality, and a variety of possible approaches in analysing a composition; hence the ambiguity, in the sense of an oscillation of attention, that others have noted in the interweaving of poetic images. It may be thought that this will hardly apply to the representation of balance between static, physical forms as opposed to the representation, in which naturalistic art excels, of movement or of stress and strain. Such immobility, however, often involves a sense of dragging weight, of the curving or swelling of a contour with which we deeply concern ourselves, since we take enormous pleasure, where good drawing makes it profitable, in feeling our way, in crawling, as it were, over a represented volume articulated to this end; many modes of draughtsmanship, or of modelling, may invite a very primitive, and even blind, form of exploration. In one of their aspects, too, relationships of colour and of texture elicit from us the same sense of process, of development, of a form growing from ., another or entering and folding up into it. And, as I have said, we find ourselves traversing represented distances, perhaps enveloped by an overpowering diffusion of light. Finally architecture, possessor of many bodily references, mirrors a dynamic or evolving process as well as the fact of construction.

It is necessary to repeat that the unitary relationship between ourselves and on-going processes represented by the aesthetic object contrasts with the integration of its parts, for which we value it as a model of a whole and separate reconstituted object. In a combination that art offers, we find a record of predominant modes of relationship, to part-objects as well as to whole objects.

I want now to remark an aspect of visual art connected with what I have called the quandaries and prejudices of visual experience that provide the possibility of a stressed language. One exploitation of these quandaries lends itself to catharsis of aggression, even of a mutilating urge that, paradoxically, is sometimes more characteristic of naturalistic art than of any other. Extreme foreshortening has been described by Arnheim (1956) as "contraction, like a charged spring". He also speaks, not altogether without justice, of "the rearrangement of organic parts through projective overlapping—hands sprouting from behind the head, ears attached to the chin, knees adjoining the chest. Even the most daring modern artists have rarely matched the paradoxical reshuffling of the human limbs that has been presented as an accurate imitation of nature", doing violence to simple patterns of structure, a desired norm—it is sometimes thought—for vision.

It may be useful to specify for a moment, if only with a handful of examples. I refer very briefly to the place of the unitary breast principle in proto-Renaissance and early Renaissance naturalism. John White (1957) has described a "growing tendency to move from the idea of things surrounded by space towards that of space enclosing and uniting things" in much art of fourteenth-century Florence and Siena. The representing of space would much later become wholly an enveloping agent, sometimes an aggressive scoop to carry us into distance, to go far beyond the canvas. But earlier, in the protoperspective space bedecked or jewelled by Giotto, Duccio, and the Lorenzetti, there exists no such manipulation or destruction of the picture surface. Moreover, at the very same time that geometric perspective was institutionalized as a cult in the first half of the fifteenth century, there calve about at the hands of those who worshipped there, particularly Piero's, a supreme use of colour, an echo between forms and intervals, whereby an equality for each shape, a lack of emphasis throughout the patterning, preserved an unified complexity of picture plane: a miraculous solution of conflicting data, perceptual and psychical, and hence of picture-making. Piero's own books reveal that he estimated perspective not at all for the new power at the artist's command of *trompe-l'oeil*, but for the extension of harmony and proportion, of the laws of optics, and, in-

deed, of a mathematically ordained universe to be learned now fully
from the image, the painting, no less than from visual experience of
which it served as an image.

Thereafter, overpowering uses for perspective have sometimes been
developed. Similarly, though little apparent until much later, from the
time of Leonardo there has been some breaking down of the constancies
that characterize the visual world, by means of the full employment of
chiaroscuro, by means of insistence on a full tonal range that disregards
the conventional aspect of an object usually seen to be constant whatever the illumination, just as perspective often utterly distorts, neglects,
a characteristic shape of an object on which conceptual art lingers.
Developing from this, we have had of late from painters the idea of a
pure sensation of colour or of light. Although the psychology of ordinary vision does not support it, the abstract quality of such observation,
analytic and truthful, has ennobled pictorial incident. Indeed, out of the
requirement for enveloping values amid the pursuit of naturalistic
detail, European artists particularly have uncovered a degree of trite-
ness in the constancies through just observations and through the bold,
embracing techniques to which they could then proceed. If what they
have thus isolated in the name of naturalism has tended to disrupt both
the picture plane and the enduring character of the represented objects
as such, these same events have called forth unparalleled efforts for
their restoration in a new, and indeed more truthful, situation of quandary, truthful especially in regard to the conflicts of the inner life.
Hence the greatness, on the whole, of our art since the Renaissance, as
well as the utter degradation to which it is prone.

* * *

I have been describing the suggestion of an overpowering process in
the painter's deployment of perceptual truth that has been largely
ignored in the exercise of practical perception. I use the word "process"
because the overpowering is felt to be going on by the spectator. I turn
now to the major overall process, a reparation, in which both the good
breast and the whole, independent mother must figure, a reparation
dependent, it seems to me, upon initial attack. I believe that in the
creation of art there exists a preliminary element of acting out of aggression, an acting out that then accompanies reparative transformation, by
which inequalities, tension and distortions, for instance, are integrated,
are made to "work". I have long held the distinction between carving
and modelling to be generic in an application to all the visual arts.
These two activities have many differences from the psychological
angle, first, I think, in the degree and quality of the attack upon the
material. Similarly, this difference of attack is relevant to the old dis-

tinction between the decorative and the fine arts where an increase of attack calls forth an increase of creativeness. But if decoration titillates, ornaments, the medium, and if larger creativeness may to some considerable extent oppose its native state, I believe that every work of art must include both activities.

A painter, then, to be so, must be capable of perpetrating defacement; though it be defacement in order to add, create, transform, restore, the attack is defacement none the less. The loading of the surface of the canvas, or the forcing upon this flat, white surface of an overpowering suggestion of perspective, depth, the third dimension, sometimes seems to be an enterprise not entirely dissimilar to a twisting of someone's arm. I am inclined to think that, more than anything else, the defacement involved of the picture plane accounts for the tardy arrival in pictorial art of an entirely coherent linear perspective. From many angles, extreme illusionism is an extreme form of art, not least in the aggressive and omnipotent attitude to the materials employed. Many— every month many more—materials are now consciously respected, set-off, in our art today; thus made purposive, their naked character bears witness to an independence of these objects. We often deprecate an entire disguise of the canvas's flatness; we advocate "preservation of the picture plane". But whereas the paint, for instance, stays paint in such works, a large part of the impact upon us may proceed from the fact that the canvas is so heavily loaded and scored. Always the strong impact of which defacement, I am convinced, is an attribute. It is "seconds out of the ring" for every writer as he opposes his first unblemished sheet, innocent of his graffiti. It is even harder to begin to paint. With the first mark or two, the canvas has become the arena in which a retaliatory bull has not yet been weakened; no substantial assault, no victory, has begun. If a painter be so blatant, so hardy, as to fling, almost heedlessly, upon the canvas, a strong impact, he will at best create an enveloping or transcendental effect of omnipotence.

Pictures in a gallery, even the pictures in the National Gallery, make an ugly ensemble; as an ensemble the bare walls would be more pleasing. There is no doubt that the most beautiful ensembles of paintings are of those that are abstract and thinly worked, unaggressive in colour. A Ben Nicholson exhibition vivifies the walls on which it is hung. Some kinds of abstract painting, then, employ a very subtle attack. But we soon reach the strange conclusion that if attack be reduced below a certain minimum, art, creativeness, ceases; *equally, if sensibility over the fact of attack is entirely lulled, denied.* The plainer tricks of perspective drawing can be easily learned and then imposed, should the knack be greedily appropriated without a thought for the numbing distortion of the surface thus worked, and so without aesthetic sensibility. A practised artist will have become habituated, of course, to his bold marks. But he cannot be a good artist unless at one time he reckoned painfully with the conflicting emotions that underlie his transformations of material, the aggression, the power, the control, as well as the belief in his own goodness and reparative aim. The exercise of power alone never makes art: indeed it reconstructs the insensitive, the manic, and often, strangely, the academic. Art requires full-dress rehearsal of varied methods that unify conflicting trends. Such presentation causes composition, the binding of thematic material, to be widely evocative. This is more clearly shown in music than in the other arts. Musicologists tend to discover that, whereas construction is easily analysed from a variety of angles, the creative element, that distinguishes a coherent web from clever dovetailing, in general eludes analysis. Hence a vague appeal, sometimes, to "organic unity". I believe that it is possible to be more specific in speaking of the deep charging of these sense-data with emotive significance, whereby the deployment of formal attributes becomes a vivid language, that is to say, symbols of objects, of relationships to objects and of processes enwrapping objects, inner as well as outer. The word "symbol" here does not indicate parallel structures, but structures wherein the component parts, though possessing no correspondence with the component parts of the original objects, are interlocked and interrelated with an intensity, sharpness, regret, or other feeling-tone that belong at least to one aspect of the original object-relationships, especially to the fact of their coexistence, interpolations, and variety.

Whereas the finished work, or the work as a whole, symbolizes integration, once again while we contemplate and follow out the element of attack and its recompense, we are in touch with a process that seems to be happening on our looking, a process to which we are joined as if to an alternation of part-objects.

At the beginning of this chapter I said that naturalistic art had need, ipso facto, for particular exertion in initiating the incantatory process, since its apparent aim sharpens the otherness of a represented incident or scene. In conclusion, and to sum up, I think I can now better make clear, in one instance of a representational aim on which everyone is agreed, how these two objectives are combined.

Consider in painting the third dimension, the suggestion of depth. No painting of whatever kind, with any merit, is absolutely flat in effect. There will be at least a suggestion of oscillation; something tends to come forward, in a manner that intrigues the senses, in front of something else, though, in general, there be no attempt to disguise the flatness of the picture plane. The surface itself seems to have bulk. Thus, at any rate to a limited degree, illusionism, a mastery in isolating generalizations that convey it, are inseparable from painting and from the artist's sense of a creative act in his determination to discover effects for the paint that are revivifying. More clearly in naturalistic painting, the first test of its merit is the degree to which we become attached to the turn of the contours, the degree to which we are compelled to feel our way into spaces, whether populated or whether empty of shapes. This matter is at the heart of painting on a flat surface, distinguishing its appreciation from an apprehension of landscape itself which the eye constructs and contemplates without ado as a three-dimensional datum.

But there are many more ways of intriguing the spectator of a painting with space than by a pedestrian representation of depth. I have emphasized the desirability of preserving the picture plane. Yet I want now to restrict the matter to the traditional aspect, the aspect dear to art schools at any rate until very recently, the aspect of which I have been reminded by a gay bit of painting of a Mediterranean harbour that I saw in a cafe. One often sees such decoration, boldly painted, perhaps without much effort and even without a visit to the south. The interesting point is that the example I have in mind, and probably most examples to be found in similar places, have no aesthetic merit, far less than photographs which, for the most part, lack that element of assertive handiwork by which the artist points to his invitation. What is so wrong with the painting, what is the most obvious reason for lack of worth? Colour, design, and application of paint are not objectionable. But the aesthete would sacrifice these merits, if such they be, to the slightest poignancy in the suggestion of space. Don't misunderstand me. There is a quay, and a boat with gay sails in the water just behind it. You can't mistake the scene. The aesthete attaches not the slightest merit to that: nothing he values can be read into the scene since, for the moment, lie places no value on blue waters, slim boats, and pretty sails in themselves. Before he can estimate and relate these things, he wants to be induced to feel his way over the stones of the quay, bit by bit. Again, he is not interested in the stones of the quay: he is interested in the breadth to the water's edge, and then in the breadth of the water between quay and boat; he wants to swim, as it were, in the empty air above them, yet again he won't mind if that which he contemplates does evocative service for, but hardly looks like, the width of a quay. There are so many ways, and always new ways, of commenting upon space, and any one of them for the moment will suffice. We want to be certain that the matter has absorbed the artist and to identify with him; we want to feel volume, density, and the air it displaces, to recognize things perhaps in the manner of the half-blind; we demand to be drawn in among these volumes, almost as if they were extensions of ourselves, and we do not tire of this process, the incantatory process at work. It is at work only because the canvas face is, in fact, flat. At the same time the restored otherness of things is asserted by these same means of true draughtsmanship, the means of all good drawings whether of things or of the figure; at the heart of aesthetic value. Surface value and depth value go hand in hand. For it is obvious that the representation of space, of depth, reflects a metaphor so unavoidable that one suspects it to be the consequence of a very old piece of concrete thinking concerning "the layers in depth" of our mental life and individuality.

Nevertheless, incantatory rhythm and movement should be approached as well from an opposite viewpoint that reveals the vibrancy and volume of objects endowed with these qualities. The felicity of art lies in its sustaining power, in a markedly dual content, in multiple forms of expression within one boundary that harmonize. It demands usually very hard work on the part of a mentality not easily seduced and satisfied by its own products. Self-expression and art are not synonymous. Art, we have seen, is mastery within the mode of certain emphases upon reconstruction. Whatever else it makes known, art transmits an enticing eloquence in regard to the *varied* attachment to objects, and in regard to the co-ordination of the self.

* * *

Since the context has been created, I want to add a note concerning an emphasis in our surroundings. I think that normal environment has always brought home to inhabitants both the otherness of things and the sense of processes that echo or amplify inner processes as such, and even dreams as such, though these meanings may merely alternate. On the other hand, I believe that everything we feel to be out of harmony with the body's image and with the ways of natural growth or change, everything we feel today to be harshly mechanical, mirrors, in a one-sided manner, an unsettlement of the inner life. In his paper on "The Uncanny" (1919h), Freud constructed an equation between the psychologically primitive and what appears weird, outlandish, *unheimlich*, unhomely. Similarly, when contemplated as a series, the mechanical apparatus that surrounds and supports our modern living, instead of stimulating a preponderant sense of otherness in the light of an unparalleled organization of outer substances, tends rather to suggest abrupt experiences that are both stranger than this and nearer to us, though without the insinuating quality of the incantatory process in art, a setting for further content. In the environment to which I now refer, there is no provision beyond the shock of it. The beauty in our streets is mostly the one of glitter, of flashing lights; surprising, momentary signals of a confusing ramification within, yet we are arrested by a sense neither of depth nor of surface. I have spoken, in regard to art, of an enveloping effect that accompanies a represented movement. In our towns today we are largely strangers to stillness, to apparent deliberateness and silence. From the street, even buildings appear to be but boundaries or targets for the movement of traffic, whereas, in the days of the horse's clop-clop, one moved within the circulation of a whole mother who still reigned fitfully. The same harsh hallucinatory quality, from the angle of utter contemplation, that is—not everyone is prepared to contemplate it at all—inevitably characterizes much modern art of merit.

The words "humanist" and "humanism" are hard to define. Whatever may be meant, I am convinced that a desideratum for the humanist is an environment stimulating awareness of otherness in harmony with hopes of an integrated object, outer as well as inner. If the depressive position itself implies humanist attitudes for the adult who has embraced it well, the paranoid–schizoid position, to which the enveloping mechanisms and disconnecting noises of limitless cities pay court, certainly does not. In the old days, art was a means of organizing the incantatory element that had been felt in the length of land or in the restless sea. Today art is entirely outmoded in the choice of such phenomena by the scintillating lack of limitation of urban things in general, though it strains all the time to keep up. But, of course, in art there exist contemplative purpose, organization, a degree of wholeness. That is why art is no less a solace now, and perhaps little less an achievement, than in great ages.

POST-KLEINIAN THOUGHT

CHAPTER SIX

The apprehension of beauty
(1973)

Donald Meltzer

It became a fundamental tenet of Melanie Klein's views on infantile development that the accomplishment of a satisfactory splitting-and-idealization of self and object was a primary requirement for healthy development. By means of this mechanism, in her view, it becomes possible for an idealized part of the infantile self to ally itself with an idealized object, in the first instance the mother's breast, as the bulwark against persecutory anxiety and confusion. The confusion particularly between good and bad in self and objects is, by this means, separated in a categorical way: exaggerated and rigid, it is true, but affording a working basis for the task of gradual reintegration of the split-off aspects in the course of development, as the values of the paranoid–schizoid position are gradually replaced by those of the depressive position, with the relinquishment of egocentricity in favour of concern for the welfare of the loved objects of psychic and external reality. This gradual shift in values has a sweeping effect upon judgement and the estimation in which are held the various attributes of human nature. Thus goodness, beauty, strength, and generosity replace in esteem the initial enthralment to size, power, success, and sensuality.

But the mode of operation of this primal mechanism of splitting-and-idealization has remained elusive and mysterious, the more so as we have become increasingly aware of the major part played by both inadequate and excessive use of it in the genesis of mental illness. Over and over again we find that the borderline, psychotic, or psychopathic patient has a fundamental defect in the differentiation of good and bad, being unable to make the distinction, or making it with rigidity bound to descriptive criteria which mock the very purpose of the operation, or even holds them in quite an inverted relation to one another. As the ubiquity of this defect in the more psychotic portion of the personality more and more pressed itself upon me in clinical experience, the more I also became aware of its conjunction with another serious defect: namely the failure of apprehension of beauty through emotional response to its perception. I noticed that whereas the more healthy of my patients recognized beauty as a *donné* without uncertainty through a powerful emotional reaction, the more ill were very dependent upon social cues, formal qualities and intellectual criteria. Often their judgement appeared sound, and in some instances even served as the basis for successful careers where aesthetic judgement was quite central. Nonetheless it was clear that, due to the lack of direct and immediate emotional response, they were deprived both of confidence in their judgement and of sincerity in their interest.

Two pieces of clinical material, some five years apart in my experience but bound together by a curious coincidence of content, have both consolidated this juxtaposition of which I speak and carried me some distance toward the solution of this interesting problem. One of them comes from a rather healthy patient with neurotic problems related to the early loss of his father, and rather late in his analysis, while the second comes from a patient suffering from bouts of depression with anorexia nervosa, very early in her analysis. I will describe and discuss them separately and then examine their relation to one another and to the problem in hand. Both centre around a single dream.

The first patient became aware that circumstance was going to oblige him to cut short his analysis, more a matter for sadness than anxiety as he was feeling quite thoroughly relieved of the symptoms for which he had originally come. In this mood he became quite acutely aware, one weekend, of the beauty of the autumnal countryside and its link with his age, which was approximately that of his father at the time of his death, and with the age he estimated the analyst to be. Sunday night he dreamed that *he was driving along the road in his new car, with which he felt very pleased, but was startled to see a bald man lying on the verge. As he drew closer he saw to his horror that the man appeared to have a branch of autumn beech leaves protruding from his chest. As the man seemed alive, my patient jumped from his car to go to his assistance, intending to draw the branch forth from the chest immediately. But to his surprise the man, despite his showing every sign of great distress, stopped him from doing so, saying, "No, call Dr. S* (a woman analyst whose paper on aesthetics my patient had recently come across), *we must first determine where the branch came from."*

Needless to say, the analyst is bald. This intelligent patient had come to understand the part which scrutiny of the countertransference plays in the method of psychoanalysis. He felt that the analyst by this means understood the nature of his pain—about his father's death, about the premature end of his analysis, about ageing, the beauty of nature, and the beauty of analytical method. Thus the branch of autumnal beech leaves expressed the quality of my patient's pain linked with the perception of beauty, of its being and ceasing to be and ever renewing itself. He was struggling to hold together within himself the joy and the pain of the truth about living and not living things, of the frailty and the feebleness of life forces pitted against the malignant, which so often seemed to be favoured by the great random factor. In other words he was seeming to shift his perception of beauty from the idealized good object to the struggle itself, thus including the malign and the random, along with the good, as participants in the drama, and thus in his love of the world.

My second patient was a young woman whose cachexia due to repeated and worsening bouts of depression and anorexia was hidden by her fashionable waifish beauty and masses of fine brown hair. From the outset of the analysis it was clear that an intelligent and sensitive but fragile adult self, identified with her paternal object, was being constantly overwhelmed by the primitive struggle between the tiny girl and an internal witch mother. In this struggle ravishment by beauty and reduction to helpless dependence were the prelude to being devoured. She could at times be so confused over the externalization of this conflict that she had to rush in panic to hide herself in bed, sleeping curled up completely covered. A few days before this material to be presented, she had had just such a panic at the dinner table when the sensation of the fat from a morsel of duck in her mouth struck terror in her connected with a recent horrifying dream image of *a seagull, denuded of feathers, flapping its stumpy wings helplessly while being swarmed over by bees.* It was just so that she herself felt often when her three little boys competed so fiercely for a place on her lap.

Some weeks following this dream image and panic one of the boys had bitten her on the finger in such an encounter and to her surprise had brought from her a torrent of tears which lasted all afternoon, in lieu of her usual flash of rage. It was at a weekend following some days of complaining about the previous month's bill, and how long was the analysis going to last, and wouldn't twice a week be enough, and mightn't she grow helplessly dependent, etc. The retreat to bed lasted three days, involved missing the first two sessions of the week, and was accompanied by rather usual getting-dressed-in-mummy's clothes type of dreams. The interpretation of the transference situation on the Wednesday brought very evident relief and the patient launched upon a rhapsody about the beauty of the huge copper beech which stood outside her bedroom window. Its leaves had just broken out and, with the morning sun shining through them, suffused an exquisite pinky, gold glow, yet they were not yet developed enough to hide the structure of the tree and the "skeleton" of its branches. But she then remembered another dream, not from the weekend but from the night before, in which *she had been riding on the upper deck of a bus, sitting on the nearside. As the bus brushed against the branches of a copper beech, they seemed to threaten to come in the patient's window and attack her face.*

Several items of history and circumstance are important to the understanding of this dream. In the first place the house in which she lives is owned by her mother and let to the young couple. Its beauty and indeed grandeur is closely linked in her mind to her mother's beauty, vitality, and social position. While the patient's hair is brown, her mother's is apparently rich auburn. It was only in the following session (when I see the patient quite early in the morning) that the sun streaming in suddenly lit up a bright red area in the patient's hair. When I commented on it she laughed, saying, "Oh, that belongs to some oriental nun, I suppose." It was in fact a hair piece, somewhat faded from its original colour, which she had been wearing the last few days, although she has in fact masses of hair of her own. The other item: In her adolescence, in a fit of jealous rage with a boyfriend, she had attacked and in fact lacerated his face with her nails. She felt ashamed and afraid that this witch-like violence in her nature could erupt on the children. Like the upper deck of the bus and her bedroom, the consulting room is also on the first floor above the ground.

I was deeply impressed by the degree and severity of the splitting-and-idealization presented by this material and by the evident role played by projective identification and confusion of identity in its perpetuation. Clearly an experience of the apprehension of beauty has been split into its joyous and terrifying components, one experienced in her waking state toward the tree outside her bedroom window, the other reserved for her dream of the tree outside the bus window. In all three locations, house, bus, and consulting room, a payment relationship is involved. In the joyous aspect of the experience, she pays tribute to the beauty of her object freely and is perhaps troubled only by the inadequacy of her language to do justice to the grandeur of her object. In the persecutory component of the experience she feels the beauty to be merely a screen for the greedy and cruel fingers of the witch-mother reaching into her to snatch away her vitality and scratch away her beauty. The redness of the bus, the hair, the beech leaves in the sun and the blood from her boyfriend's wounds seem to swim together and reveal the image of a tiny girl carried in mother's arms, close to the breast, perhaps with masses of auburn hair tumbling over the baby's face as the mother bends to kiss her. How could a mother guess the link between the baby's chortle and cooing with delight in the day and screaming beyond comfort in the night? But the hair of the "oriental nun" reveals a most important item in the configuration for it shows the contrast between the narcissistic pull of destructiveness and the object-related thrust of love. Note that the mingling of the two types of hair, the patient's own and the hairpiece implies the reverse of the image of herself in the bus, namely red hair among the brown as against a brown-haired passenger in a red bus, which in turn contrasts with copper beech leaves trying to get into the red bus. The point I am making is that the persecutor is a narcissistic object, that is, one compounded of an object and a part of the self. What is not clear to the patient, and I think we must not assume that it is clear to ourselves either, is whether the destructive bit of her self has invaded the split-off bad bit of her object, or vice versa. I can conceive of the possibility that this differentiation could be of immense prognostic importance.

How now shall we relate these two pieces of clinical material to one another and to our problem concerning beauty and primal splitting-and-idealization? In the first patient's material we see something of the pain and work which is necessary, in the course of development, to bring together the two sides of the primal split, under the economic principle and consequent values of the depressive position. In the second material we see something of the primitive terror and confusion which has been segregated off from the joy in order to make the relation to the external mother feasible for the fragile ego of the baby, and in order for it to be able to feed and survive. But does the material tell us anything about how the splitting-and-idealization comes about, say, whether as an active or passive process, or whether as a purposeful or accidental one, whether guided by external wisdom and tenderness or imposed by fortuitous triviality, etc. Clearly it tells us nothing definitive of this mysterious matter, but I think it gives some very enticing hints.

I think that the material in both instances suggests that the apprehension of beauty contains in its very nature the apprehension of the possibility of its destruction. In Bion's terms, the present object is seen to contain the shadow of the absent-object-present-as-a-persecutor. The beech tree in the spring reveals the skeleton of the beech tree in the winter, and the autumnal branch in the heart contains the recollection of the death of the father and the prediction of the death of psychoanalysis. What the fragile ego of the child cannot sustain and is riven by, the lifetime of development strives to restore, so that the beauty of the object may be looked upon directly, without doing "damage to the soul", as Socrates feared.

CHAPTER SEVEN

The delusion of clarity of insight
(1975)

Donald Meltzer

To implement his sensory equipment, tool-making man became scientific-man and developed an astonishing range of instruments for evaluating qualities and quantities in the external world. He developed an adequate notational system for assisting his memory and communication about these objects. Emboldened by this signal success, in the last century particularly, he began to try, with understandable optimism, to apply these same techniques to the description and measurement of the things of which his inner world, psychic reality, is composed.

The consequent output of instruments and data has again been impressive, but many people feel uneasy about the value and precision of these products, for in some way they seem to fall so short, in richness as well as meaningfulness, of the instruments for investigation and communication developed by poets, artists, musicians and theological figures. Some people feel that it is the conceptual background and not the instruments that is to blame. Others feel that we have come up against the limitations of language, trying, as Wittgenstein (1953) claims, to say things that can only be shown. Freud (1895d) noted quite early a very striking split in his own use of language, that his theories

---

Presented at the 29th International Psycho-Analytical Congress, London, July 1975.

rang of the laboratory and his data read like short stories. As he went on with his work he also noted over and over that, when faced with conceptual impasse, he found himself returning to the dream as his primary datum (Freud, 1918).

This seems to be a lesson of which it is easy to lose sight. We can forget that our patients, and ourselves, present a unique language in dreams, a language whose substance shapes the content, if not the aesthetic essence, of art. Dreams borrow the forms of the external world and suffuse them with the meaning of the internal world. We do, with practice, learn to read this dream-language in ourselves and our patients with some fluency, even at times with virtuosity. With its help we find a vocabulary and a music for interpretation that is at once highly personal and mysteriously universal. Our use of this dream-palette underlies the claim that psychoanalysis is truly an art-form, in itself, quite outside the question of whether any of us are good, let alone great, artificers in its employment. In this method we operate with intuitive insights supervised by scientific, conscious modes of observation and thought. It is a method which is rich enough in its potentialities to allow for the possibility of inspiration and great beauty to emerge.

In this artistic activity supervised by scientific functions the latter are deployed in several echelons. First perhaps we try to see that a formulation "covers" the material at hand. Then, in repose, we may estimate its harmony with previous material and interpretation. Subsequently we estimate its consequences for the emergence of new material and the evolution of a process. But our strength of conviction does not, I suggest, come from this wedding of insight and judgement. It comes rather from the aesthetic component of the experience, the "beauty" with which the material and the formulation cohabit, blossom, fruit, as a thing apart from ourselves.

In this slow process the richness with which interpretive possibilities arise in an analyst's mind plays a paradoxical role. While this richness lengthens the time span over which conviction must ripen and beauty emerge, the durability of the conviction is proportionately enhanced. But we can notice times at which quite another process takes place in ourselves, one which we may even confuse with inspiration. Naturally it comes more readily to our notice in our patients and I have come to think of it as " the delusion of clarity of insight". It, too, bears offspring, but not ones of beauty. Its favourite child is called " sitting-in-judgement". Others such as smugness, superciliousness, aloofness and pride follow quickly on.

It is just this juxtaposition and the basis of shifting between these two types of functioning that I wish to explore and exemplify, for I suspect that identification processes and the shift from introjective to narcissistic modes, are at its root. I say "narcissistic" identifications rather than "projective" identification (Klein, 1946) because I am not at all sure that the latter is the only means of its, the shift's, achievement. But as you will see, my material points only to a specific aspect of projective identification, one which is bound up closely with the epistemophilic instinct. Where the thirst for knowledge is still strongly dominated by motives related to envy and jealousy, the thirst for knowledge is impatient of learning either from experience, example or demonstration. It seeks rather the immediate emotional satisfaction of omniscience and this it accomplishes by intruding inside the sensory apparatus and mental equipment of its internal object. Here are three clinical vignettes to illustrate this:

Case A

A medical student had noticed recently a sharp deterioration in his capacity for clinical observation and thought during the course of an analytical break. He brought a dream that *he and his wife were walking along a country road admiring the scenery, and then they were driving in a car along a causeway between two bodies of water. Suddenly the car stopped and he realized that he had gone too far and had broken off the rubber hose which connected his car to the petrol pump.*

The point of the dream seems to be that when he is in projective identification (driving the car) his appreciation of the complexity and beauty of his data (the landscape) is narrowed to one-track-mindedness and simple ideas of causality (the causeway) until he recognizes the need for the analysis (fuel pump) to help him get beyond his present limitations.

Case B

A young author in the fifth year of his analysis was struggling with his genital Oedipus conflict, his dependence upon the analysis and upon his internal objects for the continuation of his creative powers. The prospect of termination of the analysis had come in sight and tended to throw him into a confusion of identity with his little daughter and the problem of having a second child. He dreamed that *he was with a colleague* (long recognized to be linked to the analyst) *inside a dome-like conservatory* (like the one he had been admiring near the Heath the previous day) *discussing his new book. When the colleague suggested that the two main sections of the book should be more creatively linked together in a geographical way, the patient was suddenly disturbed by a droning sound. When he looked up the sky was crowded with transparent objects, a mixture of Luftwaffe and fireflies. He felt he must rush home to protect his little girl from the bombs.*

It seemed strongly to suggest that the moment the analyst suggests that his internal objects might be allowed to come together to create a new baby, the patient's delusion-of-clarity-of-insight (inside the conservatory–breast) recognizes that this would be dangerously destructive to the little girl part of himself and that she must be protected from such an experience at all costs. It would only bombard her with Nazi-envy and preoccupation with daddy's exciting genitals (fireflies).

Case C

A young woman seemed unable to make any progress in analysis because of shallowness of a latency-period type in which she was waiting-for-daddy-to-come-to-marry-her. This had firmly attached itself to the analyst–daddy in such a way that no interpretation was taken seriously for its content but only as a countertransference activity expressing either loving or sadistic erotism. After visiting her brother's family for the weekend she dreamed that *she was taking a little boy up in a lift and kissing him, but she was somewhat afraid that her breath might smell bad.* This dream was construed to mean that she had got inside the analyst–mummy at the weekend to steal her babies but was worried that her love was contaminated by her anal sadism reflected in her addiction to smoking.

The following night she dreamed that *she was inside a glass conservatory protecting a little boy from Cary Grant, who seemed to be a raving homosexual intent on whipping the boy with his extraordinarily long penis.* As I interpreted to her at some length (sic!) that she had shifted from stealing the babies from the mummy to being one of these inside-babies masochistically submitted to the sadistic tongue–penis of the erotic daddy, the patient mainly giggled and smirked and asked why was so serious, why was I so excited, that my interpretation seemed disappointingly unoriginal, that I was probably hurt by her lack of admiration for my mind, etc.

Clearly I was unable to shift her from her state of projective identification inside the breast (conservatory) from which position the delusion-of-clarity-of-insight into the analyst's state of mind showed her unequivocally that he was hurt, excited, and sadistically whipping her with long interpretation–penises.

* * *

Clearly such examples are too anecdotal and unconvincing. They can only exemplify, leaving many doubts and unanswered questions. The broad landscape narrowing to the causeway may suggest an impoverished imagination in Case A. The simplification of modes of thought from complex linking to simple causality may be implied. The dome-shaped conservatory suggests the breast and the transparency of the Luftwaffe–fireflies may indeed imply a high degree of omniscience in Case B. The fact that Case C. is dependent on her spectacles to a degree that far outstrips her refractive error may be linked with going up in the lift, as a means of getting inside the mother's conservatory head–breast to look at the world through her eyes. But it is all only suggestive on its own. To find greater conviction as well as a richer conception of the role of such operations in a person's life-style we must look at a more longitudinal picture of an analysis.

Case D

This handsome woman in her 40s was well along in her career as a research chemist, successfully combined with marriage and children, when she came to analysis in some despair about her bad temper with the children, picking at her forehead and compulsive eating of chocolate. Her relationship with Mr D. seemed to have progressively deteriorated since they had spent an extraordinarily happy and fruitful year in Canada, each working in their somewhat related fields. From the outset she was extremely sceptical about analysis and felt that, of the many people she knew in London who had been analysed, the only one who showed distinct improvement in Mrs D's eyes was paradoxically the least enthusiastic about the method.

From the outset the work was continually confronted by a minute questioning of the validity of the method by this highly intelligent and observant woman. It was not done in a hostile way but was presented as necessary to her giving a more faultless cooperation. This indeed she did, superficially, but her attitudes suggested an underlying negativism and she admitted feeling little hope of benefit. However, she felt she could not resign herself in good conscience to the peculiarities of her character, since they affected the children, not to mention her husband's happiness, until every reasonable effort had been made. In a sense the analyst had to maintain the working-level of hopefulness and bear the full burden of the hopelessness which constantly recurred. He and analysis were put to the test while the patient waited with rather exquisitely balanced wishes for the distant outcome. When it transpired

that the presenting complaints were only small fragments of her character and symptom pathology, no improvement in other areas was
granted status. Her irritability only grew worse until it finally meta-
morphosed by the third year into a diffuse indifference and loveless-
ness towards everyone. In her tally-book the analysis had only made
her worse and indeed gave every promise of completely wrecking her
life. Yet, paradoxically, she had no desire to leave, but rather showed
every sign of settling in for the duration—of her or my life, whichever
was the shorter. In the face of this daunting loss of interest—in work,
children, sexuality, social life—it was necessary to hold fast to the
rigging of the analysis and its internal evolution.

But in fact the development of the analytical material, the evolution
of the transference and the patient's growing understanding of mental
processes left nothing to be desired, except for pleasure and enthusiasm
on her part. An early intense erotic transference had exhibited very
clear voyeuristic elements. A strong desire to look at the analyst,
minute monitoring of his noises, smells and appearance as well as those
of the rest of the house, all accompanied by intense oceanic emotionality at times, seemed, as illustrated by her dreams, to point to the impact
of early experiences in the parental bedroom. Secretiveness prolifer-
ated, along with a rather paranoid attitude about the possibility of
being recognized going to or coming from the analyst's rooms. She kept
the analysis an absolute secret from her mother, despite the fact that
their relations had grown very warm, replacing the custodial posture
Mrs D. had adopted since her father's death. When it was suggested
that this secretiveness must be part of a diffusely hurtful demeanour to
her mother, the patient tried to establish that this was not the case.
When her questions to her mother were answered by, "Well I know you
love me", Mrs D. could not see the resignation implied. In fact the
evidence all pointed in the direction of her having been a child of some
sinew, with whom a technique of compromise had been early adopted.
Her obstinacy was immense and could easily have been driven to self-
destructive activity if not appeased. In addition she had held her little
sister hostage in many ways. In the transference situation it was clear
that her need to be "right" was an overriding passion and could be
traced back with some conviction to the conjoint events of her second
year: birth of the sister, moving out of the parental bedroom, and move
to a new house.

The erotic relation to the analyst as combined parents repeated in
great detail the blissful period in the parents' bedroom and its attendant confusion of identity (Meltzer, 1967). It seemed clear from dreams
that the year abroad in Canada had been similarly experienced in the
depths so that the return to London had stirred recollections of the great

expulsion, never forgiven. Her revenge on her parents in childhood had taken the form of arrogating to herself a very sanctimonious secrecy regarding her sexuality, which was meant to parallel the establishment of the privacy of their bedroom. She became a child who confided everything else as a screen for this breach of faith and, for a long time after the erotic transference subsided, this double standard of confidentiality reappeared in the analytic situation. But gradually her dreams gave away its content of a rather diffuse anal perversity. Its enactment in her marriage was revealed and a disengagement from it was slowly effected.

In consequence of this the analytical separations were felt more keenly and this made it possible for a clear delineation to be made between the adult part of her personality and infantile structures. These latter included a very dependent baby, urgently needing the "toilet/ mummy" (Meltzer, 1967) but afraid of falling from the height of the feeding-breast; and in addition there appeared a know-it-all big sister part. This was the part that knew better than mummy and sat in harsh judgement on almost everyone. The one exception to this was seen to be. her maternal grandmother, to whom the qualities of "parental" continued to have adhered historically. This was paralleled in the analysis by the status of Melanie Klein, while the analyst, like the parents, was felt to be highly sexual but of dubious reliability.

As we proceeded into the third year of the analysis Mrs D. seemed to lapse into a desultory type of resistance to the work, bringing her material with a shrug and listening to interpretations with scarcely disguised boredom and misgivings about what seemed to her the analyst's cavalier attitude towards evidence. She explicitly considered as unworthy of respect a so-called science whose criteria of truth-function lay in the aesthetic realm, which proved nothing and could convince no one. This reached hilarious proportions one day in an incident involving a cobweb hanging from the ceiling of the consulting room. Somehow the question arose as to its origin; did it necessarily imply a spider or were other events possible, such as particles of dust adhering by static electricity. Mrs D. promptly looked it up, not in a physics or biology text but in the *New Oxford Dictionary*, and that was that. The possibility of my personal experience was ruled out in favour of definition. Whatever the analyst's experience of other phenomena might have been, they could not have been "cobwebs". He was making a linguistic error, playing the wrong "language-game" (Wittgenstein, 1953).

This debate about meaning and its relation to language came as climax to a series of dreams involving the patient's mother. Frequently the two of them were climbing hills together, having picnics on cliffs overlooking the sea or were upstairs in a house preparing food. In these many settings she was in continual conflict with her mother as to whose judgement was best. Her mother was endlessly patient, yielding and kind while she was endlessly tolerant of mother's limited knowledge, her rigidity, her age and fatigue, provincial narrowness, etc. The problem of bringing this baby into a trusting dependence on the breast was clearly aggravated by the persistence of her infantile identity being invested in the "big sister" part. It seemed quite hopeless as she lay session after session treating the analytical method in this way, bored, playing with her beads, shrugging her baby-shoulders, marching off at the end of the session with her baby-nose in the air. But a dream gave promise of a chink in the armour.

Two months earlier she had had a dream which seemed to make reference to her dislike of the timbre of her own voice: she discovered that *the piano sounded so poorly because there was a weasel hiding in it and producing a corrosive froth. But when she tried to put it out the window, it kept getting back inside despite the two big guard-dogs.* This seemed to link clearly with the acid contempt in her voice, with her eyes always ferreting out the defects and overlooking the virtues of the analyst. The way in which this operated to frustrate the breast in its attempts to fill the baby with something good and the way it was related to the perverse sexual trends found a brilliantly condensed representation in a very frightening and crucial dream with a rich associative framework. In the dream it seemed that *scripture was no longer to be taught in the schools in London as the children would not accept it unless it was called something high-flown like "moral philosophy". Then she seemed to be in a classroom where one girl was passing out pieces of cotton wool while another was making a mystic invocation to invite a giant bird to swoop down and carry off some other girl. At that moment a bird–woman appeared at the window, beating against the glass with her wings and a piece of wood. Mrs D. felt terrified she would break in.*

The associations to the dream were revealing and poignant. When they had been in Canada, living in a cottage, a robin had come every morning and beat against the bedroom window. Mrs D. thought it must have had a nest there when the cottage had stood unoccupied. On the day before the dream the patient had had to go to Oxford on business and had felt uneasy that she might see the analyst on the street there. But instead, to her dismay, on the way home she had seen her mother get off to change trains at Reading. She did not see or hear the patient call to her because Mrs D. could not open the window. She realized that she could have had the pleasure of riding with her mother had not her omniscience prevented her phoning the cousin with whom mother was staying in Oxford, so certain had she been that mother's visit was to last longer.

It was unmistakable, therefore, that the bird–woman in the dream, like the robin in Canada, represented her mother trying to get back in touch with the good baby, who, however, was being made deaf to the truth (the cotton for the ears?) and dominated by the propaganda of the know-it-all séance-holding weasel-eyed "big sister". Theoretically this would represent an inability to effect a satisfactory splitting-and-idealization of self and object (Klein, 1932).

In the months that followed an interesting and very gradual alteration in behaviour and mood took place in the consulting room. The shoulder-shrugging contempt for the psychoanalytical method and the spiteful scepticism about its efficacy, all based on her delusion-of-clarity-of-insight and sitting-in-judgement, changed to a brooding pessimism about herself and her character. She felt keenly the adamantine streak in herself and how it resisted being helped or being dependent, how it clung somehow by preference to the promise of perverse excitement, even though it no longer put this, into action. She began to note similar qualities among some of the people she had previously admired and to see how it wrecked their constructive aims and cost so much pain to the people who were fond of them. It was at first a harsh judgement on herself, one that would have passed sentence for punishment, but slowly this softened to sympathy and regret, even at tunes a bit remorseful, for the pain she inflicted on others and on herself. She felt herself to be a real "schizophrenogenic" mother and wondered at the flourishing of her children, who indeed did seem somehow to have benefited more from her analysis than she had herself. It was striking now how session after session she arrived in gloom and left cheerful. She insisted that this was just because I let her talk about her children and that was nice. Still she could recognize that the cheerfulness had something to do with the analyst's "foolish optimism" getting into her temporarily. She even was beginning to think there might be a beauty in the method that she could not see. But mainly her good feelings adhered to the analyst very personally. It was he who could bear the weasel-eyes and the shoulder-shrugging. Perhaps someday she would shed the secrecy about her love and wear her heart on her sleeve. But it would have to be very slow; she was not a plunger-in.

Almost on the anniversary of the "bird–woman" dream another amused Mrs D. and heartened the analyst, for in it *a young lion was hurling himself at her windscreen and it seemed only a matter of time before he broke through. But later she was outside the car lifting a cat in her arms and closing some gate to keep a child from straying out of the garden.* It was quite clear to her now that the delusion-of-clarity-of-insight came from being inside her object looking out its eyes and that the world, and the analysis, looked quite different from outside. The frightening lion–

breast, like the bird–woman, became the attractive cat–breast that she could now take into herself as the basis of her own motherliness.

Summary

This short paper on the psychopathology of insight and judgement has set out to demonstrate one type of disturbance which can be seen to arise from the operation of the unconscious infantile phantasy of projective identification with the internal objects, especially the mother's breast and head, experienced as the font of knowledge and wisdom. Fragments of material have been brought to illustrate the operation of the mechanism and then a more extensive description of an analysis was attempted. This latter sought to trace the relation of the patient's character pathology to a defensive structure which had been mounted in the second year of life under the pressure of disappointment and jealousy of the new baby sister. While in many ways the harshness and judgemental quality of the character was in the nature of a revenge against the parents for expelling her from a blissful confusion of identity with them, it was also a defence against ever being caught so unawares again. Thus her epistemophilic instinct and high intelligence were re-enforced by defensive as well as aggressive motives. In the transference it was necessary to work through the dissolution of the narcissistic organization illustrated best in the "bird–woman" dream. In order to do this a difficult countertransference problem of tolerating hopelessness and humiliation had to be faced, throwing light on the magnitude of the difficulties from which Mrs D's parents had retreated. It is difficult to see how parents, no matter how sterling, could have done otherwise.

The internal experience of these two mental acts, delusion-of-clarity-of-insight and sitting-in-judgment, seems to shade so subtly into their healthy counterparts, insight and judgement, that it is difficult to see how anything other than a widening of the field of introspection could distinguish them. Respect for the laws of evidence, attention to the quality of reasoning, soliciting the opinion of others in crucial matters and other safeguards may help. But such intellectual and social safety-measures also pay a price by throwing away the possible moment of inspiration that seems to have no evidential links, to which the laws of logic find no application and which may seem unintelligible when communicated to others for advice. And since all nascent creativity may be based on the seizing of such moments, Kierkegaard's (1941) "leap in the dark", there comes a time when reliance on one's own introspection, forlornly, must be attempted.

CHAPTER EIGHT

The relation of dreaming to learning from experience in patient and analyst

(1984)

Donald Meltzer

In analysis we usually study dreams to gain access to processes of thinking that concern the patient's emotional conflicts. But every once in a while, particularly with patients who are students of analysis or are professionally interested in the analytic method itself, a different sort of dream arises. These are dreams that seem to reflect the patient's thinking about how his mind works. They are what might be called "theoretical" dreams; they are not about psychoanalysis proper but the patient's own theory about his experience of his mind's operation.

Throughout the history of psychoanalysis, the so-called "theories of the mind" have been the changing models of the mental apparatus that analysts think they are using in listening to, observing and trying to understand their patients and themselves. Freud's own models changed during the course of his work. The first model postulated by him resembled some kind of telephone exchange and this he elaborated, before he started on his psychoanalytic work, in what is known as "The Project for a Scientific Psychology". This was a neurologist's model and was concerned with the apparatus that conducts messages in the brain; it had nothing to do with the meaning of the messages but only with the way in which the messages were distributed and conducted through the neural network. Once he embarked upon analytic work he elaborated a second theory which was, in a way, a supplement to the first, namely the Libido theory. This was a theory about the distribution of "mental energy" in which mental energy and sexual excitation were more or less equated with one another. But then, in the course of his work, he discovered that the central problem was conflict which had various configurations; conflict between what he called the ego and the outside world; conflict between the ego and the superego; and between the ego and the instincts. So he elaborated the Structural Theory (in the 1920s) in which he spoke of the ego as serving three masters. This envisaged the mind as an apparatus for conciliation whose central function was to reconcile the demands coming from these three directions—a negotiating instrument. It seemed natural, from the employment of that model, that this central part of the mind, the ego, should then be viewed as being mainly concerned with maintaining peace of mind (the Nirvana principle). None of the models he devised took any serious account of emotionality and its meaning—this was left for Melanie Klein to develop in her theory of the internal world. This was a great advance since it envisaged the mind as a kind of internal theatre with figures entering into emotional relationships and conflicts with one another, from which meaning was generated and deployed into the external world and external relationships. What the theory lacked was any interest in, or concern with, the thinking processes themselves; it seemed to take for granted that the mind was able to think, to perform thinking functions, as if that were not a problem for psychoanalytical investigation but could be left to the philosophers and academic psychologists.

This theory was at a similar stage of scientific development as Embryology had been before the development of Genetics. It was purely descriptive of the way the mind elaborates its particular phantasies and pictures of the world, and quite unconcerned with the means used to do this. It remained for Bion to consider this particular psychological problem further and to elaborate his Theory of Thinking which we are now beginning to explore.

Reading psychoanalytical literature gives one the impression that analysts operate in their consulting rooms using certain theories and that they make their interpretations accordingly. But it is important to remember that papers are not written in the course of analytic sessions; they are written in retrospect and they are written to be read by colleagues. They must be stated in some previously agreed language. Hence they are statements that imply the following kind of preamble: "If we accept that we are operating according to pre-existing theories, then what happens in my consulting room could be stated in this particular way." However, what in fact happens in the consulting room is basically no different from what happens in any science, which is this: we have an instrument, whose structure is analogous to the object that it is trying to study, which registers certain responses to that object, its behaviour or its structure. This holds whether we are talking about an electrical instrument for studying the inside of the cyclotron, or a photographic instrument used for photographing the sections of a cell, or any other instrument. But whatever the instrument of study, it has to have a structure analogous to the object under study in order that it can make responses that have some intelligible relationship to what is being studied. And from that point of view psychoanalysis is the perfect science because it employs an instrument not just analogous to the object but nearly identical with it. Using its harmonic response of countertransference, we study clinical phenomena.

For this reason any paper in the field of scientific psychoanalysis that is an honest report of clinical experiences is fundamentally introspective and autobiographical. Therefore, in a sense, it aspires to being a work of art. Psychoanalytic research is essentially self-scrutiny and self-description, its primary instrument being introspection. It has, therefore, a strong link with the philosophical method and can be said to take up a very comfortable methodological position in the triangle created traditionally by science, philosophy and the arts.

Psychoanalytical papers, I suggest, can also be seen as technical papers about the psychoanalytic method and how the analyst's mind seems to operate in the analytic situation. This is very similar to what happens in the arts where painters are always exploring paint as a method of representing their life experiences; musicians explore the use of sound with the same idea, and literary artists likewise are attempting the same exploration of words. A close link therefore exists between the psychoanalytic method as a research into technique, and the arts as research in craftsmanship.

As an extension of this thought I return to those dreams which I mentioned at the beginning. They are presented rarely by particularly introspective people who are interested in the psychoanalytic method; they are dreams that seem to be an exploration of problems of thinking.

The two dreams we are about to consider came after three years of analysis which had brought about significant changes in the patient's character as well as leading to her changing her professional emphasis from administration to research in her field. These dreams occurred when she was studying Bion's work on groups and his theory of thinking.

In the first dream *there was a table to be set for dinner, with maybe some six to eight places. The patient had been delegated to set out the cutlery which was all mixed up together in a drawer. It seemed a perfectly simple task. However, when she started the whole situation continually escalated in complexity; the table grew bigger, the number of places more numerous, and the variety of the different types of cutlery kept increasing and increasing; there were silver, wooden and artistic implements—knives for sculpture and modelling, pencils and pens, brushes and rulers. So she decided that she would have to change her method. She would try to accomplish the task in the same way that one would collate papers that have been duplicated, say 50 pages and 100 copies; she would organize the implements and deal them out systematically. Pretty soon it became clear that this method too was not going to be adequate to cope with the escalation, and that some other method was needed—a machine of some sort would have to be devised. She ended up by feeling that she was confronted by an impossible task, like Hercules in the Augean stables. There would have to be some sort of extremely complicated apparatus that would be able to cope both with the growing complexity as well as with the ever escalating volume of work.*

The second dream was very different. In this *she had three simple tasks to perform, and she had been given a simple instrument with which to work— a thread. First, she had to repair one of the links in a gold chain which had been given to her by her mother* (and which, in fact, she had lost just a week before). *The thread was to be used to tie the links together so that the chain could be worn. Second, there was a necklace of little polished stones* (this she had bought in an open market on a trip made some years ago). *The necklace's thread had stretched so that it was necessary to re-string the beads. Here she was concerned about whether she would be able to make the little knots that separated each bead and which held them securely so that they did not all fall off if the thread broke. Third, there was a dress in which one of the seams had become unstitched and this had to be repaired.*

This third item had a certain background in the analysis during its third month when I had told her of a six-inch split in her trouser seam because I knew that she was going to a meeting and would be very embarrassed if she discovered it later.

These two dreams came, then, at a time when the patient was studying Bion's work. She was more particularly studying the Grid [Bion, 1977] and trying to understand what alpha-function could be. It therefore seems a reasonable hypothesis that the first dream represents a way of trying to imagine what alpha-function accomplishes, while the second dream is a reference to the Grid and the kind of mental functions which the Self can perform as they are implied in the different categories of the Grid. In other words the two dreams distinguish between unconscious mental functions performed by internal objects (the breast at infantile level), and mental functions (conscious or unconscious) which lie within the capacity of parts of the Self.

Let us go back to the first dream and consider the initial situation of setting a table for six or eight people. In group psychological terms it is possible to think about people and to classify them, as in the army for instance, according to a few simple determinants—Name, Rank and Serial Number. It might be argued that this is a perfectly adequate classification and that it could be managed by the conscious mind. However, as soon as we begin to describe people as individuals rather than merely name them as members of a class, we become aware of a continually escalating complexity revealed by the on-going experience of each individual's mind and person. We soon realize that it is impossible to think about them and reach any understanding of them as individuals with our conscious mind—we have to abandon ourselves to some other apparatus over which we have no control. This is a tenable context within which the first dream could be placed.

On the other hand the second dream seems to be an investigation into what a person can do with his conscious mind, the sort of useful functions that can be controlled. It gives three examples—the gold chain, the bead necklace, and the repair to the dress. First, to put it in the context of Bion's work, each of the three different tasks in the second dream undertakes the repair of damage that has been done by "attacks on linking". (The link has been broken, stretched or disengaged.) It is also interesting to notice that the three kinds of links are all different: the gold chain is composed of links that are joined by interlocking one with another; the beads are all arranged on a single thread, but each item is separated and kept in place by a knot (which I think is also a pun meaning "a is not b, is not c, is not d" and so on, but the beads are also held firmly together by something that they all have in common); the two pieces of material are held together, like her trousers, by a thread that joins them, but it joins them in such a way that they make a shape, and the whole thing becomes three-dimensional.

In a way, of course, the second dream is much more interesting than the first which does not get any further than does Bion when he says "alpha-function"—by which he would seem to mean something that we do not understand anything about, something perhaps essentially mysterious and probably immensely complicated. However, this representation is of particular importance to this patient who has moved from preoccupation with group processes to studying the complexity of individual intimate relationships. To that extent it is characteristic of a whole series of dreams which occupied her analysis at this point. All represented in one form or another the need and fear of abandoning control and surrendering herself to emotional experience; this was sometimes represented as floating down a river, sometimes as being carried in a vehicle whose destination she did not know.

In the second dream there is the important problem of preserving and repairing what she has received from the mother, the analyst and other people. It is clearly suggested that if a link gets broken, and you do not notice it in time, you may lose the object and never be able to recover it. Whether this is true of the mental apparatus I am not sure, but it is certainly the nature of the anxiety which the dream is attempting to resolve. One might say: "If you notice the damage in time, you do have the means of repairing it with your own little thread of thinking, which may not produce gold links but it does prevent loss of the object."

Both dreams also relate to another of Bion's concepts: distinction between symbiotic and commensal relationships. We see here a representation of people being at the same table—the commensal relationship. From that point of view it can be seen that the symbolic structure of the two dreams is very similar—the places arranged around the table and the chain of gold links or necklace of beads around the neck. While the precious chain from mother is structured by linking, the necklace of common beads is held together by a common thread of separating knots. Compare this with the representation of individuals seated round the table, having something in common (commensal)—or will it be discovered when the utensils are all sorted, that each is intimately linked to its neighbour on the right and on the left (symbiotic)?

Returning to the second dream, I find that the open seam in the dress is particularly interesting because it might be seen to represent being able to make a conceptual garment that really does fit a person— you know that it is not the actual person himself; it is only a conception that you have fitted onto the person. But you have to be able to make it so that it both fits and does not fall to pieces. There is also a link with the story of the Emperor's New Clothes.

It might be said then, that the first two examples (the gold chain and the beads) have to do with the problem of understanding people's relationships to one another, how they are linked together, how they are separated, how they are similar and how they are different; but the third example, that of the seam in the dress, reflects a much more complicated approach to the individual in his own right. Thus the dream seems to be seeking an integration of the patient's former socio-political interests and her newer more psychoanalytical ones.

The first dream could also have a bearing on overcoming the delusion of independence, not only from an internal object but from objects in the external world as well. If we list the equipment that we use in our daily life, from our getting up to our going to bed again, it would include the whole technological equipment of our culture. Where does a concept of independence stand in that context? Where is the "self-made man"? What does "think for oneself" mean?

We have before us, then, a beautiful example of a person struggling to learn from experience; experience of her analysis, her reading and

experience of life in general. She has taken Bion's poetry (alpha-function, the Grid, attacks on linking, commensal and symbiotic relationships) and found her own symbolic representations in the forms of
everyday life. She has woven them together with her appreciation of
the beauty and value of the analytical experience, on to the background
of her infantile appreciation of her mother. It forms a dream tapestry of
surprising superficial simplicity and of deep complexity. Nothing that
has been said so far is in the nature of psychoanalytical interpretation of
the dream, merely a "reading" of its manifest content and implications,
knowing its background in her studious preoccupations. It adds nothing to the meaning of the dream but is, rather, a pale paraphrase. The
dream image will remain in the mind of patient and analyst long after
my prose translation of it has faded. It has "poetic diction" indeed, with
the simplicity of a Vermeer.

It can be said with confidence that by this dream operation an
intelligent and sensitive young woman is making these ideas "her own"
in the sense that Bion means by "becoming O". Furthermore by communicating her dream to me the patient has helped me to think of these
matters with a greater clarity than I had ever managed before. I had
certainly never seen so clearly the differential nature of the commensal
and symbiotic link as the one implied here by the distinction between
the gold-linked chain and the string of beads or the people seated
around the table, either symbiotically linked by varied but overlapping
equipment, or commensally linked to one another by identical implements.

CHAPTER NINE

The aesthetic object
(1984)

Donald Meltzer

This essay, which has clearly the character of a "manifesto", includes in a nutshell the themes that Meltzer was to develop in later years, outlining an innovative path of psychoanalytic thought, specifically in relation to the concepts of "aesthetic object", "aesthetic conflict, and "claustrum", with the complex clinical and theoretical problems that are linked to them.

M any will have noticed, as indeed I did, that more and more frequently I talk about "aesthetic objects". It is true that in my analytic practice there have been some changes with respect to my ideas on the nature of psychic pain and on the organization of defensive processes in relation to them. These ideas depart somewhat from those of Melanie Klein; this is due in part to the progressive absorption of the ideas of Dr Bion on what he calls the "birth break", on the transition from the condition of a water animal to the condition of an air animal. Let us focus now on this transition. We can begin by thinking of intra-uterine life, or at least at the last months of it, as a period in which the child has emotional experiences. On the basis of what the clinical material shows us, we can try to grasp conceptually the nature of this experience and the way in which it prepares the child for the transition to a life outside the mother's body. One can take into consideration something that is in the domain of instinctual preparation or, as Bion would say, of "innate preconceptions", which are already about to take their place in the uterus: the sensorial apparatuses (visual, auditory, gustative, etc.) are already stimulated by the nature of the object in which the child is, even though in an indistinct and filtered way. One can equally take into consideration that in the last two months of intra-uterine life the child feels increasingly constrained by this container; now he/she has almost no room to move, although he/she can turn and change position, but in my opinion he/she must feel terribly squeezed in there and his/her body yearns to escape from this constraint. I believe that Bion was completely right to think that the foetus has no consciousness of his/her own growth; it is much more likely that, as one can see in some dreams, he/she perceives that the claustrum is tightening around him/her.

Thus, if you think of these last months in which the senses are ready to function but receive only very muffled stimuli, in which the muscles and the body are equally ready to function but cannot do it in this terrible condition of constriction, there is no doubt that escaping from this prison must have a fantastic emotional meaning of freedom: the freedom to function. Various clinical experiences have strongly suggested to me that this exit from the tunnel, this explosion for the senses that is the apparition of the external world, must be the primary aesthetic experience. We can think, for instance, of certain dreams of patients or of certain children at the beginning of their therapy who do not seem to have developed prior to finding a therapist paying real attention to them and towards whom they have a real explosion of love.

The clinical material that we heard yesterday illustrates fully what Melanie Klein has described in relation to the oscillation between the schizoid–paranoid position and the depressive position; however this material can also be described as the oscillation between the partial object and the total object, or between a quantitative and a qualitative relationship to the world, or between the absence and the presence of meaning, or between the absence and presence of emotion. All these different aspects are implied in the distinction between schizoid–paranoid position and the depressive position made by Melanie Klein.

On the basis of clinical experiences I am increasingly inclined to believe that it is not useful to think that the equipment of the newborn is so immature that he/she can have only very primitive emotional experiences. A starting point is necessary in any case. I do not think it is useful to say: "Well, emotional experiences start at the age of four years, of four months, of four **days prior** to birth". It is certainly necessary that at a certain point one starts to have the emotional experience of the impact of the world on oneself. From a point of view that is internal to experience, and keeping in mind the model of an abrupt escape from a claustrum, we can think of an escape from the simplicity of a computer life, from a two-dimensional life, from a life where things are only what they seem to be and nothing else, from a life of causality and automaticity; escape for the sake of living in another world of experience where the essential thing is the emotions aroused in the subject by the beauty of the world. It seems to me that as long as one has not been startled by the beauty of the object, the question "Is it so beautiful inside?" cannot be raised. According to us this question is the very core of what we mean by "meaning". It seems to me that before having received the impact of the beauty of the object, and thus before having a strong inclination to ask the question "Is the inside beautiful?", we function on the simple and mechanical basis of stimulus/response. Prior to the appearance of the question "But is the inside beautiful?" we do not have anything to think about. This question corresponds well to what Melanie Klein called the nature of the epistemophile drive, which has as its first object the inside of the mother's body (today understood also as the inside of her psyche: what she thinks, feels, her intentions, her history, etc.). If we establish a link to Dr Bion's formulation or construction on the apparatus for thinking, specifically with the alpha function that enables us to think about thoughts, the stimulus for forming thoughts is the impact of the question "But is it beautiful inside?" This question, this need to raise it, will receive a response by the alpha function, the formation of symbols, the thoughts of the dream, etc.

It seems to me that it makes a big difference if in your clinical approach you think in those terms: that is, if you think of the schizoid–paranoid position not as primitive, but as the position in which one retreats in order to protect oneself from the impact of the beauty of the object, from the emotions, from the problems and the questions raised by this impact. The schizoid–paranoid position is a defensive position, it is always a defence against the pain of the depressive position.

The very essence of the depressive position is this question: "Is it beautiful inside?"—and it seems to me that this has some important repercussions on our way of working. If you think of the schizoid–paranoid position as the one which is primary from the point of view of development and which will later lead to the depressive position, you will pay much attention to the phenomenology of the schizoid–paranoid position (to all processes of scission, of projective identification, etc.) and you will work it out in all its details, thinking that in this way the transfer will develop naturally. But if, on the contrary, you think that the first experience in development is that of the explosive beauty of the object, with this distressing question: "Is it so beautiful inside?", then while observing the material your attention will always go to the traces of the impacts with aesthetic objects and also to the defences against these impacts. You will observe your material in a very different way. In addition it seems to me that if you explore the material of a schizoid–paranoid character with much interest for detail, this will have the effect of giving to this level of phenomenology a status of respectability, with a tendency towards prolonging its existence. It is almost a perversion of the analysis. Much attention paid to the details of the perverted sexual activities of a patient, to the small details of his/her obsessive activities, to the rational mixing up of his/her paranoid ideas, etc. is almost a secret complicity with the patient for preserving the ignorance of the depressive phenomenon.

But some conditions are required in the analyst himself/herself in relation to his/her outlook over the world: in fact you can adopt this position only if you consider it the only rational position that can be adopted *vis-à-vis* life and the world. Inevitably, sooner or later you will have a more pessimistic outlook over the world. But if instead of reading the newspapers you have a walk in the countryside, or at the *jeu de paume*, or read Shakespeare, etc., you will have a completely different outlook and you will see that the question that corresponds to what we are interested in is: "Ah! But is it so beautiful inside?"

CHAPTER TEN

Concerning the perception of one's own attributes and its relation to language development

(1986)

Donald Meltzer
with Mme Eve Cohen (Paris)

The differentiation in the clinical setting of psychoanalysis be
tween the manifestations of delusions and the reporting of
primitive perceptions would seem to be an area of observation
and description opened up by Bion's Theory of Thinking. By offering us
a model that enables us to conceive of such a differentiation he has
made possible our monitoring the phenomena of our consulting room
for their realizations. The theory of alpha-function and beta-elements
has already proved itself fruitful for clinical observation in the area of
communication of meaningful messages versus communication-like
missiles of meaningless stuff. In work with psychotic children it has
helped us to recognize their response to bombardment with emotional
experiences for which they have no capacity either of containment or
thought. It also gives us a basis for distinguishing between immaturity
and psychosis.

A report presented by Mme Eve Cohen at a seminar held in Paris in
April 1982 throws some valuable light on the problem. Mme Cohen's
material concerned her patient, Henri, aged twenty-six, who had had a
breakdown while abroad after six years of aimless wanderings following upon his mother's departure from the family home to live with a
lover with whom she had had a secret liaison for over ten years. Among
his complaints at the time of hospitalization there was none of the usual
delusional ideas nor was his demeanour and mode of communication
bizarre or unfriendly or secretive. On the contrary, he was very open in

describing the many phenomena of perception of himself and the world which troubled him and prevented him from maintaining any settled mode of life.

Henri, clearly, was a highly intelligent and sensitive young man, and he settled with interest and cooperativeness into psychoanalytical treatment, working out a plan of living alternate periods with mother and father while working in the father's food shop. The central complaint involved colours which he either saw or "sent out" during eating or while interacting with other people. These colour phenomena made it impossible for him to be "constant", which seemed to mean "being the same person", particularly before and after eating. This loss of constancy had become apparent to him when he had separated from his companion of long standing during his travels. At that time he became incapable of doing anything "automatically", in the sense that he could no longer remain unaware of the activities of his individual senses by focusing his attention on consensual objects. For instance the taste of the food he was eating could not distract his attention from what his eyes were seeing. The result seemed to be a bombardment of disparate *sensa* demanding to be meaningfully integrated and interpreted.

After fifteen months of therapy Henri began to complain of new phenomena which seemed to be closely related to the growing impact on him of experiences of separation in the transference. These new phenomena related to "things being added", "new attributes" which appeared as repetitive experiences during the course of certain activities. For instance, when he is cutting ham, the number 69 appears on his back. In connection with some other activity a crown of feathers appears, or coloured lines across his forehead. These "attributes" are his personal experiences but are also felt to be apprehended, not necessarily visually or even consciously, by other people. It is not clear to him whether they are phenomena which affect his feelings and relationships, or only manifest what does in fact exist.

Henri would appear, from his history, to have lived his early years in a state of great obedience to his mother, having allowed her, in effect, to do his thinking for him. In a similar way, during his travels his companion had occupied the same position. In both cases the defection of the person performing these functions had apparently left him naked to the wind of perceptual phenomena, lacking the capability of thought necessary for containing and giving meaning to his experiences. In a certain sense he had had a breakdown, but in another sense it had been what Bion calls a "break through". As he appears in the analytical sessions there is a great effort to think and to elicit his therapist's assistance in thinking. It is a very different process from an analysis in that the phenomena of the transference cannot as yet be made the focus of attention. Rather, the therapist is placed in a position of supervisor of his own efforts, variously assisting his memory so that experiences can be better linked together and at other times offering ideas about mental functioning to help him to think about his experiences. The symbol formation which more ordinarily would take place in dreaming is performed laboriously in the waking state and this at times results in his using a very poetic and idiosyncratic language.

I approach this material from two different angles: first, from the vantage point afforded by Henri's presenting us with conscious processes for forming the symbols which we are more accustomed to see fully formed in dreams; second, from the point of view of the interaction of projection and introjection at the basic level of perception of self and objects.

"These signs on the forehead probably have different meanings but I do not know them. I was fine with the bar on my forehead, not too strong. I did not feel, as I sometimes do, that I was crushing people. I don't like that. I was in harmony with people; I did not feel impoverished by something; I did not feel superior to the people I was waiting on (in the shop)."

"I think all the time that I always have something in my head; illogical things which do not help me to be myself. If I let myself go a little bit, even for a brief moment, it's a mess. For instance I have got into the habit of not looking at what I drink, for if I let myself go and cast a glance at what I am drinking, things go awry, there are colours and such things."

"What isn't normal is the fact that I cannot look when I eat; other people can do anything, at any time, but certainly not just anyhow, although it looks to me as if they let themselves go, as if they abandon themselves to the movement. I do not abandon myself to the drift but fight with myself. . . ."

"When they chew they don't pay attention; they can do anything. I am not able to chew chewing gum because I think of the gum all the time. . . ."

I have taken these examples to show the way in which Henri is observing and struggling to understand the mental phenomena which interfere with his being "constant" and "like other people" who appear to him to operate "automatically" and to be able to "do anything" without having to notice and think about their actions. When he is "thinking about the chewing gum", it is the same as when he is thinking about whether he is "crushing people" or "sending out colours" to them. In other words Henri seems to think that the spontaneity and relaxation of other people is a consequence of their being able to be unconcerned about the impact that their states of mind and actions are having on people and things. He is unable to be unconcerned in this way. He feels that there is an intimate connection between his mental phenomena and those of others, animate or not, although he recognizes that the chewing gum does not have a state of mind but must be representing something that does, a whole or a part of a living thing. It seems strongly suggested that the "colours" are representations of emotions as yet unconnected with symbolic representations which can be used for thinking. Later on he will refer to them as "vibrations" when the colour phenomena have receded. But by that time the colours have not disappeared but have begun to integrate with other formal representations to form symbols or proto-symbols: the bars of colour on his forehead, the coloured feather head-dress, the number 69 on his back. All these phenomena he calls "attributes" and explains that they are new experiences in his life.

"I have the impression that my thoughts become material. True, it is I who think, but the attributes are external to me, anyway to the extent that I really have the impression that it is material."

We have as a starting point the obvious fact that all of Henri's preoccupations concerning constancy centre round eating and its impact on himself and other people. Working as he does in his father's food shop brings the daily activities of his life into close symbolic contact with eating, and with sexuality, which is held in a state of suspension in his mind as being far beyond his capabilities of thought, let alone action. Even the nocturnal emissions which vaguely trouble him seem to have no contact with his dream-life. In fact his dream-life is not available to him in any form different from his waking preoccupations: "I do not know whether I think while I sleep. I remember the last quarter of an hour before I wake and the first ten minutes before falling asleep, but I do not remember my dreams. Yet I must be full of thoughts at night too; I cannot be without thinking. Also apparently dreaming is necessary. I do not remember any dreams except for the famous one I already told you about." (Of this dream he said: "*I was a kid; it was a long time ago. There was a well and I leaned forward and forward and saw myself as if I were double, at the same time above and below. I saw myself looking at myself and leaned so far forward that I fell. At the moment of impact I woke up in a sweat. It was a nightmare.*")

The central problem seems to be a developmental one rather than one of delusion-formation based on omnipotence. It could be stated as a problem of differentiation of the external and the internal world, of phantasy from action, of thoughts from deeds, of self from objects. We shall assume, as the observations of mothers and babies suggest, that this is the normal state of the very young infant, to whom the behaviour of other people must seem nonchalant, even cavalierly unconcerned, to

say the least. They must appear to behave as if they were either unaware or unconcerned about the enormous impact they were having
simply by existing and thinking as well as by acting. But it is true that
the organ of attention which can, in most people, be widened or narrowed, focused or unfocused, does operate to protect us from bombardment of the sort from which Henri "suffers". Or is it wrong to say that
he suffers? Is it perhaps we who suffer from this narrowing, this
scotomatization of the world by the skilled employment of our organ of
consciousness?

I would like to turn for a moment from Henri's material to a paper
which Maria Rhode presented in May 1982 to the New Imago Group,
entitled "The Parallel Structure of Words and Objects as a Stage in
Language Development". In this paper there were presented a series of
observations of very young children between the ages of eighteen and
thirty months. From the discussion about one child, whose transitions
from "private" language to conventional was exemplified, the question
arose as to the nature of "falling". Was it, as we had always assumed, a
period of vocal experimentation to achieve mastery of the physical
apparatus so that what was thought could be said to approximate to
what emerged vocally? The "private" period of speech in this child
suggested another formulation, namely that falling constituted play
with sounds in the mouth, treating the sounds as objects of imaginative
manipulation. This is not to imply a similarity to Piaget's formulation of
"egocentric speech" but rather to be part of, an extension of, the small
child's tendency to put objects in the mouth. Again we have always
assumed that this was essentially a primitive form of reality testing
where the differentiation of edible/inedible was the crucial problem.

In the observations of this child reported by Mrs Rhode the sound
"bupf" seemed to be variously split and combined with other sounds to
work out the concept covered by such words as two, both, together,
double. His play in his mouth with the sounds seemed to parallel his
play with objects, not merely as commentary on that play but as an
alternative theatre of phantasy manipulation. The conceptual formulation which might be drawn—and this is the heart of this paper—would
be as follows: lalling is to be seen as the vocal aspect of a more general
phase in cognitive development in which the physical space of the oral
cavity is utilized as the theatre of phantasy and play, a mid-point
between external play and internal thought (dream-thought or phantasy). The placing of fingers and objects in the mouth is accompanied by
the awareness of teeth, tongue, jaws, salivation and vocal capacity. In
this theatre of phantasy the sounds can be manipulated as concrete
objects devoid of fixed or determined meaning but rather driving their
meaning from the immediate juxtaposition with other sounds and buc-

cal objects. When the child moves on to accept the conventional meaning of the words in the discourse that he achieves through various forms of identification, this buccal theatre is moved outside the body because manual dexterity improves and play becomes less frustrating. But the tendency to employ the buccal theatre continues in the form of play with words based on homonymity, splitting and recombination of syllables, spoonerisms, puns, alliteration, ambiguity—in short all the devices of poetic diction.

If we now turn back to Henri's material, we can formulate an hypothesis about his state of mental organization which has an impressive cogency. May it be that we find this intelligent and sensitive young man, unaccustomed as he has been to think for himself, struggling with immature equipment to comprehend his new-found independent existence in relation to the world about him? Perhaps his equipment of thought is still somewhat fixed in this buccal stage so that the theatre of thought has not yet become located in his dream-life but is still in his mouth during waking hours. If this were so we might reasonably expect that what he does in his mouth would be poorly distinguished from actions in the inner world and thus in the outside world as well. Furthermore we might expect that his identification processes would be very volatile, since the state of objects would not be segregated into internal and external as a basis for stability of mood. Consequently any oral play or action which seemed not "in harmony", variously "crushing" or "sending out colours" for instance, would result in an immediate change in his objects of identification, namely changes characteristic of depressive illness. In fact Henri appears to be very depressive in his orientation rather than being persecuted by damaged objects.

Would this then not make sense of such complaints as his lack of "constancy", his inability to be "automatic" in his actions, his failure to be able to "let himself go"? If his buccal cavity is his theatre of thought, anything happening in his mouth might be expected to have the same impact on his view of self and world as we are accustomed for dreams to have. What sense can we then make of the new phenomenon of "attributes" such as the "69" on his back or the coloured head-dress? We would hardly notice the phenomenon if these attributes merely included such ordinary items as "looking well today", or "sexually attractive", or "my acne looks horrible". Their seemingly bizarre nature attracts our attention. Correspondingly we grow accustomed to see young people wearing sweatshirts with numbers or slogans on them, to multicoloured hair and Mohican haircuts. In what way do Henri's attributes differ from these concrete items of decoration (or disfigurement, depending on one's point of view)? Does the concept of a buccal theatre of phantasy, with its attendant failure of differentiation of internal and external, supply an adequate form of description? We cannot be satisfied unless we account also for their being "new", apparently only having appeared after some eighteen months of analysis.

I would suggest that the answer may reside in the newness of another area of experience, namely of awareness of the absent object. He has become vaguely aware that the week-end breaks have some impact on him, that he can feel "superfluous", that these feelings are linked with his mother's defection and his travelling companion's departure which had precipitated his breakdown abroad. In other words I am suggesting that what is in fact "new" is an uneasy feeling that an object from which he has become separated can notice changes in him when they become reunited. This is such an absolutely common aspect of experience that, again, we would hardly notice it as a phenomenon unless it takes such a primitive form that it appears to be bizarre. But if an adolescent patient who ordinarily comes rather well-dressed were to appear at one session in a numbered sweatshirt we would surely assume that it expressed some transferential state of mind. The difference between Henri and our more sophisticated adolescent is that Henri would notice this change, feeling as if he had the number on his back, while it would be invisible as such to ourselves. We would notice the adolescent's sweatshirt and its implications while he would be unaware of its significance.

It is in exactly this way that Henri demonstrates as a pathological state of mind the peculiarly heightened sensitivity to self and world that characterizes the artist and, in particular, the poet. While Henri has not learned to master and employ this heightened sensitivity most of us, on the other hand, have, in Wordsworth's words, "given our hearts away" for the sake of "constancy".

In order to bring this material and discussion into closer contact with problems encountered in work with children, I will review the material of Mme Cohen and Mrs Rhode from a more developmental point of view. In *Explorations in Autism* [Meltzer et al., 1975] in the chapter on mutism, I outlined a psychoanalytical theory of speech development drawing heavily on ideas put forward by such people as Susanne Langer, Wittgenstein, Cassirer, Chomsky, Russell and others. The central thesis was that language, in its genesis, is essentially two-tiered, having a primitive song-and-dance level (the most primitive form of symbol-formation) for the purpose of communication of emotional states of mind by means of the non-pathological use of the mechanism of projective identification, and that upon this foundation of deep grammar there is subsequently superimposed the lexical level of words for denoting objects, actions and qualities of the external world, that is, information. In connection with the outlining of the phenomenology of varying dimensionality in both disturbed and normal personality development, it was necessary to subscribe to a differentiation between meaningful and meaningless communications, in keeping with ideas already developed separately by Wilfrid Bion and Esther Bick.

More recently, in *Dream-Life* [1984], I explored in some detail the concept of internal space as the "theatre for generating meaning" in connection with Bion's "empty" concept of alpha-function and the format of The Grid [Bion, 1977]. The present paper can be seen to straddle the concepts of two- and three-dimensionality and to attempt to fill in some of the emptiness of the concept of alpha-function by defining a developmental space that is neither internal nor external in its implications, the "buccal theatre for generating meaning", tracing its implications both for speech development and for character. In order to carry out this task it is necessary first to discuss at some length both the concept of attention and some aspects of our ideas about symbol formation.

If we accept the idea that consciousness is best viewed, in Freud's words, as "an organ for the perception of psychic qualities", a Platonic view equating consciousness with attention, we tend to assume that we are considering an active function directed by interests derived from desires and anxieties. But that is, I suggest, only to take into account the penetrating type of attention which can be directed, narrowed or widened, focused for levels and perspectives, adjusted to levels of organization or perhaps even of abstraction. Its object are, in a sense, already "known". But there is another type of attention which is far more passive, patient, receptive, awaiting the advent of the "unknown". Bion has spoken of it in connection with what he calls "thoughts seeking a thinker", awaiting the advent of the "new idea" which the "mystic" will retail to the group, or the mystic part of the personality will transmit to the internal group (see "Dawn of Oblivion", Book III of *A Memoir of the Future* [Bion, 1991]). It is this passive type of attention which apprehends the aesthetic. The aesthetic impact of the world on the baby has been largely neglected in psychoanalytical concepts of development. For psychoanalytical material and infant observation declare, as do the poets, that the "aesthetic conflict" in the presence of the object is primary over the conflicts of separation, deprivation, and frustration to which so much thought has been devoted. The beauty of the world and its epitomization in the figure of the mother, the breast, the face, envelops the baby but brings in its train the most acute pain of uncertainty in the three-dimensional area. To what degree does the beauty of the exterior of the object correspond to the goodness of its interior, its feelings, intentions, durability? In a word, is it a "truthful" object? "Are you honest?" plagues Hamlet regarding Ophelia–Gertrude, great thinking baby that he is, not unlike our Henri.

This view, that differentiates active and passive attention, "penetration of" from "envelopment by" the object, also draws a sharp line between intrusive curiosity and thirst for knowledge. It rectifies a serious error in Melanie Klein's earlier work, drawn largely from experiences with psychotic children and only partly corrected in the *Narrative of a Child Analysis* [1975b], in which she took the view that the "epistemophilic instinct" was driven by sadism towards the contents of the mother's body. That intrusive curiosity which seeks the faults and defects of the object, stands in marked contrast to the awe and wonder at the beauty of the world which seeks to know and be known by the object. This distinction, which seems so often to separate science from art, holds more correctly for the difference between pornography and art on the one hand, and between Promethean and inspired science on the other.

The material from Henri gives strength to the formulation of a highly visual relationship between baby and mother, with eye–nipple penetrating the eye–mouth while the breast envelops the baby, and the mother and baby envelop one another in their eye-to-eye contact. The intrusive curiosity of the baby's eye–mouth counters that of the eye–nipple, which takes on the quality of the most primitive superego of the type mentioned by Freud in connection with delusions of reference. This contributes to the tendency to split nipple from breast, and for the former to take on qualities associated eventually with the father and his penis. On the other hand the mutual envelopment of the aesthetic experience between mother and baby (and it probably must be mutual to be long tolerable to either), with its passive, expectant and surrendering quality, brings the sense of mystery, of joyousness, but heavily freighted with the pain of the uncertainty of the aesthetic conflict for both. The hidden interior of the object, like the absent object, is a powerful stimulus to thought, perhaps the more powerful of the two, being in its nature far more passionate than anxious. While the anxieties engendered by the absence of the object tend to arouse violence in the service of domination and control of the object, the passion connected with the hidden interior of the aesthetic object promotes love-making, invites exploration.

Turning to the question of symbol formation before re-approaching the material from Mme Cohen and Henri, I must add an item to what has already been expressed at some length in *Dream-Life* about the nature of symbols. It is vital to understanding the way in which the "colours" have evolved into the "coloured head-dress" for instance. In the format of The Grid and his Theory of Thinking, Bion has placed alpha-function anterior to both dream-thoughts and myth, equating these two phenomena from the individual and the group. But I think this was a mistake based on the narrative form of the two which seems to me to be genuine narrative in the case of myth and contrived in the case of the dream. Myths seem to be stories, essentially true stories and therefore history. We probably do not encounter them in their original form either in folk-tale, religious literature or lay, but see them already subjected to some of the processes of condensation, ellipsis and hyperbole which will eventually boil them down, one might say, into a symbol. Think of the immense myth-content of the Cross, containing as it does both the New Testament and the Myth of the True Cross. Its power as symbol could never be comprehended without knowledge of what has been condensed within it; similarly, when symbols are brought into conjunction with one another and cross-fertilize, each being potentiated in its meaning by this conjugation. While dreams are composed of these conjugations, the narrative form they often take, which is hardly more than "and then . . . and then" etc., is the product of what Freud called the Secondary Revision. It contributes neither to their meaning nor to their significance.

My point is that myth formation is anterior to alpha-function or, more likely, is one of the components of alpha-function as the mysterious process of symbol formation. Note that this step of filling the "empty" concept with some content detracts in no way from its mystery and probably hardly lessens its essential emptiness. But it does suggest that Bion may have been wrong in thinking that the function was essentially unobservable and therefore indescribable. It seems likely that in the prehistory of the race, the first leaps of imagination were of this myth-making variety, enacted in song-and-dance, with the decoration of the dancers representing the creatures and forces of awe, similar to Henri's coloured bars on the brow or coloured feather head-dress, leaving only a short step to their graphic or sculptural representation as gods and spirits. The psychoanalytical theory of thinking proposed by Bion would suggest that this artistic move in imagination must necessarily have been both prior to, and a precondition for, the technological imagination that could invent tools and weapons.

Returning to Henri's material with these two new considerations in mind, we can recognize that his mouth is not only an area, a space, of great emotional significance to him, but that it is the scene or theatre of dramas which are monitored. minutely. In this respect we might think that his buccal equipment, especially teeth and tongue, are strongly linked to his visual imagination and stand in a strong identification with the eye–nipple in its superego function. But Henri's orientation to these events is a deeply depressive one; he cannot be unconcerned for the safety of the objects which enter his mouth, even when represented by something clearly recognized as inanimate like the chewing gum, because they are felt to be directly linked, though in mysterious ways, with external people. Early in the analysis when this concern presented as "sending out colours", it seemed delusional and perhaps hallucinatory. But as it evolved in the experience of the transference, taking on formal qualities to join the sensual ones, eventuating in the description of "attributes", this initial impression of psychotic processes gave way to the formulation of immaturity in his object relations. Throughout these first eighteen months of analysis Henri's distress was overwhelmingly depressive rather than persecutory, and when he later broke off therapy for a period to enter a mental hospital it was as a refuge from the bombardment of emotion impinging on him in the intimacy of the analysis and elsewhere as well.

When Henri compares himself with other people who seem to him to be "constant", to be able to act "automatically", to be "unconcerned", to be "able to do anything", or "to let themselves go", he seems to be describing a world of incredible nonchalance, of unthinking harmony and accommodation. And in a sense it is true: what Henri has to do with his immature, consciously controlled equipment for observation and thought, other people have long relegated to their unconscious and dream-life. But it is also true that this relegation has been accompanied by a degree, often severe, of denial of psychic reality in favour of acquiescence in custom, with a result of diminished sensibility, especially about their own impact on others. In this sense I would plead that Henri's concerns are quite realistic in their format if not necessarily in their sense of proportion. And his perception of his attributes, which is clearly not hallucinatory but imaginative, is likewise a realistic recognition of aspects of his character. The word "character" is only surprising in this context because his character, like his mood, is as unstable as a baby's.

In putting forward this formulation of the material I am depending rather heavily on the "famous" nightmare of the fall into the well. There I think we see precisely the story of his "illness" and why it may be seen more cogently as a "breakthrough" rather than a "breakdown", as Bion would say. It shows how the defection of his travelling companion, as a repetition of that of his mother, plunged him into contact (which he was, however, "leaning" towards already) with a split-off part of himself which has lived inside his object of dependence since babyhood, the part which was potentially a thinker, and perhaps a poet.

By linking Henri's material with the observations by Mrs Rhode I have framed a definitive hypothesis of a "Buccal Theatre for the Generating of Meaning" as an early stage of internalization and thought, and therefore of both internal discourse and external communication. In doing so I have perhaps added a certain definition and complexity to ideas put forward some years ago by Hanna Segal about a "third area" and by Donald Winnicott about the nature of "transitional objects". Perhaps it also has a link to the observations about "functional phenomena" in falling asleep and waking described by Silberer and rather recklessly attacked by Freud. The link also with the "envelopment by sleep" described by Schilder and recent work on REM sleep seems also suggested. But the most important implication for understanding child development probably lies in the implication that the evolution from the song-and-dance level of deep grammatical discourse of lalling and babbling, to the lexical level of social communication, is dependent on the move forward from a Buccal Theatre to a Dream Theatre for the generating of meaning.

This means that the differentiation of external and internal worlds is essential for understanding that if you want your thoughts to be communicated, you must vocalize them, a hard lesson for many to learn.

CHAPTER ELEVEN

On turbulence

(1986)

Donald Meltzer

If Bion's Theory of Thinking has some essential truth in it one must expect that new ideas, the ones which have an impact to produce catastrophic change, would appear first in dream form, only later to find some verbal and abstract representation. This is no more than to say that symbolic representations of ideas are most likely to be generated by borrowing formal elements from the outside world to portray internal world phenomena. These formal elements may implicitly include abstractions which lend themselves to analogical use in dream-life. Thus do artists and poets operate to perform their social function of giving communicable form to the new ideas nascent in the culture. To succeed in this function they must disturb us, frame questions in order to set the audience in motion to seek the answers, answers which, of course, mainly take the form of new readiness for new questions.

Psychoanalysis has come some considerable distance in defining the spectrum of emotional nuances which hold the meaning of our mental experiences. It would be a cogent view of our so-called theories that they are merely descriptive devices for outlining the structure of the variety of internal and external experiences which manifest themselves within us as emotion. But I would suggest that one whole area of emotion has as yet found no place in our body of theory because it has been assumed to stand merely in a quantitative relation. I am speaking of passions. If we adopt Bion's basic formulation of L, H and K, these passions would be "in love", "in hate" and "in awe", each with its negative counterpart, "anti-in love", "anti-in hate" and "anti-in awe". I think I am correct, certainly with regard to my own ideas, in stating that it has been assumed that passions were merely very intense emotions.

In this paper I wish to suggest another, and, I think, more interesting view, namely that passions represent states of turbulence arising from the paradoxical impact of one intense emotion on another, producing a turbulence by reason of the conflict with previously established ideas about the meaning of these emotions and their relevance to the organization of our internal world, and therefore our view of the external world. To illustrate this thesis I will bring a piece of clinical material which, while it lies outside the context of an analysis proper, has nonetheless an analytical background.

A young woman in her early thirties, a professional musician and a person of charm and beauty, asked to see me some three years after the ending of her analysis. I knew from communications and occasional follow-up visits that she had had a long struggle after the termination of the analysis to achieve a state of joyousness in her work and social relations. This had its roots in an internal situation which produced severe self-criticism and elevation of extraordinary standards in her work and in her evaluation of her behaviour with friends, standards which sapped her pleasure in accomplishments. Its origins were essentially narcissistic, deriving from a relationship with an admired and loved elder brother whose outstanding professional achievements were not paralleled in his intimate relationships. A know-it-all internal figure operated by continually raising doubts about sincerity and motivation, caricaturing analytical work.

But I had heard that in recent months this problem had seemed to give way, opening up a new area of gaiety, feelings of freedom and trust in herself. The result seemed to be a greater adventurousness in work and social relationships, accompanied by a growing confidence that she would soon find a man to lavish her love upon, to marry and have the children she was longing for. But, as she told me, something very disturbing was happening, namely that she found herself intensely drawn to a man whom she did not like. It was not a matter of disapproval of his character, for he seemed a thoroughly decent chap. She just did not like him and kept noticing things about him, ordinary little things such as turns of speech or gestures or areas of interests that she felt antagonistic towards. Then two days previously he had left her a message breaking an arrangement for the week-end without any explanation, and she found herself feeling furious. It was not an act out of keeping with their degree of intimacy which, in fact, was still on formal terms. Nor did it seem to arouse distrust or jealousy. No, she just felt furiously frustrated at the delay in getting to know him better.

She felt, in fact, that the unusual impatience had something to do with this paradoxical stage of her feelings, of feeling so strongly drawn to him yet disliking him in so many petty ways. That night she had two dreams which she found puzzling but thought interesting and wished to have my ideas about them. I too found them puzzling and interesting.

In the first dream *she was tuning a harpsichord for a woman, not in fact a professional musician but a former girlfriend of her brother, who was to give a concert. Indeed the time for the concert had already arrived and yet she had hardly begun the tuning. The trouble was that she was proceeding slowly because she was using the wrong method, namely of tuning each note to its proper pitch individually. Such a method she knew would take hours while the proper method of tuning middle C and then tuning every other note to it in fifths could be done quite quickly, simply by listening for the beats when each fifth was struck, rather than listening to the pitch.*

Actually she is a string instrumentalist and had only seen a harpsichord tuned once. There was no panic in the dream because the man running the concert was very gentle and patient with her about the delay. But she felt bad about keeping people waiting. The woman who was to play in the concert had never achieved a love relation with the brother for it had rather petered out, as had the patient's own last romance some years earlier.

In the second dream *she seemed to be standing on a high cliff overlooking a beach of silvery sand by the sea, thinking she ought to be down there sunbathing before the shadows of the cliff enveloped the beach.*

The two dreams taken together seem to make a more confident approach to meaning than either by :itself. The first clear reference point is the sense of urgency in both dreams, clearly referable to her age and impatience to get to know her new friend. Sexuality is surely indicated by the sunbathing and the word "concert". Also the wrong method is an element in both: in the one by her method of tuning; in the other by her elevated distance from the silvery sands. But the most interesting element seems to be the two methods of tuning. It is these to which I wish to turn attention.

My impression from the follow-up material of the past three years is that this young woman has achieved a fairly considerable skill in using the self-analytic method. She is able to introspect quite deeply, to follow lines of association in a most useful way and easily to recognize new representations of configurations of feeling and conflict with which she had become acquainted in the course of her rather long analysis. Consequently she had made some genuine progress on her own, of which she felt proud. Also this had increased her confidence, independence and feelings of womanliness. But one problem in her character caused her great concern, namely that she continued to feel that her life was not, somehow, being devoted to the things for which she could develop a passionate interest and devotion. Of course it was probably a matter of lacking a love relationship and children, but also professionally there was the same uneasiness. She felt sure that her capability as a musician was not a measure of her talent, which must lie elsewhere, perhaps in some way to do with children.

In the past it had been assumed by both of us that this uneasiness was part of the phenomenology of the internal doubting of sincerity generated by the internal brother-figure. But now that seemed to have been mastered, and yet. . . . Perhaps it was true that she felt more powerfully drawn to this new man than she ever had before, but it was hardly her idea of what falling in love ought to feel like. She could not say she was developing a passion for this man, but only that she felt terribly disturbed by him. Not that she had any grievances, even about the current cancellation. Her urgency to get to know him was somehow quite unpleasant, perhaps prompted by the desire to overcome being drawn to him rather than any hope of finding a love relationship with him.

I suggest that the wrong method of tuning the harpsichord may hold the secret of her mental state, namely that she is having a new experience with which she has no tried method of coping. She knows "about" the right method but has in fact never used it. And furthermore it is a method with a completely different rationale, listening for the beats when the chord (fifth) is struck rather than the pitch of each individual note. Might we call it "tuning her heart" rather than her harpsichord? Instead of paying attention to the individual emotions that she feels in the course of her experiences with her new friend, she is having to pay attention to the ways in which the various emotions harmonize or conflict with one another (the beats). Her preconception of passionate love is one of harmonious relation, of intense emotions to one another, a preconception drawn, perhaps, from the experience of splitting-and-idealization in the management of her infantile feelings. That would dispose her to split off all the qualities of her friend which she dislikes and only relate to those which "draw" her to him.

In summary: I am suggesting that this young woman, newly arrived at adulthood, is being obliged to reckon with a new value system which dislocates all her previous values of precise emotional pitch and harmonious relations. It would be similar in her professional life were she, for instance, to find herself powerfully drawn to Indian music. A capacity for passion is perhaps entering into her life in this form, obliging her to notice and value the disturbance itself as the indicator of catastrophic change.

CHAPTER TWELVE

Dénouement
(1986)

Donald Meltzer

This sort of book [*Studies in Extended Metapsychology*], which is the residue of clinical and teaching experiences rather than of any systematic research, seems a kind of compost heap. It is primarily intended to increase the fertility of the next developmental steps of others, to help them to bring to life their nascent creativity. But one also tends to hope that something alive of one's own may be found, unexpectedly, to be growing on the heap, a clump of mushrooms or a surprise of daffodils. Does the book add up to anything other than what it claims: a series of studies illustrating the use that Bion's ideas have found in my consulting room?

Bion himself was very opposed to a distinct "school" growing up around his ideas, perhaps partly because the adjective "Bionic" had such comic overtones of science fiction, gardening, electronics and quackery. But chiefly he felt, and I feel perhaps even more strongly, that the formation of "schools" is a miscarriage of science. It is naive to suppose that deep and significant differences exist. It is political to exploit them within the organizations of psychoanalysis. It fails to understand the impossible task of rendering in language the ineffable phenomena of the mind. And finally it shows little comprehension of the history of art and science. In so far as the metaphor of progress as forward movement is permissible, the development of art and science, or, in the case of psychoanalysis, art-science, moves forward in spiral fashion in some respects, or like a caterpillar in others. Those in the vanguard of development think they are miles ahead of the rear-guard when they reckon linearly, but they need only look sideways to see they are only inches in advance. Furthermore it is necessary for them to pause, and teach, and help the others to catch up before they can go on. If they fail to do this, their language, and soon their thought, becomes so idiosyncratic that they find they have departed from the social field and must find their way back. In a way this happened to Bion with *Transformations* [1965] and had to be rectified by altering his metaphors in *Attention and Interpretation* [1970].

This process of catching up tends to be misunderstood in the context of school-formation and politics as if it were some sort of clandestine plagiarism, stealing ideas and couching them in different terminology. An example of this can be seen in the development of "self-psychology" around the work of Heinz Kohut with its strong reverberation of Kleinian notions. But closer examination shows that two other processes are at work: one of these is the refinement of the language of the vanguard to fasten it more firmly to its historic roots; the other is a watering-down of the concepts to achieve a greater respectability. Both of these have their value for the social structure of the psychoanalytical movement and its relation to the surrounding intellectual and scientific community. Neither of them inhibit further forward movement in the next wave of advance.

In viewing my own work as "exploration", I like to think that some attempt should be made to trace in a more personal way what I see as the impact of Bion's ideas on my mode of life and view of the world (model of the mind, structure of history, evolution of political organizations, the role of the artist in the community, the nature of psychoanalysis as a thing, etc.).

In terms of Bion's concept of "catastrophic change" and the impact of the "new idea" there is no difficulty in establishing what this idea was and the revolution it has wrought in my ways of thinking and working . . . and also acting in general. The "new idea" was clearly something like "in the beginning was the aesthetic object, and the aesthetic object was the breast and the breast was the world". Of course I am using the word "breast" as a technical term with only an implication of description, rather than the other way round. On the one hand it seems surprising to me that this idea did not reach me through Adrian Stokes to whom it was ever vivid; on the other hand it is difficult to say whence in Bion's work it derives. It is not in the Grid [Bion, 1977]; it is only hinted at in *Transformations;* it tags along in a secondary position in *Attention and Interpretation.* Only in *A Memoir of the Future* [1991] does it find its place unambiguously. But it had reached me through Bion before that publication had crept into my thought and certainly into my consulting room. Not only had I become aware that the psychoanalytical method had taken on an aesthetic quality in my eyes but I had begun to see, mainly through dreams, that it had done so for some of my patients as well.

In retrospect I think the work on autism with its elaboration of the concept of dimensionality played an important role; the fine aesthetic sensibility of many of these children was so unmistakeable that one could not avoid wondering if their developmental failure had not been founded on processes for warding off the impact of the beauty of the world. Dismantling of the senses and two-dimensionality seemed exquisitely delicate methods for doing so without violence to the object, either externally or internally. The process of dismantling of the senses was too massive, too much like soul-murder, however, to illuminate the problem. But two-dimensionality held fascinating questions in its grip. At first it seemed that this shallowing of the world of meaning was self-explanatory, as if the dilution of meaning naturally resulted in an impoverishment of affects. Bion's ideas suggested the reverse, that a method of curtailing the intensity of affects resulted in the pallor of meaning. If this was the case, then the two-dimensional orientation to the world would be a defence against the impact of objects stirring emotions. But how? Melanie Klein's idea had been that interest in the inside of the mother, and thereby the epistemophilic instinct in general, had its origins in the intense emotionality of the mother–baby relationship. Did two-dimensionality then result from a denial of the psychic reality of the object rather than a regression to a prior stage in cognitive development?

Similarly old assumptions, tied up with Melanie Klein's delineation of paranoid–schizoid and depressive positions, were called into question. Esther Bick had revealed the identificatory processes connected with two-dimensionality (adhesive identification) so that it was feasible to think that an organization of mentality prior to the paranoid–schizoid position might exist which would strengthen the assumption of a genetic sequence with a strong internal logic, placing the depressive position at a more sophisticated level of experience. But somehow Melanie Klein's formulation of the factors operating to set the epistemophilic instinct in motion did not seem to be satisfactory. Her failure to differentiate between intrusive curiosity and thirst for knowledge as factors in the little child's interest in the inside of the mother's body, weakened the conceptual fabric. Findings with autistic children suggested strongly that sadism and splitting processes were not intensely operative in their illness but only developed in force in the process of recovery and advance in development.

Dissatisfaction of this sort with the mind-model which operated in the consulting room must gradually have influenced a shift away from thinking in terms of genetic phases of development towards a field conception. The implicit complexity seemed to demand it. I remembered Melanie Klein saying in response to critics at a meeting that it was not she who made things complicated, they just were so. Of course the human mind must be the most complicated thing in the universe within our ken. And there must be a limit to the degree to which the mind, studying itself, can penetrate its mysteries. Perhaps mystery itself is an important aspect of its essence.

Bion's emphasis on consciousness, not as a system but as an organ of the mind, the organ of attention, had already been strongly recommended by the experiences with autistic children. Their diffusion of attention with its resulting dismantling of what Bion had, half-jokingly, called "common sense" (Sullivan's "consensuality") seemed at once a powerful and yet delicately sparing way of evading the impact of life both around and within themselves. The therapeutic indication of the importance of seizing and holding their attention with interesting talk based on acute observations, had demonstrated its efficacy, if also its tendency to exhaust the therapist.

The "field" orientation which accepts multiple levels of simultaneous and more-or-less integrated functioning seems to allow the question "how" and not only "when" is the mental level called into operation to superimpose itself on the purely neurophysiological? Bion's approach to the problem, by assuming that the first operation is the creation of thoughts which then require an apparatus to think (manipulate, use) them, seems to be the crucial break with the traditional implication that thinking is prior as a function and generates thoughts. It enabled him to create the Grid and then to move on to examine the "transformations" by which thinking implements its utilization of thoughts. More than that, it provided a framework for considering false thoughts, lies, misunderstandings, un-truth, misconceptions, propaganda, cynicism. When this is compounded with the great step of opposing emotion to anti-emotion (positive and negative L, H and K) a new abacus lies to hand for thinking about thinking.

To be able to think of the mental as "level" and of its being "called into play" by the focusing of attention on the emotionality being aroused by an experience, delivers a new freedom to our consideration of the problem. And it is not merely the semantic clarification that freshens the atmosphere, for it also sweeps away the traditional primary preoccupation with logic and thereby mathematics and linguistics as our supreme source of information, from the Greeks to the

Tractatus. The "empty" concept of alpha-function is our new key. But the lock that it fits has also shifted; this is the crucial matter. We have been misled by confusing the creation of aesthetic objects as the work of rare and evolved genius with the perception of the beauty-of-the-world which Wordsworth asserted was inherent in the "clouds of glory" embodied in the mentality of children and their availability to the "splendour in the grass". Had he pursued the problem of the loss of this sensibility rather than accepting the facile explanation, essentially sociological, that "getting and spending we lay waste our powers", he would have recognized more clearly the nature of the pain that these sensibilities bring in their train.

Similarly Melanie Klein's loyalty to Freud's formulation of the duality of instinct caused her simply to by-pass the problem and explain away the evident ambivalence implicit in the epistemophilic instinct on the basis of frustration. This attitude is a bit surprising, considering that she knew very well that a certain optimal level of mental pain (frustration, persecution, envy, etc.) is necessary since development is driven by tolerable conflict. My own first glimpse of the problem was recorded in a paper called "The Apprehension of Beauty" [chapter 6, this volume], where I also failed to grasp what I had glimpsed, as I think had Hannah Segal in her famous paper on aesthetics.

And so they came together: the key of alpha-function and the lock of two-dimensionality; and an apposite metaphor it seemed. The problem area that the key of symbol formation was called into play to open, was the enigma of the inside and the outside of the aesthetic object. Its power to evoke emotionality was only equalled by its ability to generate anxiety, doubt, distrust. While the sensual qualities of the aesthetic object could be apprehended with some degree of confidence, its internal qualities, being infra- or supra-sensual, carried no such comfort. Here observation needed to be coupled with thought and judgment, and judgment depended greatly for its firmness on experience. For it was in the matching or disparity of this outside and inside of the object of awe, and wonder that its value for good or evil must surely reside. But the baby's experience of the world is almost nil. How is it to exercise such judgment? It cannot; it can only wait to see what will happen next.

This then would be the context in which absence of the object makes its crucial impact and tests the mettle. Bion has defined this problem of the absent object as "the absent object as a present persecutor" with respect to the "space where the object used to be", perhaps also by implication including Berkeley's "ghosts of departed quantities". These "times that try men's souls"[1] and find out the "summer soldier" in the depths must be infinitely more stressful for the baby when we remember their impact on Othello and Leontes, and "La Belle Dame Sans Merci". Trust would then be a compound quality of mind, like foot-pounds as a definition of work: hope–hours, or minutes or days or years. In the very young it can at times seem more to be hope–seconds as the baby's face crumples when mother turns the corner out of sight.

By defining the fundamental problem of aesthetic relations in this way and by asserting the aesthetic relationship to the world and the primal stimulus to thought, we have adopted a position compatible with a field theory that is also inherently genetic. What it does, that the differentiation of paranoid–schizoid and depressive positions fails to do in their adherence to a Life and Death Instinct foundation, is to allow for a purely mental approach to values unencumbered by biological speculation. While the issue of mental pain and tolerance thereof loses none of its clinical vibrance as an arbiter of ego strength, a new factor is introduced to the dynamism of conflict. Trust, in units of hope–time, schematically speaking, would seem to have qualitative roots in the richness of the aesthetic experience to which separation is the sequel. And this richness is surely to be found in the element of mutuality of apprehension of beauty. For the baby must be held as an aesthetic object by the mother for the experience of their love-making to reverberate and escalate in intensity.

Such a basis which allows us to conceive the "how" of the calling into action of the capacity for symbolic thought, the product of the mysterious alpha-function, more or less releases us from any great concern with the "when" of the matter. Pre-natal or post-natal, it must occur. And if this conjunction of mutuality is its essential ingredient, its inception may be widely variable in time. But, sadly, we must recognize that it may not occur at all, as in the children who do not seem to make the post-natal adjustment or whose neurophysiological apparatus is not of sufficient complexity to achieve the aesthetic level of response. The autist and the non-developer may taste it and rebel against its dominance.

But more important for clinical practice is the corollary, that the defensive operations which psychoanalysis is specially fashioned to follow may mostly, perhaps entirely, be seen as moves against the impact of the aesthetic object, although this is not apparent in the early days of an analysis. It comes, in my view, at the threshold of the depressive position, after confusions have been sorted out. How then does this view essentially differ from Melanie Klein's formulations, and what precisely are the alterations in the consulting room which are generated by it?

Undoubtedly the first and most important alteration is a diminished emphasis on the "correctness" of interpretation, perhaps a lessening of

174 POST-KLEINIAN THOUGHT

the urgency to interpret altogether. Instead the focus moves forwards, as it were, into the interaction, the relationship from which interpretive ideas emerge. The model of container–contained places a new value on receptiveness and the holding of the dynamic situation of transference–countertransference in the mind. But perhaps to state this as if the analyst were the container misses the point that it is the fitting together of the analyst's attention and attitudes to the cooperativeness of the patient that forms and seals the container, lending it the degree of flexibility and resilience required from moment to moment.

Interpretation therefore loses its explanatory function, partly from the altered nature of the situation but also because the analyst has lost his causal orientation to mental events. The field of mental states will not allow the language of linearity to assert itself, falling away in favour of attempts at description, hopelessly inadequate in a sense, as a painting would be useless as a basis for botanical research. Instead the metaphor of illumination replaces explanation. I well remember visiting a cave in the Dordogne, Combarelles I think, full of engravings of ice-age animals. As the guide moved his lamp about from one angle to another different superimposed images sprang from the wall. This image of the analyst's verbal task, to shine a light of understanding from one vertex after another, modifies the atmosphere of communication to an extraordinary degree, diminishing the authoritarian expectations of the patient and sharing the responsibility between the members of the Work Group of two. It also allows an interpretive line gradually to form. Certain dreams—the dreams and not their interpretations—establish the landmarks for both members. The function of understanding, with all its uncertainty and readiness to yield its place, by divesting the analyst of the expectation of knowing, allows him far greater freedom of speculation. Intuitions for which the evidence is not as yet obtrusive can freely be given, the degree of uncertainty being indicated by the music of the voice. Since the mystification of seeming omniscience is thus stripped from the relationship, the patient becomes more interested in the method and welcomes explanation of the rationale of the analyst's behaviour. All this, including the improved definition of the shape which the psychoanalytic process seems to be assuming, tends to erect the concept of the science, the process, the method—taken together perhaps with its personal and institutional history—as a thing-in-itself that can, eventually, be apprehended as an aesthetic object.

This has far-reaching implications for the transference and counter-transference for it establishes an object upon which are not imposed, in Freud's terms, the limitations inherent in the "particularities" of the analyst—his age, sex, appearance, known facts about his life situation, his values, politics, etc. In fact it allows for the formation of an object which the therapist and patient can examine together from a certain distance, in the same way that one steps back from most paintings to allow the composition to impinge, and then steps forward to appreciate the brush strokes and craftsmanship.

Psychoanalysis as a thing-in-itself, and its particular manifestation in the patient's own experience of analysis, comes to form a link to the internal part object, the maternal thinking–breast as combined object, breast and nipple. The functions that the analyst is felt to perform within the analytical process assume definitive shape, greatly clarifying the nature of the felt dependence. Acting out in search of substitutes during the separations stands out clearly both for the adequacy or the inadequacy of these facsimiles. The analyst is therefore in a better position to help the patient to appraise the usefulness of these alternative relationships and not merely to oppose them on the assumption that they must necessarily impoverish the transference.

It is in this connection that the externalization of the patient's narcissistic organization with the individuals and groups comes under a new and more precise scrutiny, for the basis of judgment need not rest on value alone. It is true that shifting the basis of value judgment from moral or even ethical criteria to developmental ones (which often means suspension of judgment) softens the harshness of the analyst's interventions with regard to narcissistic-based relationships, since his attitude is bound to lack a basis in demonstrable evidence, except for dreams. But when the modes of thought and avenues of communication can also be brought under scrutiny it is often possible to demonstrate the deficits in quality of thought. This is most clear when a Basic Assumption Group involvement is at issue, but even in the ganging with one or more acquaintances the "misjoyning" functions of the Negative Grid (Milton's "mimic fansie") can often be demonstrated.

This avenue of enquiry into group communication processes is surely a Bionic addition to our equipment for investigating the workings of narcissism. Nowhere is it more clear than with perverse areas of the personality which so quietly drain the vitality of object relations. And here Bion's formulation of positive and negative emotional links sheds a brilliant light. "But am I not a part of this man's emotional life?" the perverse area seems to say, claiming a certain respectability and rightful share in the world of human intimacy. A dualistic theory, of Life and Death, of Creative and Destructive drives, gives no definitive answer except a grudging, "Yes, but you must be subservient, integrated for good and creative ends", something the perverse aspect will smilingly accept, secretly triumphant. But when the perverse trends are recognized as anti-emotions, minus L, H and K, no ground need be yielded to them in compromise.

The concept of a Negative Grid and the recognition by Bion that knowledge of the truth is necessary for the construction of effective lies (lies to oneself as well as to others), has delivered a powerful tool into our hands for scrutinizing the content and operations of cynical attacks on the truth. While I have never found the Grid useful for analytic contemplation, as Bion originally suggested,[2] its format is wonderfully revealing of shifts of levels of abstraction and accompanying paradoxical statements. This leads on to greater skill in examining the defensive and evasive functions of ambiguous language usage as well as defects in logical operations, pseudo-quantifications, false equations and spurious similes.

Taken together these tools for minute scrutiny of processes of thought and communication place the analyst in a far stronger position than ever before in the struggle to wrest infantile structures from the domination or influence of destructive parts of the personality which organize the narcissistic or Basic Assumption groupings internally or in the outside world.

Finally we must examine the important matter of our private and corporate definition of psychoanalysis and its implications for our methods of work in the consulting room. I do not mean to refer to the political aspects of the problem, such as defining psychoanalysis as what members of the Psycho-Analytical Society do, or five-times-per-week by definition, or extra-institutional and so forth. These local definitions are fitted to local political problems and are not of scientific interest. The important problems are ones of private definition and public presentation to one's colleagues.

Essentially our private definition must rest on two piers, the method and the process that it engenders. Almost everyone in the field would agree that the essence of the method is the scrutiny and description of the transference by way of internal examination of the countertransference. There is far less agreement, or need of agreement, about the nature of the therapeutic process generated by these operations. It is not unlikely that the process varies from analyst to analyst, perhaps from patient to patient, in essential ways. But all would agree that each analyst needs, eventually, to have formulated his own conception of the type or range of processes that he considers useful in an analysis that is progressing. It is clear that he cannot use therapeutic criteria, either observed or reported. There is after all no need for analysts to claim any monopoly of therapeutic potency.

Having formed such a conception of type or range of process, the analyst should be in a position to be more flexible in meeting the demands of his patients with regard to frequency, duration of sessions, spacing, missing of sessions or periods of therapy, methods of payment, use of the couch, bringing or sending of written or graphic materials, interviews with relatives. Caution can replace rigidity of style and method when basic personal concepts of method and process have been established from experience with the particular patient and practice in general. Modifications in style and method introduced by the analyst should still be viewed with the greatest suspicion and avoided, probably, except for bona fide organized research. But a flexible response to a patient's requests, based on experience and firmness of concept, backed by careful scrutiny of the previous and ensuing material, can have a beneficial, humanizing and encouraging effect. The consequences for the analyst are, however, far more important. Such an orientation obliges him to engage in continual careful scrutiny of the rationale of his procedures and thus to promote his own learning from experience.

Notes

1. Tom Paine, *Common Sense* [1776].

2. See *Bion in New York and Sao Paulo* (Bion, 1980), p. 56, for his later thoughts on the subject.

CHAPTER THIRTEEN

Aesthetic conflict:
its place in the developmental process
(1988)

Donald Meltzer & Meg Harris Williams

T he evolution of the Model of the Mind which underlies the observation and thoughts of psychoanalysts has been a quiet and
covert one in many respects but its nodal points are clearly
marked by the progression Freud–Abraham–Klein–Bion. What began
as a hydrostatic model for the distribution of psychic energy in the
spirit of nineteenth century physics, gradually shifted its analogy. The
emergence of the genetic aspect brought forth the archaeological metaphor; the replacement of topography by structural imagery introduced
a social comparison (the ego serving three masters); the replacement of
"mechanism" by "unconscious phantasy", the insistence on the "concreteness of psychic reality" and the introduction of an "epistemophilic" instinct to replace Freud's "sexual researches of children",
shifted the biological model of the evolution of the individual mind
from a Darwinian to a Lamarckian basis. By 1945 the Kleinian model
had achieved this modification of the evolutionary simile of ontogeny
recapitulating phylogeny, on the basis of a strengthened position for
identification processes and thus of a view of development which emphasized relationship with objects rather than anything equivalent to
survival of the fittest. Melanie Klein's 1946 paper "Notes on Some
Schizoid Mechanisms", which introduced the ideas of projective identification and splitting processes, shattered the assumption of unity of
the mind, which Freud had already begun to do in his paper "Splitting
of the Ego in the Process of Defence" [Freud, 1940e(1938)]; it further-

more opened up a multiplication of the "worlds" of mental life in a way that even the "concreteness of psychic reality" had not envisaged. The Bionic transformation, which divides mental life into the symbolic and non-symbolic areas (alpha-function and beta elements), and places its emphasis on the mind as an instrument for thinking about emotional experiences, has only began to be felt in the consulting rooms. But Bion's firm relegation of creative thought to the unconscious dream process, and his limitation of consciousness to the "organ for the perception of psychic qualities", must in time give a decisive blow to the equation of "reason" with consciousness and profoundly alter our view of how our lives are lived. Freud's model becomes severely modified: the ego becomes the horse, shying at every unknown object in its path, always wanting to follow in the way it has gone before; while the unconscious internal objects become the rider directing it relentlessly towards new developmental experiences. How profoundly, accordingly, does our view of the psychoanalytic process change under this model; yet in a way we seem to return full circle to Freud's early view of resistance and compulsion to repeat, merely changing the venue of these anti-developmental forces from the repressed unconscious to the conservative conscious mind.

This Bionic shift in the Model of the Mind must cause us to rethink the whole problem of mental pain and the developmental process from infancy. We cannot take the newborn child as a *tabula rasa* but must consider the possibility that emotional experiences, their symbolic representation in dream thought, and their impact on the structuring of the personality, may commence *in utero*. It requires no great stretching of the imagination to conceive of the latter months of intrauterine life, *malgré* the findings of neuroanatomists about myelinization, as being fraught with emotionality. Nor is it beyond us to imagine the auditory aspects of intrauterine life, coupled to kinaesthesia, as capable of symbolic representation in the song-and-dance genre (Susanne Langer) of symbolic forms (Cassirer). It is a small step from such speculation to an "emotional" rather than a "traumatic" idea of the impact of the birth process and the first encounter with the world "outside". At the present time such speculations may seem to be beyond verification by observation, but perhaps some of the ultrasound (echographic) observations of foetal life followed after birth by infant observation and later by psychoanalysis may in time bring these fanciful ideas into more authenticated form.

But both psychoanalysis and infant observation already afford rich data for moulding these speculations into a form which can modify our image of development and mental life in the Bionic vein. It has probably escaped no-one's attention that the percentage of "beautiful" mothers recorded in the course of psychoanalysis far exceeds the national average and that this appellation clearly refers back to childhood impressions often completely out of keeping with later more objective judgements by the patients of their middle-aged parent. We will start here.

First I should like to introduce a piece of clinical material as an anchorage for further discussion and exploration. An ageing poet had entered analysis owing to the repeated failure of his love relationships to endure and deepen into marriage, for he greatly desired children as well as the stable companionship of a woman. The loss of his mother in latency had been followed by an estrangement from his father due to the extreme and probably paranoid jealousy of the stepmother who entered into his life within two years of the mother's death. Herself a widow with children, the stepmother could not bear to share her home with another woman's children and had them all sent off to boarding schools. Dread of a woman's jealousy and possessiveness had wrecked most of the patient's intimate relationships: sometimes jealousy rooted in the partner, sometimes in her mother, and sometimes provoked by the patient's enduring and close friendships with former partners or with the wives of his brothers or close friends. Being a very, attractive and able figure, it was by no means merely his phantasy that these women might have preferred him to the spouses who variously deserted and disappointed them.

During the first year of analysis the holiday breaks had not seemed to touch our poet for he had used them to undertake rather exciting trips which he had dutifully postponed to accommodate the analytic schedule. But there was evidence that the approaching Christmas, the fourth break, was beginning to rattle him a little as it drew nearer. Gardens of great beauty began to appear in his dreams along with buried hostility to an older brother whose behaviour with girls, and later with women, he considered ruthless and destructive. In the penultimate week before the break he announced in passing something about which I had heard nothing previously: that he had been overtaken by his collecting impulse. This had taken various forms since puberty, starting with stamps, then prints, antiquarian books, etc.,—each of brief but intense duration. This time it was commemorative medals, the production of which had apparently started in the seventeenth century, and examples of which—being without great monetary value—could chiefly be found in junk shops. It had been inspired by a friend whose collection he had just seen. Somehow it seemed to link with his being drawn into a marital conflict between very close friends, both of whom used him as confidant. Sensing a move closely bound up with known devices by means of which he distanced himself from the grief of his mother's sudden death, I tried to investigate this phenomenon minutely for it seemed likely that it was being invoked to abort the impact of the approaching break in analysis. The patient took umbrage at my interest, which, I fear, was a little heavy-handed and perhaps needlessly urgent.

However the urgency bore immediate fruit in dreams. To the first session of the following week, the ultimate, he brought the following two dreams:

He awoke in a little VW as if from a drunken sleep (he had drunk a little the night before and does not own a car) *to find that it was precariously perched on a cliff edge in Devon, and if he leaned forward the car tipped further quite dangerously while it did the opposite if he leaned* back (we both immediately thought of *The Gold Rush*). *Then he had arrived at the hotel owned by Jean Shrimpton to meet his friends but found the man without his wife, accompanied by another friend's girlfriend. Then he was in a garden accompanied by the couple's children and trying to climb a wall to get out. But the wall had an overhang* (sic!) *which made this impossible. However the woman then called him to come inside and suggested that he might like to trim the neighbour's hedge. But he demurred.*

We discussed various aspects of the dream: the hangover from the last week's terminal session; the starvation of the frozen "Gold Rush" type; the fact that his friend's wife was a beauty of the Jean Shrimpton type, and also his way of presenting himself as the "good" man to women disappointed in their husbands. I suggested that this was perhaps his real "collection". In the second dream:

He had been invited by another friend to remodel his mother's garden, which was already quite well planted with clumps of bamboo, clumps of Jerusalem artichokes and something that looked like a shrub of Ragged Robin. Then they went into the house in order that the friend might show the patient his "collection" which was housed in a vertical multi-sided revolving showcase. In the first section were the commemorative medals of which he had spoken in the earlier session; in the next section there were small delicate glass phials labelled "poison" (he had recently heard of a new perfume called by that name) *while in the third section there were fragments of Roman glass, beautiful in their iridescence. One flattened flask was so lovely he felt that it must be made of some precious stone. But to his surprise further rotation did not bring the return of the medals but something quite different.*

We only touched lightly on the bamboo (caning at school), Jerusalem artichokes (famous for inducing flatus), and the Ragged Robin as an idealization of his mode of ultra-casual dress and the homeless existence after his father's remarriage. What mainly engaged our attention was that the "collection" showcase was a distorted version of a kaleidoscope. Did he collect "broken" women in lieu of being broken-hearted at his mother's death? An unexpected association seemed to confirm this. Several days before, he had by chance encountered the clergyman who had delivered the oration at his mother's funeral, which he and his siblings had not attended, all being away at school. This man, he discovered, had been a friend of his mother's in her university days and waxed quite lyrical about her great beauty, charm, vivacity and intelligence. Her qualities of character the patient had never forgotten, but her great beauty came as a surprise. Were then the phials of poison/perfume little funerary tear vessels of Roman fame? Had he obviated the grief of mourning by constructing a kaleidoscopic image of his mother's character out of fragments of memory, thus replacing a more primal concept of her physical beauty by a more sophisticated one of the fineness of her personality?

Some material from the weeks prior to these events would seem to lend force to this suggestion. During the previous month I had been hearing, en passant, of pregnant women, breast-feeding women and women yearning for babies in the face of their mates' reluctance. One evening at a dinner party he had been offended, not on his own account but for the violation of the baby's privacy, when a woman fed her baby at the breast at the dinner table. That night he dreamed:

While standing on a tube platform with a male friend he noticed two girls with a man. One of them seemed to be offering her magnificent breasts for the man's admiration in a way that made the patient laugh.

It was not at all clear what his laugh had meant; certainly not derision, for the girl's attitude seemed so innocent. Perhaps he had laughed in the dream from pure joy and admiration. A second dream that night presented three rather static images contrasting with the "magnificent breasts":

The first image was an aerial view of the countryside, the receding flood waters leaving behind the hedgerows piled up mud in which dead bodies could be seen (like scenes from the recent Colombian disaster). *In the second image a film set had been constructed in a squash court consisting of a grassy hill on which a couple of stone armchairs rested; in the third he was surprised at how tatty the décor of the opera seemed until a young girl*

*pulled a lever to show him the two magnificent monsters that leaped from
two great boxes on the stage* (they were like the "wonderful" monsters
drawn by Sendak in *Where the Wild Things Are*).

In summary I suggested that these images could be condensed into a
single statement of the disastrous effect upon him of suddenly seeing
his mother's breasts emerge from her brassiere (the hedgerows–squash
court–boxes) to feed his baby sister, a "monstrous" thing for her to do
right in front of him at the age of four.

In the light of the later material I am inclined to make two further
connections: first of all, between the stone armchairs and the flask that
was so beautiful he thought it must be made of precious stone rather
than glass; and secondly between the dead bodies in the mud behind
the hedgerows and the collection of commemorative medals (perhaps
showing draped and undraped figures in bronze?).

I propose now to leave this splendid material hovering in the background, to be referred back to as I proceed to the main body of the
exposition. The psychoanalytical stance regarding emotions or affects
has probably been severely hampered by Freud's early neurophysiological model, in which quantities of excitation of the mental apparatus were seen to be apprehended subjectively as emotions. On the other
hand Freud clearly espoused Darwin's attitude that emotions are experienced as the consequence of the perception of one's own social behaviour, with affective display being a relic of primitive modes of social
communication. The paradoxicality of embracing both views was lessened by the separating-off of mental pain under the general rubric of
"anxiety", again viewed as a quantitative representation of dammed up
impulse. The essential failure to distinguish between the experience of
emotion and the display of emotional states placed the theory of the
meaning of emotions in a kind of conceptual limbo. Even Melanie
Klein's more detailed dissection and differentiation of emotions failed
to correct this. The classical juxtaposition of emotion and reason, with
its implied denigratory contrasting of female and male mentality, akin
to primitive/civilized and infantile/adult, failed to find any correction
until Bion's Theory of Thinking.

In many ways the object-relations direction set by Abraham in his
"Short Study of the Libido" [1924(105)], with its exciting delineation of
part-object and whole-object relationships, mapped the perimeter of a
territory it failed to explore. The objects were left with their anatomical
state as their substantiating feature, while the meaning of this fragmentation remained largely unnoticed in theory although under continuous
exploration in the consulting room. In the clinical material it was probably clear to most workers that the partial anatomical reference was the

consequence of a limitation in meaning: that partial objects had been deprived of their essential mentality, their capacity for feeling and thought and judgement, while retaining their formal and sensual features. They could be used, valued, feared, placated but they could not be loved and admired, protected and served. Only the fetishist, with his partial (or even more dismantled) object, could succeed in caricaturing the passions which whole objects could arouse.

It was perfectly natural for Melanie Klein, therefore, working on the assumption of unity of the mind and Darwinian expectation of evolution of the individual from simplicity to complexity, to place her formulation of the paranoid–schizoid position in chronological primacy. The "red in tooth and claw" implication of the equation of immaturity with primitiveness saw no need to think twice. Pain and persecution could simply be taken as synonymous. But the 1946 paper on schizoid mechanisms changed all that. The gross simplification of mental life presented by psychoanalytical theory could hardly even be taken as a skeletal structure upon which phenomenological flesh derived from the consulting room could be hung. A far more complex model was required to describe the follies, inconsistencies and astonishing self-ignorance of human beings. It was no longer sufficient to cleave to a medical model that could assume that the absence of disease constituted mental health, as if the mind functioned by a physiology and embryology directly analogous to the body. It became necessary to take into account the whole spectrum, like the Rat Man's father declaring of his enraged child that he would grow up either to be a great man or a great criminal.

Outside the invisible walls of psychoanalytical thought it is probably generally accepted, again unthinkingly I would say, that the brain is a giant computer and that the mind is the brain, any other description being mere metaphor. But of course that is exactly the point: the mind is the metaphor-generating function which uses the great computer to write its poetry and paint its pictures of a world scintillating with meaning. And meaning is in the first instance the fundamental manifestation of the passions of intimate relationship with the beauty of the world.

Once one has taken on board Bion's description of "an emotional experience" as the primary developmental event, it becomes clear that his "empty" concepts of alpha-function and beta-elements make, essentially, a distinction between symbol formation and thought on the one hand, and a computation using signs and simple modes of extrapolation from past experience and received ideas, on the other. The creation of idiosyncratic symbols as opposed to the manipulation of conventional signs, marks the watershed between growth of the personality and adaptation. The tension between the two is the essence of what

Freud labelled as "resistance to enquiry". Bion's distinction between "learning from experience" and "learning about" the world is precise. It is likewise marked by the distinction we make between narcissistic forms of identification (projective and adhesive) which produce an immediate and somewhat delusive alteration in the sense of identity, and the introjective process by which our internal objects are modified, setting up gradients of aspiration for the growth of the self.

Our lives are greatly occupied by relationships which are not intimate. Rousseau's Social Contract well describes the way in which we move about the world, using the lubrication of manner and custom, of conformity and social invisibility to minimize the friction and thus the wear and tear on our psyche–soma. And it is probably in this area that the majority of psychosomatic dislocations take place. The "hostages to fate" aspect of our posture towards the casual world of teeming humanity, where "everything threatens the head that I love", intimidates us beyond our wildest imaginings. We strive to create, through our apparent docility to the requirements of the community, a private space in which to enjoy the usufruct of our inheritance without "let or hindrance". These manoeuvres create the social armour which Wilhelm Reich described so wonderfully. But we are confronted with the problem of removing it when "at home" and donning it again in time to sally forth. We dread to send our little children naked into the world of the nursery and the school, and, later, to see them swallowed up by the great combine harvester of the adolescent community.

Of the people who do not manage the enclosure of this space of privacy and intimacy, two distinct classes, at the antipodes of the body of the community, can be distinguished. The first of these, comprising the mentally and socially ill, are cut off from intimacy by the severity of their delusional ideas: either from living in states of projective identification, or from a gross failure of development of the personality, or from such perseverance in infantile modes of relationship that intimacy of an adult sort cannot develop. The second class are the artists, whose pained perception of the inhumanities daily in force about them, juxtaposed to a vision of the beauty of the world being vandalized by these primitive social processes, forbids them to squander the huge blocks of lifetime required for adaptation. If lucky they are spared by the community from total neglect or persecution, but at the expense of having their work appropriated and misused, ridiculed and imitated, all at the same time. The recent vogue in literary criticism is a precise example of acting-out ambivalence and hostility towards the artists. At best they are treated as members of the amusement industry.

The huge majority of caring parents, seeing all about them the misery of maladaptation, cannot help being primarily concerned, in their methods of upbringing, with armouring their children against the inhumanities inflicted on both the poorly adapted and on those whose naked sensitivity makes them vulnerable to the grossness of inconsiderate behaviour in casual and contractual relations. Similarly our schools cannot resist the pressure from parents and government alike to direct their efforts toward producing employable grown-ups. One must see the facts without seeming to pretend that any alternative is close at hand. We wish to prepare our children for the beauties of intimacy but our anxieties for their survival overcome our judgement so that we find ourselves joining in the training process, knowing quite well that it will dampen their thirst for knowledge and constrict their openness to the beauties to which they stand heir.

Although this process reaches its climax in the establishment of the so-called latency period, close observation of family life and of the mother–infant relationship reveals evidence of its early commencement. No event of adult life is so calculated to arouse our awe of the beauty and our wonder at the intricate workings of what we call Nature (since we hesitate nowadays to cite first causes), as the events of procreation. No flower or bird of gorgeous plumage imposes upon us the mystery of the aesthetic experience like the sight of a young mother with her baby at the breast. We enter such a nursery as we would a cathedral or the great forests of the Pacific coast, noiselessly, bareheaded. Winnicott's stirring little radio talks of many years ago on "The Ordinary Devoted Mother and her Baby" could just as well have spoken of the "ordinary beautiful devoted mother and her ordinary beautiful baby". He was right to use that word "ordinary", with its overtones of regularity and custom, rather than the statistical "average". The aesthetic experience of the mother with her baby is ordinary, regular, customary, for it has millennia behind it, since man first saw the world "as" beautiful. And we know this goes back at least to the last glaciation.

Correspondingly it is only the limitations in our ability to identify with the baby that leaves him, in our thoughts, denuded of mentality. This ordinary beautiful baby does come trailing Wordsworthian clouds of glory in his openness to the apprehension of the world about him, if not the wisdom that can make him "father to the man" (although, to do Wordsworth justice, his "little philosopher" is five years, and not five days, old). Proto-aesthetic experiences can well be imagined to have commenced *in utero*: "rocked in the cradle of the deep" of his mother's graceful walk; lulled by the music of her voice set against the syncopation of his own heart-beat and hers; responding in dance like a little seal, playful as a puppy. But moments of anxiety, short of foetal distress, may also attack the foetus: maternal anxiety may also transmit itself through heartbeat, rigidity, trembling, jarring movements; perhaps a coital activity may be disturbing rather than enjoyable, perhaps again dependent on the quality of maternal emotion; maternal fatigue may transmit itself by loss of postural tone and graceless movement. Perhaps above all the foetus may feel his growth as the narrowing of his home in typical claustrophobic fashion and deduce that life exists beyond its familiar bounds, a shocking idea to a natural flat-earther. Imagination is a foraging impulse; it will find food for thought in the desert.

How, then, may the bombardment of colour, form and patterned sound of such augmented intensity as greets the newborn, impinge upon his mind? This we must ask the moment we consider that the baby's mind may already have begun its functions of imaginatively and thoughtfully exploring the world of its emotional interest. The great variety of demeanour and behaviour of the newborn is too obvious for anyone seeing them in the mass, as in an obstetrical department, to ignore; but of course this has always been ascribed to variation in constitution, or temperament, or differing degrees of foetal distress during birth, etc. The making of such ascriptions has neither descriptive nor explanatory power and merely dismisses the problem. Certainly it is no more speculative to say that babies experience the birth process and the first encounters with the world of intense *sensa* with differing attitudes, ranging from complete aversion to ecstatic wonder at the "brave new world". Two great allegories that define these two poles of birth experience, namely Harold Pinter's *Birthday Party* and Shakespeare's *The Tempest*, both define with great clarity the baby's relation to the placenta and its transformations. Our poet's kaleidoscope-collection cabinet inside the house is an attacked placental image just as the three images of the next dream reveal the jealously attacked "magnificent breasts". Bion's paper on "The Imaginary Twin" [1950] pursues this same theme of the imagery of the placenta; but only in his last work, the trilogy *A Memoir of the Future* [Bion, 1991], does he discuss the implications of prenatal mental life and the role that the cut-off prenatal parts of the personality play in later psychopathology.

This type of imaginative conjecture cannot aspire to any status other than that of being credible, or at least as credible as such unimaginative formulations as "constitution", "heredity", or "just like his father was as a baby". At any rate for our purpose here it is quite sufficient to establish credibility as a basis for interest in the wider speculation for which, however, we do have evidence that is more than merely suggestive. Since this wider speculation is the heart of the matter of this book it needs a small preamble of its own in the context of the history of psychoanalytical ideas.

Although it may not have found its official statement until *The Ego and The Id* [1923b], from at least the time of "Little Hans" Freud was aware that mental pain and mental—that is, intrapsychic—conflict were absolutely bound together. Such was Freud's Darwinian bias towards action as the ultimate goal of mental functioning that varieties of mental pain, generally lumped together as "anxiety", including even the grief of mourning, needed to be given a heuristic value as "signal" of some danger. I say even the grief of mourning for his emphasis is upon this emotion as a signal that hopes and aspirations connected with the lost one require to be relinquished in the "work" of mourning.

There is a subtle though immensely significant change in attitude towards mental pain in the work of Melanie Klein. Its most obvious item is the classification of mental pains into persecutory and depressive, but this represents an expansion and clarification of Freud rather than a fundamental change in attitude. It is true that her classification somehow carries the implication that persecutory pain is "bad" and depressive pain "good" because they have reference to regressive and progressive developmental trends respectively. But the more important alteration, growing out of her forward-looking, developmental orientation, as compared to Freud's essentially backwards-looking, psychopathological interest, is her insistence that a certain level of mental pain, different though it is for different people, is essential for development of the personality. It is true that she assumed that the basic developmental schema was inbuilt, either by genetics, pre-history, social process or internal logic, but she saw clearly that an optimal level of anxiety favoured developmental conflict and its resolution, while both too much and too little of such pain favoured stagnation or regression.

Important as these differences from Freud may be, the basic area of agreement was there: that mental pain was in one way or another related to frustration of impulse life. Only in the 1957 paper, "Envy and gratitude", did she break with this blanket assertion. Envy of the good object for possession of its good attributes was established, yet even here it was hedged about with such ideas as "the breast that feeds itself", circling back to the thesis of frustration. This ambiguity seemed resolved by Bion in *Learning from Experience* [1962], when he described emotions as "links" and threw over the traditional dualities of love and hate in favour of a more complex and philosophically far more penetrating confrontation. First of all he extended the range of passionate links to include, along with loving and hating, knowing (L, H, and K links). But further in the tradition of Milton, Blake and Coleridge, he made the imaginative leap of confronting positive with negative emotional links: love (L) with anti-love (minus L), hate with anti-hate (minus H) and thirst for knowing with philistinism (K with minus K).

Moreover he demonstrated how intertwined are the positive links with one another, as did Blake in "The Marriage of Heaven and Hell". Likewise for the negative ones—Coleridge's "foul fiend". This immediately threw a brilliant light on hypocrisy, for instance, for may not anti-hate parade as love, and may not philistinism present itself as the guardian of scientific truth? Wordsworth says much the same thing, that "hating falsehood is not the same as loving truth".

But even Bion did not depart from the fundamental link of mental pain and frustration until Chapter 10 of *Attention and Interpretation* (1970), where he introduced the idea of "catastrophic change", a concept he later greatly expanded in *A Memoir of the Future* (Bion, 1991), especially in the third book, *The Dawn of Oblivion*. Throughout his work he had cleaved to the Keatsian formulation, "beauty is truth, truth beauty"; but only in these last works did he begin to spell out its implications. It is the "new idea" which impinges on the mind as a catastrophe for, in order to be assimilated, this sets in flux the entire cognitive structure. This view, which Darwin stated and Freud so stirringly enlarged, while not difficult to grasp in the intellectual aspect they expound, challenges imagination at the emotive level. If we follow Bion's thought closely we see that the new idea presents itself as an "emotional experience" of the beauty of the world and its wondrous organization, descriptively closer to the noumenon, to Hamlet's "heart of mystery".

The vista opened by Bion's formulation on mental pain and mental pleasure implies that the intrinsic conflict of both the positive and negative emotional links, surrounding desire and interest, is always present and that, therefore, at the passionate level—which is the level at which dream life pursues its course—pleasure and pain are inextricably bound together. But this essential conflict (from whose matrix the "learning from experience" evolves to produce structural change as opposed to augmented information,) must find its symbolic representation (alpha function) in order to become available for dream thoughts, transformation into verbal language (or other symbolic forms, as in the arts) and elaboration through abstraction, condensation, generalization and other instruments of sophisticated thinking. [These processes have been discussed at greater length by Bion and by the author in *Dream Life* (1983)]. Toleration of this conflict, which is the heart of the matter of ego strength, resides in the capacity that Bion, after Keats, has called "negative capability": the ability to remain in uncertainty without irritably reaching after fact and reason (see Keats's Letter to his brothers George and Tom, April, 1817).

In the struggle against the cynical power of the negative links this capacity to tolerate uncertainty, not knowing, the "cloud of unknowing", is constantly called upon in the passion of intimate relations and is at the heart of the matter of aesthetic conflict. Traditionally it has been shelved in the form of the concept of "first causes", which has never proved satisfactory because of the problem of "free will". Moses could talk directly with God but his followers had to have faith in him, which repeatedly disintegrated and had to be renewed by miracle or affliction.

"The spirit of the LORD was upon him and he did prophesy" sufficed for the prophets but eventually it was necessary for God himself to become incarnate in Jesus to be convincing—to some—part of the time. Kierkegaard's "leap in the dark" expresses the difficulty. How does the baby ever manage it? In terms of external reality, where Plato's ideal forms are continually set aside by the great random factor, neither the baby nor the adult ever does manage it. But fortunately the evolution of mind had not stopped at living in the outside world. The human mind constructs an inner world where meaning is displayed figuratively and justice prevails. "Let faith oust fact; let fancy oust memory; I love deep down and do believe".

And so our imaginative conjecture posits that every baby "knows" from experience that his mother has an "inside" world, a world where he has dwelled and from whence he has been expelled or escaped, depending on his point of view. The "evidence", if it will be admitted as such, is overwhelmingly in favour of the expulsion theory. But perhaps people in whom the denial of psychic reality is dominant may disagree. Freud's early view of the unconscious, and perhaps his later views of the superego, suggest that he too might have preferred the escape theory. Only in the paper "On Fetishism" did he seem to allow for the concreteness of the world of phantasy of the inside of the body, of child and mother alike.

If we may turn back to my poet's material, the friend's wife who invites him to enter from the walled garden and to "trim the neighbour's hedge" is not merely inviting him to a coitus in revenge for her husband's infidelity; she is also the mother inviting him to explore her inner world in compensation for the father's closeness to the older sister (and later his intimidation by his second wife). There, inside, he finds the deadness of the collection, the fragmentation representing the mother's death, on the one hand, and his jealous attacks on her consequent to seeing his baby sister fed at the breast. The collection, like the kaleidoscope, idealizes the fragmentation of her beauty, which he cannot remember.

At last we have arrived at the core of our discourse. I will try to state the thesis precisely, then to pursue its implications. The ordinary beautiful devoted mother presents to her ordinary beautiful baby a complex object of overwhelming interest, both sensual and infra-sensual. Her outward beauty, concentrated as it must be in her breast and her face, complicated in each case by her nipples and her eyes, bombards him with an emotional experience of a passionate quality, the result of his being able to see these objects as "beautiful". But the meaning of his mother's behaviour, of the appearance and disappearance of the breast and of the light in her eyes, of a face over which emotions pass like the shadows of clouds over the landscape, are unknown to him. He has, after all, come into a strange country where he knows neither the language nor the customary non-verbal cues and communications. The mother is enigmatic to him; she wears the Gioconda smile most of the time, and the music of her voice keeps shifting from major to minor key. Like "K" (Kafka's, not Bion's), he must wait for decisions from the "castle" of his mother's inner world. He is naturally on guard against unbridled optimism and trust, for has he not already had one dubious experience at her hands, from which he either escaped or was expelled—or perhaps he, rather than his mother, was "delivered" from the danger! Even at the moments of most satisfactory communication, nipple in mouth, she gives an ambiguous message, for although she takes the gnawing away from inside she gives a bursting thing which he must expel himself. Truly she giveth and she taketh away, both of good and bad things. He cannot tell whether she is Beatrice or his Belle Dame Sans Merci. This is the aesthetic conflict, which can be most precisely stated in terms of the aesthetic impact of the outside of the "beautiful" mother, available to the senses, and the enigmatic inside which must be construed by creative imagination. Everything in art and literature, every analysis, testifies to its perseverance through life. But what is its role in development and in the structure of psychopathology? For it is the human condition. What man knows the heart of his beloved, or his child, or his analysand, as well as he knows the heart of his enemy?

It is more than analogical to say that analysts have the same type of aesthetic conflict in their love affair with the psychoanalytical method and its framework of theory of the personality and therapeutic process. Clearly the method, with its intimacy, privacy, ethics, attentiveness, forbearance, non-judgemental stance, its continuity, open-endedness, implicit readiness for sacrifice on the analyst's part, commitment to recognize errors, sense of responsibility towards the patient and his family—all of which is embodied in the dedication to scrutinize the transference–countertransference process—all of these facets, bound together by systematic effort, make the method unequivocally an aesthetic object. But within the method is the theory by which it is practised, and this theory is notoriously open to suspicion; among the list of often mutually exclusive accusations which have been levelled against it, one may include those of being reductionist, bourgeois, cynical, simplistic, hypocritical, unscientific, messianic, satanic, anti-Christian, paternalistic, mechanistic, sexist, anti-sexual, amoral, moralistic. Every one of these slanders—for in the gross they are slanders—has a grain of truth in it. And yet the analysts of today may be laying the foundations of a science of great grandeur in the future, in the way that the alchemist laid the groundwork for modern chemistry and its astonishing accomplishments.

This may seem a harsh judgement, but the facts are there. Compared to the complexity of what transpires in our consulting rooms, our descriptions of them are fairy tales both in their simplicity and crudeness. Take the clinical material I have reported as a background to discussion: it is just a story of my memory of my impression. No amount of tape recording or video filming will help, because the heart of the matter of what transpired between my poet and myself was ineffable, infrasensual, in the air, and furthermore so complicated that my feeble organ of consciousness can at best notice its grossest landmarks, such as what we call dreams and associations.

The history of the theory of the psychoanalytical method reads like a fairy story indeed, like a logical extension of "The Emperor's New Clothes". Once upon a time there was an Emperor whose name was Freud and his patients defrauded him by clothing him in transference so that he believed that he was good and handsome and wise. But then a child called Dora laughed at him and he realized that he was just naked Freud. But then a great man, Freud, understood that the clothing of the transference had its own psychic reality and that accepting his nakedness beneath it gave him a strange beauty and power to heal his patients' minds. But later on others discovered that wearing this clothing of the transference did really effect some developmental change in wisdom and benevolence (recognition of the countertransference); while failure to remember the nakedness underneath bred grandiosity, complacency, greed. Still later it was discovered that this recognized fiction of their relationship also enabled both partners to use their minds for thinking to a degree that neither was able to do by himself (Bion). But then it began to become clear that in fact they were not using their minds, their minds were using them. Some time later . . .

The point that I am trying to make is that our theories are essentially retrospective. We gradually become aware of what we have been doing, of what has been happening in our consulting rooms, and we try, using the grossly unsatisfactory medium of language, *faute de mieux*, to describe it. But to our dismay it always sounds as if we were explaining, not just describing. And then we begin to believe our language of "because" and forget what hindsights we are expressing and we fall into militant elitist groups using the same words, and consequently became easy prey for our critics, the fashionable exponents and enemies of psychoanalysis. Our academicism makes us vulnerable.

Furthermore the teaching of psychoanalysis has taken an institutional form which has perpetuated these elitist groupings and created what Bion would call the Fight–Flight Basic Assumption mentality between groups and a Dependency BA mentality within each. To make matters worse, the publishing of scientific findings has resided within these institutions, in collusion with a ruthlessly capitalist book-publishing community. Consequently the shibboleth significance of jargon words has tended to replace their clinical descriptive meaning as derived from the aesthetic quality of the method. No outsider reading this literature (viz., my own clinical material) could ever guess the beauty of the method. It may reveal something of the beauty of the working of the mind but nothing of the aesthetic of the method by which this is made manifest.

It is my distinct impression that this poisoned atmosphere of institutionalized psychoanalysis has bred a certain shyness about speaking of love in the transference and countertransference, for fear of appearing sentimental or of colluding in the covert aggression of the erotic transference. The term "good" has come to mean little other than "gratifying", while "truth" has lost its intentional quality and has been replaced by "verisimilitude" or a purely technical meaning something akin to "accurate", or perhaps "similar" in its geometric sense. Of course there is always the danger of the sharp edge of psychoanalytic instruments being blunted by the rubbery qualities of Humanism (what Meg Harris Williams calls "soft humanism") and Sociological Relativism. The absence of the vocabulary of aesthetics in the literature of psychoanalysis, at least in its theoretical vocabulary, is nowhere more stunningly illustrated than in Melanie Klein's *Narrative of a Child Analysis* [1975b]. The terse and even harsh language of her theories, and their preponderant concern with the phenomenology of the paranoid–schizoid position, stands in astonishing contrast to the emotional, and certainly at times passionate, climate of her relationship to Richard and of his overwhelming preoccupation with the vulnerability of the beauty of the world to Hitler's destructiveness and his own.

Thus it is that the literature of psychoanalysis, anxious for medical and scientific respectability, has also gone along unthinkingly with certain cultural preconceptions about babies. Everyone is agreed that mental life, in all its richness of emotionality, thought, judgment and decision, must start at some time. Systematic observation of the mother–infant relationship, as developed by Esther Bick and practised in the training of child psychotherapists at the Tavistock Clinic from as early as 1950, reveals unmistakeably the meaningfulness of what to casual observation seem to be the random patterns of the baby's activities. These early patterns, watched through their evolution in the first two years of life, tell a story of character development and lend emphasis to the importance of the matrix of relationship and communication between mother and infant from the very first moments of post-natal life. Similarly the impact of interferences such as prematurity, incubation, early separations, failures of breast feeding, physical illness in mother or baby reveal themselves in character development as unmistakeably as the "shakes" in a piece of timber mark early periods of drought.

It is necessary to plead for this recognition because the period of maximal beatification between mother and baby arises very early, soon to be clouded by varying degrees of post-partum depression in the mother and, as I am asserting, the baby's reaction against the aesthetic impact. The picture of Madonna-and-child is not always very enduring, but it is deeply convincing. One can see its power repeated in later years when a grandmother holds her distressed grandchild, waiting for its mother to return to feed it; thirty years drop from her visage as the bliss of success in calming the child spreads through her being. It is this moment when the ordinary beautiful devoted mother holds her ordinary beautiful baby and they are lost in the aesthetic impact of one another that I wish to establish in all its power—and all its afterimage of pain. "Isn't it a pity that they have to grow up!" What congruent shaft of pain goes through the baby?

> Why did I laugh tonight? No voice will tell:
>   No god, no Demon. of severe response,
> Deigns to reply from Heaven or from Hell.
>   Then to my human heart I turn at once—
> Heart! thou and I are here and alone;
>   Say, wherefore did I laugh! O mortal pain!
> O Darkness! Darkness! ever must I moan,
>   To question Heaven and Hell and Heart in vain.
> Why did I laugh? I know this being's lease
>   My fancy to its utmost blisses spreads;
> Yet could I on this very midnight cease,
>   And the world's gaudy ensigns see in shreds.
> Verse, fame, and Beauty are intense indeed,
>   But Death intenser—Death is Life's high meed.
>
> [John Keats]

I think Melanie Klein was wrong to assume that the paranoid–schizoid position in object relations was anterior to the depressive position. This preconception coloured her language and distorted her thought about the processes of development. The depressive position was "reached", or "attained" or "achieved" by three months, she thought; and the evidence for it was a noticeable change in the baby's eyes. But this entailed a tragic view of the depressive position, a relic of the "romantic agony" which plays such a role in Freud's thought about the Oedipus Complex. It stands human values on its head, looking back at the relinquished object instead of forward to development and the possibility of an enriched object which the very relinquishment makes attainable. It has, as it were, a linear structure of possession and loss, rather than a complex image capable of gathering both past and future into the immediacy of a present experience. Bion has seen it more correctly in his little formula $Ps \leftrightarrow D$ as the repeated oscillation in integration and values that must be traversed with every "catastrophic change" throughout life.

Keats's poem might appear, on a superficial reading, to be an expression of the "romantic agony". Indeed he had to explain to his friends, who were alarmed at his poem, that he was not extolling death but rather the way in which the idea of death is central to the experience of life and beauty, as he explained shortly after:

> She dwells with Beauty—Beauty that must die;
> And joy, whose hand is ever at his lips
> Bidding adieu . . .
>
> ["Ode on Melancholy"]

The tragic element in the aesthetic experience resides, not in the transience, but in the enigmatic quality of the object: "Joy, whose hand is ever at his lips / Bidding adieu." Is it a truthful object that is always reminding the lover of the transience, or a tantalizing one, like La Belle Dame? The aesthetic conflict is different from the romantic agony in this respect: that its central experience of pain resides in uncertainty, tending towards distrust, verging on suspicion. The lover is naked as Othello to the whisperings of Iago, but is rescued by the quest for knowledge, the K-link, the desire to know rather than to possess the object of desire. The K-link points to the value of the desire as itself the stimulus to knowledge, not merely as a yearning for gratification and control over the object. *Desire makes it possible, even essential, to give the object its freedom.*

In my experience this is the heart of the essential shift manifest in the threshold phenomena between Ps and D. It is true, as Melanie Klein spelled out, that the shift involves the transformation from self-interest in safety and comfort to concern for the welfare of the loved object. But that does not describe the modus operandi of the shift. For in the interplay of joy and pain, engendering the love (L) and hate (H) links of ambivalence, it is the quest for understanding (K-link) that rescues the relationship from impasse. This is the point at which Negative Capability exerts itself, where Beauty and Truth meet. Consider our poet's delicately balanced "Gold Rush" state of mind, awakening from a drunken state in his VW (?fuck-wagon, masturbation chamber?) Why did he laugh when he saw the "magnificent breasts" so innocently offered in the dream, as with the woman feeding her baby at the dinner table? Joy and outrage seem to have been placed in conflict, depending on whether he was identifying with the baby or seeing it as his baby sister, as evidence of the parental sexuality, or of his mother's insensitivity? Or cruelty? Or flamboyant exhibitionism? How quickly he was tipped over into seeing the breast as full of dead babies (the bodies in the mud) or as exhibitionist and hard (the film-set hill with the stone armchairs) or as tatty with child-frightening nipples (the monsters from *Where the Wild Things Are* [Sendak, 1963]).

If, in fact, for the ordinary beautiful baby with his ordinary devoted beautiful mother, this aesthetic impact is what greets his emergence into the world outside the womb, then the aesthetic conflict and the depressive position would be primary for development, and the paranoid–schizoid secondary—the consequence of his closing down his perceptual apertures against the dazzle of the sunrise. In Plato's terms he would hasten back into the cave. But such metaphors tell us nothing of how it happens. Perhaps Wordsworth's "getting and spending / we lay waste our powers" can give us a hint if we apply it to the transactions of infancy and early childhood. Who, after all, is more materialistic than the small child? And the "Gold Rush" implications of our poet's dream? There was a moving little scene in that masterpiece of the screen *The Treasure of Sierra Madre*, when the old prospector, Walter Huston, insists against the opposition of the greedy and paranoid Humphrey Bogart, that, having been allowed to remove a fortune in gold from the mountain's interior, they must, in gratitude, repair her wound by returning all the rubble from which the gold had been extracted.

There could well be countless babies who do not have ordinary devoted beautiful mothers who see them as ordinary beautiful babies, and who are not greeted by the dazzle of the sunrise. Yet I cannot claim with conviction that I have ever seen one in my consulting room. Not even in my extensive experience of schizophrenic patients and psychotic children have I failed to find evidence of their having been touched by the beauty—and recoiled wildly from it, as they do again and again in the course of analysis. There is much evidence (cf. Spitz) to suggest that being thus untouched is not compatible with survival, or at least with the survival of the mind.

As an addendum to existing theory this book is a piece of hindsight. I feel confident that in our consulting rooms, whether consciously or not, depending largely on the random factor of the training group and its particular chauvinist jargon, psychoanalysts in general, for at least the last thirty years, have been treating the phenomena which Melanie Klein labelled as paranoid–schizoid and depressive positions in the way I am describing. The psychopathology which we study and allege to treat has its primary basis in the flight from the pain of the aesthetic conflict. The impact of separation, of deprivation—emotional and physical, of physical illness, of oedipal conflict—pregenital and genital, of chance events, of seductions and brutality, of indulgence and over-protection, of family disintegration, of the death of parents or siblings—all of these derive the core of their significance for the developmental process from their contribution as aspects of the underlying, fundamental process of avoidance of the impact of the beauty of the world, and of passionate intimacy with another human being. It is necessary for our understanding of our patients, for a sympathetic view of the hardness, coldness and brutality that repeatedly bursts through in the transference and countertransference, to recognize that conflict about the *present* object is prior in significance to the host of anxieties over the *absent* object.

To end this and to illustrate what is meant by "wildly recoil from the impact of the aesthetic of the object", I offer some material from the analysis of a psychotic young woman.

Siegrie is now 30 years old and has been an acute or ambulatory paranoid schizophrenic patient under care of the community since the age of 17 when, while in Uganda with her family, during a period of political turmoil, she became paranoid and deluded towards her mother. She saw her as extremely beautiful with lights shining from her eyes, felt that she was feeding her LSD with the food and that she was intending to make her into a homosexual. At times of acute breakdown she has fits of religious delirium, is violent and requires locked-ward care and heavy medication. Siegrie has had analytic therapy for five years with the Director of the ward for research on psychotherapy of the psychoses in a large, old-fashioned and rather splendid hospital outside Oslo.

The most significant features and events of her history are these: she was the first child, conceived before marriage, of a student couple, the father remaining at University to take his degree during the patient's first half year of life. At 14 months, when the father was planning to take the family to the United States where he was to study for a higher degree, the mother decided to go back to work to save money for the trip and she placed Siegrie in a Salvation Army Children's Home where she remained for four or five months until severe bladder and respiratory illness made it necessary that she be returned to the mother. While in the United States she started to stray away from home almost as soon as she could walk and she showed a distinct preference for the company of a neighbouring family. Siegrie's family returned to Norway when the patient was three, the mother then being pregnant with a boy who died three months after birth. There was no apparent cause of death which was put down as a "cot death". A brother was born when Siegrie was five and a sister when she was ten. When she was fifteen the family went to Uganda where the father took a temporary teaching post, and while there the patient was converted to an American Pentecostal Church, much against the parents' wishes.

Following her first breakdown, ending soon after her repatriation, the patient finished her secondary schooling but subsequent breakdowns prevented her from acquiring any higher education or following any form of vocational training although she is an intelligent girl and is also, apparently, artistically gifted. She is attractive in appearance although somewhat plump.

The therapy has been conducted three times weekly, with the patient seated opposite the therapist; the patient has only recently consented to use the couch but still finds this disturbing after only a few minutes on each occasion. She knows the therapist's wife who was a nurse on the ward before marriage and Siegrie knows that the couple now have two children. During periods of remission she lives in a hostel connected with the hospital with three other ex-patients, all women; the hostel is unstaffed although monitored by hospital personnel.

While the therapy has made quite steady progress in lessening the frequency and duration of acute attacks of paranoid delusion and agitated confusional states, the therapist feels that it has plateaud to a supportive relationship which neither of them is willing to run the risk of intensifying by increased frequency, or use of the couch, deeper and more conflictual interpretations, etc. The patient's family also seems to prefer to play-it-safe, being friendly but keeping their distance socially. The patient went on holiday to the Mediterranean last summer with the whole family and this went reasonably well. But the mother will not give the patient a flat in the house which she owns where both the brother and sister have flats. She receives her at most once a week for Sunday lunch. In fact the patient prefers telephone contact to visits.

The two dreams that I wish to report and discuss come from the period after the summer break. At the time the general feeling was that the fire was starting to burn and that another breakdown was not far away, ostensibly springing up over the issue of the flat but also clearly arising over analytic issues between patient and analyst, each feeling that the other was holding back, settling in, keeping things comfortable. The analyst increasingly felt parasitized and was impatient for Siegrie to get on with her education.

In the first dream

> *the patient was in her hostel with her companions and someone said that there was not enough light. So Siegrie climbed up into the loft to open a window. But outside on the roof was a horde of homosexual women led by a very beautiful woman, who wanted to get in but the patient hurriedly closed the window. Then there was a knock at the front door, and when Siegrie opened it, once more there was the beautiful woman and her horde. So Siegrie invited them in. One of them had very short hair and surgical tape on her head. This woman said that she had had a brain operation for a sex change and that the patient could have one too. But at this point the beautiful woman leader looked fat and ugly and so Siegrie refused the offer.*

In the second dream

> *Siegrie was in the bath and was having a pleasant telephone conversation with the favourite of her several boyfriends and she felt a stirring of genital desire or excitement.*

Siegrie is still a virgin, finding it impossible to have intercourse although fond of boys, and she is attractive to them; she is able to be affectionate and fairly erotic with the one on the telephone. There does not seem to be any tincture of homosexuality in her relations with her three house-mates. That seems almost entirely reserved for her delusional states.

I wish to approach this material from the viewpoint of the light it throws on the problem of intolerance to aesthetic impact. The dreams can be read as follows:

When the newborn Siegrie first opens her eyes and sees the beauty of her mother's face and all the parts of her body the impact is overwhelming, enveloping, invasive, stirring powerful tendencies towards surrender. From this she can withdraw by closing her eyes but she is unable to close her genital area from being stirred into excitement indistinguishable from having a full rectum. But the impact is far less compelling to surrender (her word) since the element of beauty has vanished.

It is better, as the second dream declares, to stay in the warm waters inside mother and just commune by auditory means with a less beautiful, though also frightening object like a father. In fact Siegrie is far more comfortable with her steady, reasonable and unemotional father and would rather telephone than visit her mother.

The fight-for-the-flat that took shape in subsequent months parallels and, to some extent, replaces the fight over the use of the couch and encounter with the maternal transference. Historically it would seem that the four or five months in the Salvation Army Home was a threat to her life more from change of geography than from the separation from her mother as an external object. Changes of geography such as the trips to the United States and Uganda have similarly unhinged Siegrie. Through painting, where she can as yet only produce very faint, gossamer-like figures, she seems to be trying to accustom herself to see the beauty of humans and of the world but one feels that it will need to be worked out at the storm centre of the transference before she can emerge into emotional and intimate contact with another human being, using her eyes and containing her passions.

CHAPTER FOURTEEN

The place of aesthetic conflict in the analytic process

(1988)

Donald Meltzer

In considering the conflict of emotion aroused by the aesthetic impact of the object, it is necessary to relate this struggle to our exist ing model of the mind in its various dimensions, in the sense of extended metapsychology. Earlier chapters have dealt mainly with the dynamic, economic, genetic and geographical aspects, but aesthetic conflict has an important relation to mental structuring also. Insofar as the conflict over the manifest exterior and the ambiguous interior of the object stirs the epistemophilic instinct, it clearly makes an important—perhaps the major—contribution to the shaping of the place of K in the balance of L, H and K in the knowledge-seeking life of the individual. Melanie Klein and Bion, in particular, have traced the importance of the qualities of the object with regard to the evolution of the superego functions of internal and external objects. The vigilance, intelligence and incorruptibility of these objects are surely the infantile basis of honesty; for long before an ethical preference can be embraced, despair of being able to deceive one's objects enforces integrity. The policeman at one's elbow is an essential bar to self-deception; love of the truth comes much later.

But the contribution of aesthetic conflict to the development of the ego-ideal functions of objects is less apparent. When objects are fully formed and loved their force in promoting aspiration towards excellence seems unnecessary of explanation. But aspiration, even in the sense of Milton's aspiration "to become a true poem", is not the same as inspiration. And, unless we propose to deal with inspiration as mere allegory, we must take account of the "Muse" in our consideration of ego-ideal functions. The psychoanalytical literature is unclear about the modus operandi of the inspirational role of the ego-ideal in promoting development, although it seems clear to many workers that the efficiency of introjective identifications derives from its aspirational stimulus, thus accounting for the gradual emergence of *identified qualities* in contrast to the immediacy of the effect on the *sense* of identity induced by narcissistic forms of identification. This absence of a clear psychoanalytical view of inspiration can be seen to have the same roots as the failure to take account of the aesthetic impact of objects on personality development. Probably the tacit assumption has been that children have emotions but not passions, while on the other hand passions have never been given status among the emotions except on a quantitative basis as intense or excessive emotions. Certainly one of the aims of this book is to establish the term "passion" as a specific response to aesthetic objects: as a *qualitatively* distinct consortium of L, H and K, which is therefore subject to very specific forms of attack by negative links. One need hardly document the virulence with which the anti-aesthetic forces in the mind, as in the culture, mount their attacks on aesthetic objects and aesthetic experience.

Much of this thesis on the attacks against the breast as an object of trusted dependence, was outlined in the chapter on the "Threshold of the Depressive Position" in *The Psycho-Analytical Process* [1967]. But at that time my attention was mainly focussed on the breast as part object, valued and even loved for its functions. These functions were mainly seen in Kleinian terms related to introjective processes, for the work of Bion had not as yet really found its place in my consulting room. The thinking breast, the assimilation of the mother's eyes to her nipples, the function of her reverie in making available to the baby the food for thought, the alpha-elements and dream-thoughts (rows B and C of the Grid [Bion, 1977]) that enable the baby to deal with emotional experiences rather than to evacuate them—none of this had worked its way into my theoretical framework or model of the mind. Consequently the conflicts over the feeding breast, while recognized as structured in terms of the outside versus the inside of the object, were viewed mainly from the point of view of greed, envy, and possessive jealousy (of the inside-babies).

At present I would think all of that as substantially tenable, but from the viewpoint of recovery, rather than the achievement, of the depressive position. The superego aspect of this primal part-object was attributed to the nipple as the paternal element of the combined object of breast and nipple, endowed with qualities of strength and authority, presiding over the feeding process. I would now see the nipples as associated primarily with the mother's eyes whereas their secondary link to the father's penis opens the way to erotization and zonal confusion. On the other hand the ego-ideal function of the combined object of breast and nipple was felt then to reside in the depressive problem of the shift in values, from ego-centric to object-related concern, consequent to and intrinsic to the shift to a depressive economic principle.

I think still that this is a useful way of looking at the ego-ideal functions of internal objects. The depressive orientation is essentially aspirational in its ethos; worthiness as a goal is at the heart of the experience of love and gratitude. But, it seems to me, it cannot cogently describe the inspirational aspect, which must be at the root of the transition from useful productivity—using received equipment of ideas, knowledge and skills—to true creativity. I do not wish to use this term loosely, bandied and battered as it is by promiscuous employment. Studying letters, essays and diaries of great artists suggests that even among such persons inspiration is a rare and fleeting phenomenon. How momentary or non-existent must it be among lesser figures? But it is a phenomenon and our model of the mind must be able to describe it, though we bow before its essential mysteriousness.

Psychoanalytical contributions to any theory of inspiration and creativity must, of course, be derived from experience of the analytical process. In my opinion, although reference to aesthetic experiences past and current must necessarily make up some part of the patient's material, the entry into the transference of an aesthetic apprehension of the analyst's modes of thought, of the analytical method and of the process of development that it generates, makes a late appearance in the therapy. It is by no means coincidental that its appearance tends to be simultaneous with another phenomenon: the tendency to impasse at the threshold of the depressive position, as described in *The Psycho-Analytical Process* in 1967. At the time of writing the paper "The Apprehension of Beauty" (1973) [chapter 6, this volume], I read a paper on impasse to my colleagues which was fiercely resisted. I ascribed this characteristic tendency to inertia and impasse in the therapeutic process to the economics of mental pain in a general way. That is, I reported my observations on the waning of persecutory anxieties and the incipiency of depressive pain, as primarily related to "the writing on the wall" or the "whiff of grapeshot" of inevitable weaning and termination of the dependence.

I still think this is a legitimate generalization, but more point and descriptive power can be added to the concept by correlating the tendency to impasse with the emergence of aesthetic experience in the transference and its attendant problem of the love of truth. Two recent clinical experiences have helped me to clarify the inter-relation of these two ideas—namely, of the ego-ideal functions of the aesthetic impact of the primal objects, and the relation between the appearance of aesthetic conflict in the transference with the crisis of the Threshold of the Depressive Position, and its attendant tendency to impasse.

The first experience illustrates the emergence of the aesthetic conflict in the transference as a new experience for the patient and the crucial role it plays in the evolution of love for the truth. A young woman, slim and attractive, coming from abroad but speaking perfect, if somewhat inaudible English, had been seconded by the charitable organization for which she had worked for some fifteen years, to study personnel management in this country for a period of three years. During this time she undertook an analysis as part of her training and had been in therapy four times per week for some five years at the time of the present material. These five years had seen very extensive changes in her character, which had been chaste, withdrawn and colourless, deeply religious and asexual. A moderate degree of coming to life was reflected in changes in her interests, mode of dress, attraction to men, improved liveliness and lessening of her piety. When her personnel training was completed she asked to stay on to do a further training in counselling, to which her parent organization agreed in view of her long service at a very low stipend. Eventually she asked to be released from her contract, to which the officers of the charity not only acquiesced, but gave her a bonus of some seven thousand pounds as a severance gift. At that time, one year before the current material, we had agreed that she should continue the analysis at the greatly reduced fee that her organization had been paying, on the assumption that she would barely survive economically even with the help of her bonus until she returned to her country at the end of the analysis.

Within the next six months she completed her counselling course, found some rather menial employment and made preparations to leave when her student's visa would expire. Her analytic progress was slow and there seemed reason to doubt that time would be adequate for a satisfactory resolution of the difficulties that prevented her forming relationships of any depth of intimacy, especially with men. The same problems appeared in the analysis as very stilted communication, colourlessness of voice and vocabulary, a marked tendency to rehearse inwardly before speaking, and an adamant insistence that the relationship was necessarily impersonal because of her lying on the couch and because the analyst gave no information about himself. However she was a fine reporter of dreams and grudgingly developed some understanding of the spitefulness and princessly pride which held her back from acknowledging or showing feelings.

During the next months her social life seemed to pick up, her style of dress became markedly more youthful and attractive and the material began to revolve more around the men she met, mostly at her work. She talked of moving closer to the area of the analysis, now that she was no longer having to go to her course on the other side of town, and this seemed also to imply that she could now rely on public transport and save the expense of running a car. However she did not move, did not give up the car. Then one day she brought a simple little dream that *she was carrying a typewriter from one room to another and dropped it, but it was not damaged.* Inquiry elicited the information that it was not her type-writer, but an electric one which she does in fact borrow from a fellow lodger, who does not actually own it either. It seems to belong to a woman who had gone back to her native land, leaving the machine to be shipped to her. How long ago was this? Several months. Why had it not been shipped? Oh, the girl didn't seem to be in any hurry to have it!

The cat was out of the bag. I began to review her financial situation with her and discovered that she was now working full time, also had some private clients (illegally), had never touched the seven thousand pounds nor even the interest on it, since she was planning to buy a flat for her sole occupancy in order to have more privacy and to see her clients. Had she considered raising her fee to me to approximate my regular charge? Yes, she had thought about it but decided that the analyst had been satisfied with the low fee during the previous years. The brazen ingratitude rather took my breath away.

Having clarified the problem, I rather left her to struggle with it, which her sullen demeanour reflected and her dreams documented. She grudgingly offered a compromise, to pay three quarters rather than half my regular fee, but seemed quite unable to grasp the issue of the cheating and the money that represented it. She was just like a monkey who gets his fist in the bowl of nuts and cannot get it out because he cannot let go of the nuts. She argued, she sulked, she flattered, she wept, but fortunately she also dreamt. *She was on a train going through exquisitely beautiful country in the vicinity of a city called Queenstown, but she was standing in the driver's cab rather than sitting in a passenger carriage. There was also present an attractive man and a young boy. She was looking at the man, wondering was he married, was he perhaps homosexual.* When I inquired about the driver the patient replied that she didn't know, she didn't notice him. I suggested that this train journey was meant to represent the analysis and her training which had finally brought her into a state of mind where she could notice the beauty of the world and this life, not relegating it all to Heaven; that Queenstown was London and the driver whom she didn't notice—being too busy finding a hus-band—was myself.

This dream had some effect and led to some movement towards understanding the enormity of her ingratitude and dishonesty with me as the parents who help her to develop towards womanhood in a world of beauty and sexuality. Two weeks later she had a dream clearly a sequel to the Queenstown one, that *she was sitting in the back seat of a car behind a couple; they might have been her parents or the analyst and his wife. The car came over the brow of a hill and revealed a magnificent vista of valleys and hills with the sea in the distance. But coming towards them was an articulated lorry, a Juggernaut, and she felt frightened it would crash into them. Then she noticed by the side of the road a splendid horse, unsaddled and riderless, but with a bridle on its head.* I felt that the juggernaut represented that part of herself which attacks the parents as a combined object and which threatened to destroy the progress she was making towards acknowledging her dependence. The man of the Queenstown dream seemed to be replaced by the splendid horse, which I suggested implied that she was now more able to see the possibility of beauty in a man and his genital instead of simply husband-hunting in a predatory way. There was perhaps a pun, bridle–bridal.

The charming thing about this material is that the acting-in-the-transference is so transparently childish, and in a sense innocent, prior to thought. We need not be amazed (since Bion), that people can go far in their contractual adaptation to the "world" without being encumbered by this troublesome faculty—imaginative thought. But intimacy cannot far proceed without it, for its evolution depends upon getting to know one another. These imaginative incursions into the ambiguous interior of the other's mind, which my patient attempts in her dream regarding the man in the train-cab, are little facilitated by simply looking. There must be interaction and communication to supply the unconscious with that wealth of data which can comprise an emotional experience. The mere aesthetic impact of the other person's exterior, even when it delivers a hammer-blow to the heart, as in love-at-first-sight, cannot generate the alpha-elements from which thoughts spring forth. This lady's habit of rehearsing her communications so impoverishes her vocabulary and the music of her voice that she fails to make an "impression" on another person's mind. It is clear that without her excellent recall of dreams—which, however, must always be supplemented with interrogation for detail—little comprehension would ever have germinated in my mind. The analysis would have remained as drought-stricken as her other relationships.

Clearly this young woman is not an unethical person. She is an unthinking one, and therefore insensitive to the position, feelings, needs and attitudes of others. All little children pilfer. To some degree it has the meaning of scavenging, but this can hardly be the case when a child systematically steals from her mother's handbag, buys sweets or is hoarding her loot to buy a dolly. The innocence is shown in the naiveté of their self-revealing crimes. Had I been more alert I would have noticed the parade of new clothes long before the typewriter dream gave the game away. The role of projective identification and attendant confusion of identity in this naiveté is shown in a dream the patient had a few weeks after the juggernaut one: *she was in her parents' bedroom and her mother came in, saying that there was dirty water left in the bath, implying that the patient should clean it up. But she was annoyed because she felt sure that it was mother who had taken the bath.* It is as if to say that she comes to analysis to afford me the opportunity of correcting my misconceptions about her. In such an instance, thinking in terms of mechanisms of defence, one cannot say with certainty whether the patient is confused or is employing confusion as a defence. In the latter case, in more epistemological terms, the truth is being bowdlerized by means of projective identification. In that case we must come to the question of love for the truth and its relation to the aesthetic level of experience of the primal objects.

The second piece of material, which takes us back to our poet, four months on, bears directly on this problem. Following the material reported earlier about the "magnificent breasts" and his "collection" of other men's women, we entered on a period of some turbulence both in analysis and his external life situation. A young protégé who was almost like an adopted son left the country to rejoin his estranged family, and the patient abandoned the job which was his financial mainstay owing to political differences. But I felt that the central disturbance was reflected in his analytic material, which pursued the theme of attacks on the breast shown in the trio of dreams introduced by the "dead bodies in the mud". The issue of jealousy of the next baby became unequivocal in his dreams, showing a savagery that quite astonished him. As a result a fairly deep split in his personality, consisting of the poet and lover of truth versus an ambitious, greedy and sly infantile aspect, declared itself openly, although it had been suspected earlier for historical reasons. Distrust of the analyst and of the analytic method introduced a certain reserve and tentativeness into his previously open and enthusiastic participation, as a certain loneliness and restless sense of inertia suffused his daily life.

Indecision about the future course of his work pushed him to accept an assignment for three weeks to Nicaragua, attracted by the money, the danger and the political turbulence. On return, after missing this period of analysis, he found himself able to write up his experience

with a speed and vividness that paralleled the enthusiasm and camara-
derie which he had found and entered upon so wholeheartedly there.
He had been particularly attracted by a woman, an American, who
seemed to have made herself completely at home amidst the danger
and confusion, quite completely "gone native".

Without any apparent diminution of his satisfaction with the analyst's work or reneging of his former conviction of the benefits that the
two years of work had reaped for him, he decided that he had had
enough help. The justification for this was a bit disingenuous, for, while
he was now contemplating pursuing a career of free-lance roving jour-
nalism, he harked back to an earlier discussion in the analysis. At that
time he had expressed some anxiety that the analytic resolution of
infantile conflicts might adversely affect his poetic inspiration. I had
agreed at that time that it was an issue about which my experience was
too limited to express any contrary conviction. My private thought,
which I have eventually shared with him, is that balking at the threshold of the depressive position (as I think he was contemplating), might
certainly damp creative thought for reasons that the following material
illustrates.

Shortly after his return from Nicaragua, in the midst of his pleasure
at writing so well, with such ease, and at far greater length than he had
expected, the following dream arrested his attention. In the dream *he
was defecating but gold and silver coins were mixed up with his faeces.* This
rather surprised him for moneymaking had never been a passion. Yet
he could see the implication: journalistic productivity that brought in
the money was not the same as poetic inspiration, which certainly did
not. Two weeks later an even more arresting dream appeared, in the
context of his having made a definite decision to stop the analysis on
the eve of his departure for his next, and far more protracted, journalistic venture. *There was a house, large but not particularly grand, at the top of
some monumental steps, like the Spanish Steps, and on a balcony high up were
the surviving members of the family of a man who had committed suicide. The
house was to be taken over and converted, perhaps to a pub or museum and the
architect was explaining to him some of the problems of conversion. The
patient himself was particularly concerned with the task that would confront
them, of removing from the steps all the political slogans that had been daubed
on to them. But the architect assured him that this was no problem, for they
had a new method. This involved painting some substance over the daubings
which, when it dried, enabled them to lift whole sheets of the paint off, revealing the stone beneath.* The patient commented that the pavements and
walls in Nicaragua were daubed with slogans, one of them being "A
Nicaraguan is worth dying for." I thought that our problem had to do

with what was worth living for, and that political slogans, which are intended to make creative thought unnecessary, are the stuff of which the steps to mental suicide are paved. What impressed me most about the dream was the way in which the slogans which hide the truth of the enduring stone beneath, also hide the monumental beauty of the steps in development—that is, evolution rather than revolution.

In Chapter IX of *Studies in Extended Metapsychology* [1986], I described some clinical material which seemed to suggest that lies do not destroy the truth in the mind but only obscure it. This material is another example and would seem to be a tribute to the "new method" of psychoanalytic inquiry, into language usage and dreams, which enable the lies to be lifted off. But it is also a testimony to the Keatsian dictum, "Beauty is truth, truth beauty". Whether it is "all ye know on earth and all ye need to know" is another matter. But I would agree that "the great beauty of Poetry is, that it makes every thing every place interesting—" (letter to George and Georgiana Keats, September 1819).

This seemingly banal statement about poetry and the power of its aesthetic impact, that it makes everything interesting, I take to mean "makes it food for thought". This seems to me to be the nub of the matter, the core of my thesis. The most adequate description of "passion" would seem to be that our emotions are engaged in such a way that love, hate and the yearning for understanding are all set in motion. The quantity or intensity can be disregarded. It is the consortium that is essential. Many objects and events arouse one or the other; we love this, hate that, wish to understand the other. Our passions are not engaged. Our interest is in abeyance; we wish to engage with the object of love, to avoid or destroy the object of hate, to master the object that challenges our understanding. But when we encounter something that engages our *interest*, when we see it as a fragment or instance or sample of the beauty of the world, we wish to ascertain its authenticity, to know it in depth. And at that moment we encounter the "heart of (its) mystery", along with the severe limitations in our capacities for knowledge. We enter upon the realms of science and art, the cathedral of the mind hidden in the forest of the world.

The emotional flavour of our passions, of awe and wonder, surely become jaded with time. I do not refer to the crushing of passion by the child's education in and out of the family, from which he has an opportunity of recovery in adolescence. I mean rather the filling-up of the apparatus of interest and questioning by the bombardment of explanation to which we are subjected, by science today as by religion in the past. The double-helix type of discovery dispels the "cloud of unknowing"; fatigue and the yearning for comfort reach out for such explanatory morsels, without noticing that the little bit of nourishment they offer is accompanied by a strong dose of the lotus. Whereas to see with passionate eyes is to see the Poetry.

This is the solipsistic plight; its depth of loneliness fosters the urge for communication, the need to share, the hunger for intimacy, to say what can be said—and to show what cannot.

CHAPTER FIFTEEN

New considerations on the concept of the aesthetic conflict

(1990)

Donald Meltzer

At a year's distance from the publication of *The Apprehension of Beauty* [chapter 6, this volume], the author traces a historical reconstruction of the psychoanalytic journey from Freud to Bion via Melanie Klein—a route which reconsiders the relationship between psychoanalysis and art, as well as the important role of beauty in intimate relations, above all between mother and baby. Other concepts appear pertinently in Meltzer's short essay: the theory of passions, the attack on links, infantile development as "learning from experience" which modifies significantly the attitude to childhood of those who bring up babies. The essay continues allowing the romantic poets to speak directly. The aesthetic conflict is found in the final phase of analysis, when aesthetic feelings arise together with live passions (links L, H, K) and "negative capability" (Keats) is also manifested, "which renders possible the toleration of doubt and uncertainty without irritable reaching after fact and reason".

I do not wish to bore you with too much history, but it is not possible to understand psychoanalytic theory without having recourse to history, which is also the individual history of every single psychoanalyst. I have had two types of psychoanalytic training (besides psychiatric training): a Freudian analytic training in the United States and another of the Kleinian variety in London. Thus the development of my conception of mental development is, in certain ways, parallel to the history of the development of psychoanalytic theory.

The main feature of the development of psychoanalysis is that of having departed from being a sub-species of psychiatry, with very precise aims and limits, that is the cure of specific mental symptoms, in particular hysteria. The method developed by Freud was born to explain certain phenomena on the basis of the experience of one's development/upbringing. Thus psychoanalysis started out as an explanatory science, part of the more general science of medicine. It then developed into something very different, thanks to the ideas of Klein and of those who, like Bion, then developed those ideas.

Little by little this was transformed into an art form to describe mental phenomena and the human mind. In the course of this development of a science for explaining mental phenomena, psychoanalysis became concerned with mental pain, but very little with mental pleasure.

The general formulation on the subject of mental pain was that of anxiety and anguish, which seems to have been descriptive, in its first phases, but also later, like a fear of something whose nature one does not understand, a very mysterious type of fear. Freud reached the idea of anxiety as the signal of an unknown danger. In addition he subdivided this into anxieties which could come from various directions: from the id, from the superego, from the ego, from the external world; fundamentally, however, it remained a signal of an unknown danger.

Melanie Klein made the first great revolution in the theory of mental pain, distinguishing in that area between persecutory and depressive pain.

These two types of pain are reciprocal, but basically both of these two types of pain can be understood in terms of the theory of the danger signal: persecutory pain represents a danger that derives from a hostile object; depressive pain represents the danger that our own hostility constitutes for the loved object. In this way Klein introduced into psychoanalysis that which we may define as a system of values.

In Freudian theory the only value considered was the safety and the well-being of the self. Thus even if this view did not introduce a real system of values, this unique concept of the well-being of the self had a noteworthy influence on the way of understanding the human condition, insofar as it implied that every human being was profoundly egocentric: all his efforts were directed toward regaining a state of tranquillity, the so-called *nirvana principle*, thus outlining a set of values that was extremely pessimistic, almost cynical.

Freud had besides to confront the problem of explaining the highest conquests of man. He resolved it by introducing the concept of sublimation, which is perhaps a sort of expedient, of deception. He thus arrived at a theory by which all the greatest achievements in the arts and in science are the fruit of a sublimation of male homosexuality (thus omitting all female achievements). In the field of the aesthetic, this theory led to a view of artistic and scientific achievement that came to be termed "psychobiography", which led to attempts to explain works of art on the basis of the psychological biography of the artist, as though the work of art were a sort of symptom. This view, initiated by Freud, had a great flowering in the 1920s and 1930s; as you can imagine, this approach alienated a large part of the artistic world from psychoanalysis. Artists felt profoundly offended at this way of seeing them.

Furthermore it is interesting to note, reading Freud, that he treated in the same way—that is to say, as a symptom—his own aesthetic experience: for example, when he relates his emotional experience before the Acropolis, he describes it as though it was an aberration in his own personality. This tendency, which has changed since the first works of Melanie Klein, which began in 1946 with her work on the paranoid–schizoid and depressive positions, in fact sets out a first value system.

Within the theory of the paranoid–schizoid and depressive positions, Klein developed what can be considered a theory of aesthetics. Even though this was no longer a cynical or pessimistic view like Freud's, it was nevertheless a theory of artistic functioning and of aesthetic creativity, which linked works of art to the struggles within the artist's personality. This aesthetic theory considers that within the depressive position the damage done to the loved objects by aggressive attacks, whether within or externally, must be repaired; essentially this is a matter of reparation in relation to the loved object. In so far as, in Melanie Klein's view, the infant's love for the object is fundamentally aroused by the benefits which the object provides, this reparation—for the damage which the subject has inflicted on the object—is aimed at obtaining again these same benefits. . . .

This is curious also because, if one looks at the Klein's clinical material with children, the problem of the beauty of the object is always present. In the case of Richard, he constantly speaks of the beauty of his therapist, of the countryside, of the starry sky etc.

If one looks at that first theory using Bionic theory, we can now understand what the problem was at that time. It consisted in a postulate that is present in almost all of the human race from the very beginning—that is, that love and hate are set in opposition to each other. This leaves no space to define passion, unless in quantitative terms, where passion is a very intense love; but hate is also a very intense passion. In addition to this problem, related to a theory of emotions, there is also the fact that both Freud and Klein considered the development of the personality in a strongly biological way, as though it was programmed in the same way as bodily development, as though it were a sort of embryology of the personality, sited within the genetic structure.

Two people have questioned this biological model of the development of the personality, each from his own point of view, namely Bion and Money-Kyrle. They emphasized that personality is something other than the brain, that it is something that has to be constructed on the basis of experience, thought, and learning from experience. This approach, which makes clear the self-development of personality, has put an end to psychoanalysis as an explanatory science, whereby pathology was explained on the basis of earlier bad experience or the absence of good experience—as though there were a causal link between these earlier experiences and current experiences. The causal theory of development has been replaced by the concept of development as the field of experience, in which even in the womb the baby has a field within which he operates and from within which he selects experiences and objects, about which he thinks.

This has had a great effect on the concept of responsibility. It has led to a great change in the way of presenting oneself in relating to children, who should no longer be trained, but need protection from bad experience. In other words, this has led to more live emotional relationships. If we think that the baby is responsible for its choice of experiences, we see the function of parents as that of helping them to take account of and take note of their experiences and to think about them.

This attitude towards children has the effect of respecting their individuality and their ability to create their own self, thereby making the responsibility of parents much more like that of the analyst. It has also changed the idea of the responsibility of the analyst.

While the analyst previously considered his function to be that of investigating difficulties in the resolution of conflicts derived from experiences in the past, now he has made a great step forward. First he thought he had a goal towards which to direct the patient; now he only has to remain behind the patient, following the direction that the patient has taken. This view of the child as accomplishing his own self-development and constructing his own self was not new at all: it had already been outlined by several English poets about 150 years ago.

Three English poets in particular have described clearly this view of the child and his development—Wordsworth, Keats, and Coleridge. The most succinct description comes from Keats, in a letter to his brother: "People say that we live in a vale of tears, I say that we live in a vale of soul-making." This is a much more optimistic view of human development and of the type of world in which we live.

These three poets, together with Blake, emphasize the beauty of the world—in contrast to traditional western culture, which saw all beauty in an earthly paradise, while the real world was a place where one had to scrape up the leavings of life from an arid terrain, which gave nothing.

The change in the way of viewing the emotions introduced by Bion allows us to have a different view of love and of hate. What has produced this change is treating the emotions as "links": when there is a relationship between two persons or between a person and an object, an emotional impact is created, and this constitutes a link.

But a person may break this link and withdraw from its emotional impact in the way that Bion described when he added to the mechanisms of defence described in psychoanalytic theory another type of defence, "attacks on linking". He suggested that there are three fundamental types of emotional links, one of love, one of hate and a third, more important for development, which is that of the desire to know the object. This link, referred to by Bion as "K" (for Knowledge), has its origin in the so-called epistemophilic instinct.

This type of link was by no means unknown in the Freudian theory of the mind, but Freud thought that the origin of the desire to know resided in what he defined as sexual researches, placed in the years from 3–5—that is, in the Oedipal phase. Freud considered that the sublimation of sexual curiosity formed the origin of the development of scientific thinking. Melanie Klein, without basically changing this theory of knowledge, changed it in time and changed its object, saying that the first object of the child's curiosity was the inside of the mother's body.

Bion's description of the links between emotions, comprising these three links (hate, love, knowledge), allows us to point out another configuration of emotions, in which all three of these links act at the same moment: this is passion.

Bion's theories were elaborated in the 1960s and 1970s and have allowed the description of three different areas of clinical experience, which come together in the theory of the aesthetic conflict. Besides their usefulness in therapeutic relationships, they have allowed us to see the mother/infant relationship more clearly as well as, with echography, the behaviour of the foetus, and it has also helped us to describe from a new perspective what occurs at the end of a successful analysis.

As regards foetal behaviour as shown in echography, the theory of emotions has allowed us to understand better the vital experience of the foetus in his particular environment. In fact, it allows us to see the experience of birth as an emotional experience arising from one type of environment to another. As regards the observation of the mother/ infant relationship, this theory allows us to gather which aspects of the relationship have to do with the baby's way of experiencing, as he regards the mother simultaneously with wonder and with fear. It has allowed us besides to understand that the baby does not only respond with love to the mother's services or with hate resulting from his frustrations, but that he responds in a passionate way to the mother as a total object, to the whole personality of the mother.

Already in the course of analyses we often pick up little episodes in which the patient has an aesthetic experience, before a landscape, at a visit to a museum, or in relation to the analyst seen as a marvellous person. But these experiences of love seem to be separate from those of hate, for example in relation to the analyst or his method, or from the desire to known the analyst as a person, to know his internal experience, his personal evolution. For about 8–10 years I have begun to notice, towards the end of analyses, experiences that Bion defined as "passions": here the patient experiences simultaneously curiosity, great feelings of love, and violent feelings of hate toward the analyst and his method.

I will give a brief example of a woman patient, a retired doctor in her sixties, who had had a terrible relationship with her mother from the birth of a little brother when she was two.

When she began analysis, not only was she still in love with her father, she was convinced that he was the real love of her life. She had had three husbands, and from the first two (good husbands) she had 5 children, while the third was a horrible man. In the course of the analysis, first her father died, then her mother, then the divorced wife of the terrible husband. At this point there was a rethinking of her relationship with her father. When her mother grew old, her father had very brutally put the mother away into a hospice and gone to live with a younger woman with whom he had had a relationship for about 20 years, but of whom the patient had had no knowledge.

Her new evaluation of the relationship with the father allowed her to separate from her husband and to also to evaluate differently her relationship with her mother, which then only changed on her mother's death: the patient took into account her intense maternal transference and her infantile dependence in relation to me in the course of the analysis. To the extent that she took account of the maternal transference, she also became able to live intense aesthetic experiences with music, art, landscapes, paintings. . . .

These kinds of experiences, which we find at the end of analyses, when patients show passionate responses in which there co-exist love, hate, and the desire for knowledge (curiosity), are also linked to observations of the relationship of baby/mother and to foetal situations evidenced in echography. This has allowed us to formulate a new theory of the aesthetic conflict.

We formulate it thus: when the baby opens its eyes to the beauty of the world represented by its mother, it has a passionate experience of hate, love, and the desire to know the inside of this object which externally is so beautiful (as Melanie Klein had already said). Then its conflict is not only between hate and love, but also between what is observable and what is not observable, between the exterior of the mother (observable) and the interior of the mother (not observable), marking the prototype of doubt about the sincerity of the other person in these terms: are the exterior and the interior really comparable or not?

Another aspect of Bion's theories is that he longer regarded anxiety as a danger signal, but as a manifestation of uncertainty. Bion in fact describes the strength of the ego as "negative capability"—that is, as the capacity to tolerate uncertainty. In this theory of the aesthetic conflict, which is added to the theory of values outlined by Melanie Klein, the emphasis is not only on the ability to hate the object but also on the capacity to tolerate a passionate relationship with the world. This implies that a passionate relationship is full of uncertainty and that uncertainty is a great stimulus to thought.

The definition of "negative capability" comes from Keats: it is the capacity to tolerate uncertainty "without irritable reaching after fact and reason", it is the capacity to wait for later confirmation. We are dealing with a basic function in the formation of the self, which is created through a passionate experience, through uncertainty, through the capacity to think for oneself.

Bion's theory predicts that, through emotional experience, alpha function leads to the formation of symbols which make possible dreaming and thinking; the alternative to this process, where the individual elaborates his own symbols on the basis of his own emotional experiences, is another possibility, in which the individual receives preformed symbols formed by others.

This enables us to understand why creativity is a rather rare human phenomenon, since it requires the capacity to think for oneself, tolerating a passionate experience made up of hate, love and tremendous curiosity. Even when one succeeds in experiencing emotions passionately, there is still the need to wait until the mind can think about these experiences "without irritable reaching" for symbols provided by others, and using these to understand the experience.

All of this throws a new and different light on our way of looking at the problems of development. With Melanie Klein, we are used to recognizing the problems related to the processes of splitting of the object, but not to thinking about a splitting of our own experiences, whereby the experiences of love, hate and curiosity can be directed toward three different objects. This splitting of our experience is different from the splitting of the object or of the self but is more like what Bion has called "attacks on links". This allows the analyst to give his attention to aspects which at times are hidden, for example that the loved objects, the hated objects and the objects which are founts of our curiosity are part of the same object, and thus the links re-unite the same object.

The theory of the aesthetic conflict is not a substitute for Freudian and Kleinian theories, but is added to them, enriching them. It allows us to think about the self-development of the personality, and is the first satisfactory attempt at a psychoanalytic explanation of creativity.

CHAPTER SIXTEEN

The geographic dimension of the mental apparatus

(1992)

Donald Meltzer

In the model of the mind that I am using the geographical dimension can be subdivided, for phenomenological purposes, into six distinct areas: the external world, the womb, the interior of external objects, the interior of internal objects, the internal world, and the delusional system (geographically speaking "nowhere"). The first five subdivisions comprise areas that have psychic reality. The external world also has a concrete reality which calls forth adaptational processes, fundamentally meaningless. The delusional system is also meaningless in a different way, being delusional in its significances and bizarre in its objects.

To the outside world, beyond our adaptational moves, which are learned largely by infra-mental processes of mimicry (one dimensional) and trial-and-error, we may deploy meaning when the impact of events and objects impinges on us emotionally and are subjected to processes of imagination, that is, to symbol formation (alpha function) and thinking. But we are not limited in this matter to the impact of events and objects; we also have the capacity to deploy emotion and thus infuse with meaning, potentially, events and objects whose impact is not in themselves substantial. In *The Apprehension of Beauty* [Meltzer & Harris Williams, 1988] I proposed a terminology which grows out of Bion's affect theory, plus and minus L (love), H (hate) and K (interest, knowing). I suggested that our innate response to the beauty-of-the-world, that is aesthetic responsiveness, contains an integration of all three of these positive links, L, H and K, but that the pain of the ambivalence combined with the necessity of tolerating uncertainty, makes it very difficult to hold these links together. The splitting processes bring relief by deploying the links to separate objects, thus also splitting the, self in its emotional capabilities and experiences. These splitting processes do not necessarily reduce the experiences to an adaptational level—in which thinking about meaning, which necessarily includes value, would be replaced by scheming, logic derived from basic assumptions, and actions aimed at success (triumph).

Where meaningfulness can be preserved despite the splitting of the passionate links, we are in the realm of Melanie Klein's paranoid–schizoid position in terms of values, but the processes of projection and introjection remain active. Modification becomes possible, because action can be restrained in favour of thought. But this commerce between external world experience and internal world processes is dependent on observation and the restraint of premature intellection and story making. Unconscious dream thoughts must be given time to form so that thinking and transformations can occur. The contained must be allowed to enter the container, in Bion's model.

Certain types of clinical experience, when combined with what can be learned from baby observation and echography, suggest that emotional experiences and rudimentary symbol formation and thought commence in the latter months of gestation and form the background upon which the experience with the world outside, and in particular the first encounters with the mother's body and mind, make their crucial impact. Bion's suggestion that infantile parts may be left behind at birth, remain enwombed, is strongly suggested in patients in whom a traumatic factor complicates their gestation: maternal illness, infarction of the placenta, prematurity, foetal distress, to name a few. This is an area still to be worked out: its impact on character, its appearance as states of withdrawal, its part in sleep patterns. I mention it here to distinguish it from those aspects of projective (intrusive) identification with which this book is so particularly concerned.

These states of mind, whether central to the character or only contributory, require division into two categories: those contingent upon intrusion or those resulting from passive induction into external objects. These latter seem to result in various pathological states such as *folie à deux*, multiple personality, demoniacal possession. Where an external object carries infantile transference, introjection easily ensues on separation. None of these states seem to concern us here for they all present primarily identificatory manifestations of a narcissistic type, without the claustrophobic phenomena.

But the intrusive identification with internal objects seems always to show both aspects, the identificatory and the projective (claustrophobic). The internal object of these processes is par excellence the internal maternal object and its special compartmentalization. Where projection into the internal paternal object is obtrusive, it seems to be as a means of entry to the mother's body. It has important identificatory consequences but little of the claustrophobic in its own right. These identificatory aspects, of projective identification with internal and external objects, have been extensively studied. It is almost exclusively the intrusive, projective ones that concern us here, from the theoretical viewpoint, while their intermingling in the clinical situation will concern us with regard to the technical problems.

All of these considerations require differentiation from the relationships of the self to its internal objects insofar as their boundaries of inviolable individuality and privacy are respected at all levels. I think it fair to say that internal objects impinge on the self, at various levels, because of both their qualities and their functions. Unlike external objects, emotions are not deployed to these objects, they are evoked by them. It is at this level of psychic reality that form and function are experienced as wedded so that beauty is truth, truth beauty.

As the various children of a single family discover eventually that, experientially, they have "different" parents, so it is that the different parts of the self have different internal objects. For some parts of the self objects are at a partial object level, for others they are invaded and altered by projections; for some the paternal and maternal are far apart while for others they are combined; for some they are held under omnipotent control, while other parts of the self can give their internal objects their freedom. From this point of view reintegration of the self is contingent upon the reintegration, in a sense the rehabilitation, of the internal objects. And upon this integration the further development of the internal objects becomes a possibility, going beyond what Freud envisioned as their accruing qualities from outside the family, from heroes and heroines of the present and past. The integrated internal combined object learns from experience in advance of the self and is almost certainly the fountainhead of creative thought and imagination.

In pitiful contrast to the glorious possibilities of growth for self and objects which the links of positive LH and K embrace, the anti-life and anti-emotion forces which dedicate themselves to minus LH and K, to Puritanism, hypocrisy and Philistinism, construct a Pandemonium of the delusional system. Their tools are stupid, essentially. Negative mimicry builds a world of delusional ideas and bizarre objects from the debris of alpha-function-in-reverse, aided by transformations in hallucinosis and the format of the negative grid [Bion, 1977]. This would seem to be the Bionic formulation whose evocation clinically we cannot pause to consider here. (It has some mention in Chapter 8, Meltzer, 1992.)

CHAPTER SEVENTEEN

The compartments
of the internal mother

(1992)

Donald Meltzer

Although the clinical realizations which gave rise to the conception of the compartmentalization of the internal mother's body go back to the early 1960s, the autism research group that finally produced *Explorations in Autism* [Meltzer et al., 1975], and particularly to the late Doreen Weddell's work with "Barry", it was not until twenty years later that the full significance came through to me. Out of clinical work and teaching and the literary companionship of Martha Harris and her daughters the conception of aesthetic conflict arose to alter considerably my view of personality development and the human condition. In between came the various essays collected and organized in *Sexual States of Mind* [1973] where the internal compartmentalization of the internal mother's body, its reference to orifices and the polymorphous nature of adult sexuality, added substance to the formal description.

It is clear that two new ideas which, by gaining clarity, made the descriptions in this present book possible, are Bion's affect theory, plus and minus L, H and K, and the central part in the oscillations $Ps \leftrightarrow D$, played by the aesthetic conflict. In seeing this as a tormenting uncertainty about the interior qualities of the aesthetic object, it becomes possible to express the idea of ego strength as negative capability. When the dimension strength/weakness becomes thus observable in its operation and not merely construed from its consequences, we seem to move to a new level of precision in clinical observation (and self-scrutiny).

What emerges in the consulting room and in supervisions is a greatly clarified distinction between immaturity and psychopathology. On the one hand one can range the manifestations of infantile confusions of both a geographic and zonal nature along with Money-Kyrle's thesis of developmental misconceptions. In contrast to this are the pathological constructions which arise from what Bion calls "lies" or column 2 of the grid, failure of alpha-function perhaps induced by what I have called "storytelling" reversal of alpha-function with a debris (beta-elements-with-traces-of-ego-and-superego) from which bizarre objects and the delusional system are shaped by the forces of minus LHK, and finally the operation of omnipotent mechanisms (splitting processes, omnipotent control of objects and intrusive identification).

From the point of view of model-of-the-mind, it is necessary to trace development both in terms of self and of objects. My own emphasis previously, along with the general trend in Kleinian descriptions, has been on the evolution of the self, particularly from the structural aspect. Here, where we are attempting an exploration of the consequences of the intrusive side of the dual phenomena of projective identification, we need to attempt a description primarily of the geography and qualities of the internal objects and secondarily to trace the metapsychological implications for the self. This latter consideration will include the consequences for structure of the self and also for its view-of-the-world. As a basis for our central investigation into the implications for the internal objects and for the self of the operation of the intrusive side of projective identification as an aspect of psycho-pathology, we need first to clarify the direction and extrapolation of the evolution of the internal objects during the maturational process in order to understand the distortions in objects and self consequent to the intrusion.

The first thing that must be clarified is the difference between a conception of the inside of the internal mother derived from imagination and one that is the product of the omnipotent intrusion, and thereby of omniscience. Clinical material is able to be quite explicit and precise in regard to the latter, but the former, the interior of the mother as construed from the outside, respecting the privacy of her interior, must be a product of the patient's and the analyst's imagination. But we have another source as well, that given to us by artists and poets. From clinical material one can see that the functions of the different parts of the mother carry an assumption of interior structure, but here of course the forms are borrowed by imagination from those of the outside world. This borrowing of forms has a reflexive consequence for our construing the meaning of the outside world from which the forms have been borrowed. By contrasting the two views—that constructed by imagination and that "discovered" by intrusion—we can also gain a meaningful differential of views-of-the-world as they are determined by psychic reality, in health and in disturbance. The pathological consequences are discussed in Chapter 5 on "Life in the Claustrum" [Meltzer, 1992].

Here it would be most useful to outline the direction of development of the internal objects insofar as it is reflected in the imaginative conception of the inside of the internal mother. The general movement is clearly from a vast space, undifferentiated and simply containing all forms of life—the Earth Mother—to a compartmentalized but largely partial object mother whose functions for the child (augmented by desires aroused in the child) determine its imaginative constructions. This unintegrated interior is formed in clusters around the assumption of analogy between the infant's experiences of his own orifices vis-à-vis the mother's services. Thus are eyes drawn to eyes, ears to the mother's mouth, baby mouth to the nipples, nose to the mother's aroma; and thus is the baby's integration gradually brought together into consensuality by the mother's integrated behaviour: baby head to maternal head/breast. But a correspondingly integrated conception of her interior must be a far more difficult task, hampered by both ambivalence aroused by failures in her functions and the aesthetic conflict about the uncertainty of her interior. Particularly is this true of the more problematic areas of excretory processes and erotic genital trends. Probably the desires to penetrate and be penetrated inherent in all orifices greatly complicate the baby's acceptance of dependence for services to these highly erogenous zones. The anxieties about emptying the mother or poisoning her with excrements form a contrapuntal arrangement to the possessiveness and tyrannical trends. It is this mother-in-danger which presses the child away from viewing the father as a rival towards enlisting him for the preservation of this indispensable and treasured object. Of the three orifices assumed open to the father, his functions in feeding and cleaning the mother are more easily accepted than his genital baby-nurturing one. And thus the genital oedipal conflict can hardly be joined until the pregenital ones have been largely resolved.

The consequence of this difficulty in integrating the functions of the mother, insofar as they influence the baby's imaginative conception of her interior, predispose to the image of three compartments in relative or absolute isolation from one another. The inside babies must neither get at the food of the breast nor occupy the mother's thoughts; the rectal rubbish bin must not spill into the breast nor poison the babies in the genital. The forms chosen to represent these compartments and their functions must be borrowed from what is observable of family life, and

family life is reflexively imbued with the meaning of these compartments and the anxieties attendant. Thus there ensues a continual commerce between outer world and inner world, a commerce in which the
formal qualities are introjected and the meaning externalized. The route
of the extrapolation in the maturational process is clearly towards
integration and the combined object. But to give substance to these
generalizations, we must turn to the artists and poets:

> Beneath him with new wonder now he views
> To all delight of human sense expos'd
> In narrow room Natures whole wealth, yea more,
> A Heav'n on Earth: for blissful Paradise
> Of God the Garden was, by him in the East
> Of *Eden* planted; *Eden* stretched her Line
> From *Auran* Eastward to the Royal Towrs
> Of great *Seleucia,* built by *Grecian* Kings,
> Or where the Sons of *Eden* long before
> Dwelt in *Telassar:* in this pleasant soile
> His farr more pleasant Garden God ordained;
> Out of the fertil ground he caus'd to grow
> All Trees of noblest kind for sight, smell, taste;
> And all amid them stood the Tree of Life,
> High eminent, blooming Ambrosial Fruit
> Of vegetable Gold; and next to Life
> Our Death the Tree of Knowledge grew fast by,
> Knowledge of Good bought dear by knowing ill.
> Southward through *Eden* went a River large,
> Nor chang'd his course, but through the shaggie hill
> Pass'd underneath ingulft, for God had thrown
> That Mountain as his Garden mould high rais'd
> Upon the rapid current, which through veins
> Of porous Earth with kindly thirst up drawn,
> Rose a fresh Fountain, and with many a rill
> Water'd the Garden; thence united fell
> Down the steep glade, and met the neather Flood,
> Which from his darksom passage now appeers,
> And now divided into four main Streams,
> Runs divers, wandring many a famous Realme
> And Country whereof here needs no account.

[Milton, *Paradise Lost, IV,* 205–235]

The geography of the Garden, originally raised by God for his own
pleasure and in which he is wont to walk, is of this strange construction,
that a hill has been raised above a river, thus making it an underground
river which reappears "from his darksom passages" to unite with the

rills which had risen from the fountain on top of the mountain, whose waters had been "through veins of porous earth with kindly thirst up drawn". Reunited, the flood is then divided into four main streams which "runs divers, wandering many a famous Realme / And Country whereof here needs no account". This imaginary vascular system clearly is only of interest to Milton insofar as it nourishes the breasts and head, the Tree of Life "High eminent, blooming Ambrosial Fruit / Of vegetable Gold; and next to Life / Our Death the Tree of Knowledge grew fast by".

It is a powerful invocation of the interior of the mother's body and the separate motives which draw the intruding part of the personality inwards, into the sensual delight of the breast or the omniscience of the mother's (library) head. Of the two it is only the Tree of Knowledge that is forbidden and consequently it is to the longing for Godlike knowledge that Satan appeals in his seduction of Eve. Homer's view of sexuality is less guilt-ridden:

> This hand the wonder framed; an olive spread
> Full in the court its ever verdant head.
> Vast as some mighty column's bulk, on high
> The huge trunk rose, and heaved into the sky;
> Around the tree I raised a nuptial bower,
> And roofed defensive of the storm and shower;
> The spacious valve, with art inwrought, conjoins;
> And the fair dome with polished marble shines.
> I lopp'd the branchy head; aloft in twain
> Sever'd the bole, and smooth'd the shining grain;
> Then posts, capacious of the frame, I raised,
> And bore it, regular, from space to space:
> Athwart the frame, at equal distance lie
> Thongs of tough hides, that boast a purple dye;
> Then polished the whole, the finished mould
> With silver shone, with elephant and gold.

> [Homer, *The Odyssey*, Book XXIII (Pope's translation)]

Here the voice of the poet evokes for us the nuptial chamber. Again we see the tree, this time the olive, around which this indestructible and sequestered haven is constructed.

But the Odyssey is also a compelling image of the function of the internal father on his return, through the act of love, to rid the internal mother of the persecutors and projected rubbish of the bad and naughty children. This debris, collected in the mother's rectum and removed by the internal father as a Herculean task like the Augean Stable, makes another point at which the relationship of the external parents supports or weakens the child's unconscious concept of the relationship between the internal parents at partial and whole object levels.

These descriptions, taken, as it were, from the vertex of the Telemachus part of the infantile personality vis-à-vis the bad and naughty brothers and sisters, fraught of course with savage infantile competitiveness, represent the consequences of splitting and idealization of the objects. The "bad" parents are represented as well in phantasy, and in the *Odyssey* they can be found in other aspects of both Ulysses and Penelope. He is the adventurer who stays too long away from the home and is soon off again on his travels. Penelope is also the bad mother whose weakness, unsupported, finds recourse to deception and placation in dealing with the bad children (of the narcissistic gang). But even in their "badness" the idealized parents illustrate the goodness to which, unhampered by infantile projective identifications (of adolescent qualities, for instance in Ulysses and Penelope), the internal objects can develop. The firm establishment of the compartmentalization would seem to be the precondition for the evolution of the qualities of mind of these parental figures, extrapolating to the infinity of truthfulness, goodness and wisdom—to godhead.

[The alterations wrought in these compartments are discussed elsewhere.] But I cannot leave this tribute to the inspiration coming from the poets and artists without mentioning the great display of this compartmentalization seen through the sin-racked and plague-tormented mentality of the end of the fifteenth century. Bosch's triptych, usually called "The Garden of Earthly Delights", displays the indolence, the sensuality and the claustrophobia of the three compartments consequent to the "first disobedience", the intrusion upon the parental prerogatives.

CHAPTER EIGHTEEN

Disorders of thought

(1994)

Donald Meltzer

Two years after *The Claustrum* [1992] Donald Meltzer returns, in a pleasantly discursive style, to the ways of function of thought processes, symbol formation and the role of truth in mental life. With the aid of two clinical cases which illustrate two different disorders of thought linked to misunderstandings of symbols. Interesting but still to be developed is the concept of "skeleton of the symbol"—differing from Bion as regards the possibility of observing symbol formation, Meltzer was pointing out the places in which symbol formation " is interrupted and deformed".

Bion's theory of thinking furnished us with an instrument for thinking about thinking and we now only have to try to use it to understand how it works, where it works, and where it does not work. To summarize briefly, it starts from the idea that our mind produces thoughts that can be used for thinking. Thoughts are produced through a mysterious process which Bion called "alpha function" and which consists in the transformation of emotional experiences into symbols. These symbols are formed during dreams in the way which Freud himself called "dream work". These dreams are therefore raised to ever higher levels of abstraction through a reflexive process, returning to nourish the mind and to promote further thought processes. . . . This system, which generates thoughts and which uses them for thinking, can also be interrupted at any point and the products of thinking can be used as a basis for action.

When this occurs, one puts an end to thinking and introduces a new process called "experimental action". The fundamental characteristic of experimental action is that it is not concerned to verify the truth within the thinking process, but is only concerned to see if it works in the external world. . . .

Thinking is thus not a ubiquitous process. For many people this mode of functioning, in which the process of thinking is interrupted at a certain point and experimental action prepared, is their habitual way of proceeding. Many people base themselves on the idea of things working, not on their being true, so that love of the truth is not a dominant element in their lives. Naturally, however, this view is very important from a psychoanalytic point of view.

Most patients who come into therapy are satisfied when they are successful, and are not very interested in understanding whether their functioning is based on the truth, on lies or on delusion. Bion's theory of thinking furnishes us with an instrument for recognizing the way in which people think, whether on the basis of truth or less than that. . . .

I want to give two clinical examples that required a certain amount of exploration to reach some degree of truth. The questions about truth occur on at least two different levels: the first concerns the trustworthiness of the observation of facts, the other concerns what was done with the truth in terms of symbol- and dream-formation.

The first patient of whom I shall speak is a bony, angular woman who came into the consulting room almost brushing the wall and threw herself onto the couch like a dead weight.

She is a woman who complained a lot about her bones and her muscles.

This complaining seems to have gone back to her birth. She appeared to complain of her bone structure, of the way in which her muscles were attached to her bones and their functioning, as though this was something that had begun from her birth. She tried to solve these problems in all possible ways, from masseurs to fortune-tellers.

When she came to me, this woman was on the point of giving up an academic career in a university department. On the one hand it was as though she had been "fired" by the department in which she worked and made herself incredibly unpopular. On the other hand she had been made a slave of the department, doing every possible sort of work. She had left the department, giving up a secure and well-paid post to try private work in her profession; this was extremely precarious, and she risked not having enough money to pay for the analysis. The patient told me all this at our first meeting.

The first year of analysis was very interesting. She had a considerable verbal capacity, was very intelligent, with very twisted thinking and logic. It was evident that the patient was involved in a very intrusive and complicated relationship with her mother, who was about 70 at the time, which included minute control of her mother through continuous discussions.

I will speak to you about something that was not exactly a dream but was something like a dream and may constitute a sort of model for understanding her mode of functioning.

One day, unlike her usual way, the patient left her car walking very securely, entered the consulting room decisively, and lay down delicately on the couch. I remained very surprised and waited to understand what had happened. The woman began speaking, saying that she had had a wonderful experience. I waited to hear her tell me that she was in love, but instead she recounted that she had just visited the natural history museum. I know this museum vaguely and have retained the impression of a terrifying Victorian structure, though with very interesting specimens. The patient referred to having seen the skeleton of a little elephant, together with the skeleton of its mother. At a certain point the woman, looking at the skeletons of the little elephant and its mother, had seen the dome of the museum, which appeared to her to be extraordinarily beautiful.

This seemed to me the equivalent of a dream. It had to do with her identification on the basis of the skeleton: her link with her mother was a skeletal link.

In the live example that I have described, the skeleton had the same function that Bion defined as "alpha function". Looking at the two skeletons, the patient was able to see the dome of the museum as a thing of great beauty. This seemed extraordinary to me, because, considering Bion's theory of thinking, I [now] had the idea that alpha function allowed one to see the beauty of an object and to recover its aesthetic significance.

This has led me to think about symbol formation and the way in which it relates to our body, to our skeletal structure and to our musculature.

I have asked myself whether symbol formation, symbols, and each particular symbol has its own skeleton, and if misunderstandings could arise from the fact of confusing the perception of the skeleton of the symbol with the symbol itself. There are various reasons for thinking that this is the case. To see and "affirm" the aesthetic value of an object in the outside world or in an artistic representation we need the intervention of alpha function. Thinking of this woman's experience with the skeletons of the little elephant and its mother as she looked at them, it seemed to me that I understood how one can speak of a work of art in terms of artistic technique or of its composition without gathering its complex essence.

Another example is provided by a patient whom I have had in analysis for several years and who appears very resistant to the exploration of his psychic reality, remaining very attached to the concrete aspects of reality.

He is married, has four children, the last of whom is still very young, and although he is a very devoted father and a paediatrician he is unable to be effective in what he does. He seems to me a very concrete person with little imagination, who is flat on an affective level.

About three years ago he planned to build a garage near his house, but he did not manage to complete that plan. His original plan was to construct a garage with his father-in-law, a man very expert in DIY. When his father-in-law died, he gave up this project and substituted the idea of building a playroom for the children, given that a fourth child had been born. He thought at this point of building a new room on the model of a barn near his home. He went to this barn and studied its architecture, reproduced its designs, and thought even of buying it in order to dismantle it and use the wood to construct the new room. When he went to see the barn, he realized that it was in very bad condition, but persisting in his original plan he decided to buy material similar to that of the barn for the building of his room. I felt rather encouraged by the perseverance shown by the patient at the time; I had not taken into account his pre-occupation with the causes of the bad condition of the barn. The patient convinced me to think about strategies for making weatherproof the beams that he had bought.

He had read in the newspaper that the roof of York Minster had caught fire and had been reconstructed using a material that was particularly resistant to water and to fire. He recalled having visited the Minster and having been struck by the luminosity of the new beams. Merely on the basis of this, the patient thought he had understood how that was possible. He had read in the newspaper that they had then used beams that had been burnt preventatively. His phantasy was that the new beams had been burnt to make them very resistant and were then treated and polished. When he spoke of this in the session, I drew to his attention to the fact that what he considered a proof was something insignificant. The patient became angry at what I said, and the result was that he telephoned the architect who had reconstructed the

Minster at York to have him explain in what way he had treated the beams.

The architect was very helpful and explained to the patient that they had taken huge wooden beams, had carbonized them, and had then scraped away the burnt parts and had used what remained, a small beam, for the construction.

The night following our telephone contact, the patient had an interesting dream. He dreamed that *he had gone with a friend to a conference where they explained the method of building houses with roofs made of bamboo cane covered with mud. At the end of the conference the patient explained to his friend that this material was arranged at various angles according to whether they were building the walls or the roof of the house: for the latter they used right angles, which evidently did not make sense.*

In the course of this tale, at a certain point the patient began to speak of what had actually happened the night before: at around eleven he had interrupted some work he was doing to go to his wife, who was breast-feeding their youngest child. Seeing this scene, he had felt very angry, but he could not understand why, given that feeding during the night had also been a custom with the older children, as also to feed them beyond their first year.

I knew that from the first months of the last pregnancy the patient had not had sexual relations with his wife. I asked the patient at this point what were the couple's arrangements at night. The patient said that the little baby slept in a bed placed at the foot of the parents' bed in a position that allowed him to see them. This arrangement had been thought of by the patient himself, with the idea that in this way the boy would feel more secure, being able to have the parents in his sight.

At this point I was able to understand something more of the dream. I thought that the explanation that he gave his friend in the dream about the arrangement of the bamboo canes represented something that strengthened the family and which related to the particular arrangement of the baby's bed in relation to the parents' bed, which was felt as a rather good thing for the family.

Two days later the patient arrived at the session saying that he had moved the baby from the room and had made love to his wife for the first time for a year. I did not manage to understand if the patient had finally intuited something or if he was only going along with the analyst's interpretation. . . . I had interpreted the dream as something in which a linguistic metaphor had been used to build a structure. When the patient described the position of the baby and of his parents at a right angle to each other, using the expression "encroaching", he was expressing some sort of conflict. So I he was trying to think, using a metaphor represented by a verbal expression that could describe the positions taken by the baby and his parents.

These are the points that I put on a trial by fire when studying disturbances of thought: one is the use of the skeleton of a symbol as though it were the symbol itself, the other is the use of a metaphor as a symbol: both result in disturbances of in thinking.

Bion justified having called this "alpha function", maintaining that symbol formation cannot be observed. Probably this is a mistake on his part because there are a variety of ways in which one may observe the formation of symbols. If we think of symbol formation as a process, we can examine this process and pick out some places in which it is interrupted or distorted. We can also observe symbol formation where there is a reversal of alpha function: this is a process of cannibalization of the symbol in which we find fragments of alpha function and traces of beta elements and of ego- and superego functioning. These elements cannot be used for thinking, only for hallucination and delusion-formation.

Mythology begins with a story which then undergoes a continuous process of condensation, and perhaps this is what happens in the process of symbol formation. This last concept shows that we do not form our own symbols, but use symbols that are conveyed to us through the generations. Thus the symbols that we receive and commonly use in our thinking and our communication are not the same symbols that are created autonomously under the effect of the inspiration that is present in artists.

CHAPTER NINETEEN

The lobby of dreams

(1988)

Donald Meltzer & Meg Harris Williams

Hamlet's immediate reaction to the Ghost's revelations is, following his university training, to write something down— not only in the "table of his memory" ("the book and volume of my brain"), but literally in his "tables". But he seizes them in vain, since the real problem is impossible to formulate, and he can only arrive at the platitudinous precept that "one may smile, and smile, and be a villain". He finds that telling a story requires aesthetic correlatives, not merely the instinctive urge to spill it out. Throughout the play, he is then plagued by the sense that everyone else wants to write his story, play upon his stops, pluck out his mystery, before he can even envisage himself: "Ere I could make a prologue to my brains, / They had begun the play". His antic disposition protects him in one way but exposes him in another, as an object of curiosity whose "very cause of lunacy" may by some process of detective riddle-solving be ferreted out and explained: "by indirections find directions out". The idea of "playing" therefore becomes a byword for manipulation, rather than for discovery-through-art; in *Hamlet*, all types of acting and action tend to be false moves rather than fictions about revelation; they are all "actions that a man might play". Instead, playing is contrasted with the idea of "holding", the capacity to observe without interpreting, which comes to focus substantially on Hamlet's relationship with Horatio: as in, "If thou didst ever hold me in thy heart . . ." or in Hamlet's declaration of love immediately before the play-within-a-play begins, standing out in contrast to its anti-revelatory nature:

> blest are those
> Whose blood and judgment are so well commeddled
> That they are not a pipe for Fortune's finger
> To sound what stop she please. Give me that man
> That is not passion's slave, and I will wear him
> In my heart's core, ay, in my heart of heart,
> As I do thee.

And although Hamlet speaks here as if Horatio had always held this significance for him, our impression is on the contrary, that the context of events and of Horatio's reaction to them, make the idea of Horatio more meaningful and eventually indispensable to Hamlet; thus on his first appearance, Hamlet appeared barely to recognize Horatio, did not travel from Wittenberg with him, and was unaware that he had been present at Elsinore throughout the funeral, marriage and coronation. Horatio's integrity as an observer is also stressed by the small detail that even Claudius employs him at one point to keep an eye on Ophelia (a post in which, since he can never affect the active course of events, he might seem to fail dismally—except that by some obscure means, the drowning of Ophelia shortly comes to the Queen's notice). He complements Hamlet's function as misfit or Fool through also being an outsider, always on the fringes of the court yet never receiving nor requiring "advancement", so remaining "poor"; and "why should the poor be flattered?" Despite or rather because of his passivity, Horatio comes to provide a vital aesthetic dimension to the story of the Mind of Denmark. Where everyone else is engaged in action, he is one who "in suffering all, suffers nothing"—that is, though seeing and feeling all that is done, he does not disintegrate or allow his self to become denatured. Without Hamlet's depths of exploration, he is not of princely or heroic calibre, but neither does he slip into defensive omnipotence (like Claudius and Polonius) in the face of phenomena he does not understand. And although he has few words to speak, his presence in the play is strongly felt. At the end, when Fortinbras the simple soldier-prince (an outsider in the sense of being uncontaminated by ideas) receives the election of the state, bequeathed with Hamlet's "dying voice", Horatio receives the legacy of Hamlet's "story". He is still there to hold together the facts of the story, just as he was there at the beginning to introduce Hamlet and us to the Ghost, though he is no more a protagonist than are we ourselves. So in terms of the spatial quality of *Hamlet* as a whole, the Horatio dimension, which is defined gradually and almost imperceptibly, is essential to the reader's grasp of

Hamlet's "act"—the drama of dreams which is taking place between the lines, and which, unlike the linear plot, does not end definitively in a dying voice.

Horatio's un-prominent significance begins to take shape only after Hamlet's heroic effort to explore alone the "undiscovered country" of his mind in the "To be or not to be" soliloquy. This is an exploration which terminates abortively in the nunnery scene with Ophelia, and is never resumed so hopefully. The soliloquy stands at the centre of the play, in spatial as well as temporal terms; it is the eye at the centre of the whirlwind; its implications radiate outwards from this key point in the Hamlet consciousness. In terms of linear plot progression, this speech appears to have no business here—embedded as it is in the midst of the Mousetrap sequence, between Hamlet's first meeting with the players and the fruition of his scheming to "catch the conscience of the king". The plot is thickening and gathering speed, and this introspective and abstract soliloquy seems to stand in the way of the main action of the play, which has finally got going—so much so that sometimes in productions it has been lifted out of context and placed nearer the beginning, where Hamlet is more depressed and less manic. Yet, as we shall see, this detachment from the main action of the revenge tragedy (the play's superficial form) is essential to the play's *latent* drama, with its conflict between an omnipotent detective mentality and an exploratory, symbolic mentality. The soliloquy is given in the Lobby, where Hamlet is known to walk for hours on end, pacing his chosen cage and masticating "words, words, words", thereby reinforcing his sense that "Denmark's a prison" (as he tells Rosencrantz and Guildenstern). The Lobby is partly open to the sky, making a sort of artificial outside within the claustrophobic heart of the court; it is the place where Polonius and Hamlet discuss the shapes of the clouds, and Hamlet implies that the shape of the prince he is looking for is not that of a camel or a weasel or a whale; a place which Hamlet regards as but one step from the grave, as when Polonius asks him: "Will you walk out of the air, my lord?" and he answers "Into my grave?" The Lobby as a space, also echoes the Ghost's "prison-house" of purgatory, whose "secrets" he is "forbid to tell". All in all, it is ambiguous as to whether the Lobby is a chamber of dreams or a prison for nightmares. In it the prince is bounded in a nutshell, rehearsing the interaction between infinite space and bad dreams.

In "To be or not to be", the latent spatial tensions of the underlying dream-play in *Hamlet* take on an almost microscopic character, barely visible to the naked eye. Here Hamlet makes an approach to the cloud of unknowing which contains the shape of the undiscovered country at the heart of his mystery:

To be, or not to be, that is the question:
Whether 'tis nobler in the mind to suffer
The slings and arrows of outrageous fortune,
Or to take arms against a sea of troubles,
And by opposing end them. To die—to sleep,
No more; and by a sleep to say we end
The heart-ache and the thousand natural shocks
That flesh is heir to: 'Tis a consummation
Devoutly to be wish'd. To die, to sleep;
To sleep, perchance to dream—ay, there's the rub;
For in that sleep of death what dreams may come,
When we have shuffled off that mortal coil,
Must give us pause . . .

As Dr Johnson saw, the speech "shows connections rather in the speaker's mind, than on his tongue"; if one reads only the argument, it appears to be the refined expression of a string of Renaissance commonplaces; but if one reads the images beyond the "tongue", it evokes in a semi-abstract way the tentative journey of a soul tasting a new world in a way which transcends the sterility of "words, words, words". The "sea of troubles" echoes the sea of madness figured by Horatio in the ghost-scene, towards which Hamlet was led by the armed Ghost, who was himself invulnerable to the soldiers' sword-stabs; and the beating of the waves on rocks lies faintly behind the "shocks" on "flesh", the soul's armour and sounding-board, just as the "mortal coil" suggests both tightly-wound rope and a snake shedding its skin. The mind's body no longer seems a "sterile promontory", but quivers in anticipation. Hamlet's evocation of "the heartache, and the thousand natural shocks / That flesh is heir to" opens a new perspective on the observation of everyday suffering, as if through a microscope: expressing the drama which escapes the stage, the shock of feeling which normally goes unnoticed. Hence it stands in stark contrast to the play-within-a-play which is being engineered in the background, and the bombastic rhetoric of the players, which one part of Hamlet regards as a travesty of genuine feeling: "What's Hecuba to him, or he to Hecuba, that he should weep for her?" Hamlet's picture of the newly-transmuted soul which has "shuffled off this mortal coil" and "pauses", disoriented in its new nakedness, for unknown "dreams to come", is a startlingly poignant revision of the standard image of release from the body's prison. We remember the tranquil, secure sleep in which the Ghost was painfully assaulted by a kind of dream of being poisoned—the fundamental dream-sequence to which Hamlet is "heir", both fulfilling and undermining the "consummation" of life. This underlies the emotional upheaval which is the genesis of the poetic exploration in "To be or not to be", and which leads out of the smooth nutshell to "the pale cast of thought". Now the embryonic prince pauses, at the threshold of the land of dreams, the undiscovered country, then crosses back to the world to capture aspects of worldly injustice ("Th' oppressor's wrong, the proud man's contumely, / The pangs of dispriz'd love"); then again makes another approach to the caesura of death, the moment of change, at which

> the dread of something after death,
> The undiscover'd country, from whose bourn
> No traveller returns, puzzles the will . . .

At the very threshold again, "dread" is strangely transmuted into disorientation, as "must give us pause" becomes "puzzles the will"; and the word "puzzles", emphatically placed, gives the idea of confusion an almost physical impact as in "amazed". Yet it is still delicately contained on a spiritual plane; the idea of "something after death" is no longer that of the hell-fire torments threatened in the Ghost's "eternal blazon" speech; these have melted away, like "too too solid flesh", leaving—not a filled-in picture—but a pause and a space for the "undiscovered country" at the heart of the mystery, a glimpse of a landscape whose features are unknown. The rhythm of the verse carries the voyaging soul into death and back again.

The values hinted at by this pause in the overt argument (whose logic has lost its impetus) deprive worldly enterprises, including those of "great pitch and moment", of even "the name of action":

> Thus conscience does make cowards of us all,
> And thus the native hue of resolution
> Is sicklied o'er with the pale cast of thought,
> And enterprises of great pitch and moment
> With this regard their currents turn awry
> And lose the name of action.

The new prince is no longer sure, not only of what action to take and when, but of what constitutes "action"—what kind of action has reality. The Ghost's injunction was to "pursue the act" without "tainting his mind"; now the question arises, what "act" is Hamlet really pursuing? For in this soliloquy the revenge-action and the superficial question about Claudius's guilt have been far transcended. Hamlet puts in the background the melodramatic blazonry which surrounds the idea of the revenge-act and other pseudo-actions usually considered heroic or important, and concentrates instead on the poetic and genuine aspects of the Ghost's suffering, the "unhousel'd" infant soul on its lonely journey. He retraces the Ghost's travels through a refinement of imagery, by "suffering in the mind", until the traveller who returns from the undiscovered country is no longer the same as the one who went. The Ghost who was "unhearsed" and "cast up" from the grave, is given a place in "conscience"; the literal disfigurement of his body ("bark'd about most lazar-like") is transmuted into "sicklied o'er with the pale cast of thought"; the blood coursing through the "gates and alleys of the body, curdled 'like eager droppings into milk'", becomes the "currents [which] turn awry" as action metamorphoses into thought. The pure milk which fed the infant soul becomes contaminated at the moment of simultaneous sin and thought, when the boundaries of the mind extend beyond the womblike nutshell which it believed was infinity, and a glimpse of the undiscovered country hoves in view. The very process of "suffering in the mind" expands the horizons of thought, in a way antithetical to the process which Hamlet in the previous scene had described as "unpacking my heart with words". The latent imagery of "To be or not to be" occupies a space between the lines which is as far beyond "words, words, words" as "action" is beyond its "name". It exemplifies Hamlet's struggle to get beyond philosophy into poetry, to exchange riddling for the heart of the mystery, to achieve "beneficence in space" (to use Stokes's phrase).

Immediately at the end of the soliloquy, without even half a line's pause, Ophelia appears:

> Soft you now,
> The fair Ophelia! Nymph, in thy orisons
> Be all my sins remember'd.

Her presence at this point seems to derive from two opposing lines of force, the real "mighty opposites" which govern the drama of the Mind of Denmark: on the one hand, she appears the answer to Hamlet's dream of an "undiscovered country", and his spiritual voyage seems to conjure up her presence (though it seems she has in fact been present in the background all the time); on the other hand, she has been planted as bait by Claudius and Polonius, who have arranged themselves as "lawful espials" behind a pillar in the Lobby while "To be or not to be" is being spoken and Ophelia is "loosed" to Hamlet. The clash between these two forces meeting in the person of the innocent Ophelia, arouses an explosive violence in Hamlet which is matched only by his verbal attack on the other woman he loves, his mother, for being soiled by experience. The name "Ophelia" (according to the Arden edition notes) seems to have two derivations: in a word meaning "succour", and in "Apheleia" meaning "simplicity", described by Ben Jonson as "a nymph pure and simple as the soul or as an abrase table". As the partner to Hamlet's soul, or the earthly image of his own soul, Ophelia both offers succour to the "puzzled" embryonic prince within him, and stresses its vulnerability. As Laertes later tells the priest, "A ministering angel shall my sister be / While thou liest howling". Hamlet fresh from "crawling between earth and heaven", immediately addresses her as if she might somehow provide a container for his "sins", for the puzzled, howling, crawling child within him which she may "remember" through innate knowledge. Yet her *tabula-rasa* quality reacts two-dimensionally, appearing simply to reflect back his sins in the form of returning his gifts: "My lord, I have remembrances of yours / That I have longed to redeliver. I pray you now receive them". She acts in automatic obedience to her father who told her to "lock up" her "chaste treasure". Hamlet intuits the fact that, as *tabula rasa*, she is merely acting as a vehicle for another force, but far from excusing her, this inflames him because it is the very force which he regards as his enemy—the enemy of the true aesthetic action which, he implies, can somewhere "shape" offences into thoughts:

> Get thee to a nunnery. Why, wouldst thou be a breeder of sinners? I am
> myself indifferent honest, but yet I could accuse me of such things that
> it were better my mother had not borne me. I am very proud,
> revengeful, ambitious, with more offences at my beck than I have
> thoughts to put them in, imagination to give them shape, or time to act
> them in. What should such fellows as I do crawling between earth and
> heaven?

The very act of birth makes a sinner; the infant exploring the territory of his world-mother between its upper and lower regions, is sinning and simultaneously seeking for a mould of mental form, a shaping spirit of imagination. Hamlet implies that if Ophelia merely redelivers offences, instead of shaping them, her proper place is in a "nunnery"—a type of chastity which has, in his view, associations with bawdery; he feels Ophelia is displaying herself towards him in a way that is not herself but a species of "painting" or false art: "I have heard of your paintings. . . . God hath given you one face and you make yourselves another". The nunnery and the brothel are both places where the real body or self is hidden, a tantalizing but immune secret. In these passages Hamlet is really speaking to the Polonius-behind-Ophelia, whom he calls a "fishmonger" (bawd) and warns not to let his daughter "walk i' the sun" (with a pun on "son"—namely himself), "lest she may conceive". For it is Ophelia's stance, rather than any literal suspicion of the eavesdroppers on their conversation, which prompts him to see the ghost of her father in her, and to make the sudden accusation: "Where's your father? . . . Let the doors be shut upon him, that he may play the fool nowhere but in's own house". Hamlet feels Polonius too belongs in a nunnery or asylum, in return for engineering the false non-meeting of minds which occurs in the nunnery scene and which converts the Lobby of Dreams into a cage, as if Hamlet and Ophelia were animals in a zoo marked out for insemination in captivity, "breeding maggots". (Hence after the forthcoming murder, Hamlet against all rationality insists on "stowing" Polonius in a cupboard on the stairs, on the way up to the Lobby—not to disguise his crime, but because it seems to him an appropriate confinement.) Polonius regards the mystery of whatever may be "brewing between" the young lovers much as he regards the mystery of the madness inside Hamlet—as something which can be trapped for inspection, a phenomenon which may be encompassed by the politic language of bargaining, manoeuvring, hunting, playing and selling.

Yet Hamlet's rage against Ophelia derives not only from his antipathy to Polonius, but from his own failure to communicate with her—the conventional absurdity of his love-letters, which belong just as much to the realms of courtly artifice as do Polonius' manoeuvres, rather than to the true expression of feeling; and in particular, his unspoken guilt at his behaviour during his last meeting with her, when he intruded half-dressed into her closet while she was sewing in order to project onto her his anxiety after the meeting with the Ghost. In Ophelia's account (for this offstage encounter constitutes yet another dream-image, expressing Ophelia's intuition of Hamlet's state of mind), he came "As if he had been loosed out of hell / To speak of horrors", and echoing the Ghost's torments, with a sigh that seemed "to shatter all his bulk / And end his being". Hamlet's attempt to convey his experience of the Ghost is beset by the devils of aggressive artifice and "blazonry", echoing his difficulty in receiving the real experience from the ambiguous Ghost in the first place. Hence his intrusion into the closet is less a communication than a species of attack, a type of play-acting or false art in the same mode as the Mousetrap. The vision of the teasing, frightening Ghost is directed at Ophelia without any digestion or modification of the image, and it is inevitable that it should simply reflect back again without understanding. In a sense Hamlet gets his just deserts in the nunnery scene, since the anti-aesthetic element in his relations with Ophelia is initiated by himself not Polonius; he has never presented his sins or "remembrances" in a form which gives her a proper chance to receive or remember them. Ultimately Ophelia, in her effort to understand him and receive his image truly, takes the weight of his madness upon herself (she is the only character with a literal belief in it, and it affects her literally), and sinks with all his sins remembered, drowning. The "rose of the fair state" and the "rose of May" are at the same time idiot-fool and innocent-fool, suggesting a fundamental bond of sympathy which never finds any language of interaction, any aesthetic correlation. After the nunnery scene, therefore, Hamlet's mania redoubles in energy, and he includes Ophelia, too, among the participants in a poisoned marriage whom he tries to trap in the play-within-a-play.

CHAPTER TWENTY

Aesthetic appreciation through symbolic congruence

(1988)

Donald Meltzer & Meg Harris Williams

> the calm
> And dead still water lay upon my mind
> Even with a weight of pleasure, and the sky
> Never before so beautiful, sank down
> Into my heart, and held me like a dream.

In these lines from the *Prelude* Wordsworth captures the essence of aesthetic appreciation through symbolic congruence: the "fitting" of the individual mind to the aesthetic object, in such a way that boundaries merge and yet the independent integrity of both partners in the drama—internal and external world—is affirmed and radiates significance. He does this without any self-conscious rhetoric relating to the "pathetic fallacy"; no "as ifs" or personifications; it is simply described as a fact, that the mind at the bottom of the lake of consciousness is pressed upon by the weight of water reflecting the sky, in such a way that it both holds and is held by this ethereal expanse of light which has taken on a quality of weight and density—sinking "down" (as if like a stone) yet in fact like a "dream". The alternation of down and up-movements, suggesting increase and decrease in density, confirms the sense of dissolving and reforming boundaries as mind seeks congruence in nature and through this, the experience of becoming known. Likewise, Adrian Stokes speaks of architecture as being a "solid dream", in which "directions and alternatives and the vague character

of a weighty impress" are captured, held, integrated with "full cognizance of space", until the "changing surfaces, in–out, smooth–rough,
light–dark, up–down, all manner of trustful absorption by space, are
activated further than in a dream". And as an extension of this, Stokes
describes aesthetic response in general, as recalling and holding the
"feel" of a dream:

> Appreciation is a mode of recognition: we recognise but we cannot
> name, we cannot recall by an effort of will: the contents that reach us
> in the terms of aesthetic form have the "feel" of a dream that is
> otherwise forgotten . . . ["The Luxury and Necessity of Painting", in
> *Three Essays*, 1961]

At the heart of aesthetic appreciation lies the problem of holding, recognizing, the feel of the dream which is evoked between the dreamer and
the aesthetic object (whatever form this may take). This is a diaphanous
cloud of unknowing, which seems composed nevertheless of solid elements with shape and texture, awaiting capture into a symbolic correspondence. As Stokes says: "Owing to the corporeal nature of the
adult's inner objects, it seems that a dream can deposit a residue of
sensations of shape, as does art the more general . . . perception of inner
objects" (*Painting and the Inner World*, 1963a). So, holding the dream has
to do with a congruence or reciprocity between internal and external
objects: with "full cognizance of space". And in the fields of art and
literature, for example, the artist's experience as embodied in the art
form, serves as a model for the aesthetic mentality: not just by providing an aesthetic object as a thing in itself, but also by exemplifying the
process of symbol formation which is what will enable the viewer to
hold the dream in his mind, under observation, until such time as it
becomes meaningful.

   In this chapter I want to focus on the implications of this for literary
criticism: first by expanding the definition of "symbolic congruence",
with the help in particular of Adrian Stokes; then by exploring the
apprehension of beauty in Wordsworth's sonnet "On Westminster
Bridge".

   In academic literary culture in recent years, so strong has been the
grip of the soft humanist mentality—upholding the polarity between
thought and feeling, reason and intuition—that any attempt to under-
mine its supremacy and to investigate the aesthetic foundation of creative thought is doomed to make one feel like Sisyphus pushing his stone
up the hill. The only popular alternative at present seems to be the
recurrent mechanistic one of linguistic behaviourism, in the form of
structuralism and pseudo-Freudian interpretation. And inspected more
closely, this turns out not even to be an alternative, but merely another

version of the same thing, only presented under the aegis of prep-school verbal trickery, rather than that of complacent liberal maturity. Altogether the prevailing academic view of art seems to be one in which oral or anal gratification, ineffectively checked by conscious efforts at didactic morality or reasonableness, is displayed (acted out) under the pressure of social adaptation. There is on the whole no concept of psychic change.

Among the false or anti-aesthetic approaches to what should prop-erly be seen as an aesthetic concern, one may include such things as: the notion of art's "incompleteness", as if its social function were to titivate the intellect of the cultured bourgeoisie in order to complete itself; the notion of the critic (or the "normal" aspect of an artist) imposing some "secondary process" on art's "primary process" to keep it in order; all criticism based on the phantasy of uncovering the "secrets of the uncon-scious" (thereby employing no distinction between secrecy and mys-tery); and all criticism which shows no awareness of the distinction between sign-systems and symbolic forms (so that the art-symbol is talked about as if it were merely a manifestation of society's basic assumptions).

Yet the critic who is aware of these distinctions, who has a grasp of the aesthetic quality of the material he is handling, and tries to ap-proach it in an aesthetic manner, is hampered by the weight of the stone he is pushing—not just in terms of convincing others, but owing to the task itself; shouldering "the burden of the mystery". In effect, he has a task analogous to that of the artist, in trying to evolve a language which is capable of containing the implications and reverberations of an emo-tional experience—yet probably without the degree of talent for discov-ering and expressing mental life through symbolic forms, which is the artist's most essential characteristic. In aesthetic criticism, therefore, he is heavily dependent on using a faculty of receptive congruence to the formal structures evolved by the artist for the containing of "meaning" or "artistic import". He is dealing with the same mysterious phenom-ena, the life of the mind in process; yet owing to his smaller stature is under perhaps even greater pressure not to call infantile omnipotence to his aid, not to penetrate intrusively the mystery of the aesthetic object and explain it away by providing (even implicitly) the ultimate inter-pretation. No critic can attain the same felicity of expression as the artist who is his subject and guide. Yet without certain qualities he would be incapable of doing his job. From the aesthetic critic we are entitled to expect, therefore, some ability to tolerate the uncertainty of the cloud of unknowing aroused by confrontation with the aesthetic object, without irritable reaching after fact and reason; some capacity to look steadily at the subject until eventually a pattern emerges. That is, we expect the concern with "knowing" to dominate the inevitable academic background of "knowing about". We also expect some means of verbal expression which, however inadequate it may be, is nonetheless in intention geared towards receiving the inherent expressiveness of the art-symbol, rather than towards superimposing the critic's preconceptions. Above all, though most elusive to define or locate, we expect from the critic who is genuinely involved in the aesthetic mentality, some overriding sense that his encounter with art constitutes one of his life's formative experiences: that it is, to use Bion's terms, a species of "identifying with the evolution of O"—"O" being the "absolute essence" or "central feature" of an emotional situation, translated by Bion and others as equivalent to "the state of being in love". The network of identifications into which the viewer is drawn by the invisible tensions and forces materializing in aesthetic forms, activates the heart of passionate experience, the source of the world's meaningfulness. The structure of this experience, if not its intense daring, is the same for the viewer or critic as for the artist who was "the first that ever burst / Into that silent sea" (in Coleridge's phrase). So the aesthetic critic's prime responsibility in holding the dream for the reader, is to show by example how it is possible to think *with* the book, rather than showing what to think *about* it. To do this he has to avoid both intrusive curiosity (converting the aesthetic object into a secret), and also, buttressing himself through judgement and evaluation (as if he were self-elected guardian of the object).

The language of aesthetic criticism, should therefore, by means of its own deep-laid metaphor, image a goal of generating new realms of meaning through exploration and discovery, based on passionate congruence between the forms of the inner self and those of the aesthetic object. Commitment should be to a process rather than to an interpretation: to the vale of soul-making, the evolution of O, the "vision of a former world and a future" (Byron's definition of poetry). The aesthetic critic, by contrast with the solely academic critic, needs to respond to what Stokes calls the "envelopment" or " incantatory" factor in art, rather than standing guard over the external qualities of the object as a museum piece. As in that archetypal model for aesthetic criticism, Keats's "Ode on a Grecian Urn", he must revere the object's inviolate world-of-its-own, yet at the same time allow its sculptured contours to melt and mingle with his own state of mind, together with the anxiety, excitement and confusion entailed as it "pipes to the spirit ditties of no tone". This transcendental music, this penumbra of significance beyond the lexical connotations of words, begins to impinge on the observer as he ceases to be a mere observer. He becomes a partaker, and also the one who is being observed. Feeling himself drawn in to the aesthetic object, and responding to the psychic tensions captured by its formal qualities, his own inner mental structure is inevitably modified. This drawing-in aspect of aesthetic experience is described by Adrian Stokes in *The Invitation in Art* [chapter 5, this volume], as "a vehemence beyond an identification with realised structure, that largely lies . . . in a work's suggestion of a process in train, of transcending stress, with which we may immerse ourselves". While at the same time, Stokes continues, "under the spell of this enveloping pull, the object's otherness, and its representation of otherness, are the more poignantly grasped":

> The great work of art is surrounded by silence. It remains palpably "out there", yet none the less enwraps us; we do not so much absorb as become ourselves absorbed.

The two modes or rather aspects of aesthetic response—incorporation and envelopment, observing and being observed, holding and being held—are complementary and mutually enriching. Unless the viewer or critic can respond to the "incantation" of art, there is no sense of self-exploration. And if there is no self-exploration, then neither is there full appreciation of the objective qualities of the art-symbol. "Knowing" as opposed to "knowing about" can never be objective in the academic sense; yet it is clear that the kind of subjectivity which is required by an aesthetic response, is very different and in fact antithetical to what is usually meant by the term "self-expression", since it is rigorously tied to the formal structure of the object. It is in fact, as Emily Brontë said, "when the eye begins to see and the ear begins to hear". The Urn, archetype of the mother's body—being the subject of our primary aesthetic experience—does not yield the *meaning* of its message "Beauty is truth, truth beauty" to the viewer who has not committed his *self* for observation and exploration. Those words may mean nothing, and may mean everything, depending on the character of the viewer's progression through the rest of the poem; they materialize on the surface of the Urn at the end of the poem, as if emerging from within and only now becoming readable. To the conscientious critic who has painstakingly laboured through to this point, they appear like a slap in the face from the poet, who tells him that his entire mode of evaluation has been inadequate. In order to read the Urn, or to read a poem on the Urn, it is necessary to find a mode of procedure which can take account of the aesthetic object's infiltration of and—in effect—*attack* upon the viewer's own established ego-structure, so that it re-forms from the vertices of "love, hate and knowledge" in response to the recognition of "Beauty". "The import of an art symbol", writes Susanne Langer, "cannot be built up like the meaning of a discourse, but must be seen *in toto* first":

Artistic import, unlike verbal meaning, can only be exhibited, not demonstrated, to anyone to whom the art symbol is not luced . . . [The articulation of the art symbol] may be traced, but it can never be constructed by a process of synthesis of elements, because no such elements exist outside it. [*Feeling and Form*, 1953]

The problem is how to know that which, however concrete, is ineffable—in such a way that we are discovering ourselves at the same time, and responding to the invitation in art. Our immediate reaction to a great work of literature may be one of amazement, awe, disturbance; we may intuitively see its truth, yet not recognize this new experience. Yet our desire to "know" the work better may be an ambivalent one, a type of self-defence, if it is based on explaining-away, unearthing secrets, diagnosing the psychopathology of its author—even perhaps the apparently harmless scholarly pursuit of establishing sources and references. And the usual way we read, a species of daydreaming, is no less an indulgence in preconception than is the more systematic procedure of academic interpretation. Nevertheless the work of art does demand for us to know it, in a more essential sense; it exists for the use of mankind, to awaken and give shape to our need to be known and to know ourselves. We confront the work of art; an emotional experience occurs, which needs to be integrated within the mind in the form of a reciprocal symbol, such that its meaning may become known; "but first a container must be found to hold the experience" (Bion, Meltzer). Then in the interaction between the mind of the viewer and the artist's mental process as embodied in the art form, a new emotional event germinates. The meaning of the art-symbol crosses beyond art's material boundaries, into that desolate no-man's land where as Keats said "the sedge is withered from the lake / And no birds sing": the "undiscovered country, from whose bourn / No traveller returns". This is the area in which aesthetic criticism operates.

Tolstoy uses the image of a field of battle, as yet untouched by contending forces, its boundaries quivering in anticipation of some strange transformation, to describe the threshold of knowledge:

One step beyond that line, which is like the bourne dividing the living from the dead, lies the Unknown of suffering and death. And what is there? Who is there? Thmere beyond that field, beyond that tree, that roof gleaming in the sun? No one knows, but who does not long to know? You fear to cross that line, yet you long to cross it; and you know that sooner or later it will have to be crossed and you will find out what lies there on the other side of the line, just as you will inevitably have to learn what lies the other side of death. [*War and Peace*, tr. R. Edmonds]

This is what Bion calls the "caesura" between commensal worlds, which comes to vibrate with meaning as a "discovery" is heralded, and the idea of a mutually penetrating "common sense" takes shape. The importance is paramount of being able to construct a space where "it" can happen, by means of a struggle both active and passive, a relationship with some inspirational power experienced as outside the self. Without some underlying spatial metaphor—Urn or battlefield—to give internal objects a chance to achieve symbolization, the dreamer or viewer or critic may feel overwhelmed by the cloud of unknowing, and unable to hold its meaning or be held by its meaningfulness. Like Tolstoy's battlefield shaped between its opposing armies, Milton makes a dual approach to the "void and formless infinite". The formless space is defined by two reciprocal movements: on the one hand, by holy Light investing the "rising world of waters dark and deep", and on the other, by the flight of the poet's soul "through utter and through middle darkness". The soul is seeking a return to the place where light gave the world meaning and safety ("Thee I revisit safe"); but light no longer seems to give the secure (and familiar) form of Nature's "book of knowledge fair" to the formless infinite. In fact all form is lost in space, until another area for light's operation is discovered as its rays are forcefully reflected in the direction of the unknown: "shine inward, and the mind through all her powers irradiate". From this confrontation between the self and a higher power in the realms of infinite space, the poet forges a new container for meaning—the world of the mind: a world which he now has the higher power's aid in observing.

Our aesthetic reception of poetry has to be modelled on the poet's own struggle for symbolic form; poets and artists are, inevitably, among our main guides to aesthetic experience. Yet even with the poet as guide (as the poet has holy Light, or the Muse), the process of working towards a symbolic congruence is so difficult that one is tempted to lapse into hopelessness about the point of it all, and thence into complacency. The gap between the poet's experience and our own might seem so vast (when we try to take it seriously), that we prefer to relegate it to the spheres of romance and daydream; we find that astronomical conjectures are not relevant to our late-twentieth-century selves who are in the adulthood of mankind's evolution and don't have to depend (like Milton) on imagination and a glimpse through Galileo's telescope, to discover the mysteries of space; such flights of fancy can have no bearing on grown-up thought and reason. The temptations to demean or recoil from aesthetic experience are strong, especially when we don't know what to do with it. Yet the universal infant within everyone would not regard as remote or meaningless the experience of flying through utter and middle darkness, or of the "universal blank" at the withdrawal of the "human face divine", or of food for the soul as well as the body when "eyes" are "planted inward", mist is dispersed, and the mind expanded and fulfilled. Adrian Stokes describes mental life as "a laying out of strength within, in rivalry as it were, with the instantaneous world of space":

> For all the blaring echoes, there are many cries to which we are normally untuned. Yet so vast is emotion, we come to feel that cries from the heart rebound to us from the astronomical distances of the universe. [*Inside Out*, 1947]

Milton's space, prophetic though it was of later scientific discoveries, is first and foremost a field for "tuning in" to the ineffable qualities of emotional life, those "ditties of no tone". It dramatizes what Tolstoy calls the "bourne between the living and the dead"; what Stokes calls the "line of equivalence between emotion and the outer world":

> By means of expression, his perennial activity, the mind of man views with the world in outwardness: deeper things come forward. An expressive token of all expressiveness, the face of the stone is made to show through the stone; and in the evening light there is a moment when mind seems to become extension, stands revealed in the eyes. [*Venice*, 1945]

Along this line of equivalence, between classical and romantic zones, or "carving" and "enveloping" modes of contact between self and object, the dream is evoked and contained; the drama of the inner world finds its symbolic form. The infant-soul's interaction with the body-spaces of the world-mother constitutes the formation of Mind—a sort of "extension" of the solid object in the changing light: the inside emerging outside, the outside sinking in and holding like a dream. Donald Meltzer stresses the primordial quality and centrality of the aesthetic sense, beginning with the baby at the breast or even earlier, and being what separates "protomental" activity (nominative, externally factual, quantitative) from true "mental" experience—symbolic and qualitative, carrying meaning in the sense of imaginative import. Aesthetic congruence, under the aegis of the Mother/Muse, is the source and foundation of all developmental thought-processes, of essential "knowing" above and beyond "knowing about"; based on simultaneously exploring and being explored. Responding to the aesthetic object's incantation, and incorporating its function of observing our internal processes, we enter the world of coming-to-knowledge. In Bion's words: "What is to be sought is an activity that is both the restoration of good (the Mother) and the evolution of good (the formless, infinite, ineffable)" (*Attention and Interpretation*, 1970). The reason why we need a clearer grasp of what aesthetic experience is, through recognizing and evaluating it, is not therefore to swell the numbers of artists or musicians or psychoanalysts, but to locate and develop that aspect of our mental life which governs the meaningfulness of our attitudes and relationships in other spheres.

CHAPTER TWENTY-ONE

Keats: soul-making

(1991)

Meg Harris Williams

> Imperceptibly impelled by the awakening of the thinking principle—
> within us—we . . . get into the Chamber of Maiden-Thought . . . in-
> toxicated with the light and the atmosphere, we see nothing but
> pleasant wonders, and think of delaying there for ever in delight.
> However among the effects this breathing is father of is that tremen-
> dous one of sharpening one's vision into the heart and nature of
> Man—of convincing one's nerves that the World is full of Misery and
> Heartbreak, Pain, Sickness and oppression—whereby this Chamber
> of Maiden Thought becomes gradually darken'd and at the same
> time on all sides of it many doors are set open—but all dark—all
> leading to dark passages We see not the balance of good and evil. We
> are in a Mist We are now in that state—We feel "the burden of the
> Mystery".
>
> [Keats, letter to Reynolds, 3 May 1818][1]

K eats's beautiful metaphor of life—that is, the life of the mind as
a "mansion of many apartments", describes his personal state at
the end of his poetic apprenticeship, in the foreshadow of his
inspired poetry of 1819. It is a prototypal parable of the infant soul's
explorations in the world of the mind, and also includes Keats's conception of a "general and gregarious advance of intellect" in cultural
history, in which new minds can take advantage of previous endeav-
ours without having to rely totally on their "individual greatness of

Mind" for every step forward in development.[2] In this context, Milton's "philosophy" (conscious doctrine) is simple by comparison with Wordsworth (whom Keats also regarded as "a great Poet if not a Philosopher")[3]; Keats saw Wordsworth as having arrived at this point partly by virtue of previous poets, and his "Genius" as being "explorative of those dark Passages. Now if we live, and go on thinking, we too shall explore them."[4] In the event, it was not Wordsworth but Keats who took over the "grand march of intellect" at this point of poetic Mist and Mystery. He established a relationship with his internal world which enabled him to "go on thinking". The Chamber of Maiden Thought is at the heart of the mind's mansion, and all doors open from it. From its original "infant or thoughtless Chamber", the soul is "imperceptibly impelled" to the next chamber by innate forces beyond its control, by forces which have strangely "awakened", on the lines of Coleridge's recognition that "at times we should awake and step forward", or Ibsen's *When We Dead Awaken*. It is not the "bright appearance" of Maiden Thought which motivates, though the chamber stands invitingly with its "wide open door"; rather, it is this innate "thinking principle". Indeed, "we care not to hasten to it, but are at length impelled". Such is the nature of the poetic principle of self development, activated by internal forces beyond the self's volition, despite the self's reluctance. Once in the second chamber, the infant soul is "intoxicated" by the sensuous wonder of its brave new world; yet its very "breathing" of that new world, incorporating it into the fibres of its own being, "is father to" the poison of heartbreak and sickness, as an inevitable part of its growing condition. This is the thought-sickness of which Hamlet complained; or in Keats's own words, "Until we are sick, we understand not."[5] And eventually, the dark doorways send their emanations into the Chamber of Maiden Thought, so the condition of "straining at particles of light in the midst of a great darkness" (as Keats puts it later)[6] becomes unavoidable. Now the poetic mind is shrouded in mist, which expresses the knowledge of "Mystery", at last felt upon the pulses. Keats leaves his extended metaphor at this point, on the threshold of a new chamber of discovery—saying he has not "arrived" any further.

The initial intoxication of Maiden Thought conveys Keats's own first experience of poetry, which "swam into his ken" like a "new planet",[7] and on which he seized with a "Leviathan" appetite for its emotional food. As he wrote the year before: "I find that I cannot exist without poetry—without eternal poetry—half the day will not do—the whole of it—I began with a little, but habit has made me a Leviathan."[8] From the beginning, this passionate need for the immense store of riches which the young Keats sensed were embodied within poetry, co-existed with the daunting fear of "flattering oneself into the delusion of being a great poet" and thus blaspheming against poetry's god, Apollo, through presumption or hubris—the "crime" of being a "selfdeluder".[9] And for Keats, writing poetry was the necessary response to reading it; writing constituted the process of digestion of the riches bequeathed by "great men" such as Shakespeare and Milton who (in Keats's early "Ode to Apollo") vibrate passions and roll thunders under their god's command. So, Keats wrote, "I have asked myself so often why I should be a Poet more than other Men,—seeing how great a thing it is."[10] Keats's world of poetry was inhabited by gods and god-like poets whose identities pressed on his own. His wholehearted and (to superficial appearance) childlike conviction of their reality, was a key factor in his capacity to "go on thinking" and continually grow out of himself. He paid more than lip-service to these deities within his breast, and this enabled him to override issues which might otherwise have inhibited and would certainly have delayed his poetic quest—such as the criticism (or praise) of his contemporaries, or his own savage self criticism. Keats was always conscious of the preciousness of time and the unknown imminence of death (perhaps from the early deaths of his father and mother, and certainly from the death of his beloved brother Tom in December 1818, which was on the horizon from almost the start of Keats's career as a poet). This probably clarified his own aim to be faithful to the "Genius of Poetry" as an internal principle, and to establish his "Humbleness" in relation to these internal objects; in contrast with this, deference to the opinions of society or of selfhood was really a type of egotism, or "Pride".[11] As he wrote in a rage to his publisher, regarding the "slipshod Endymion" (whose four thousand lines of blank verse Keats saw as a test of his own capacity to stay the course):

> Had I been nervous about its being a perfect piece, & with that view asked advice, & trembled over every page, it would not have been written; for it is not in my nature to fumble—I will write independently. . . . The Genius of Poetry must work out its own salvation in a man: It cannot be matured by law & precept, but by sensation and watchfulness in itself—That which is creative must create itself—[12]

Keats never had any doubt about the nature of real ideas as "constitutive" not merely "regulative", which Coleridge formulated as the most important problem in philosophy. In the mental orientation in which the creative creates itself, the self's function is to "sense" and "watch" the internal manifestations of the Genius of Poetry—the thinking principle, motivated by "the eternal Being, the Principle of Beauty,—and the Memory of great Men".[13] The operation of this principle is "allegorical"—as opposed to "literal", "consequitive", or "by law and precept"; thus,

> they are very shallow people who take everything literal—A Man's life of any worth is a continual allegory—and very few eyes can see the Mystery of his life—a life like the scriptures, figurative—[14]

Keats here uses the term "allegory" differently from Blake or Coleridge, without its mechanistic connotations; it has the same quality as their "vision" or "symbol", as the container for "mystery". He makes an equivalent contrast between mechanic and organic qualities when he distinguishes between "cutting a figure" and "being figurative"—saying Byron is the former, and Shakespeare the latter.[15] It was in relation to his own strenuous quest to become "figurative" himself as a poet (to "be a true Poem", as Milton said), and to conquer the temptation to cut figures, that he furiously insisted he should "ever consider [people] as debtors to me for verses, not myself to them for admiration".[16]

"Shakespeare led a life of Allegory; his works are the comments on it." Inevitably, key figures in the internal drama of the thinking principle's progress, were Shakespeare and Milton (towards whom Keats was more ambivalent, though his admiration was as intense). At the very end of his writing career, Keats wrote that "Shakespeare and the Paradise Lost every day become greater wonders to me";[17] and though shortly afterwards, when giving up *The Fall of Hyperion*, he was to say that "life to [Milton] would be death to me",[18] this rejection of his inspiring force was made in the context of suspecting that—as he put it later—the "continued stretch of his imagination had killed him", and that he refused to "sing in a cage".[19] At that point, Milton and the poetic principle were mutually identified and equally hated. Likewise, when Keats was writing the original *Hyperion* during Tom's illness, in the context of both Milton's "hateful siege of contraries" and Tom's "identity pressing" on him, he felt: "I live now in a continual fever—it must be poisonous to life although I feel well."[20] But when extricated from the complexities of this tragic context, both Shakespeare and Milton, as creative minds, were seen by Keats as providing not laws and precepts but models for experience: symbolizing through their works the mystery of existence. Keats was determined to internalize their thoughts and their thinking processes:

> I am "one that gathers Samphire dreadful trade" the Cliff of Poesy Towers above me. . . . I remember your saying that you had notions of a good Genius presiding over you. . . . Is it too daring to Fancy Shakespeare this Presider?[21]

Like Wordsworth's pursuing cliff in *The Prelude*, or Coleridge's pursuing forces in *The Ancient Mariner*, the cliff (from *King Lear*) threatens to swallow the tiny figure of the poet. In the same way, Keats half humorously accused Milton of "gormandizing" society's limited allowance of "intellect" owing to the enlargement of his own imagination, so "leaving the shore pebble all bare".[22] Yet Keats, instead of shooting the Albatross and denuding his internal world, faces the aesthetic conflict squarely, and derives from the awesome overpoweringness of the object a reciprocal "good Genius" aspect, presiding over his own development. The aesthetic mentality which Blake had exemplified in "The Tyger" and Wordsworth in the London of "Westminster Bridge", was to become characteristically and almost unwaveringly Keats's own mode of experience. In the same context as the Shakespearean cliff, he formulates what will become a consistent principle, and the foundation for his "Vale of Soul-making" two years later: "difficulties nerve the Spirit of a Man—they make our Prime Objects a Refuge as well as a Passion".[23] The Keatsian pattern for creative thought is one of being assimilated into the world of the aesthetic object and then restored to a changed self whose identity has new boundaries. The Grecian Urn, the Nightingale's tree, the bower of Psyche, the vale of Saturn in *Hyperion*, are all symbols of potential new worlds leading outwards from the Chamber of Maiden Thought, each with their governing deities; and in exploring them, the poet each time feels his own boundaries dissolve by means of outward and inward-moving communications, and then reform. Though the Muse has flown, an aspect of knowledge has been incorporated within the very structure of his mind.

In the context of analysing whether Milton did "more harm or good" to the world, Keats allegorizes the condition of the "Spiritual Cottager" who is about to be drawn away from his "mental Cottage of feelings quiet and pleasant—[his] Philosophical Back Garden", towards unknown realms:

> For as the spiritual Cottager knows there are such places as France and Italy and the Andes and the Burning Mountains—so the spiritual Cottager has knowledge of the terra semi incognita of things unearthly; and cannot for his Life, keep in the check rein—[24]

Milton was one of his supreme guides to the terra incognita of things invisible to mortal sight: modelling the process of awakening the thinking principle. In his marginal notes to *Paradise Lost*, Keats writes:

> A poet can seldom have justice done to his imagination—it can scarcely be conceived how Milton's Blindness might here aid the magnitude of his conceptions as a bat in a large gothic vault.[25]

In the process of "one Mind's imagining into another", the home for conceptions—the spiritual cottage—is magnified like a cathedral in its proportions, as are the conceptions themselves. Earthly obstacles such as blindness are metabolized into spiritual tools, their sensuous implications reversed. Keats internalized this model for expanding the mind, in his own process of metabolizing emotional obstacles by "etherealizing", "alchemizing", or "digesting" (frequent metaphors of his), such that they become developmental aids in the Vale of Soul-making, "nerving the spirit". In this way the Chamber of Maiden Thought becomes a Gothic vault. Keats called this searching for "the principle of beauty in all things", or "the Beautiful, the poetical in all things"[26]; it is the principle which underlies superficial ugliness or fearsomeness and makes "disagreeables ... evaporate",[27] to reveal the beauty of their spiritual meaning—or as Blake would say, the line of the Almighty. It is in fact the "thinking principle" of the Maiden Thought model. Keats saw Milton therefore as "committed to the Extreme":

> Milton in every instance pursues his imagination to the utmost he is "sagacious of his Quarry", he sees Beauty on the wing, pounces upon it and gorges it to the producing his essential verse.[28]

This quality of "extremity" refers to the bat-like sensing of the ultimate boundaries of the mind's chamber in its expanded condition; the idea of Beauty is the quarry and the food which produces in the poet "essential verse" (in Keats's sense of a "fellowship with essence").[29] This is what Keats means by his desire for a philosophical mode which will "widen speculation" and "ease the Burden of the Mystery".[30] He is not looking for "precepts" or "consequitive reasoning" to keep his imagination or feelings in order; he is looking for a mode which will reveal inherent structure, as well as content:

> The difference of high Sensations with and without knowledge appears to me this—in the latter case we are falling continually ten thousand fathoms deep and being blown up again without wings and with all [the] horror of a bare shouldered Creature in the former case, our shoulders are fledge, and we go thro' the same air and space without fear.[31]

The "fledged" poet is not one of modified but of *contained* emotionality, able to divine the meaning and the exploratory or developmental purport of his catastrophic emotional experiences. He can go through the "same air and space without fear" a spatial description of symbol formation. Ultimately this culminates in the Vale of Soul-making model of the mind.

In an analogous way, Keats takes two examples of Shakespearean conceits on apparently un-beautiful subjects (the "barren" trees of winter, and a wounded snail), to show how they become beautiful through the "intensity of working out conceits"—that is, how they embody an underlying metaphor about Shakespeare's mind in the process of working. He quotes:

> As the snail, whose tender horns being hit,
> Shrinks back into his shelly cave with pain,
> And there all smothered up in shade doth sit,
> Long after fearing to put forth again:
> So at this bloody view her eyes are fled,
> Into the deep dark Cabins of her head.[32]

Like Keats's own dispossessed Saturn later, retired into the shady sadness of a vale where he feels smothered and suffocated, Shakespeare's snail symbolizes the poet's venturing soul which has received a painful blow (in Saturn's case, like Lear's, to his omnipotence), and retires back into the Chamber of Maiden Thought. It is "his view" but "her eyes", as if themselves wounded through this identification, retiring bloodied into the cave. Keats comments that Shakespeare like Milton with his "gormandizing" of intellect "has left nothing to say about nothing or anything". Yet again Keats metabolizes this obstacle—the sense of his own snail-like insignificance—and converts it into a feature of self development under the aegis of Shakespeare as presiding genius (and also of Milton as epic explorer):

> Deep in the shady sadness of a vale
> Far sunken from the healthy breath of morn,
> Far from the fiery noon, and eve's one star,
> Sat grey-haired Saturn, quiet as a stone,
> Still as the silence round about his lair;
> Forest on forest hung about his head
> Like cloud on cloud. No stir of air was there,
> Not so much life as on a summer's day
> Robs not one light seed from the feathered grass,
> But where the dead leaf fell, there did it rest.
> A stream went voiceless by, still deadened more
> By reason of his fallen divinity
> Spreading a shade; the Naiad 'mid her reeds
> Pressed her cold finger closer to her lips.

In these fine opening lines of *Hyperion* (1818), Keats fuses the voices and style of Milton, Shakespeare and Wordsworth. Saturn, as king of the fallen pre-Olympian dynasty, will shortly lament his lost creative powers in terms equivalent to Lear's, having lost his infantile omnipotence: "Saturn must be King. . . . But cannot I create? / Cannot I form? Cannot I fashion forth / Another world, another universe . . .?" (I. 125–43). The answer to this question is contained in the original picture in which "fallen divinity" (the only abstract concept in a concrete picture) itself spreads the shade of its claustrophobic silence and absence of expressive power. The Naiad, a former agent of nature's animism, seals her lips in confirmation of the passage's echo-less resonance ("stone, still, no stir, not so", etc.), whose poetry consists in the ability to express the ugly deprivation of music: "voiceless, nerveless, listless, realmless". The extreme sensuousness of the passage conveys mental space and organic suspension, symbolizing the dispossession of Saturn's organizing powers—an enforced passivity and claustrophobia, like Milton's Satan within his serpent prison, expressing the first stage in poetic inspiration. The history of Keats's writing of *Hyperion* is complicated by Tom's death, which Keats associated with the deathly strictures of false art; and the next stage of inspiration by the Muse does not come to fruition here, but only in Keats's later poetry. Nevertheless, before this happens, Keats is aware from his imagining—into the minds of his mentors Shakespeare and Milton, of the potential beauty of this snail-like condition of lost power or lost eyesight. Thus he formulates the "trembling and delicate snail-horn perception of Beauty" which emerges from "those innumerable compositions and decompositions which take place between the intellect and its thousand materials".[33] The snail-poet's pain becomes one of those innumerable, infinitesimal dissolvings of the identity by the imagination (which as Coleridge said, "dissolves to recreate"), hence a feature of the principle of beauty in all things. In the same way, Keats singled out two passages from *Paradise Lost* as being of a "very extraordinary beauty": one being Orpheus torn to pieces by the rout, and the other describing Ceres' search for her lost daughter Proserpine, "which cost Ceres all that pain", after she had been gathered into the cavernous underworld.[34] Yet Proserpine, like the snail, is ready to re-emerge. Both passages are myths about the poetic principle's vulnerability when it becomes separated from its internal deities (Proserpine from Ceres, Orpheus from the Muse)—"nor could the Muse / Defend her son". Keats had an unparalleled capacity to internalize the experience of the poetic forebears who formed part of his own internal objects or mental deities; he made their symbolizations his food for thought and "essential verse", and allowed their experience to structure his own unfledged identity: "for axioms in philosophy are not axioms until they are proved upon our pulses: we read fine things but never feel them to the full until we have gone the same steps as the Author."[35] Keats himself "pounded" and "gorged" on the quarry of beauty which these poems embodied, and through which he intended to essentialize his own poetic identity.

We see therefore that the beauty–truth equivalent whose most famous expression is contained in the last lines of the "Ode on a Grecian Urn", runs constantly through all Keats's writings. Keats always regarded a sense of beauty as the first step in recognizing the richness of any potential mind-forming experience; and by "beauty", as we have seen, he included a range of complex "sensations" such as pain, ugliness, blindness, etc.: "I have the same idea of all our Passions as of Love—they are all in their sublime, creative of essential Beauty."[36] "The Idea of Beauty" is the hub of all Keats's other critical criteria; such concepts as "intensity", "negative capability", "disinterestedness", "wise passiveness", "abstraction", "fellowship with essence", all radiate outwards from it. "Essential beauty"—the beauty that is truth—is something which has to be created in the eye of the beholder, "from his own inwards" as Keats wrote in the context of another characteristic soul-making metaphor, that of the spider spinning its web:

> Memory should not be called knowledge—Many have original Minds who do not think it—they are led away by Custom—Now it appears to me that almost any Man may like the Spider spin from his own inwards his own airy Citadel—the points of leaves and twigs on which the Spider begins her work are few and she fills the Air with a beautiful circuiting: man should be content with as few points to tip with the fine Webb of his Soul and weave a tapestry empyrean—[37]

Keats's idea of creative knowledge, as opposed to mechanical memory or "consequitive reasoning",[38] is one in which the soul weaves a sort of receiving-net full of fertile crossing-points ("symbols for the spiritual eye"), from which experience can be drawn and radiated back to the centre. The mind—he continues to elaborate—"receives" like a flower, as well as "gives" like a bee; and becomes a complex entity with points of contact in both the "empyrean" vertex and the subsoil, "mould ethereal":

> Minds would leave each other in contrary directions, traverse each other in Numberless points, and [at] last greet each other at the Journeys end— . . . thus by every germ of Spirit sucking the Sap from mould ethereal every human being might become great, and Humanity instead of being a wide heath of Furse and Briars with here and there a remote Oak or Pine, would become a grand democracy of Forest Trees.[39]

Keats, like Blake and Coleridge, saw the possibilities for the collective mind of humanity as modelled on the individual creative mind: both seen in relation to some infinite source of spiritual nurture which Keats described variously in terms of etherealized earth, essential substance, abstracted sensuousness. This is the shaping spirit of imagination, the frame of emotional tensions delicately balanced between giving and receiving, from which "essential beauty" is evolved—the truth which can make every mind great.

Moreover, the imagining-into faculty is secondary to (perhaps consequent on) the being-imagined-into faculty which (in Coleridge's terms) "reflects" the mystery of being:

> Several things dovetailed in my mind, & at once it struck me, what quality went to form a Man of Achievement especially in Literature & which Shakespeare possessed so enormously—I mean *Negative Capability*, that is when man is capable of being in uncertainties, Mysteries, doubts, without any irritable reaching after fact & reason—Coleridge, for instance, would let go by a fine isolated verisimilitude caught from the Penetralium of mystery, from being incapable of remaining content with half knowledge. This pursued through Volumes would perhaps take us no further than this, that with a great poet the sense of Beauty overcomes every other consideration, or rather obliterates all consideration.[40]

Keats implicitly regards his own philosophical formulation (made when he was aged 22) as an extension of Coleridge's; yet even he is accused of a sort of premature systemization before the implications of the "beauty" of the idea he is following have been fully spun out, and the web of mystery established. He probably correctly divined Coleridge's shrinking before the ultimate frightening or "disagreeable" connotations attendant on the idea of "Beauty" in the Keatsian sense (of a legacy symbolized in *The Ancient Mariner*), substituting "reason" at the fountain-head of his value-system. Keats recognized that ultimately, reason—even in its sophisticated Coleridgean sense—would not suffice as the supreme guide to the penetralia of the mystery.[41] For Keats, the "Sense of Beauty" which is elaborated in response to the spidery eye of the beholder weaving in his darkening Chamber of Maiden Thought, is the governing force in the principle of thinking. His criterion of "Beauty" itself speaks "volumes", and in its complexity subsumes all other formulations of the poetic principle. Only in response to "Beauty", can the mind match its tentative explorations to the holding-points of die web of the mystery of its own being, in which it discovers a symbolic congruence. Thus in *The Fall of Hyperion* at the end of his career (two years later), Keats describes the formation of a tapestry empyrean when "the lofty theme . . . hung vast before my mind, / With half unravelled web" (I. 306–8), as the identity of a poet begins to grow out of that of fanatic and dreamer. When this structural web begins to form, the mind is "fledged" and set on a course of self development.

Keats began this process of "fledging" his mind when he set out on a walking tour of Scotland with his friend Brown in the summer of 1818, determined to "learn poetry" and to "harvest" beauty. In the course of the tour he encountered not only the "countenance or intellectual tone" of the mountains and natural wonders,[42] but also new images for the "birthplace" of poetry—including Milton's Lycidas guarding Fingal's Cave, and the spirit of Burns in his cottage of degradation, which "sicklied" Keats's Grecian ideal of beauty on the lines of Hamlet's "sicklied o'er with the pale cast of thought".[43] By the end of the tour Keats found himself on the top of Ben Nevis "blind in mist":

> Here are the craggy Stones beneath my feet;
> Thus much I know, that a poor witless elf
> I tread on them; that all my eye doth meet
> Is mist and Crag—not only on this height
> But in the World of thought and mental might—[44]

In effect, he has walked himself into the position of clouded unknowing which occurs when Maiden Thought becomes darkened, and which enables him to imagine-into the condition of Saturn at the beginning of *Hyperion* (begun on his return from Scotland, all in the context of Tom's illness). Under the strain of this, *Hyperion* collapses and Keats blames Milton and the artistic imagination (as he will a year later when *The Fall of Hyperion* is written under the shadow of his own death). For a period he feels severed from poetry and the Muse: "Poetry and I have been so distant lately I must make some advances soon or she will cut me entirely."[45] Yet within a few months, and in the context of falling in love with Fanny Brawne, Keats has regained the adventurous quality of the poetic "mist" and Socratean "ignorance", describing himself as "straining at particles of light in the midst of a great darkness" and "striving to know [him]self", and suddenly exorcizes the concept of a deathly false art through writing "La Belle Dame Sans Merci".[46] The silent Naiad of *Hyperion* becomes the Belle Dame with "language strange" which is both understood and misunderstood by the infant poet on his "pacing steed", recognizing a language of love yet not conceding his own powerlessness and inability to possess the object of love, with its magical poetic food of "honey wild and manna dew". The knight poet's "starv'd lips" and tubercular flush of false poetic roses derives from a misconception which the very telling of his story exorcizes by symbolically containing it within the mind of the questioner in the poem (his alter-ego, the next poet-to-be). The knight's steed and binding flowers evaporate, for in poetry (as Keats writes in a sonnet of the same time) the

Muse should be "bound with garlands of her own". This is the leap forward which raises Keats from the stalemate of Saturn's hellish vale, and results in his formulation of the world as a "Vale of Soul-making". In this, Keats's personal myth of the mind's creativity, he describes how "intelligences or sparks of the divinity" which occur universally, come to "acquire identity" and become "souls"—"each one personally itself :

> How, but by the medium of a world like this? . . . Do you not see how necessary a World of Pains and troubles is to school an Intelligence and make it a soul? A Place where the heart must feel and suffer in a thousand diverse ways! Not merely is the Heart a Hornbook, It is the Minds Bible, it is the Minds experience, it is the teat from which the Mind or intelligence sucks its identity—[47]

This is Keats's "system of salvation" or of "spirit-creation", which he feels will relieve mankind of its reliance for happiness on a "seldom-appearing Socrates", by setting its own happiness in evolution. The web is spun "from its own inwards", and only then can link up with the "teat" or growth-points through which the ethereal sap flows to build up the mind's identity. And in this process, though Socrates himself cannot help if there is no internally motivated thinking principle, the mind may make use of "Mediators and Personages" such as those in heathen mythology, who (like Keats's own use of the poet-gods) can mediate between the intelligence and the spirit-world.

Immediately on clarifying this system of spirit-creation, Keats writes the first of his beautiful spring odes, the "Ode to Psyche". All the odes (and all Keats's inspired poetry, including the agonizing struggle with *Hyperion* and its later dream-form *The Fall*) are about creativity, but the "Ode to Psyche" springs directly from his myth of Soul-making, and represents the breakthrough heralded by the "Belle Dame"; thus it establishes the mental orientation for them all. In it, Keats makes the inspired recognition that a "heathen goddess" had been "neglected" and that he is the knight come to rescue her. The goddess of the mind is discovered, not through becoming her lover (as in the "Belle Dame") but through "singing" her "secrets". As he will write later: "The Soul is a world of itself and has enough to do in its own home."[48] In this ode, the curtains are drawn back on the soul's own home, and the source of the thinking principle—the vision of beauty—is revealed.

> O Goddess! Hear these tuneless numbers, wrung
>   By sweet enforcement and remembrance dear,
> And pardon that thy secrets should be sung
>   Even into thine own soft-conchèd ear.
> Surely I dreamt to-day, or did I see
>   The wingèd Psyche with awakened eyes?

The poet's "awakened eyes" are cleansed doors of perception, marked off from everyday actuality by the initial disorientation of seeming a "dream"; the sudden revelation complements the agonizing emotional work which lies behind it, "wrung by sweet enforcement and remembrance dear". In echoing the opening lines of "Lycidas", Keats is also reminding the goddess of his own struggle with poetry's destroyed garlands, and making a plea for their restoration. It is implied that this restoration may occur if his "tuneless numbers" (syllables, rhymes) are heard by this internal deity, who represents *his* soul as well as the Soul. The "tuneless numbers" begin by representing his own musical or poetic insufficiency (without divine aid), as in La Belle Dame's "And no birds sing"; but when reflected in the "ear" of the goddess, they become ambiguous, and foreshadow the suprasensuous music of the Grecian Urn's "Pipe to the spirit ditties of no tone", or of the negated "virgin choir" later in this ode. The poet's condensed invocation, with its reminder of his "tuneless" state, is a condition of "wandering thoughtlessly" (suggesting both unfledged, and unreasoning). He sees the lovers' bower, but we suspect would never have recognized Psyche were it not for his instant recognition of Cupid: "The winged boy I knew; / But who wast thou . . . ? His Psyche true!" That is, the love whom he "knows" as part of himself, leads him to the essential beauty of the mind, which though within is also in a sense beyond himself. The mists of Maiden Thought clear before the light of the non-virgin goddess whose story (classically taking place in darkness) becomes illuminated by the poet's own awakened, "inspired" eyes:

> O latest born and loveliest far
>   Of all Olympus' faded hierarchy!
> Fairer than Phoebe's sapphire-regioned star,
>   Or Vesper, amorous glow-worm of the sky;
> Fairer than these, though temple thou hast none,
>   Nor altar heaped with flowers;
> Nor virgin-choir to make delicious moan
>   Upon the midnight hours—

The "faded hierarchy" of Olympian Apollo who had been Keats's god of poetry hitherto, and who had refused to die-into-life according to the poet's command in *Hyperion*, here transfers all its sensuous richness to the new goddess or Muse. In herself she outshines all these attributes, which are delivered as outgrown negatives; then suddenly the poet realizes what his appropriate and reciprocal response must be if he is truly to internalize the vision, and establish Psyche as his soul's deity. His earlier, doubtful "Surely I dreamt . . . or did I see . . . ?" becomes emphatically not dream but vision:

I see, and sing, by my own eyes inspired.
So let me be thy choir and make a moan
    Upon the midnight hours—
Thy voice, thy lute, thy pipe, thy incense sweet
    From swinged censer teeming;
Thy shrine, thy grove, thy oracle, thy heat
    Of pale-mouthed prophet dreaming.

Yes, I will be thy priest, and build a fane
    In some untrodden region of my mind,
Where branched thoughts, new grown with pleasant pain,
    Instead of pines will murmur in the wind:
Far, far around shall those dark-clustered trees
    Fledge the wild-ridged mountains steep by steep;
And there by zephyrs, streams, and birds, and bees,
    The moss-lain Druids shall be lulled to sleep;
And in the midst of this wide quietness
A rosy sanctuary will I dress
With the wreathed trellis of a working brain, . . .

Once the aesthetic reciprocity is achieved (by the poet echoing the features of worship such that they become a tracing of Psyche's attributes), Psyche truly becomes a symbol for his inner world, whose beauty he can match with numbers which are no longer tuneless, since they are symbiotically linked with their imaginative source—"With all the gardener Fancy e'er could feign, / Who breeding flowers will never breed the same". Keats's "Fancy" is not a mechanical mode but a servant of imagination, breeding poetry's flowers from their fertile and inexhaustible source, and echoing Richard II's words: "these two beget / A generation of still-breeding thoughts". The pattern of reciprocation is what links the spider–poet's web with the ethereal mould of his inner world (the shrine in the midst of terra incognita, "some untrodden region of my mind"); his mind is "fledged" by branched pine thoughts. Moreover the branchings will become innumerable once the shrine has been established, as will the figures enclosed within them (zephyrs, streams, etc.)—all intelligences or sparks of identity waiting to become schooled into souls. The ridged, branched mountain-surface is the "wreathed trellis of a working brain", in which—the poet promises—"shadowy thought" together with the "bright torch" of his own reciprocal inner illumination, will always be waiting "To let the warm Love in!"—to continue the fertilizing of the Chamber of Maiden Thought.

The "Ode to Psyche" is thus the symbolic presentation of Keats's system of spirit-creation, in which unknown areas of the mind or of the collective mind of humanity can become fertilized and linked in a complex pattern of emotional tensions and identifications, under the aegis of an underlying principle of beauty which will eventually enable each spark of identity to become "each one personally itself". The mind feeds and grows by means of this continual process, in which not only itself but also its internal objects (or the idea of Mind itself) shed previous identities and "hierarchies" which they have outgrown, to be re-born as bright new stars which have retained the essence of their original beauty. Keats became the greatest of the Romantic poets owing not to effortless facility in the display of talent, but to intense work on his internal relations and his determination to see the beauty of truth. For him, "learning poetry" and "making the soul" were the same thing. His own beautiful model of the mind therefore subsumes and transcends that of other philosophers of his own—and later—generations.

Notes

Keats's poetry is quoted from *Poems,* ed. M. Allott (1970), London: Longman.

1. Keats, *Letters of John Keats,* ed. R. Gittings (1987), Oxford University Press, p. 95.

2. Ibid., p. 95.

3. Letter to G. and T. Keats, 21 February 1818, ibid., p. 69.

4. Letter to Reynolds, 3 May 1818, ibid., p. 95.

5. Ibid., p. 93.

6. Journal-letter to George and Georgiana Keats, February–May 1819, ibid., p. 230.

7. See his sonnet "On First Looking into Chapman's Homer".

8. Letter to Reynolds, 18 April 1817, *Letters,* ed. R. Gittings (1987), p. 7.

9. Letter to Haydon, 10, 11 May 1817, ibid., pp. 13–14.

10. Letter to Hunt, 10 May 1817, ibid., p. 10.

11. Letter to Taylor, 27 February 1818, ibid., p. 70.

12. Letter to Hessey, 8 October 1818, ibid., pp. 155–156.

13. Letter to Reynolds, 9 April 1818, ibid., p. 85.

14. Journal-letter to G. and G. Keats, February–May 1819, ibid., p. 218.

15. Keats likewise condemned Wordsworth for the "sketchy intellectual landscape" and "comfortable moods" which were not a "search after Truth" (ibid., p. 31). Keats's hostility to Byron was in part returned (see *Don Juan,* XII.60), presumably because Keats stirred Byron's feelings of guilt in relation to poetry. Yet Byron was equally aware of the mask of intellectual pseudity: compare their identical satirization of Castlereagh in *Don Juan,* IX.49 and *Letters,* ed. R. Gittings (1987), p. 78.

16. Letter to Taylor, 23 August 1819, ibid., p. 280.

17. Letter to Bailey, 14 August 1819, ibid., p. 277.

18. Letter to G. and G. Keats, 17–27 September 1819, ibid., p. 325.

19. As reported by his friend Severn (*The Keats Circle,* ed. H. H. Rollins, cited by W. J. Bate, *John Keats,* New York, Oxford University Press, 1966, p. 688); see also letter to Fanny Brawne, 1 March 1820, *Letters,* ed. R. Gittings (1987), p. 365.

20. Letter to Dilke, 20, 21 September 1818, ibid., p. 153.

21. Letter to Haydon, 10, 11 May 1817, ibid., p. 12.

22. Letter to Rice, 24 March 1818, ibid., pp. 77–78.

23. Letter to Haydon, 10, 11 May 1817, ibid., pp. 11–12.

24. Letter to Rice, 24 March 1818, ibid., p. 77.

25. Keats's marginalia to *Paradise Lost*, in *Poetical Works and Other Writings*, ed. H. and M. Buxton Forman (1883, 1938–39), vol. 3, p. 21.

26. Letter to F. Brawne, February 1820, *Letters*, ed. R. Gittings (1987), p. 361; and letter to Bailey, 3 November 1817, ibid., p. 33.

27. Letter to G. and T. Keats, 21, 27 December 1817, ibid., p. 42.

28. Marginalia to *Paradise Lost*, in *Poetical Works and Other Writings*, ed. H. and M. Buxton Forman (1883, 1938–39), Reeves & Turner, vol. 3, pp. 19, 28.

29. *Endymion*, 1.779; see letter to Taylor, 30 January 1818, *Letters*, ed. R. Gittings, 198), p. 59, in which he refers to this passage as a "stepping of the Imagination towards a Truth".

30. See, for example, letter to Reynolds, 3 May 1818, ibid., p. 92.

31. Ibid., p. 92.

32. Shakespeare's "Venus and Adonis", cited in Keats's letter to Reynolds, 22 November 1817, ibid., p. 40.

33. Letter to Haydon, 8 April 1818, ibid., p. 83.

34. See marginalia to *Paradise Lost*, IV.268–272 and VII.32–38, in *Poetical Works and Other Writings*, ed. H. and M. Buxton Forman (1883/1938–39), Reeves & Turner, vol. 3, p. 27.

35. Letter to Reynolds, 3 May 1818, *Letters*, ed. R. Gittings (1987), p. 93.

36. Letter to Bailey, 22 November 1817, ibid., p. 37.

37. Letter to Reynolds, 19 February 1818, ibid., p. 66.

38. Letter to Bailey, 22 November 1817, ibid., p. 37.

39. Letter to Reynolds, 19 February 1818, ibid., p. 66.

40. Letter to G. and T. Keats, 21, 27 December 1817, ibid., p. 43.

41. Emily Brontë uses the same word (penetralium) in a context of identical emotional significance; see *Wuthering Heights*, ed. D. Daiches (1965), Harmondsworth, Penguin, p. 46.

42. See letter to T. Keats, 25–27 June 1818, *Letters*, ed. R. Gittings (1987), p. 103.

43. See Keats's sonnet "On Visiting the Tomb of Burns", quoted in ibid., p. 109.

44. "Read me a lesson, muse", quoted in ibid., p. 148.

45. Journal-letter to G. and G. Keats, February–May 1819, ibid., p. 224.

46. See ibid., pp. 230–231, 243–244.

47. Ibid., pp. 249–251.

48. Letter to Reynolds, 24 August 1819, ibid., p. 282.

CHAPTER TWENTY-TWO

Entry to the claustrum

(1992)

Meg Harris Williams

It is the figure of Lady Macbeth which enables Shakespeare to probe the full implications of the state of mind exemplified in Macbeth. Although the air is thick with equivocation, confusion and murderous potential after the fighting, it is she who ensures that his downward course of "success" is irrevocably precipitated into action ("screwed" to the "sticking place" in her phrase). In another poetic juxtaposition, Shakespeare suddenly transfers king, family, courtiers and generals that very night to the confines of Lady Macbeth's castle. It is done with lightning speed and a sense of frantic urgency, with messengers "almost dead for breath" and the king trying to outride Macbeth—whose "great love, sharp as his spur" nonetheless makes him win the race. Those who do not make it to the castle that night are knocking at the gate before dawn the next morning—to be welcomed all by the "devil–porter" as "equivocators" on their way to the "everlasting bonfire". The castle is presented as a feminine enclosure: as when Lady Macbeth (referring to the breathless messenger who brings the "great news" of Duncan's arrival) says:

> The raven himself is hoarse
> That croaks the fatal entrance of Duncan
> Under my battlements.

> [I.v.38—40]

On the outside, she and her castle appear "fair": an idyllic haven or "cradle" in which "temple—haunting martlets" may nest (I.vi.4), a place of security and nurture for infant souls. In this context, Duncan is described as if he were a satisfied infant put to sleep, retiring to bed "shut up / In measureless content", surrounded by other images of childhood, including his young sons; even his bodyguards are mere children, easily seduced and slaughtered. But the castle is a place of equivocation, an extension of the fairytale witches' cauldron, a murder-ous trap. It comes to symbolize Lady Macbeth's explicitly perverted femininity, which has been emptied of the milk of human kindness and filled with "gall" or evil spirits:

> Come, you Spirits
> That tend on mortal thoughts, unsex me here,
> And fill me, from the crown to the toe, top-full
> Of direst cruelty! make thick my blood,
> Stop up th'access and passage to remorse; . . .
> Come to my woman's breasts,
> And take my milk for gall, you murth'ring ministers,
> Wherever in your sightless substances
> You wait on Nature's mischief! Come, thick Night,
> And pall thee in the dunnest smoke of Hell,
> That my keen knife see not the wound it makes,
> Nor Heaven peep through the blanket of the dark,
> To cry, "Hold, hold!"

> [I.v.40–54]

Her language invokes the blood-smoked haze associated with the witches and with Macbeth's prowess on the battlefield ("Unsex . . . from crown to toe" echoing "unseam . . . from nave to chops"). It is literally an unsexing, a perversion of femininity (not an ambiguous extension of it): focussing on the body as a claustrophobic trap with its passages of communication stopped up, only penetrable by wound-ing, and with the idea of masculinity (her husband) present only in the form of her "knife", a mere mechanical instrument of destruction. This is her castle, her "battlements", in which she is about to receive Duncan with his saintly and childlike connotations—himself like an infant peeping through the blanket, whose glance encounters no re-sponding ray of sight from "sightless substances" and their "mur-thering ministers".

Lady Macbeth's imagery finds its counterpart of ambiguity in Macbeth's next soliloquy, his first genuine attempt to ask himself what he really feels about the murder, now that his wife has confronted him with its execution and both he and Duncan are placed together under her roof. Macbeth has to leave the supper table early in order to have even the shortest space of time alone in which to consider his decision. At first, his ability to think is hampered by the prevailing fuzz of equivocation, with its punning upon the concepts of "sequence" "cease" and "success".

> If it were done, when 'tis done, then 'twere well
> It were done quickly: if th' assassination
> Could trammel up the consequence, and catch
> With his surcease success; that but this blow
> Might be the be-all and the end-all—here,
> But here, upon this bank and shoal of time,
> We'd jump the life to come.
>
> [I. vii. 1–7]

Ostensibly Macbeth is considering the "consequences" of both eternal and then earthly judgement and retribution, in this speech. But the significant message, relayed through poetry rather than argument, is that for him "success" is a condition with no consequence in the sense of no future: would Duncan's "surcease" constitute a "be-all and an end-all" also for Macbeth himself, a cessation of life's trials at one "blow"? The foul fact of murder seems a mere formality ("done—done—done"), slithered over through the sounds of the wordplay, as if it were itself a mere noise: "assassination–consequence—surcease–success", the single blow of success. And the fair face which covers it is, for Macbeth, a state of finite security, an escapist longing, more passive than Lady Macbeth's desire to control and command others: it is a conflict-free haven, a succession free from consequences of any kind, not merely retributive; in effect a type of death (as in Keats's "cease upon the midnight with no pain"). After the murder, he will say of Duncan: "After life's fitful fever he sleeps well". But even before the murder, for Macbeth in his deep depression, life is already a fitful fever, and the imagery indicates his envy bf the sleeping and the dead. It is not only the afterlife of eternity but his own future life which he would like to successfully cease, marooned upon a sandbank and removed from the flux of existence. This would be his goal in possessing the crown. If one blow could make him king in this sense, being-all and ending-all, he would do it.

It is not until Macbeth considers Duncan himself, in the light of his own relation to him (which is at the moment a paternal one—being his host) that he comes into contact with his own emotional core, and seems to wake up for the first time in the play:

> Besides, this Duncan
> Hath borne his faculties so meek, hath been
> So clear in his great office, that his virtues
> Will plead like angels, trumpet-tongu'd, against
> The deep damnation of his taking-off;
> And Pity, like a naked new-born babe,
> Striding the blast, or heaven's Cherubim, hors'd
> Upon the sightless couriers of the air,
> Shall blow the horrid deed in every eye,
> That tears shall drown the wind.—I have no spur
> To prick the sides of my intent, but only
> Vaulting ambition, which o'erleaps itself
> And falls on th'other—
> (*Enter* Lady Macbeth)

[I.vii:16–28]

"Taking off", a euphemism for destroy (as in "takes your enemy off", II. 1.104), is associated with "jumping" the life to come; but here it also, ambiguously, becomes a metaphor for achieving a spiritual life, focussed on the new-born babe who is surrounded by angels ("trumpet-tongu'd" so able to speak meaningfully) and riding the horses of the winds (elemental couriers and carriers of passion). Duncan becomes the new-born babe Pity, guarded by the cherubim (angels of spiritual knowledge); and in turn this becomes a representation of Macbeth's own soul, newly-born because newly seen. In this symbolic cloud-formation (illustrated by Blake) "sightless couriers" direct their ray of feeling into "every eye", thus contrasting with Lady Macbeth's "sightless ministers" who inhabit the witch-like fog of equivocation, the blanket of the dark, which can be pierced only with knives not sight; it contrasts also with the artificially cocooned "shoal of time" in its unfeeling limbo. The poetry of this passage therefore conveys a process of perception in Macbeth, achieved by opening up a means of internal communication—the "access to Remorse" whose passage Lady Macbeth had vowed to stop up. As a visual expression of emotional reality it is, potentially, Macbeth's strongest defence so far against committing the murder.

But Macbeth is unable to translate the feeling which he has suddenly discovered into terms of active argument; he is still a novice in the field of thinking. He immediately falls back into a passive state of non-responsibility: "I have no spur / To prick the sides of my intent"— that is, nothing is goading him onwards, so there is no need for him to proceed; events can sort themselves out without his "stir" (as he said earlier). His own horse of "ambition" seems out-matched by the heavenly ones and he is content to let them win the course—but without making the crucial step of personal commitment. He is therefore doubly vulnerable when Lady Macbeth enters, precisely on cue, and shows herself to be the "spur" which Macbeth hoped he lacked. During the ensuing section of dialogue, Macbeth becomes ensnared helplessly in her trap. He does not attempt to convey any of the force of the feeling from the soliloquy, but instead argues lamely that he does not want to lose the "golden opinions" he has just won "from all sorts of people"; he would like to wear these for a while "in their newest gloss, / Not cast aside so soon". Macbeth was already feeling uncomfortable (albeit flattered) by being "dressed in borrowed robes"—loaded with titular honours and pressed into a false intimacy with the king; yet they suited his ambition, and he had hoped they would appease his ambitious "partner of greatness", his wife (I.v.11). The theme of false clothing which does not express the inner man is used by Shakespeare throughout the play in association with the theme of equivocation. For Lady Macbeth it is the externalities which make the man, rather than vice versa; she retaliates furiously: "Was the hope drunk, / Wherein you dress'd yourself?" The golden crown is the only clothing worth having since it overrides any number of golden opinions; she is not interested in appearance as a means of social facilitation but only in the power which it denotes, and as she asks uncomprehendingly in her later sleepwalking: "What need we fear who knows it, when none can call our power to accompt?"

Macbeth is doomed, but he makes one final heroic attempt to save himself from the degradation which she is thrusting upon him, with the words:

Pry'thee, peace.
I dare do all that may become a man;
Who dares do more, is none.

The words are few but meaningful, particularly in the wider context of the play's imagery. He implies his own definition of integrity and manliness is as something distinct from the gloss of other people's opinions and from power: some deeds are "becoming" and some are not, but their measure is internally not externally taken. But Lady Macbeth, faced with this unexpected rebellion, rounds on her "beast" of a husband savagely with her own definition of manhood as one who dares to "do" what he phantasizes, rather than being "unmade" by it; the occasion, opportunistically seized, becomes the man:

When you durst do it, then you were a man;
And, to be more than what you were, you would

Be so much more the man. Nor time, nor place,
Did then adhere, and yet you would make both:
They have made themselves, and that their fitness now
Does unmake you.

Lady Macbeth had claimed she would vanquish her husband through the "valour of her tongue"; but what ultimately overpowers him is not her direct chastisement. Rather, it is her instinctive recognition of his Achilles' heel, which she earlier called the "milk of human kindness", and which she now interprets in terms of the new-born babe of his soliloquy:

I have given suck, and know
How tender 'tis to love the babe that milks me:
I would, while it was smiling in my face,
Have pluck'd my nipple from his boneless gums,
And dash'd the brains out, had I so sworn
As you have done to this.

The image of the babe lay at the heart of his temporary rebellion against her, resulting in the definition of manhood which she found so infuriating. Macbeth is at his most vulnerable at the moment when he begins to think for himself; his capacity for thinking is itself new-born and undeveloped, and his habitual passivity prevents him from protecting it. Lady Macbeth's brazen image of infanticide is taken by him (as she intended) as an attack on his own infant soul, her knife cutting through his blanket of equivocation. He feels paralysed, in effect by terror, owing to what he calls her "undaunted mettle", her pseudomasculinity. Using the language of admiration—"bring forth men-children only!"— he acknowledges his subservience to her, as a witch in woman's clothing, and submits to being recruited as her agent. In this way, Shakespeare uses dramatic irony and poetic ambiguity to pursue to the utmost the implications of Macbeth's wavering condition—the origins of the "mind diseased" which might otherwise have remained obscured by equivocation's shadowy cloak.

CHAPTER TWENTY-THREE

Parallel directions in psychoanalysis
(1991)

Margot Waddell

> The human nature unto which I felt
> That I belonged, and reverenced with love,
> Was not a punctual presence, but a spirit
> Diffused through time and space, with aid derived
> Of evidence from monuments, erect,
> Prostrate, or leaning towards their common rest
> In earth, the widely scattered wreck sublime
> Of vanished nations.
>
> [Wordsworth, *The Prelude*][1]

In his definitive statement of the life of the mind as "The Vale of Soul-making",[2] Keats distinguishes between those who are genuinely able to explore the further chambers, the inner recesses and dark passages of what he had earlier called the "large Mansion of Many Apartments"—human life, and those who stopped thinking, or at least did not "think into the human heart".[3] The Soul-*making* emphasis in the experience of life, lies in the capacity to tolerate the perception that "the world is full of Misery and Heartbreak, Pain, Sickness and oppression".[4] That knowledge is co-terminous with the realization that it is in apprehending that very reality that the many doors open from the Chamber of Maiden Thought. In a world of Circumstances, it is the

Heart which is "the teat from which the Mind or intelligence sucks its identity".[5]

In considering how the embodiment in literature of the development of the life of the mind has illuminated the task of psychoanalysis, their congruent goals become apparent: to explore the process whereby truthful emotional experiences evolve and to participate in the growth of the mind. Founded, as it is, in the notion that all cognition is primarily emotion, that knowing is essentially an imaginative experience, "The Vale of Soul-making" offers a description of the human condition that is shared by the Romantic poets, by mid-nineteenth-century writers and late-twentieth-century, post-Kleinian psychoanalysts alike. By establishing the necessity of placing emotionality at the heart of the matter, it focuses attention on recognizing the place for meaning and value in human affairs—the absolute values of psychic reality as opposed to the relativity of social values. The promotion of the evolution of such values has always required that thought have its anchorage in feeling. In pursuing this same process in the context of psychoanalytic thinking, we follow the central preoccupation of the great creative artists, to oppose the dissociation of thought from feeling.

In this sense a similarity of *direction* may be asserted between Shakespeare's work, that of Milton, of the Romantic poets, of Emily Brontë and of George Eliot, and the way psychoanalysis has developed. This direction could be characterized by its stress on the necessity of value—whether explicitly or implicitly expressed—and a commitment to an organic principle of growth. ("Organic" does not imply that, given the right conditions, the seed of the human mind will grow, blossom and eventually die, but rather that the mind is a living thing with its own processes of development and principles of growth, related to, but by no means determined by, external conditions.) This way of thinking represents an alternative to the positivist view that all life is ultimately reducible to laws operable in the organic and inorganic world alike (an aspiration which Freud struggled to relinquish).

The congruence of direction between literature and psychoanalysis resides in their both being based in this embracing of emotion as lying at the heart of meaning, symbol formation being the entree to thinking about meaning. Hence it is reasonable for Shelley to say that the "poets are the unacknowledged legislators of the world", and for the psychoanalysts to say that the mother/baby relationship determines the direction of development for the child. The congruence has become clear through the work of Bion, who represented the mother's functioning— the primary instrument for the reception of symbol formation—as being, in turn, the basic necessary mode of functioning for the baby. The transference, at the level of the infant/breast relationship, is the vehicle for all fundamental change through psychoanalysis. The "thinking" breast becomes the unconscious "legislator" of the baby's world. The symbolizing processes of the artist and his or her relationship with the community involve a similar reciprocity—through the symbolic value of the work—to the relationships alike between mother and baby and between therapist and patient.

Bion's theory is that symbol formation is initially a function of the internal object rather than of the self. Alpha function, as he calls it, is first a capacity on the mother's part, stemming from her internal object. It is experienced as the breast, or the "thinking" breast. In good circumstances she aids in the establishing of, and gives form to, the baby's object—that is when the mother is able to hold, and transform, the baby's mental state, and when the manner and matter of the baby's projections are not too overwhelming. The creating of symbols as the basis for thinking remains a function of that internal object. Most behaving, thinking, speaking, even dreaming, occurs with received symbols. Individuality, however, lies in the generating of autonomous, idiosyncratic symbols—in giving form to "Ideas, in the highest sense of that word" (Coleridge), in finding a "local habitation and a name". It is in embracing these idiosyncratic symbols of emotional experience, initially made available in dreams, that the individuality of each person evolves through self creative thinking. These "Ideas" embody "the shaping spirit of Imagination". The alternative is to operate with received symbols which are utilized as signs for adaptation, risking the imposition of preconceptions and the insistence that the world, or the world of the mind, conform to them rather than allowing the ideas to modify the mind.

"The Vale of Soul-making" is the symbol Keats has offered, available for having meaning poured into it. For what is shaped by Imagination with the use of symbols is an idea of the world and of self in-the-world. We contribute to shaping the world in accordance with that vision of self in-the-world, the nature of which it is the shared task of the patient and therapist to illuminate. In Deronda's case, this process involved thinking himself out of his egocentricity into being-in-the-world—such that "his own personality would be no less outside him than the landscape".[6]

In the process of analysis, the patient's essential self, that is the experiencing rather than the adaptive self (the endo-skeletal as opposed to exo-skeletal personality), becomes available for understanding through the symbolic content of the "dream" being transformed into the symbolic form of language by the interpretation. For this to be

achieved, the therapist has to "follow" the material—holding a candle
behind the individual, the better to illuminate what lies before, rather
than shining a directive, pedagogic "light" in front, to lead. ("Does my
way of seeing it help you to see it more clearly your way?") For the
patient in the consulting room, the development of such capacity for
understanding lies in the opportunity to engage with the mind of a
therapist who is genuinely open to the idea of carrying the transference
image. This function of carrying the transference, by which the therapist aids the forward movement of the patient's development and thus
does not repeat the disappointments and disillusionments of past figures, is dependent on the therapist's openness to being apprehended as
bearing internal qualities which s/he knows, having overcome egocentricity, s/he not only does not, but in their particularity cannot, possess.
With Deronda, for example, there is a far more rich sense of the qualities which are attributed to him than of those which he actually has. The
mind's self creation occurs according to the degree of truthfulness
existing in the relationship between subject and internal object.

In *Middlemarch*, the crisis and culmination of the growth of
Dorothea's mind is expressed in terms of this same symbolic congruence between subject and object. Her development in the course of the
novel is from short-sighted aspiration of a projective kind to a much
broader and more humble vision of the nature of humanity and of her
place therein. She undergoes her final, and profoundest, disillusion-
ment when,

> with a consciousness which had never awakened before, she stretched
> out her arms towards [that bright creature whom she trusted] and
> cried with bitter tears that their nearness was but a passing vision: she
> discovered her passion to herself in the unshrinking utterance of
> despair?[7]

George Eliot describes how Dorothea did not linger long "in the narrow
cell of her calamity, in the besotted misery of a consciousness that only
sees another's lot as an accident of its own".[8] Rather,

> She opened her curtains, and looked out towards the bit of road that
> lay in view, with fields beyond, outside the entrance-gates. On the
> road was a man with a bundle on his back and a woman carrying her
> baby; in the field she could see figures moving perhaps the shepherd
> with his dog. Far off in the bending sky was the pearly light; and she
> felt the largeness of the world and the manifold awakenings of men to
> labour and endurance. She was part of that involuntary, palpitating
> life, and could neither look out on it from her luxurious shelter as a
> mere spectator, nor hide her eyes in selfish complaining.[9]

Dorothea's catastrophic change, which she embraced and accepted, initiated for her a wider vision of the world and altered her experience of herself and her place therein, thus changing her understanding of the relationship between the two. (Dorothea has an inner strength which enables her to undergo these traumatic experiences and to learn from them. It may be that her orphaned state stimulated her to develop certain capacities by cleaving the more to her internal mother. Gwendolen, by contrast, who existed in a mutually childlike emotional dependency with her mother needed a mediating figure to enable her to undergo similar experiences.)

The regenerative process in Dorothea is expressed through her emotional apprehension of external reality, uncluttered by the author's imposition of preconception or by the intrusion of sentimentalism. The author simply describes Dorothea's mental processes. Her character's internal landscape has been opened up to aspects of experience to which she had hitherto been blind, ones which had laid no place in "that part of her world which lay within park palings".[10] In this kind of writing no self consciousness as to the nature of the relationship between subject and object obtrudes; none of the confusion which clouds questions of perception and so-called "objectivity", so well put by Coleridge: "The chameleon darkens in the shade of him who bends over it to ascertain its colours."[11] For in the process of Soul-making, of becoming more known to herself, Dorothea's experience finally takes her back to "the teat from which the Mind or intelligence [could] suck its identity". The links of relatedness, as George Eliot makes clear elsewhere—particularly in *The Mill on the Floss*, stem from the "mute dialogues", as Wordsworth describes them, which a baby holds with his mother's heart; from that "infant sensibility" which is "the Great birthright of our Being"[12]—akin to George Eliot's "landscape of childhood" as the imagination's mother-tongue.[13]

George Eliot's definition of imagination in one of her last essays offers a vivid description of the best of her own writing, where the symbolic representations of experience are expressed in a decreasingly discursive and more idiosyncratic and active way. The words might also be taken to describe, with equal clarity, the nature of the psychoanalytic process:

> Powerful imagination is not false outward vision, but intense inward representation, and a creative energy constantly fed by susceptibility to the various minutiae of experience, which it reproduces and reconstructs, in fresh and fresh wholes; not the habitual confusion of provable fact with the fictions of fancy and transient inclination, but a breadth of ideal association which informs every material object,

> every incidental fact, with far reaching memories and stored residues
> of passion, bringing into new light the less obvious relations of hu-
> man existence.[14]

Writing after the completion of the last novel, George Eliot here offers a
formulation about the relationship between art and life towards which
her entire oeuvre had been moving. It is about vision and the making-
available-of vision. Art, poetry, symbol formation/alpha function are
to do with "making vision available". The nature of the reciprocity
between mother and baby is a relationship *vis-à-vis* the world in which
the mother's understanding and vision are presented to the baby.
Powerful imagination may similarly be described as manifest in the
evolution of the analytic process—the unconscious transaction of transference and countertransference. The patient and analyst or therapist
may thus observe, and try to comprehend, the process, and, in a sense,
yield themselves to it. Resistance or defence in either tend to take up
their positions against the emotional experience and its forward movement, that is, against development. George Eliot's description may be
taken as a statement about the orientation of therapist and patient
together observing and trying to understand the shared emotional experience. It is a mutual experience in which, as George Eliot says, "The
coercion is often stronger on the one who takes the reverence. Those
who trust us educate us."[15]

To be an honest baby requires an honest breast—a flexible container
which is able to change and adapt without losing its essential integrity.
Only so can the individual be open to, in terms of having the courage to
undergo, catastrophic change. In the course of the experience meaning
emerges through the shared symbolic process of the interpretative
mode. The capacity of patient and therapist alike to tolerate the trans-
ference/countertransference process is akin to Keats's "Negative Capability", "when man is capable of being in uncertainties, Mysteries,
doubts, without any irritable reaching after fact and reason"—the quality which, above all, went to form a Man of Achievement.[16]

The final dream of a young model, Sarah, who was facing a premature interruption of therapy for external reasons, rather beautifully
indicated that some such process was beginning to occur. Sarah had
sought help for her depression—desperate to break a pattern of relating
to men in which she found herself in a state of clinging dependency,
masochistically unable to separate until, like a climbing plant, she had
some alternative supporting structure to which to attach herself.

The pain of mutual relinquishment in the final sessions had been
acute. Being the fourth of six siblings, her life had, from the first,
constituted a type of group experience, in which the Basic Assumption

mentality described by Bion predominated: attitudes were stereotyped around notions defined either by their acceptability, or by their opposition, to the dominant culture of the group at the time. Leaving therapy was yet another in a long series of premature weanings, evoking intense feelings of desolation, loss, and anger—her early experiences all too emotionally immediate.

In this dream *she found herself in the ante-chamber of a large and beautiful house. There were doors which opened into the interior, dark passages leading off to which she felt she had access and was on the point of entering, but felt uncertain and apprehensive. This small room was itself lovely. Panelled, as in her childhood home, with many recesses and alcoves in which there were exquisite, precious objects—china ornaments, glass, wood carvings. The room was pervaded by a smell of spices—myrrh and frankincense, she thought. Her eyes alighted on one object in particular, a blue glass bowl of extraordinary fragility and beauty. She gazed at it half believing that it belonged to her and that she had the right to take it with her, yet feeling too that that might be to steal. A tall, dark, mysterious woman entered apparently the owner. As they looked at each other, Sarah "knew" that the object was indeed her own.*

This "knowledge" was essentially, as she said at the time, an imaginative experience rather than an aspect of reality. Evidence of the prematurity of her leaving lies, perhaps, in the uncertainty about to whom the bowl belonged. Was it really hers or was it that of the tall dark woman? Yet there did seem to have occurred an awakening of "the thinking principle within", impelling her beyond the ante-chamber. The context made it clear that it derived from having been enabled, albeit briefly, to have an experience of the mysterious psychoanalytic process as a breast which awoke in her an imaginative vision of her ordinary self creative potential. The house evoked memories—the internal landscape of the parental home—memories and "shared residues of passion" which she could now "use" rather than merely bitterly "recall"; "Those shadowy recollections", as Wordsworth put it in the *Immortality Ode,*

> Which, be they what they may
> Are yet the fountain light of all our day,
> Are yet the master light of all our seeing

—those "memories in feelings", as Klein called them, the "mother tongue of our imagination".

Sarah's sense that the bowl was related to the imminent possibility of moving into the main part of the house was an aspect of an awakened vision "into the heart and nature of Man", as Keats had described it in his "Mansion of Many Appartments".

The pervasive perfumes offered intimations both of a new birth and of mourning. In beginning to allow herself, with apprehension, to depend on the internal object to help her carry "the burden of the Mystery", it seems that she was also beginning to relinquish the external pseudo-supportive structures which had characterized her relations hitherto. She was standing at a threshold, mourning a loss, fearful that she had brought it about, but willing to draw on an internalized resource—the blue glass bowl. The dream is full of possibility. Yet there is a shared apprehension, related to the premature leaving of the Chamber of Maiden Thought aspect of the transference. Perhaps she was going into the dark passages inadequately equipped, having internalized less the strong, functional qualities of the object than its non-functional fragility and preciousness. The therapist might be apprehensive as to what exactly Sarah was taking away—the image of the bowl was ambiguous, either ready to be filled with meaning, or simply, empty.

This worrying ambiguity was absent from the dream material of a second patient, 34-year-old Stephen, whose therapy was able to take its course over a number of years. A successful young academic, he had always used intellectuality as an effective defence against a range of infantile anxieties, above all, against the pain of intimacy. Knowledge as a form of power rather than as a source of understanding had long provided a serviceable carapace—this knowledge gradually including the latest psychoanalytic theory, particularly those aspects which he thought most interested his therapist. His quest for knowledge had a quality which was more in tune with a desire to possess and occupy than to understand; to steal secrets and with them inoculate himself against pain, rather than genuinely to take in, and identify internally with, the functions of the object.

This state of mind is well caught in an brief early dream. The contrast to another dream some three years later, which drew on similar images, measured a long period of intense struggle with his fledgling self. The different use of the same image in each dream encapsulates the nature of the developmental process which is described here—something of the possibility of coming out of projective identification, overcoming grandiosity, of risking adventure rather than selling for ambition—in keeping with the ways in which Dorothea and Gwendolen were finally able to place themselves in the world.

In the early dream, *there were beautiful glass spheres, contained each in its own convex cup—spheres which he smashed with a heavy ball-bearing, gathering the broken pieces into a mixing bowl and putting the ball-bearing on top, with a complacent air of "what a good boy am I"*. In this competitive caricature of analytic work, the self congratulatory "good boy" Stephen was able to deceive himself as to the cup-filling confection—as if it constituted an actual cake/breast rather than a mockery of the psychotherapeutic method.

After three more years of hard work an external event occurred, aptly described by Stephen as "a bombshell", for it introduced a mode of perception and a quality of feeling the capacity for which had only ever been hinted at before. The eruption of a long quiescent skin condition, eczema, coincided with a visit to his home in Ireland, during the weekend when the eldest of his three younger sisters was due to give birth. Tormented over this weekend by his infantile feelings of distress, among other things at the recurrence of the very symptom which had originated at the birth of this same sister thirty-two years earlier, he had the following dream: *he resided in the place where children ore before being born—existing as protoplasmic blobs, suspended in a bluish pink atmosphere above cups—themselves seemingly attached, as if by a line of some sort, to a lily pad on the surface of the water. The children were talking together. One conversation was distinct, between himself and an unborn girl. They were discussing his fear of death: "If you are born you have to die"; he said, "and that feels too terrifying." She disagreed—the real courage lay in allowing yourself to be born in the first place. Once you'd done that you had already taken care of the fear of death. Dying didn't seem anything like so bad afterwards. What you had to do was meet the cup, get down into it and be born. Then you could bear the rest. With that she did get down into the cup and went ahead, leaving Stephen lingering behind, fearful, and yet infused with courage and expectancy.*

This dream seems rather a remarkable representation of the birth of the mind, the hitherto unborn parts of Stephen's personality—the bluish, pink dawning of the thinking principle. It seems to place the Chamber of Maiden Thought prior to birth (recovered at the breast with all the dark passages). The foetus feels encouraged to proceed by the capacity to hold a dialogue with the part of the self which now knows that the cup constitutes a safe internal container—linked both to internal worlds and external by way of the lily pad/umbilical cord. Held in that container Stephen could allow himself to consider being born—to "think", in Bion's sense of a preconception meeting a realization engaging with the cup of life, the internal mother—and thereby being able to proceed with his development. The cup had now become a genuinely containing object in which his mind might be fledged and set on a course of self creation. The contrast with former states of mind is well caught in George Eliot's description of that between being egotistically enclosed within a mind which takes the world "as an udder to feed the supreme self",[17] and forming a sense of connectedness with all ordinary human existence:

It is an uneasy lot at best to be what we call highly taught and yet not
to enjoy: to be present at this great spectacle of life and never to be
liberated from a small hungry shivering self—never to be fully possessed by the glory we behold, never to have our consciousness
rapturously transformed into the vividness of a thought, the ardour
of a passion, the energy of an action, but always to be scholarly and
uninspired, ambitious and timid, scrupulous and dim-sighted.[18]

... encased within what she elsewhere calls, "that troublous fitfully-
illuminated life".[19]

In the vast imaginative worlds of her novels, some characters manage to be born just as, in the process of novel writing, George Eliot's
creative capacity was born—decreasingly insistent on imposing preconceptions and discursively moralizing, but committed rather to an
ethical position related to understanding the truthfulness of the world
within, that "unmapped country" where the mind is given space to
breathe and create itself, "through the medium of the Heart in a world
of Circumstances". The experience of catastrophic change initiates a
process of self development whereby the mind may become possessed
by the glory we behold and not remain shut up within its own short-
sighted egotistical enclosure.

In Bion's theory, change involves the birth of a new idea which,
in turn, entails the relinquishing of the old form: in order to be born
a letting-go has to occur to allow for the transformation of the existing state of mind, or the superimposition upon it of the new idea—
the internal catastrophic change. The process, as Keats clearly states,
is impelled from within—it is not a matter of wilful fantasizing
(Coleridge's "Fancy"), but one which depends on a capacity for growth
and change initiated by the internal object.

In the period between Stephen's two dreams it seemed that a shift
had taken place—the necessity of coming out of his projective identification and previous states of mind had become apparent. The second
dream shows his trepidation about emerging and having to face both
the fact that his younger sister had so obviously moved ahead of him in
development, and the situation which had bowled him over in childhood, the birth of the next sibling. This shift was marked (not brought
about) by the "bombshell" of the birth of his nephew; "marked" because that event occurred in a psyche which seemed prepared also to be
born, to suffer the consequences of leaving the manic projective identification. With that event his shell of false identity was felt to have
shattered—the shell of "Custom" and "Memory", with which lie had
resisted growth and its associated turbulence, and into which he had
withdrawn from any experience of joy or passion.

With Keats, the poems become the serial representation of the changing internal container. An aesthetic reciprocity is established between internal and external objects whereby a new container of meaning is evolved by way of the mind's development. So too with George Eliot, the successive novels may be thought of in terms of her efforts to find a container for meaning—a meaning which clearly did not reside in the contemporary theories of the mind and psychology with which she was so familiar, but which became increasingly located in the internal aspects of her characters' existence, albeit finely tuned by the vicissitudes of their external life and by wider cultural and historical phenomena. The function Deronda performed internally for Gwendolen is George Eliot's most evolved expression of the process whereby a mind's development is initiated and assisted by the changing quality of the internal object. For Deronda was himself wrought upon by Gwendolen's experience, of her life and his impact upon it. He was able to "receive" that experience without being overtaken by her feelings to digest her pain and hand it back to her as food for thought.

With the patients described, the contrast is clear between Keats's notion of creative knowledge—which both Sarah and Stephen were struggling towards—and the "consequitive reasoning",[20] whereby each had lived their lives hitherto. Thinking in these creative terms (as opposed to pseudo-thinking which may amass "knowledge" as information or fact) is mind-building, soul-making—a process which involves the struggle between the impelling nature of the desire to be born, Coleridge's "innate principle of self development", and the resistant pull away from the fear and pain of the unknown, represented as death.

The central metaphor for the interlocking of internal and external lives in *Middlemarch* is the web. Soul-making too belongs to the ordinariness and the beauty of the spider spinning her web, making from her own inwards her own airy citadel. Stephen was slowly becoming "schooled" in learning to spin from his own inwards, not to suck his knowledge from the entrails of host objects, as was his wont in "Alien" identifications in days gone by. Similarly, Sarah had to struggle to weave her internal web, or fashion and strengthen her beautiful glass bowl, such that she could feel some confidence that her mind was being born, or fledged—outgrowing its previous identity. For each, the Basic Assumption conformity, with family configurations in Sarah's case, and with ambitious, social expectations of academic success in Stephen's, provided an exo-skeletal mentality which had confined, rather than protected, their respective personalities.

Bion describes catastrophic change as an internal group process whereby these basic assumptions are disrupted by that part of the personality, "the mystic", which receives the new idea, or the new concept. Internal change has to occur in the personality in order for this new idea to be assimilated. Sarah had clung to the shifting surfaces of the fashion world, moving from relationship to relationship, continuously adhered to the desiccated structures of unions already past, despite knowing that their life had long since drained away. Stephen had remained enslaved to the academic hierarchy, despite conscious attempts to dismantle those structures (literally, as he once put it, to remove the mantle of his beetle/self), that aspect of the superstructure which commanded both his obedience and his illicit contempt.

Each case makes it clear that development in life, or the evolution of the psychoanalytic experience is not a continuous linear process. They both suffered, rather, the impact of certain nodal points (leaving therapy prematurely and the crisis of "birth", respectively) which constituted growth points, or "epochs", as George Eliot would describe them. Uncertainly in Sarah's case, and more confidently in Stephen's, these epochs initiated a move forward in development. Each had become able to "receive" back projections which had been worked on in the therapeutic relationship, making it possible, thereby, to make use of their experience and to suffer the internal change consequent upon it.

In *The Prelude*, Wordsworth addresses the twin processes of projection (as an ordinary and necessary mode of communication) and receptivity, which epitomize the creative act and which describe the literary model of the human mind as a thing whose characteristic activity is self creation. The lines could equally well convey the reciprocity of the relationship between therapist and patient—both being "willing to work and to be wrought upon"—by the analytic process.

> That is the very spirit in which they deal
> With all the objects of the universe;
> They from their native selves can send abroad
> Like transformations, and from themselves create
> A like existence, and, whene'er it is
> Created for them, catch it by an instinct;
> Them the enduring and the transient both
> Serve to exalt; they build up the greatest things
> From least suggestions, ever on the watch,
> Willing to work and to be wrought upon,
> They need not extraordinary calls
> To rouze them, in a world of life they live
> By sensible impressions not enthralled
> But quicken'd, rouz'd and made thereby more apt
> To hold communion with the invisible world.

[XIII.91–105]

In the clinical material described, we find the infant soul on the threshold of exploring the life of the mind, at the point of acceptance of the Chamber of Maiden Thought—and the dark passages that lead off it—able, now, to perceive the man with the bundle on his back, the woman carrying her baby; hopefully to spin from their own inwards an airy citadel. Previous identities have had to be shed, and reborn in the bowl or the cup of the internal object—born of aesthetic reciprocity, inspired by that internalized process, whereby the goddess "Psyche" can be recognized as the deity of the mind's truthfulness.

Notes

1. The lines from Wordsworth's *Prelude* (1850 edition) are quoted by George Eliot as the Epigraph to Chapter 69 of *Daniel Deronda*, Penguin Classics (1986), p. 864.

2. *Letters of John Keats*, ed. R. Gittings (1987), Oxford University Press, p. 249.

3. Ibid., pp. 95–96.

4. Ibid., p. 95.

5. Journal-letter to G. and G. Keats, February–May 1819, ibid., p. 250.

6. *Daniel Deronda*, Penguin Classics (1986), ch. 17, p. 229.

7. *Middlemarch*, Penguin Classics (1985), ch. 80, p. 844.

8. Ibid., ch. 80, p. 845.

9. Ibid., ch. 80, p. 846.

10. Ibid., ch. 77, p. 829.

11. *Aids to Reflection* (1905), Edinburgh: Grant, p. 70.

12. See Wordsworth's *Prelude*, II.240–7.

13. *The Mill on the Floss*, Penguin Classics, ch. 5, Book 1, p. 94.

14. *Theophrastus Such*, London, Cabinet Edition (1978), ch. 13, p. 197.

15. *Daniel Deronda*, ch. 35, p. 485.

16. Letter to G. and T. Keats, 21, 27 December 1817, *Letters*, p. 43.

17. *Middlemarch*, ch. 21, p. 243.

18. Ibid., ch. 29, p. 314.

19. Ibid., ch. 30, p. 324.

20. Letter to Bailey, 22 November 1817, *Letters*, ed. R. Gittings (1987), Oxford University Press, p. 37.

REFERENCES AND BIBLIOGRAPHY

Abraham, K. (1924[105]). A short study of the development of the libido, viewed in the light of mental disorders. In: *Selected Papers of Karl Abraham, M.D.* (pp. 418–501). London: Hogarth Press, 1927; reprinted London: Karnac, 1988.

Allott, M. (Ed.) (1970). *Poems*, London: Longman.

Apollinaire, G. (1914). *Alcools* [Alcohols]. Paris, 1913; Middletown, CT: Wesleyan, 1995.

Arnheim, R. (1956). *Art and Visual Perception: A Psychology of the Creative Eye.* London: Faber.

Bate, W. J. (1966). *John Keats.* New York: Oxford University Press.

Bell, C. (1914). *Art.* London: Chatto & Windus.

Berenson, B. (1950). *Aesthetics and History.* London: Constable.

Bion, W. R. (1950). The imaginary twin. In: *Second Thoughts: Selected Papers on Psycho-Analysis.* London: Heinemann; reprinted London: Karnac, 1984.

Bion, W. R. (1962). *Learning from Experience.* London: Heinemann; reprinted London: Karnac, 1984.

Bion, W. R. (1965). *Transformations: Change from Learning to Growth.* London: Heinemann; reprinted London: Karnac, 1984.

Bion, W. R. (1970). *Attention and Interpretation.* London: Tavistock; reprinted London: Karnac, 1984.

Bion, W. R. (1977). *Two Papers: The Grid and Caesura.* Rio de Janeiro: Imago Editora; revised edition London: Karnac, 1989.

Bion, W. R. (1980). *Bion in New York and São Paulo.* Strath Tay, Perthshire: Clunie Press.

Bion, W. R. (1991). *A Memoir of the Future*. London: Karnac.
Bion, W. R. (1995). *La sindrome di Stendhal*. Florence: Ponti alle Grazie.
Bléandonu, G. (1994). *Wilfred Bion, His Life and Work 1897–1979*. London: Free Association Books.
Britton, R. (1999). Existential anxiety: Rilke's *Duino Elegies*. In: *Belief and Imagination, Explorations in Psycho-Analysis*. London: Routledge.
Brontë, E. (1850). *Wuthering Heights*, ed. D. Daiches. Harmondsworth: Penguin, 1965.
Buxton Forman, H., & Buxton Forman, M. (Eds.) (1883/1938–39). *Poetical Works and Other Writings*. London: Reeves & Turner.
Caudwell, C. (1937). *Illusion and Reality*. London: Lawrence & Wishart.
Coleridge, S. T. (1825). *Aids to Reflection*. Edinburgh: Grant.
Contini, G. (1946). Introduction to *Dante Alighieri, Rime* [Verses]. Turin: Einaudi.
Ehrenzweig, A. (1948). Unconscious form creation in art. *British Journal of Medical Psychology, 21* (Parts II & III).
Eliot, G. (1860). *The Mill on the Floss*. Harmondsworth: Penguin, 1986.
Eliot, G. (1871–72). *Middlemarch, A Study of Provincial Life*. Harmondsworth: Penguin, 1985.
Eliot, G. (1876). *Daniel Deronda*. Harmondsworth: Penguin, 1986.
Eliot, G. (1879). *Theophrastus Such*. London: Cabinet Edition, 1978.
Etchegoyen, R. H. (1991). *The Fundamentals of Psychoanalytic Technique*. London: Karnac.
Fairbairn, W. R. D. (1938). The ultimate basis of aesthetic experience. *British Journal of Psychology, 29* (Part II).
Fano Cassese, S. (1998). Il sublime e el peturbante nell'opera di D. Meltzer [The sublime and the disturbing in the work of D. Meltzer]. *Contrapunto, 22*.
Fano Cassese, S. (2002). *Introduction to the Work of Donald Meltzer*. London: Karnac.
Fenichel, O. (1946). *The Psycho-Analytic Theory of Neurosis*. London: Kegan Paul.
Freud, S. (1895d) (with Breuer, J.). *Studies on Hysteria. S.E. 2.*
Freud, S. (1900a). *The Interpretation of Dreams. S.E. 4–5.*
Freud, S. (1908e[1907]). Creative writers and day-dreaming. *S.E. 9.*
Freud, S. (1910c). *Leonardo da Vinci and a Memory of His Childhood. S.E. 11.*
Freud, S. (1911b). Formulations on the two principles of mental functioning. *S.E. 12.*
Freud, S. (1913f). The theme of the three caskets. *S.E. 12.*
Freud, S. (1914). *Essays in Applied Psycho-Analysis, Vol. II*. London, 1951.
Freud, S. (1914b). The Moses of Michelangelo. *S.E. 13.*
Freud, S. (1917e [1915]). Mourning and melancholia. *S.E. 14.*
Freud, S. (1918b [1914]). From the history of an infantile neurosis. *S.E. 17.*
Freud, S. (1919h). The uncanny. *S.E. 17.*
Freud, S. (1923b). *The Ego and the Id. S.E. 19.*

Freud, S. (1925). *Contributions to Psycho-Analysis, 1921–45*. London, 1948.

Freud, S. (1926d [1925]). *Inhibitions, Symptoms and Anxiety. S.E. 20*.

Freud, S. (1927d). Humour. *S.E. 21*.

Freud, S. (1940e[1938]). Splitting of the ego in the process of defence. *S.E. 23*.

Freud, S. (1950 [1892–1899]). Poetry and "fine frenzy" (1897). In: *The Origins of Psycho-Analysis: Letters to Wilhelm Fliess*, Draft N. London: Imago, 1954.

Fry, R. (1920). *Vision and Design*. London: Chatto & Windus.

Fry, R. (1926). *Transformations*. London: Chatto & Windus.

Gaburri, E., & Ferro, A. (1988). Gli sviluppi kleiniani e Bion. In: A. A. Semi (Ed.), *Trattato di psicoanalisi*. Milan: Raffaello Cortina Editore.

Galimberti, E. (2000). *Wilfred R. Bion*. Milan: Bruno Mondadori.

Gay, P. (1988). *Freud: A Life for Our Time*. New York: Norton.

Gittings, R. (Ed.) (1987). *Letters of John Keats*. Oxford: Oxford University Press.

Gosso, S. (1997). *Paessaggi della mente*. Milan: Franco Angeli.

Grinberg, L., Sor, D., & Tabak de Bianchedi, E. (1993). *Introduzione al pensiero di Bion*. Milan: Raffaello Cortina Editore.

Grosskurth, P. (1986). *Melanie Klein*. London: Hodder & Stoughton.

Harris Williams, M. (1987). *A Strange Way of Killing*. Strath Tay, Perthshire: Clunie Press.

Harris Williams, M. (1988). Holding the dream: The nature of aesthetic appreciation. In: D. Meltzer & M. Harris Williams, *The Apprehension of Beauty: The Role of Aesthetic Conflict in Development, Art and Violence* (pp. 178–199). Strath Tay, Perthshire: Clunie Press.

Harris Williams, M., & Waddell, M. (1991). *Chamber of Maiden Thought: Literary Origins of the Psychoanalytic Model of the Mind*. London: Routledge.

Heimann, P. (1942). A contribution to the problem of sublimation and its relation to processes of internalization. *International Journal of Psycho-Analysis, 23* (Part I).

Heimann, P. (1950). On countertransference. *International Journal of Psycho-Analysis, 31*.

Heimann, P. (1952). *Developments in Psycho-Analysis*. London: Hogarth Press.

Hinshelwood, R. D. (1989). *A Dictionary of Kleinian Thought*. London: Free Association.

Hodges, H. A. (1944). *Wilhelm Dilthey, An Introduction*. London: Oxford University Press.

Jones, E. (1914). The Madonna's conception through the ear. In: E. Jones, *Psycho-Myth, Psycho-History: Essays in Applied Psychoanalysis*. New York: Hillstone, 1974.

Jones, E. (1916). The theory of symbolism. In: *Papers on Psycho-Analysis*. London: Baillière Tindall & Cox, 1948.

Jones, E. (1948). *Papers on Psycho-Analysis*. London: Baillière, Tindall and Cox.

Jones, E. (1953–57). *The Life and Work of Sigmund Freud (Vols. 1–3)*. London: Hogarth Press.

Jones, E. (1954). *Hamlet and Oedipus*. New York: Doubleday.

Jung, C. (1933). *Psychological Types*. London: Kegan Paul.

Kafka, F. (1902). *Letters to Friends, Family, and Editors* (trans. R. Winston & C. Winston). New York: Schocken Books, 1987.

Kafka, F. (1924). *The Castle*. Harmondsworth: Penguin, 1987.

Keats, J. (1987). *Letters of John Keats*, ed. R. Gittings. London: Oxford University Press.

Kierkegaard, S. (1941). *Fear and Trembling*. Princeton, NJ: Princeton University Press.

Klein, M. (1927). Criminal tendencies in normal children. In: *Contributions to Psycho-Analysis, 1921–45*. London: Hogarth Press. Also in: *Love, Guilt and Reparation and Other Works* (pp. 170–185). London: Hogarth Press, 1975.

Klein, M. (1928). Early stages of the Oedipus conflict. *International Journal of Psycho-Analysis, 9* (Part I).

Klein, M. (1932). *The Psycho-Analysis of Children*. London: Hogarth Press, 1975; reprinted London: Karnac, 1998.

Klein, M. (1935). A contribution to the psychogenesis of manic-depressive states. *Contributions to Psycho-Analysis, 1921–45*. London: Hogarth Press, 1948. Also in: *Love, Guilt and Reparation and Other Works* (pp. 262–289). London: Hogarth Press, 1975.

Klein, M. (1940). Mourning and its relation to manic-depressive states. In: *Contributions to Psycho-Analysis, 1921–45*. London: Hogarth Press, 1948. Also in: *Love, Guilt and Reparation and Other Works* (pp. 344–369). London: Hogarth Press, 1975.

Klein, M. (1946). Notes on some schizoid mechanisms. In *Developments in Psycho-Analysis*. London: Hogarth Press, 1952. Also in: *Envy and Gratitude and Other Works* (pp. 1–24). London: Hogarth Press, 1975.

Klein, M. (1948a). *Contributions to Psycho-Analysis, 1921–45*. London: Hogarth Press.

Klein, M. (1948b). On the theory of anxiety and guilt. *International Journal of Psycho-Analysis, 29*: 113–123. Also in: *Envy and Gratitude and Other Works* (pp. 25–42). London: Hogarth Press, 1975.

Klein, M. (1955). On identification. In: M. Klein, P. Heimann, & R. Money-Kyrle (Eds.), *New Directions in Psycho-Analysis* (pp. 309–345). London: Tavistock. Also in: *Envy and Gratitude and Other Works* (pp. 141–175). London: Hogarth Press, 1975.

Klein, M. (1957). Envy and gratitude. In: *Envy and Gratitude and Other Works* (pp. 176–235). London: Hogarth Press, 1975.

Klein, M. (1958). On the development of mental functioning. In: *Envy and Gratitude and Other Works* (pp. 236–246). London: Hogarth Press, 1975.

Klein, M. (1963a). *Our Adult World and Its Roots in Infancy*. London: Heinemann.

Klein, M. (1963b). Some reflections on *The Oresteia*. In: *Our Adult World and Other Essays*. London: Heinemann, 1963. Also in: *Envy and Gratitude and Other Works* (pp. 275–299). London: Hogarth Press, 1975.

Klein, M. (1975a). *Love, Guilt and Reparation and Other Works*. London: Hogarth Press; reprinted London: Karnac, 1992.

Klein, M. (1975b). *Narrative of a Child Analysis: The Conduct of the Psychoanalysis of Children as Seen in the Treatment of a Ten-Year-Old Boy*. London: Hogarth Press; reprinted London: Karnac, 1996.

Klein, M., Heimann, P., & Money-Kyrle, R. (1955). *New Directions in Psycho-Analysis*. London: Tavistock.

Kristeva, J. (1984). *Revolution in Poetic Language* (trans. Margaret Waller). New York: Columbia University Press.

Langer, S. (1942). *Philosophy in a New Key*. Cambridge, MA: Harvard University Press.

Langer, S. (1953). *Feeling and Form*. New York: Charles Scribner's Sons.

Laplanche, J., & Pontalis, J.-B. (1973). *The Language of Psychoanalysis*. London: Hogarth Press.

Lee, H. B. (1939). A critique of the theory of sublimation. *Psychiatry, 2* (May).

Lee, H. B. (1940). A theory concerning free creation in the inventive arts. *Psychiatry, 3* (May).

Listowell, Earl of (1933). *A Critical History of Modern Aesthetics*. London: Allen & Unwin.

Meltzer, D. (1966). The relation of anal masturbation to projective identification, *International Journal of Psycho-Analysis, 47*: 335–342. Also in: E. B. Spillius, *Melanie Klein Today, Vol. 1* (pp. 102–116). London: Routledge, 1988.

Meltzer, D. (1967). *The Psycho-Analytical Process*. London: Heinemann Medical; reprinted London: Karnac.

Meltzer, D. (1973). *Sexual States of Mind*. Strath Tay, Perthshire: Clunie Press.

Meltzer, D. (1978). *The Kleinian Development* (3 vols.). Strath Tay, Perthshire: Clunie Press.

Meltzer, D. (1984). *Dream-Life: A Re-Examination of the Psycho-Analytical Theory and Technique*. Strath Tay, Perthshire: Clunie Press.

Meltzer, D. (1986). *Studies in Extended Metapsychology: Clinical Applications of Bion's Ideas*. Strath Tay, Perthshire: Clunie Press.

Meltzer, D. (1992). *The Claustrum. An Investigation of Claustrophobic Phenomena*. Strath Tay, Perthshire: Clunie Press.

Meltzer, D. (1994). *Sincerity and Other Works: Collected Papers*. London: Karnac.

Meltzer, D., Bremner, J., Hoxter, S., Wedell, D., & Wittenberg, I. (1975). *Explorations in Autism: A Psychoanalytical Study*. Strath Tay, Perthshire: Clunie Press.

Meltzer, D., & Harris Williams, M. (1988). *The Apprehension of Beauty: The Role of Aesthetic Conflict in Development, Art and Violence*. Strath Tay, Perthshire: Clunie Press.

Milner, M. [Joanna Field] (1950). *On Not Being Able to Paint*. London: Heinemann.

Nussbaum, M. (1987). *The Fragility of Goodness*. Cambridge: Cambridge University Press.

Rank, O. (1932). *Art and Artists*. New York: Knopf.

Read, H. (1931). *The Meaning of Art*. London: Faber & Faber.

Read, H. (1934). *Art and Society*. London: Faber & Faber.

Read, H. (1951a). *Art and the Evolution of Man*. London: Freedom Press.

Read, H. (1951b). Psycho-analysis and the problem of aesthetic value. *International Journal of Psycho-Analysis, 32*.

Rickman, J. (1940). The nature of ugliness and the creative impulse. *International Journal of Psycho-Analysis, 21* (Part III).

Rilke, R. M. (1923). *Duino Elegies* (trans. J. B. Leishman & S. Spender). London: Hogarth Press, 1957.

Riviere, J. (1959). The inner world in Ibsen's "Master Builder". In: M. Klein, P. Heimann, & R. Money-Kyrle (Eds.), *New Directions in Psycho-Analysis* (pp. 370–383). London: Tavistock, Also in: A. Hughes (Ed.), *The Inner World and Joan Riviere: Collected Papers 1920–1958* (pp. 332–347). London: Karnac, 1991.

Rosenfeld, H. (1952). Notes on the psycho-analysis of the super-ego in an acute schizophrenic patient. *International Journal of Psycho-Analysis, 33*: 111–131. Also in: M. Klein, P. Heimann, & R. E. Money-Kyrle (Eds.), *New Directions in Psycho-Analysis* (pp. 180–219). London: Tavistock.

Sachs, H. (1940). Beauty, life and death. *American Imago, 1*: 81–133.

Scott, W. C. M. (1949). The body scheme in psychotherapy. *British Journal of Medical Psychology, 22*.

Segal, H. (1968). *Introduction to the Work of Melanie Klein*. London: Karnac and The Institute of Psychoanalysis, 1988.

Semi, A. A. (Ed.) (1988). *Trattato di Psicoanalisi, Vol. 1: Teoria e tecnica*. Milan: Raffaello Cortina.

Semi, A. A. (Ed.) (1989). *Trattato di Psicoanalisi, Vol. 2: Clinica*. Milan: Raffaello Cortina.

Sendak, M. (1963). *Where the Wild Things Are*. New York: HarperCollins Publishers.

Sharpe, E. (1930). Certain aspects of sublimation and delusion. *Collected Papers on Psycho-Analysis*. London: Hogarth Press, 1950.

Sharpe, E. (1935). Similar and divergent unconscious determinants underlying the sublimations of pure art and pure science. In: *Collected Papers on Psycho-Analysis*. London: Hogarth Press, 1950.

Sharpe, E. (1937). *Dream Analysis*. London: Hogarth Press.

Steiner, R., & King, P. (1994). *The Freud/Klein Controversies* 1941–45. London & New York: Tavistock/Routledge.

Stevenson, R. L. (1887). *Memories and Portraits*. London: Chatto & Windus, 1912.

Stokes, A. (1945). *Venice: An Aspect of Art*. London: Faber & Faber.

Stokes, A. (1947). *Inside Out: An Essay in the Psychology and Aesthetic Appeal of Space*. London: Faber.

Stokes, A. (1955). Form in art. In: M. Klein, P. Heimann, & R. Money-Kyrle (Eds.), *New Directions in Psycho-Analysis* (pp. 406–420). London: Tavistock.

Stokes, A. (1961). *Three Essays on the Painting of Our Time*. London: Tavistock.

Stokes, A. (1963a). *Painting and the Inner World*. London: Tavistock.

Stokes, A. (1963b). Concerning the social basis of art. In: D. Meltzer & M. Harris Williams, *The Apprehension of Beauty*. Strath Tay, Perthshire: Clunie Press, 1988.

Stokes, A. (1965). *The Invitation to Art*. London: Tavistock Publications.

Symington, J., & Symington, N. (1996). *The Clinical Thinking of Wilfred Bion*. London: Routledge.

Tolstoy, L. (1899). *War and Peace* (trans. R. Edmonds). Harmondsworth: Penguin, 1982.

Winnicott, D. W. (1945). Primitive emotional development. *International Journal of Psycho-Analysis, 2*. Also in: *Collected Papers: Through Paediatrics to Psycho-Analysis* (pp. 145–156). London: Tavistock, 1958.

Winnicott, D. W. (1948). Paediatrics and psychiatry. *British Journal of Medical Psychology, 21*. Also in: *Collected Papers: Through Paediatrics to Psycho-Analysis* (pp. 157–173). London: Tavistock, 1958.

Winnicott, D. W. (1951). Transitional objects and transitional phenomena. *International Journal of Psycho-Analysis, 34* (1953): 89. Also in: *Collected Papers: Through Paediatrics to Psycho-Analysis* (pp. 229–242). London: Tavistock, 1958.

Winnicott, D. W. (1958). *Collected Papers: Through Paediatrics to Psycho-Analysis*. London: Tavistock.

Winnicott, D. W. (1971). *Playing and Reality*. London: Tavistock.

Wittgenstein, L. (1918). *Tractatus logico-philosophicus*. London: Routledge, 2001.

Wittgenstein, L. (1953). *Philosophical Investigations*. Oxford: Blackwell.

Wordsworth, W. (1798). Preface. In: W. Wordsworth & W. T. Coleridge, *Lyrical Ballads*. London: Methuen, 1968.

Wordsworth, W. (1805). *The Prelude*. 1850. London: Oxford Paperbacks, 1970.

Zambrano, M. (1988 [1977]). *Claros del bosque*. Barcelona: Biblioteca de Bolsillo.

NAME INDEX